ALBANIA

MINING LAWS AND REGULATIONS HANDBOOK

STRATEGIC INFORMATION AND BASIC LAWS

International Business Publications, USA
Washington DC, USA - Albania

ALBANIA

MINING LAWS AND REGULATIONS HANDBOOK

STRATEGIC INFORMATION AND BASIC LAWS

UPDATED ANNUALLY

Cover Design: **International Business Publications, USA**

We express our sincere appreciation to all government agencies and international organizations which provided information and other materials for this handbook

2018 Updated Reprint International Business Publications, USA
ISBN 1-4330-7688-8

This handbook provides basic information for starting or/and conducting business in the country. The extraordinary volume of materials covering the topic, prevents us from placing all these materials in this handbook. For more detailed information on issues related to any specific investment and business activity in the country, please contact Global Investment Center, USA

Please acquire the list of our business intelligence and marketing reports and other business publications. We constantly update and expand our business intelligence and marketing materials. Please contact the center for the updated list of reports on over 200 countries.

For additional analytical, business and investment opportunities information, please contact Global Investment & Business Center, USA at (703) 370-8082. Fax: (703) 370-8083. E-mail: ibpusa3@gmail.com Global Business and Investment Info Databank - www.ibpus.com

Printed in the USA

ALBANIA
MINING LAWS AND REGULATIONS HANDBOOK
STRATEGIC INFORMATION AND BASIC LAWS

TABLE OF CONTENTS

BUSINESS AND DEVELOPMENT PROFILES

STRATEGIC PROFILES

Capital and largest city	Tirana 41°19′N 19°49′E
Official languages	Albanian
Demonym	Albanian
Government	Unitary parliamentary constitutional republic
• President	Ilir Meta
• Prime Minister	Edi Rama
Legislature	Kuvendi
Formation	
• Principality of Arbanon	1190
• Anjou Kingdom of Albania	February 1272
• Princedom of Albania	1368
• League of Lezhë	2 March 1444
• Proclamation of independence from the Ottoman Empire	28 November 1912
• Principality of Albania (Recognised)	29 July 1913
• Albanian Republic (1st republic)	31 January 1925
• Albanian Kingdom	1 September 1928
• People's Republic of Albania (2nd republic)	11 January 1946
• People's Socialist Republic of Albania (3rd republic)	28 December 1976
• Republic of Albania (4th republic)	29 April 1991
Current constitution	28 November 1998
Area	
• Total	28,748 km^2 (11,100 sq mi) (140th)
• Water (%)	4.7
Population	
• January 2017 estimate	2,876,591
• 2011 census	2,821,977
• Density	98/km^2 (253.8/sq mi) (63rd)
GDP (PPP)	2018 estimate
• Total	$37.923 billion
• Per capita	$13,193[3]
GDP (nominal)	2018 estimate
• Total	$14.120 billion
• Per capita	$4,912
Gini (2013)	34.5 medium

HDI (2015)	▲ 0.76 high · 75th
Currency	Lek (ALL)
Time zone	CET (UTC+1)
• Summer (DST)	CEST (UTC+2)
Date format	dd/mm/yyyy
Drives on the	right
Calling code	355
ISO 3166 code	AL
Internet TLD	.al

Albania officially the **Republic of Albania** is a country in Southeastern Europe. The country spans 28,748 square kilometres (11,100 square miles) and had a total population of 3 million people as of 2016. It is a unitary parliamentary constitutional republic with the capital in Tirana, the country's most populous city and main economic and commercial centre. The country's other major cities include Durrës, Vlorë, Sarandë, Shkodër, Berat, Korçë, Gjirokastër and Fier.

Albania lies in the southwestern portion of the Balkan Peninsula bordered by Montenegro to the northwest, Kosovo to the northeast, the Republic of Macedonia to the east, and Greece to the south and southeast. Most of the country is mountainous, including the Albanian Alps in the north, the Korab Mountains in the east, the Ceraunian Mountains in the south and the Skanderbeg Mountains in the center. The country's coast touches the Adriatic Sea to the west and the Ionian Sea to the southwest that forms the Albanian Riviera. It is less than 72 km (45 mi) from Italy across the Strait of Otranto, which connects the Adriatic to the Ionian.

Previously in classical antiquity, Albania has been populated by various Illyrian, Thracian and Greek tribes, as well as several Greek colonies established in the Illyrian coast. In the third century BC, the region was annexed by the Roman Empire and became an integral part of the Roman provinces of Dalmatia, Macedonia and Illyricum. The unified Principality of Arbër emerged in 1190, established by archon Progon in the Krujë, within the Byzantine Empire. In the late thirteenth century, Charles of Anjou conquered the Albanian territories from the Byzantines and established the medieval Kingdom of Albania, extending from Durrës along the coast to Butrint in the south. In the mid-fifteenth century, it was conquered by the Ottomans.

The modern nation state of Albania emerged in 1912 following the defeat of the Ottomans in the Balkan Wars.

The modern Kingdom of Albania was invaded by Italy in 1939, which formed Greater Albania, before becoming a Nazi German protectorate in 1943. After the defeat of Nazi Germany, a Communist state titled the People's Socialist Republic of Albania was founded under the leadership of Enver Hoxha and the Party of Labour. The country experienced widespread social and political transformations in the communist era, as well as isolation from much of the international community. In the aftermath of the Revolutions of 1991, the Socialist Republic was dissolved and the fourth Republic of Albania was established.

Albania is a democratic and developing country with an upper-middle income economy. The tertiary sector dominates the country's economy followed by the secondary and primary sector.

Following the end of communism in 1990, the country went through a process of transition from a centralized economy to a market-based economy. It also provides universal health care and free primary and secondary education to its citizens.

Albania has a high Human Development Index and is ranked 13th in the Happy Planet Index, 38th in the Global Gender Index, 52nd in the Social Progress Index and 37th for Life Expectancy. The country is a member of the United Nations, World Bank, UNESCO, NATO, WTO, COE, OSCE and OIC. It is also an official candidate for membership in the European Union. In addition it is one of the founding members of the Energy Community, including the Organization of the Black Sea Economic Cooperation and Union for the Mediterranean.

GEOGRAPHY

Location: Southeastern Europe, bordering the Adriatic Sea and Ionian Sea, between Greece and Serbia and Montenegro

Geographic coordinates: 41 00 N, 20 00 E

Map references: Europe

Area:
total: 28,750 sq km
land: 27,400 sq km
water: 1,350 sq km

Area—comparative: slightly smaller than Maryland

Land boundaries:
total: 720 km
border countries: Greece 282 km, The Former Yugoslav Republic of Macedonia 151 km, Serbia and Montenegro 287 km (114 km with Serbia, 173 km with Montenegro)

Coastline: 362 km

Maritime claims:
continental shelf: 200-m depth or to the depth of exploitation
territorial sea: 12 nm

Climate: mild temperate; cool, cloudy, wet winters; hot, clear, dry summers; interior is cooler and wetter

Terrain: mostly mountains and hills; small plains along coast

Elevation extremes:
lowest point: Adriatic Sea 0 m
highest point: Maja e Korabit (Golem Korab) 2,753 m

Land use:
arable land: 21%
permanent crops: 5%
permanent pastures: 15%
forests and woodland: 38%
other: 21%

Irrigated land: 3,410 sq km

Natural hazards: destructive earthquakes; tsunamis occur along southwestern coast

Environment—current issues: deforestation; soil erosion; water pollution from industrial and domestic effluents

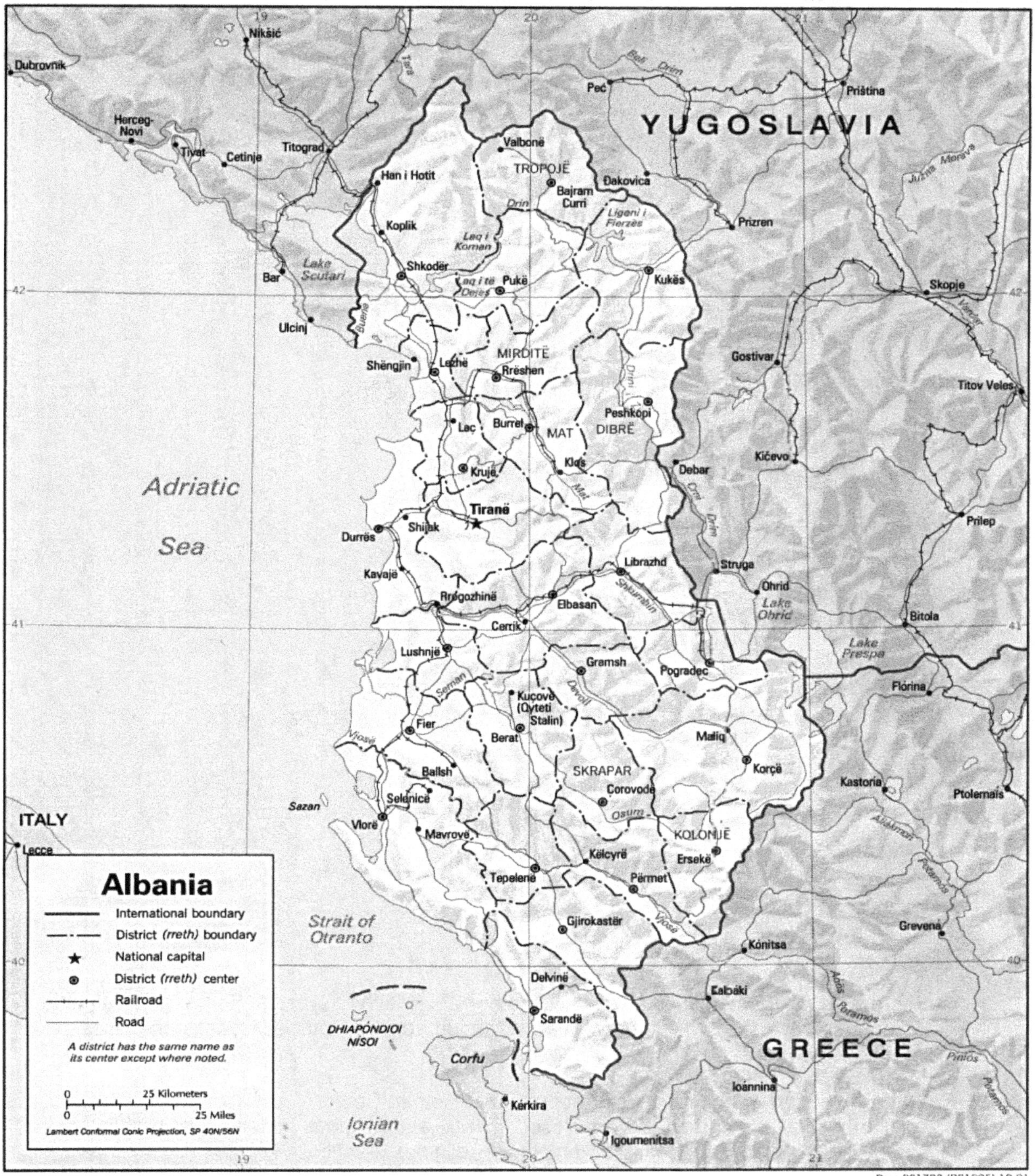

Base 801723 (B01095) 10-91

Environment—international agreements:
party to: Biodiversity, Climate Change, Wetlands
signed, but not ratified: none of the selected agreements

Geography—note: strategic location along Strait of Otranto (links Adriatic Sea to Ionian Sea and Mediterranean Sea)

Natural resources: petroleum, natural gas, coal, chromium, copper, timber, nickel

PEOPLE

Population: 3,364,571

Age structure:
0-14 years: 33% (male 568,642; female 530,088)
15-64 years: 61% (male 957,561; female 1,105,870)
65 years and over: 6% (male 84,280; female 118,130)

Population growth rate: 1.05%

Birth rate: 20.74 births/1,000 population

Death rate: 7.35 deaths/1,000 population

Net migration rate: -2.93 migrant(s)/1,000 population

Sex ratio:
at birth: 1.08 male(s)/female
under 15 years: 1.07 male(s)/female
15-64 years: 0.87 male(s)/female
65 years and over: 0.71 male(s)/female
total population: 0.92 male(s)/female

Infant mortality rate: 42.9 deaths/1,000 live births

Life expectancy at birth:
total population: 69 years
male: 65.92 years
female: 72.33 years

Total fertility rate: 2.5 children born/woman

Nationality:
noun: Albanian(s)
adjective: Albanian

Ethnic groups: Albanian 95%, Greeks 3%, other 2% (Vlachs, Gypsies, Serbs, and Bulgarians)
note: other estimates of the Greek population ranged from 1% (official Albanian statistics) to 12% (from a Greek organization)

Religions: Muslim 70%, Albanian Orthodox 20%, Roman Catholic 10%
note: all mosques and churches were closed in 1967 and religious observances prohibited; in November 1990, Albania began allowing private religious practice

Languages: Albanian (Tosk is the official dialect), Greek

Literacy:
definition: age 9 and over can read and write
total population: 93%

GOVERNMENT

Country name:
conventional long form: Republic of Albania
conventional short form: Albania
local long form: Republika e Shqiperise
local short form: Shqiperia
former: People's Socialist Republic of Albania
etymology: the English-language country name seems to be derived from the ancient Illyrian tribe of the Albani; the native name "Shqiperia" is derived from the Albanian word "Shqiponje" ("Eagle") and is popularly interpreted to mean "Land of the Eagles"

Government type:
parliamentary republic

Capital:
name: Tirana (Tirane)
geographic coordinates: 41 19 N, 19 49 E
time difference: UTC+1 (6 hours ahead of Washington, DC, during Standard Time)
daylight saving time: +1hr, begins last Sunday in March; ends last Sunday in October

Administrative divisions:
12 counties (qarqe, singular - qark); Berat, Diber, Durres, Elbasan, Fier, Gjirokaster, Korce, Kukes, Lezhe, Shkoder, Tirane, Vlore

Independence:
28 November 1912 (from the Ottoman Empire)

National holiday:
Independence Day, 28 November (1912) also known as Flag Day

Constitution:
history: several previous; latest approved by the Assembly 21 October 1998, adopted by referendum 22 November 1998, promulgated 28 November 1998
amendments: proposed by at least one-fifth of the Assembly membership; passage requires at least a two-thirds majority vote by the Assembly; referendum required only if approved by two-thirds of the Assembly; amendments approved by referendum effective upon declaration by the president of the republic; amended several times, last in 2016 (2017)

Legal system:
civil law system except in the northern rural areas where customary law known as the "Code of Leke" prevails
International law organization participation:
has not submitted an ICJ jurisdiction declaration; accepts ICCt jurisdiction

Citizenship:
citizenship by birth: no
citizenship by descent only: at least one parent must be a citizen of Albania
dual citizenship recognized: yes
residency requirement for naturalization: 5 years

Suffrage:
18 years of age; universal

Executive branch:
chief of state: President of the Republic Ilir META (since 24 July 2017)
head of government: Prime Minister Edi RAMA (since 10 September 2015); Deputy Prime Minister Niko PELESHI

cabinet: Council of Ministers proposed by the prime minister, nominated by the president, and approved by the Assembly

elections/appointments: president indirectly elected by the Assembly for a 5-year term (eligible for a second term); a candidate needs three-fifths majority vote of the Assembly in 1 of 3 rounds or a simple majority in 2 additional rounds to become president; election last held in 4 rounds on 19, 20, 27, and 28 April 2017 (next election to be held in 2022); prime minister appointed by the president on the proposal of the majority party or coalition of parties in the Assembly

election results: Ilir META elected president; Assembly vote - 87 - 2 in fourth round

Legislative branch:
description: unicameral Assembly or Kuvendi (140 seats; members directly elected in multi-seat constituencies by proportional representation vote to serve 4-year terms)
elections: last held on 25 June 2017 (next to be held in 2021)

election results: percent of vote by party - PS 48.3%, PD 28.9%, LSI 14.3%, PDIU 4.8%, PSD 1%, other 2.7%; seats by party - PS 74, PD 43, LSI 19, PDIU 3, PSD 1

Judicial branch:
highest court(s): Supreme Court (consists of 17 judges, including the chief justice); Constitutional Court (consists of 9 judges, including the chairman)

judge selection and term of office: Supreme Court judges, including the chairman, appointed by the president with the consent of the Assembly to serve single 9-year terms; Constitutional Court judges appointed by the president with the consent of the Assembly to serve single 9-year terms with one-third of the membership renewed every 3 years; chairman elected by the People's Assembly for a single 3-year term
subordinate courts: Courts of Appeal; Courts of First Instance

Political parties and leaders:
Democratic Party or PD [Lulzim BASHA]
Party for Justice, Integration and Unity or PDIU [Shpetim IDRIZI] (formerly part of APMI)
Social Democratic Party or PSD [Skender GJINUSHI]
Socialist Movement for Integration or LSI [Monika KRYEMADHI]
Socialist Party or PS [Edi RAMA]

Political pressure groups and leaders:
Confederation of Trade Unions of Albania or KSSH [Kol NIKOLLAJ]
Omonia [Leonidha PAPA]
Union of Independent Trade Unions of Albania or BSPSH [Gezim KALAJA]

International organization participation:
BSEC, CD, CE, CEI, EAPC, EBRD, EITI (compliant country), FAO, IAEA, IBRD, ICAO, ICC (national committees), ICCt, ICRM, IDA, IDB, IFAD, IFC, IFRCS, ILO, IMF, IMO, Interpol, IOC, IOM, IPU, ISO (correspondent), ITU, ITUC (NGOs), MIGA, NATO, OAS (observer), OIC, OIF, OPCW, OSCE, PCA, SELEC, UN, UNCTAD, UNESCO, UNIDO, UNWTO, UPU, WCO, WFTU (NGOs), WHO, WIPO, WMO, WTO

Diplomatic representation in the US:
chief of mission: Ambassador Floreta FABER (since 18 May 2015)
chancery: 2100 S Street NW, Washington, DC 20008
telephone: [1] (202) 223-4942
FAX: [1] (202) 628-7342
consulate(s) general: New York

Diplomatic representation from the US:
chief of mission: Ambassador Donald LU (since 13 January 2015)
embassy: Rruga e Elbasanit, 103, Tirana
mailing address: US Department of State, 9510 Tirana Place, Dulles, VA 20189-9510
telephone: [355] (4) 2247-285
FAX: [355] (4) 2232-222

Flag description:
red with a black two-headed eagle in the center; the design is claimed to be that of 15th-century hero George Kastrioti SKANDERBEG, who led a successful uprising against the Ottoman Turks that resulted in a short-lived independence for some Albanian regions (1443-78); an unsubstantiated explanation for the eagle symbol is the tradition that Albanians see themselves as descendants of the eagle; they refer to themselves as "Shqiptare," which translates as "sons of the eagle"

National symbol(s):
black double-headed eagle; national colors: red, black

National anthem:
name: "Hymni i Flamurit" (Hymn to the Flag)
lyrics/music: Aleksander Stavre DRENOVA/Ciprian PORUMBESCU
note: adopted 1912

ECONOMY

Albania, a formerly closed, centrally-planned state, is a developing country with a modern open-market economy. Albania managed to weather the first waves of the global financial crisis but, the negative effects of the crisis caused a significant economic slowdown. Since 2014, Albania's economy has steadily improved and economic growth reached 3.8% in 2017. However, close trade, remittance, and banking sector ties with Greece and Italy make Albania vulnerable to spillover effects of possible debt crises and weak growth in the euro zone.

Remittances, a significant catalyst for economic growth, declined from 12-15% of GDP before the 2008 financial crisis to 5.8% of GDP in 2015, mostly from Albanians residing in Greece and Italy. The agricultural sector, which accounts for more than 40% of employment but less than one quarter of GDP, is limited primarily to small family operations and subsistence farming, because of a lack of modern equipment, unclear property rights, and the prevalence of small, inefficient plots of land. Complex tax codes and licensing requirements, a weak judicial system, endemic corruption, poor enforcement of contracts and property issues, and antiquated infrastructure contribute to Albania's poor business environment making attracting foreign investment difficult. Since 2015, Albania has launched an ambitious program to increase tax compliance and bring more businesses into the formal economy. In July 2016, Albania passed constitutional amendments reforming the judicial system in order to strengthen the rule of law and to reduce deeply entrenched corruption.

Albania's electricity supply is uneven despite upgraded transmission capacities with neighboring countries. However, the government has recently taken steps to stem non-technical losses and has begun to upgrade the distribution grid. Better enforcement of electricity contracts has improved the financial viability of the sector, decreasing its reliance on budget support. Also, with help from international donors, the government is taking steps to improve the poor road and rail networks, a long standing barrier to sustained economic growth.

Inward FDI has increased significantly in recent years as the government has embarked on an ambitious program to improve the business climate through fiscal and legislative reforms. The government is focused on the simplification of licensing requirements and tax codes, and it entered into a new arrangement with the IMF for additional financial and technical support. Albania's three-year IMF program, an extended fund facility arrangement, was successfully concluded in February 2017. The Albanian Government has strengthened tax collection amid moderate public wage and pension increases in an effort to reduce its budget deficit. The country continues to face high public debt, exceeding its former statutory limit of 60% of GDP in 2015 and reaching 72% in 2016.

GDP (purchasing power parity):

$35.87 billion (2017 est.)
$34.59 billion (2016 est.)
$33.46 billion (2015 est.)
note: data are in 2017 dollars
unreported output may be as large as 50% of official GDP
country comparison to the world: 126

GDP (official exchange rate):
$13 billion (2017 est.)

GDP - real growth rate:
3.7% (2017 est.)
3.4% (2016 est.)
2.2% (2015 est.)
country comparison to the world: 85

GDP - per capita (PPP):
$12,500 (2017 est.)
$12,000 (2016 est.)

$11,600 (2015 est.)
note: data are in 2017 dollars
country comparison to the world: 122

Gross national saving:
15.6% of GDP (2017 est.)
15.9% of GDP (2016 est.)
16.3% of GDP (2015 est.)
country comparison to the world: 122

GDP - composition, by end use:
household consumption: 77.6%
government consumption: 10.9%
investment in fixed capital: 27%
investment in inventories: 0%
exports of goods and services: 29.7%
imports of goods and services: -45.2% (2017 est.)

GDP - composition, by sector of origin:
agriculture: 22.6%
industry: 23.8%
services: 53.7%
(2017 est.)

Agriculture - products:
wheat, corn, potatoes, vegetables, fruits, olives and olive oil, grapes; meat, dairy products; sheep and goats

Industries:
food; footwear, apparel and clothing; lumber, oil, cement, chemica s, mining, basic metals, hydropower

Industrial production growth rate:
3.5% (2017 est.)
country comparison to the world: 83

Labor force:
1.407 million (2017 est.)
country comparison to the world: 135

Labor force - by occupation:
agriculture: 41.8%
industry: 11.4%
services: 46.8% (2017 est.)

Unemployment rate:
14% (2017 est.)
15.2% (2016 est.)
note: these official rates may not include those working at near-subsistence farming
country comparison to the world: 170

Population below poverty line:

14.3% (2012 est.)

Household income or consumption by percentage share:
lowest 10%: 4.1%
highest 10%: 19.6% (2015 est.)

Distribution of family income - Gini index:
29 (2012 est.)
30 (2008 est.)
country comparison to the world: 136

Budget:
revenues: $3.486 billion
expenditures: $3.765 billion (2017 est.)

Taxes and other revenues:
26.8% of GDP (2017 est.)
country comparison to the world: 105

Budget surplus (+) or deficit (-):
-2.1% of GDP (2017 est.)
country comparison to the world: 88

Public debt:
71.3% of GDP (2017 est.)
72% of GDP (2016 est.)
country comparison to the world: 50

Fiscal year:
calendar year

Inflation rate (consumer prices):
2.1% (2017 est.)
1.3% (2016 est.)
country comparison to the world: 98

Central bank discount rate:
1.25% (31 December 2017 est.)
1.75% (31 December 2016 est.)
country comparison to the world: 125

Commercial bank prime lending rate:
7.2% (31 December 2017 est.)
9.65% (31 December 2016 est.)
country comparison to the world: 117

Stock of narrow money:
$3.979 billion (31 December 2017 est.)
$3.397 billion (31 December 2016 est.)
country comparison to the world: 112

Stock of broad money:

$6.665 billion (31 December 2017 est.)
$5.75 billion (31 December 2016 est.)
country comparison to the world: 122

Stock of domestic credit:
$8.147 billion (31 December 2017 est.)
$7.065 billion (31 December 2016 est.)
country comparison to the world: 114

Current account balance:
-$1.201 billion (2017 est.)
-$899 million (2016 est.)
country comparison to the world: 139

Exports:
$960.9 million (2017 est.)
$789.1 million (2016 est.)
country comparison to the world: 159

Exports - commodities:
apparel and clothing, footwear; asphalt, metals and metallic ores, crude oil; cement and construction materials, vegetables, fruits, tobacco

Exports - partners:
Italy 50.5%, Serbia 8.1%, Kosovo 7.5%, Greece 4.2%

Imports:
$4.084 billion (2017 est.)
$3.671 billion (2016 est.)
country comparison to the world: 132

Imports - commodities:
machinery and equipment, foodstuffs, textiles, chemicals

Imports - partners:
Italy 29%, Germany 9.4%, China 8.7%, Greece 7.8%, Turkey 7.8%, Serbia 4.1%

Reserves of foreign exchange and gold:
$3.274 billion (31 December 2017 est.)
$3.109 billion (31 December 2016 est.)
country comparison to the world: 102

Debt - external:
$8.579 billion (31 December 2017 est.)
$8.421 billion (31 December 2016 est.)
country comparison to the world: 120

Stock of direct foreign investment - at home:
$6.056 billion (31 December 2016 est.)
$5.459 billion (31 December 2015 est.)
country comparison to the world: 102

Exchange rates:
leke (ALL) per US dollar -
121.9 (2017 est.)
124.14 (2016 est.)
124.14 (2015 est.)
125.96 (2014 est.)
105.48 (2015 est.)

ENERGY

Electricity - production:
4.726 billion kWh (2014 est.)
country comparison to the world: 120

Electricity - consumption:
7.793 billion kWh (2014 est.)
country comparison to the world: 100
Electricity - exports:
288.5 million kWh (2014 est.)
country comparison to the world: 74

Electricity - imports:
3.355 billion kWh (2014 est.)
country comparison to the world: 48

Electricity - installed generating capacity:
1.878 million kW (2015 est.)
country comparison to the world: 109

Electricity - from fossil fuels:
5.2% of total installed capacity
country comparison to the world: 203

Electricity - from nuclear fuels:
0% of total installed capacity
country comparison to the world: 40

Electricity - from hydroelectric plants:
94.8% of total installed capacity
country comparison to the world: 9

Electricity - from other renewable sources:
0% of total installed capacity (2015 est.)
country comparison to the world: 151

Crude oil - production:
20,510 bbl/day (2014 est.)
country comparison to the world: 69

Crude oil - exports:
23,320 bbl/day
country comparison to the world: 57

Crude oil - imports:
3,440 bbl/day
country comparison to the world: 79

Crude oil - proved reserves:
168.3 million bbl (1 January 2015 est.)
country comparison to the world: 63

Refined petroleum products - production:
2,228 bbl/day (2012 est.)
country comparison to the world: 107

Refined petroleum products - consumption:
25,000 bbl/day (2015 est.)

country comparison to the world: 121
Refined petroleum products - exports:
354.2 bbl/day (2012 est.)
country comparison to the world: 117

Refined petroleum products - imports:
20,770 bbl/day (2012 est.)
country comparison to the world: 109
Natural gas - production:
19 million cu m (2015 est.)
country comparison to the world: 89

Natural gas - consumption:
19 million cu m
country comparison to the world: 112

Natural gas - exports:
0 cu m (2015 est.)
country comparison to the world: 55

Natural gas - imports:
0 cu m (2015 est.)
country comparison to the world: 155

Natural gas - proved reserves:
849.5 million cu m (1 January 2014 est.)
country comparison to the world: 105

Carbon dioxide emissions from consumption of energy:
3.962 million Mt (2012 est.)
country comparison to the world: 130

COMMUNICATIONS

Telephones - fixed lines:
total subscriptions: 250,000
subscriptions per 100 inhabitants: 8 (2014 est.)

country comparison to the world: 123

Telephones - mobile cellular:
total: 3.4 million
subscriptions per 100 inhabitants: 111 (2014 est.)
country comparison to the world: 133

Telephone system:

general assessment: despite new investment in fixed lines, teledensity remains low with roughly 10 fixed lines per 100 people; mobile-cellular telephone use is widespread and generally effective

domestic: offsetting the shortage of fixed-line capacity, mobile-cellular phone service has been available since 1996; by 2011, multiple companies were providing mobile services, and mobile teledensity had reached 100 per 100 persons; Internet broadband services initiated in 2005, but growth has been slow; Internet cafes are popular in Tirana and have started to spread outside the capital

international: country code - 355; submarine cable provides connectivity to Italy, Croatia, and Greece; the Trans-Balkan Line, a combination submarine cable and land fiber-optic system, provides additional connectivity to Bulgaria, Macedonia, and Turkey; international traffic carried by fiber-optic cable and, when necessary, by microwave radio relay from the Tirana exchange to Italy and Greece (2011)

Broadcast media:

3 public TV networks, one of which transmits by satellite to Albanian-language communities in neighboring countries; more than 60 private TV stations; many viewers can pick up Italian and Greek TV broadcasts via terrestrial reception; cable TV service is available; 2 public radio networks and roughly 25 private radio stations; several international broadcasters are available (2010)

Radio broadcast stations:

AM 13, FM 46, shortwave 1

Television broadcast stations:

65 (3 national, 62 local); 2 cable networks

Internet country code: .al

Internet hosts: 15,528
country comparison to the world: 124
Internet users:
total: 1.7 million
percent of population: 56.5% (
country comparison to the world: 104

TRANSPORTATION

Railways:
total: 447 km (none electrified)
standard gauge: 447 km 1.435-m gauge (1995)

Highways:
total: 18,000 km
paved: 5,400 km
unpaved: 12,600 km

Waterways: 43 km plus Albanian sections of Lake Scutari, Lake Ohrid, and Lake Prespa (1990)

Pipelines: crude oil 145 km; petroleum products 55 km; natural gas 64 km (1991)

Ports and harbors: Durres, Sarande, Shengjin, Vlore

Merchant marine:
total: 8 cargo ships (1,000 GRT or over) totaling 28,394 GRT/41,429 DWT

Airports: 9

Airports—with paved runways:
total: 3
2,438 to 3,047 m: 3

Airports—with unpaved runways:
total: 6
over 3,047 m: 1
1,524 to 2,437 m: 1
914 to 1,523 m: 2
under 914 m: 2

Heliports: 1

MILITARY

Military branches: Army, Navy, Air and Air Defense Forces, Interior Ministry Troops, Border Guards

Military manpower—military age: 19 years of age

Military manpower—availability:
males age 15-49: 763,949

Military manpower—fit for military service:
males age 15-49: 622,013

Military manpower—reaching military age annually:
males: 32,954

Military expenditures—dollar figure: $60 million

Military expenditures—percent of GDP: 2%

TRANSNATIONAL ISSUES

stateless persons: 7,443

Disputes—international: the Albanian Government supports protection of the rights of ethnic Albanians outside of its borders but has downplayed them to further its primary foreign policy goal of regional cooperation; Albanian majority in Kosovo seeks independence from Serbian Republic; Albanians in The Former Yugoslav Republic of Macedonia claim discrimination in education, access to public-sector jobs, and representation in government

Illicit drugs: increasingly active transshipment point for Southwest Asian opiates, hashish, and cannabis transiting the Balkan route and—to a far lesser extent—cocaine from South America destined for Western Europe; limited opium and cannabis production; ethnic Albanian narcotrafficking organizations active and rapidly expanding in Europe

IMPORTANT INFORMATION FOR UNDERSTANDING ALBANIA

OFFICIAL NAME: Republic of Albania

Geography

Area: 28,748 sq. km. (slightly larger than Maryland).
Major cities: *Capital*--Tirana (600,000, est.). *Others*--Durres (200,000, 2005 est.), Shkoder (81,000, 2005 est.), Vlore (72,000,est.).
Terrain: Situated in the southwestern region of the Balkan Peninsula, Albania is predominantly mountainous but flat along its coastline with the Adriatic Sea.
Climate: Mild, temperate; cool, wet winters; dry, hot summers.

People

Population (est.): 3,600,523.
Growth rate (est.): 0.529%.
Ethnic groups (2004 est., Government of Albania): Albanian 98.6%, Greeks 1.17%, others 0.23% (Vlachs, Roma, Serbs, Montenegrins, Macedonians, Balkan Egyptians, and Bulgarians).
Religions: Muslim (Sunni and Bektashi) 70%, Albanian Orthodox 20%, and Roman Catholic 10%.
Official language: Albanian.
Health (est.): *Life expectancy*--males 74.95 years; females 80.53 years. *Infant mortality rate*--20.02 deaths per 1,000 live births.

Government

Type: Parliamentary democracy.
Constitution: Adopted by popular referendum November 28, 1998.
Independence: November 28, 1912 (from the Ottoman Empire).
Branches: *Executive*--President (chief of state), Prime Minister (head of government), Council of Ministers (cabinet). *Legislative*--140-seat unicameral People's Assembly or Kuvendi Popullor (100 members elected by direct popular vote; 40 by proportional vote; all serve 4-year terms). *Judicial*--Constitutional Court, High Court, multiple district and appeals courts.
Suffrage: Universal at age 18.
Main political parties: Democratic Party of Albania (DP); Albanian Socialist Party (SP); Socialist Movement for Integration (LSI); Albanian Republican Party (PR); Demo-Christian Party (PDK); Union for Human Rights Party (PBDNJ); New Democracy Party (PDR); Social Democratic Party (PSD); Social Democracy Party (PDS).

Economy
Natural resources: Oil, gas, coal, iron, copper and chrome ores.

GEOGRAPHY

Albania shares a border with Greece to the south/southeast, Macedonia to the east, Kosovo to the northeast, and Montenegro to the northwest. Western Albania lies along the Adriatic and Ionian Sea coastlines. Albania's primary seaport is Durres, which handles 90% of its maritime cargo.

PEOPLE AND HISTORY

Over 90% of Albania's people are ethnic Albanian, and Albanian is the official language. Religions include Muslim (Sunni and Bektashi), Albanian Orthodox, and Roman Catholic.

Scholars believe the Albanian people are descended from a non-Slavic, non-Turkic group of tribes known as Illyrians, who arrived in the Balkans around 2000 BC. After falling under Roman authority in 165 BC, Albania was controlled nearly continuously by a succession of foreign powers until the mid-20th century, with only brief periods of self-rule.

Following the split of the Roman Empire in 395, the Byzantine Empire established control over present-day Albania. In the 11th century, Byzantine Emperor Alexius I Comnenus made the first recorded reference to a distinct area of land known as Albania and to its people.

The Ottoman Empire ruled Albania from 1385-1912. During this time, much of the population converted to the Islamic faith, and Albanians also emigrated to Italy, Greece, Egypt and Turkey. Although its control was briefly disrupted during the 1443-78 revolt, led by Albania's national hero, Gjergj Kastrioti Skenderbeu, the Ottomans eventually reasserted their dominance.

The League of Prizren (1878) promoted the idea of an Albanian nation-state and established the modern Albanian alphabet, updating a language that survived the hundreds of years of Ottoman rule despite being outlawed. By the early 20th century, the weakened Ottoman Empire was no longer able to suppress Albanian nationalism. Following the conclusion of the First Balkan War, Albanians issued the Vlore Proclamation of November 28, 1912, declaring independence and the Great Powers established Albania's borders in 1913. Albania's territorial integrity was confirmed at the Paris Peace Conference in 1919, after U.S. President Woodrow Wilson dismissed a plan by the European powers to divide Albania among its neighbors.

During the Second World War, Albania was occupied first by Italy (1939-43) and then by Germany (1943-44). After the war, Communist Party leader Enver Hoxha, through a combination of ruthlessness and strategic alliances, managed to preserve Albania's territorial integrity during the next 40 years, but exacted a terrible price from the population, which was subjected to purges, shortages, repression of civil and political rights, a total ban on religious observance, and increased isolation. Albania adhered to a strict Stalinist philosophy, eventually withdrawing from the Warsaw Pact in 1968 and alienating its final remaining ally, China, in 1978.

Following Hoxha's death in 1985 and the subsequent fall of communism in 1991, Albanian society struggled to overcome its historical isolation and underdevelopment. During the initial transition period, the Albanian Government sought closer ties with the West in order to improve economic conditions and introduced basic democratic reforms, including a multi-party system.

In 1992, after the sweeping electoral victory of the Democratic Party, Sali Berisha became the first democratically elected President of Albania. Berisha began a more deliberate program of economic and democratic reform but progress on these issues stalled in the mid-1990s, due to political gridlock. At the same time, unscrupulous investment companies defrauded investors all over Albania using pyramid schemes. In early 1997, several of these pyramid schemes collapsed, leaving thousands of people bankrupt, disillusioned, and angry. Armed revolts broke out across the country, leading to the near-total collapse of government authority. During this time, Albania's already inadequate and antiquated infrastructure suffered tremendous damage, as people looted public works for building materials. Weapons depots all over the country were raided. The anarchy of early 1997 alarmed the world and prompted intensive international mediation.

A UN Multinational Protection Force restored order, and an interim national reconciliation government oversaw the general elections of June 1997, which returned the Socialists and their allies to power at the national level. President Berisha resigned, and the Socialists elected Rexhep Meidani as President of the Republic.

During the transitional period of 1997-2002, a series of short-lived Socialist-led governments succeeded one another as Albania's fragile democratic structures were strengthened. Additional political parties formed, media outlets expanded, non-governmental organizations and business associations developed. In 1998, Albanians ratified a new constitution via popular referendum, guaranteeing the rule of law and the protection of fundamental human rights and religious freedom. Fatos Nano, Chairman of the Socialist Party, emerged as Prime Minister in July 2002.

On July 24, 2002, Alfred Moisiu was sworn in as President of the Republic. A nonpartisan figure, he was elected as a consensus candidate of the ruling and opposition parties. The peaceful transfer of power from President Meidani to President Moisiu was the result of an agreement between the parties to engage each other within established parliamentary structures. This "truce" ushered in a new period of political stability in Albania, making possible significant progress in democratic and economic reforms, rule of law initiatives, and the development of Albania's relations with its neighbors and the U.S.

The "truce" between party leaders began to fray in summer 2003 and progress on economic and political reforms suffered noticeably due to political infighting. The municipal elections of 2003 and national elections of 2005 were an improvement over past years, adding to the consolidation of democracy despite the continued presence of administrative errors and inaccuracies in voter lists.

In 2005, the Democratic Party and its allies returned to power, pledging to fight crime and corruption, decrease the size and scope of government, and promote economic growth. Their leader, Sali Berisha, was sworn in as Prime Minister on September 11, 2005.

Since the election, Prime Minister Berisha's government has made the fight against corruption and organized crime a priority, although the former has met with limited success. The opposition has criticized the government's approach to fighting corruption and crime as unconstitutional and an attempt to undermine independent institutions. While previously relations between the government and opposition SP party were characterized as antagonistic, both sides have at times shown willingness to work together to achieve major policy objectives, such as the constitutional reforms of early 2008.

Another politically contentious process was the pre-electoral period prior to the 2007 local elections. Although the February 18, 2007 local elections were generally peaceful and democratic, over-politicized debate during the preceding months resulted in procedural and administrative problems during the conduct of the elections. A major positive step forward was the performance of the police force.

The fragility of the Albanian electoral system was tested again during the parliamentary by-election in zone 26 (Shijak) on March 11, 2007. The left-wing opposition parties withdrew their commissioners from the polling stations and the counting center, in spite of prior concessions from the Central Elections Commission (CEC) to the opposition's demands. Opposition commissioners left and took with them one of the seals that mark the ballots. By midday, the opposition candidate also announced his withdrawal from the parliamentary race. However, the right of citizens to vote prevailed and the process continued thanks to the technical arrangements of the CEC. The only visible sign of violence was the wounding of a Democratic Party commissioner, who was fired upon by a militant.

Both elections were an indication of lack of political will to cooperate and of the need for a comprehensive electoral reform of the Albanian electoral system.

On July 20, 2007 President Bamir Topi was elected within Parliament after six members of the opposition coalition broke ranks to vote for his candidacy. Out of 90 deputies present at the session, 85 voted for Topi, while Neritan Ceka, head of the opposition Democratic Alliance party, won five votes. Topi, 50, a former agriculture minister, succeeded President Alfred Moisiu for a five-year mandate.

GOVERNMENT AND POLITICAL CONDITIONS

The unicameral People's Assembly (Kuvendi Popullor) consists of 140 seats, 100 of which are determined by direct popular vote. The remaining seats are distributed by proportional representation. All members serve 4-year terms. The Speaker of Parliament (Jozefina Topalli) has two deputies, who along with eight permanent parliamentary commissions assist in the process of legislating Albanian affairs. Parliamentary elections were held on June 28, 2009; as of end-June, results were not yet finalized.

The President is the head of state and elected by a three-fifths majority vote of all Assembly members. The President serves a term of 5 years with the right to one re-election. Although the position is largely ceremonial, the Constitution gives the President authority to appoint and dismiss some high-ranking civil servants in the executive and judicial branches, and this authority can have political implications. The President is also commander in chief of the armed forces, and chairs the National Security Commission. The current President's term expires on July 23, 2012.

The Prime Minister is appointed by the President and approved by a simple majority of all members of the Assembly. The Prime Minister serves as the Chairman of the Council of Ministers (cabinet), which consists of the Prime Minister, Deputy Prime Minister, and other ministers. Members of the Council of Ministers are nominated by the Prime Minister, decreed by the President, and approved by a parliamentary vote.

Albania's civil law system is similar to that of other European countries. The court structure consists of a Constitutional Court, a Supreme Court, and multiple appeal and district courts. The Constitutional Court is comprised of nine members appointed by the Assembly for one 9-year term. The Constitutional Court interprets the Constitution, determines the constitutionality of laws, and resolves disagreements between local and federal authorities. The Supreme Court is the highest court of appeal and consists of 11 members appointed by the President with the consent of the Assembly for 9-year terms. The President chairs the High Council of Justice which is responsible for appointing and dismissing other judges. The High Council of Justice is comprised of 15 members--the President of the Republic, the Chairman of the High Court, the Minister of

Justice, three members elected by the Assembly, and nine judges of all levels elected by the National Judicial Conference.

The remaining courts are divided into three jurisdictions: criminal, civil, and military. There are no jury trials under the Albanian system of justice. A college of three judges, sometimes referred to as a "jury" by the Albanian press, renders court verdicts.

Principal Government Officials
President--Bamir Topi
Prime Minister--Sali Berisha
Deputy Prime Minister--Genc Pollo
Minister of Defense--Gazmend Oketa
Minister of Foreign Affairs--Lulzim Basha

ECONOMY

Currency	Lek (ALL)
Fiscal year	Calendar year
Trade organisations	WTO, BSEC
Statistics	
GDP	$32.259 billion (PPP, 2015), $14.520 billion (Nominal, 2015)
GDP rank	96th (PPP, 2015 est.)
GDP growth	2.1% (Real, 2014 est.)
GDP per capita	$11.700 (PPP, 2015 est.) $5.260 (Nominal, 2015)
GDP by sector	agriculture: 18.4%, industry: 16.3%, services: 65.3% (2014 est.)
Inflation (CPI)	2.0% (CPI, 2012 est.)
Population below poverty line	10.3%
Gini coefficient	34.5
Labour force	1.280 million
Labour force by occupation	Agriculture: 18.4%, Industry: 16.3%, Services: 65.3% (December 2014 est.)
Unemployment	13.3%
Average gross salary	385 € / 430 $, monthly
Main industries	perfumes and cosmetic products, food and tobacco products; textiles and clothing; lumber, oil, cement, chemicals, mining, basic metals, hydropower
Ease-of-doing-business rank	68th
External	
Exports	$2.47 billion
Export goods	textiles and footwear; asphalt, metals and metallic ores, crude oil; vegetables, fruits, tobacco
Main export partners	Italy 43.3% China 9.7% Spain 8.4% Kosovo 7.4% India 6.1%

Imports	$5.067 billion (2014)
Import goods	machinery and equipment, foodstuffs, textiles, chemicals
Main import partners	Italy 36.1% Greece 9.6% China 7.2% Turkey 5.7% Germany 4%
Public finances	
Public debt	$7.825 billion (December 2014)
Revenues	$3.3 billion (Budget 2014)
Expenses	$4.50 billion (Budget 2014)
Economic aid	recipient: ODA: $366 million (top donors were Italy, EU, Germany) (2003 est.)
Credit rating	Standard & Poor's: B (Domestic) B+ (Foreign) BB+ (T&C Assessment) Outlook: Positive
Foreign reserves	$2.825 billion (December 2014)

The **economy of Albania** has undergone a transition from its Communist past into an open-market economy since the early 1990s. The country is rich in natural resources, and the economy is mainly bolstered by agriculture, food processing, lumber, oil, cement, chemicals, mining, basic metals, hydro power, tourism, textile industry, and petroleum extraction. As of 2014, exports seem to gain momentum and have increased 300% from 2008, although their contribution to the gross domestic product is still moderate (the export of products per capita as of 2014 is around $1,100).

Albania's transition from a socialist centrally planned economy to free-market capitalism has been largely successful. There are signs of increasing investments, and power cuts are reduced to the extent that Albania is now exporting energy. In 2012, its GDP per capita (expressed in Purchasing Power Standards) stood at 30% of the EU average, while AIC (Actual Individual Consumption) was 35%.Still, Albania has shown potential for economic growth, as more and more businesses relocate there and consumer goods are becoming available from emerging market traders as part of the current massive global cost-cutting exercise. Albania, Cyprus, and Poland are the only countries in Europe that recorded economic growth in the first quarter of 2010. International Monetary Fund (IMF) predicted 2.6% growth for Albania in 2010 and 3.2% in 2011.

Albania and Croatia have discussed the possibility of jointly building a nuclear power plant at Lake Shkoder, close to the border with Montenegro, a plan that has gathered criticism from Montenegro due to seismicity in the area. In addition, there is some doubt whether Albania would be able to finance a project of such a scale with a total national budget of less than $5 billion. However, in February 2009 Italian company Enel announced plans to build an 800 MW coal-fired power plant in Albania, to diversify electricity sources. Nearly 100% of the electricity is generated by ageing hydroelectric power plants, which are becoming more ineffective due to increasing droughts. However, there have been many private investments in building new hydroelectric power plants such as Devoll Hydro Power Plant and the Ashta hydropower plant.

The country has large deposits of petroleum and natural gas, and produced 26,000 barrels of oil per day in the first quarter of 2014 (BNK-TC). Natural gas production, estimated at about 30 million m^3, is sufficient to meet consumer demands.

Other natural resources include coal, bauxite, copper and iron ore.Albania has the largest onshore oil reserves in Europe. Albania's crude output amounted to more than 1.2 million tonnes in 2015, including 1.06 million by Canada's Bankers Petroleum, 87,063 tonnes from Canada's Stream Oil and 37,406 tonnes by Albpetrol on its own. Three foreign firms produced the rest.

Agriculture is the most significant sector, employing a significant proportion of the labor force and generating about 21% of GDP. Agriculture in Albania employs 47.8% of the population and about 24.31% of the land is used for agricultural purposes. Domestic farm products accounted for 63% of household expenditures and 25% of exports in 1990. As part of the pre-accession process of Albania to the EU, farmers are being aided through IPA 2011 funds to improve Albanian agriculture standards. Albania produces significant amounts of tobacco, olives, wheat, maize, potatoes, vegetables, fruits, sugar beets, grapes; meat, honey, dairy products, and traditional medicine and aromatic plants, figs (13th largest producer in the world) and sour cherries. Albania's proximity to the Ionian Sea and the Adriatic Sea give the underdeveloped fishing industry great potential. World Bank and European Community economists report that Albania's fishing industry has good potential to generate export earnings because prices in the nearby Greek and Italian markets are many times higher than those in the Albanian market. The fish available off the coasts of Albania are carp, trout, sea bream, mussels, and crustaceans.

"Tourism is gaining a fair share of Albania's GDP with visitors growing every year. As of 2014 exports seem to gain momentum and have increased 300% from 2008, although their contribution to the GDP is still moderate (the exports per capita ratio currently stands at 1100 $) . Although Albania's growth has slowed in 2015 tourism is expanding rapidly and foreign investments are becoming more common as the government continues the modernization of Albania's institutions

Albania's economy has improved substantially over recent years and has outperformed many other countries in the region. However, it is still considered one of the poorest countries in Europe. According to the Bank of Albania, per capita income was $3,675 in 2008, expected to reach $4,000 in 2009. According to some preliminary data by the World Bank's Poverty Assessment Program, 12.4% of the population lived below the poverty line in 2008, marking a considerable improvement from 25.4% in 2002. The official unemployment rate is 12.7%. Almost 60% of all workers are employed in the agricultural sector, although the construction and service industries have been expanding recently. Tourism has been boosted significantly by ethnic Albanian tourists from throughout the Balkans. The GDP is comprised of services (50%), agriculture (19%), industry (12%), construction (14%), and transport and communication (6%). The Albanian economy has been partially sheltered from the global financial crisis and the economic downturn. In April 2009, the International Monetary Fund (IMF) predicted that Albania would be one of two countries in Europe to enjoy a positive growth rate for 2009, but lower remittances from Albanian workers abroad (approximately 9.6% of the GDP in 2008), mostly in Greece and Italy, and smaller exports will put a strain on economic activity.

The global financial crisis has reduced Albanian citizens' trust of commercial banks, even though the domestic banking sector has remained largely insulated from the crisis. Although bank deposits dropped by 10% since September 2008, withdrawals have diminished recently and deposits have stabilized during the second quarter of 2009. Lower liquidity has forced commercial banks to tighten lending procedures. In February 2009, the growth rate of loans dropped to 29% from 35% in 2008. In general, the banking sector remains viable and able to further finance the economy, as the ratio of loans to deposits, approximately 65%, is still low compared to western standards.

Albania was the last of the central and eastern European countries to embark upon democratic and free market reforms. Furthermore, Albania started from a comparatively disadvantaged position due to Hoxha's catastrophic economic policies. The transition from a centrally planned economy to a market-oriented system has been almost as difficult for Albania as the country's communist period.

The democratically elected government that assumed office in April 1992 launched an ambitious economic reform program meant to halt economic deterioration and put the country on the path toward a market economy. Key elements included price and exchange system liberalization, fiscal consolidation, monetary restraint, and a firm income policy. These were complemented by a comprehensive package of structural reforms, including privatization, enterprise and financial sector reform, and creation of the legal framework for a market economy and private sector activity.

Results of Albania's efforts were initially encouraging. Led by the agricultural sector, real GDP grew, and Albania's currency, the lek, stabilized. The speed and vigor of private entrepreneurial response to the opening of Albania's economy was better than expected. In 1995, however, progress stalled. The collapse of the infamous pyramid schemes of the late 1990s and the instability that followed were a tremendous setback, from which Albania's economy continues to recover.

The Albanian Government signed a free trade agreement (FTA) with the European Union (EU) as part of its Stabilization and Association Agreement negotiations. The interim agreement entered into force in December 2006, with a duty-free regime for almost 90% of agricultural and industrial products. On the fiscal side it will also significantly reduce revenue collection.

Albania has FTAs with Macedonia, Croatia, Bulgaria, Romania, Bosnia, Turkey, and Moldova. Albania also previously established an FTA with the UN Interim Administration Mission in Kosovo (UNMIK), which was transferred to the Republic of Kosovo in 2009. In April 2006, these bilateral agreements were replaced by a multiregional agreement that entered into force in May 2007 based on the Central European Free Trade Agreement (CEFTA) model.

The EU remains, by far, Albania's main trading partner, providing 60.7% of Albania's imports and receiving 79.7% of exports for 2008. Trade with Italy and Greece represent the largest share of EU trade, with a combined 67.7% of imports and 88.6% of exports. The impact of CEFTA in Albania's trade with member countries has been insignificant.

U.S. trade with Albania is very low. In 2008, U.S. exports to Albania totaled $67 million compared with $49 million in 2007, an increase of 36.7%. Part of this increase was due to the 8% depreciation of the dollar against the domestic currency. U.S. imports from Albania decreased 26% in 2008 ($5.1 million) from $6.9 million in 2007. However, there are some discrepancies between U.S. and Albanian trade figures. Major U.S. investment to date has been limited to large-scale infrastructure contracts with the government; Lockheed Martin and Bechtel are principal U.S. participants. In 2008, Refinery Associates of Texas became the first significant U.S. investor representing 20% of the consortium that privatized 85% of the shares of the state-owned oil refinery ARMO.

Albania is trying to attract foreign investment and promote domestic investment, but significant impediments exist. The Albanian Government faces the daunting task of standardizing and uniformly applying business laws, improving transparency in business procedures, resolving property ownership disputes, restructuring the tax systems (including tax collection), and reducing corruption.

Business growth has been hampered by Albania's inadequate energy and transportation infrastructure despite some significant investments in both sectors during the last few years. The capital, Tirana, and the main port of Durres generally receive electricity most of the day, but frequent power outages plague every other city, small town, and rural village. Although recent steps have been taken to improve the transportation infrastructure, Albania has a limited railway system and just one international airport. Because of the mountainous terrain and poor road conditions, overland goods transport is arduous and costly. However, the government has invested heavily in road construction over the last three years, and the country now sports a new, modern highway along its entire coastline, from Shkoder in the north to the southern resort city of Sarande. In addition, completion of the 170-kilometer Durres-Kukes highway in fall 2009 will provide a major transportation corridor connecting markets in the central Balkans through Kosovo to the port of Durres.

MILITARY AFFAIRS

Since the fall of communism in Albania in 1991, the country has played a constructive role in resolving several of the interethnic conflicts in south central Europe, promoting peaceful dispute resolution and discouraging ethnic Albanian extremists. Albania sheltered many thousands of Kosovar refugees during the 1999 conflict. Albania is part of the international force serving in Bosnia (EUFOR), and Albanian peacekeepers are part of the International Security Assistance Force (ISAF) in Afghanistan and previously contributed to the international stabilization force in Iraq prior to its mandate expiring in December 2008. While in Iraq, Albania was one of only four nations to contribute troops to the combat phase of Operation Enduring Freedom.

Albania worked with the international community to restructure its armed forces and strengthen democratic structures, including addressing military reforms, in its pursuit of NATO membership. Since 1999, Albania has spent approximately $108 million annually on military expenditures, roughly 1.35% of its GDP. According to Government of Albania projections, military expenditures were to reach 2% of GDP in 2008. With bilateral and multilateral assistance, the Ministry of Defense is transitioning to a smaller, voluntary, professional military, and reducing the vast amounts of excess weaponry and ammunition that litter the country and pose a significant public hazard and proliferation risk. The Albanian Government and the international community are working together on a project that will make Albania a mine-free country by 2010. Most high- and medium-priority mine clearance has been completed in the mined areas of northeast Albania, a legacy of the 1999 Kosovo crisis. However, a significant amount of unexploded ordnance remains to be demilitarized in the country.

Albania and the U.S. enjoy a military partnership and are signatories to treaties including the 2003 Prevention of Proliferation of Weapons of Mass Destruction and the Promotion of Defense and Military Relations and the 2004 Supplementary Agreement to the Partnership for Peace Status of Forces Agreement, which defined the status of American military troops in Albania, further enabling military cooperation. In May 2003, Albania, Croatia, Macedonia, and the U.S. created the Adriatic Charter, modeled on the Baltic Charter, as a mechanism for promoting regional cooperation to advance each country's NATO candidacy. In spite of strong EU objections, Albania also signed in May 2003 a bilateral agreement with the United States on non-surrender of persons, based on Article 98 of the statute of International Criminal Court.

In 2004 President George W. Bush authorized the use of the Nunn-Lugar Cooperative Threat Reduction program funds for projects in Albania, marking the first time such funds were used outside the former Soviet Union. With this funding the United States has assisted the Government of Albania with the destruction of a stockpile of chemical agents left over from the communist regime. Under this program, Albania became the first nation in the world to complete destruction of declared chemical weapons holdings under the Chemical Weapons Convention in July 2007.

Albania received an invitation to become a NATO member at the April 2008 NATO Summit in Bucharest. The U.S. Senate unanimously ratified Albania's Protocols of Accession to NATO on September 25, 2008, and President Bush signed the Accession Protocols on October 24, 2008. Albania became a member of NATO on April 1, 2009.

FOREIGN RELATIONS

Albania is currently pursuing a path of greater Euro-Atlantic integration. Its primary long-term goals are to gain EU membership and to promote closer bilateral ties with its neighbors and with the U.S. Albania is a member of a number of international organizations, as well as multiple regional organizations and initiatives, including NATO, the Organization for Security and Cooperation in Europe (OSCE), the UN, the Stability Pact, the Adriatic Charter, and the World Trade Organization (WTO). In June 2006, Albania and the EU signed a Stabilization and Association Agreement, the first step to EU membership, which will focus on implementing essential rule of law reforms and curbing corruption and organized crime. Albania filed its application for EU candidacy on April 28, 2009.

Albania maintains good relations with its neighbors. It re-established diplomatic relations with the Federal Republic of Yugoslavia following the ousting of Slobodan Milosevic in 2000, and maintains excellent relations with the Republic of Montenegro, which gained its independence after the dissolution of the Serbia and Montenegro union in 2006. Albanian, Macedonian, and Italian law enforcement agencies are cooperating with increasing efficiency to crack down on the trafficking of arms, drugs, contraband, and human beings across their borders. Albania has also arrested and prosecuted several ethnic Albanian extremists on charges of inciting interethnic hatred in Macedonia and Kosovo. Tensions occasionally arise with Greece over the treatment of the Greek minority in Albania or the Albanian community in Greece, but overall relations are good.

U.S.-ALBANIAN RELATIONS

Albania enjoys friendly and cooperative bilateral relations with the U.S. Pro-U.S. sentiment is widespread among the population. Even while the U.S., which had closed its mission to Albania in 1946, was being vilified by communist propaganda during the Hoxha regime, ordinary Albanians remembered that Woodrow Wilson had supported Albanian independence in 1919. Albanians credit the NATO bombing of Serbia in 1999 with saving thousands of Kosovo Albanians, and they greatly appreciate the U.S. Government's continued support for a stable, free, and democratic Kosovo.

In 2003, Albania and the U.S. signed and ratified a number of agreements, including a treaty on the Prevention of Proliferation of Weapons of Mass Destruction and the Promotion of Defense and Military Relations; the Adriatic Charter; and an agreement regarding the non-surrender of persons to the International Criminal Court. The U.S. strongly supports Albania's EU membership goal, as it did Albania's pursuit of NATO membership. Working toward NATO membership, the U.S. and Albania signed a Supplementary Agreement to the Partnership for Peace Status of Forces Agreement, an important step in strengthening bilateral cooperation and enhancing security, peace, and stability in the region. The U.S. Senate unanimously ratified Albania's Protocols of Accession to NATO on September 25, 2008, and President Bush signed the Accession Protocols on October 24, 2008.

Since FY 1991, the U.S. has provided Albania with more than $616 million in assistance, not counting U.S. Department of Agriculture (USDA) food aid. The aid has served to facilitate

Albania's transition from the most isolated and repressive communist state in Europe to a modern democracy with a market-oriented economy, and to support long-term development. In 2007, the U.S. gave over $21.1 million to Albania under the Support for East European Democracy (SEED) Act program. Albania was among the first countries selected to participate in the Threshold Program under the Millennium Challenge Account, winning a grant of $13.8 million and a second Threshold grant of $16 million in 2008. The program targets two critical stumbling blocks to development--corruption and rule of law.

Despite daunting problems at home, Albania has wholeheartedly supported U.S. anti-terrorism efforts by freezing terrorist assets, shutting down non-governmental organizations (NGOs) with possible links to terrorist financing, expelling extremists, and providing hundreds of military troops for the U.S.-led actions in Afghanistan and Iraq. Albania has played a moderating role in the region and has fully supported UN mediation efforts in Kosovo.

Principal U.S. Embassy Officials

chief of mission: Ambassador Donald LU (since 13 January 2015)

Donald Lu was sworn in as U.S. Ambassador to the Republic of Albania on December 17, 2014. Prior to that assignment, he worked on the Ebola crisis in West Africa as Deputy Coordinator for Ebola Response in the State Department. His overseas postings include Deputy Chief of Mission in India, Azerbaijan and Kyrgyzstan. He also served for a year as Chargé d'Affaires at the U.S. Embassy in Azerbaijan.

Deputy Chief of Mission--Stephen Cristina
Political/Economic Section Chief--Paul Poletes
Political Officers--Tony Baird, Michael Gray
Economic/Commercial Officer--Victor Myev
Consular Officer--Abigail Aronson
USAID Director--Roberta Mahoney
Public Affairs Officer--Bix Aliu
Defense Attaché--Brian Moore
Regional Security Officer--Patrick Leonard
Management Officer--vacant

The U.S. Embassy is located at 103 Tirana Rruga Elbasanit, Tirana; telephone: [355] (4) 224-7285; facsimile: [355] (4) 223-2222.

TRAVEL AND BUSINESS INFORMATION

The U.S. Department of State's Consular Information Program advises Americans traveling and residing abroad through Country Specific Information, Travel Alerts, and Travel Warnings. **Country Specific Information** exists for all countries and includes information on entry and exit requirements, currency regulations, health conditions, safety and security, crime, political disturbances, and the addresses of the U.S. embassies and consulates abroad. **Travel Alerts** are issued to disseminate information quickly about terrorist threats and other relatively short-term conditions overseas that pose significant risks to the security of American travelers. **Travel Warnings** are issued when the State Department recommends that Americans avoid travel to a certain country because the situation is dangerous or unstable.

For the latest security information, Americans living and traveling abroad should regularly monitor the Department's Bureau of Consular Affairs Internet web site at http://www.travel.state.gov, where the current Worldwide Caution, Travel Alerts, and Travel Warnings can be found. Consular

Affairs Publications, which contain information on obtaining passports and planning a safe trip abroad, are also available at http://www.travel.state.gov. For additional information on international travel, see http://www.usa.gov/Citizen/Topics/Travel/International.shtml.

The Department of State encourages all U.S. citizens traveling or residing abroad to register via the State Department's travel registration website or at the nearest U.S. embassy or consulate abroad. Registration will make your presence and whereabouts known in case it is necessary to contact you in an emergency and will enable you to receive up-to-date information on security conditions.

Emergency information concerning Americans traveling abroad may be obtained by calling 1-888-407-4747 toll free in the U.S. and Canada or the regular toll line 1-202-501-4444 for callers outside the U.S. and Canada.

The National Passport Information Center (NPIC) is the U.S. Department of State's single, centralized public contact center for U.S. passport information. Telephone: 1-877-4-USA-PPT (1-877-487-2778); TDD/TTY: 1-888-874-7793. Passport information is available 24 hours, 7 days a week. You may speak with a representative Monday-Friday, 8 a.m. to 10 p.m., Eastern Time, excluding federal holidays.

Travelers can check the latest health information with the U.S. Centers for Disease Control and Prevention in Atlanta, Georgia. A hotline at 800-CDC-INFO (800-232-4636) and a web site at http://wwwn.cdc.gov/travel/default.aspx give the most recent health advisories, immunization recommendations or requirements, and advice on food and drinking water safety for regions and countries. The CDC publication "Health Information for International Travel" can be found at http://wwwn.cdc.gov/travel/contentYellowBook.aspx.

Further Electronic Information

Department of State Web Site. Available on the Internet at http://www.state.gov, the Department of State web site provides timely, global access to official U.S. foreign policy information, including Background Notes and daily press briefings along with the directory of key officers of Foreign Service posts and more. The Overseas Security Advisory Council (OSAC) provides security information and regional news that impact U.S. companies working abroad through its website http://www.osac.gov

Export.gov provides a portal to all export-related assistance and market information offered by the federal government and provides trade leads, free export counseling, help with the export process, and more.

MINERAL AND MINING SECTOR: STRATEGIC INFORMATION

ALBANIA

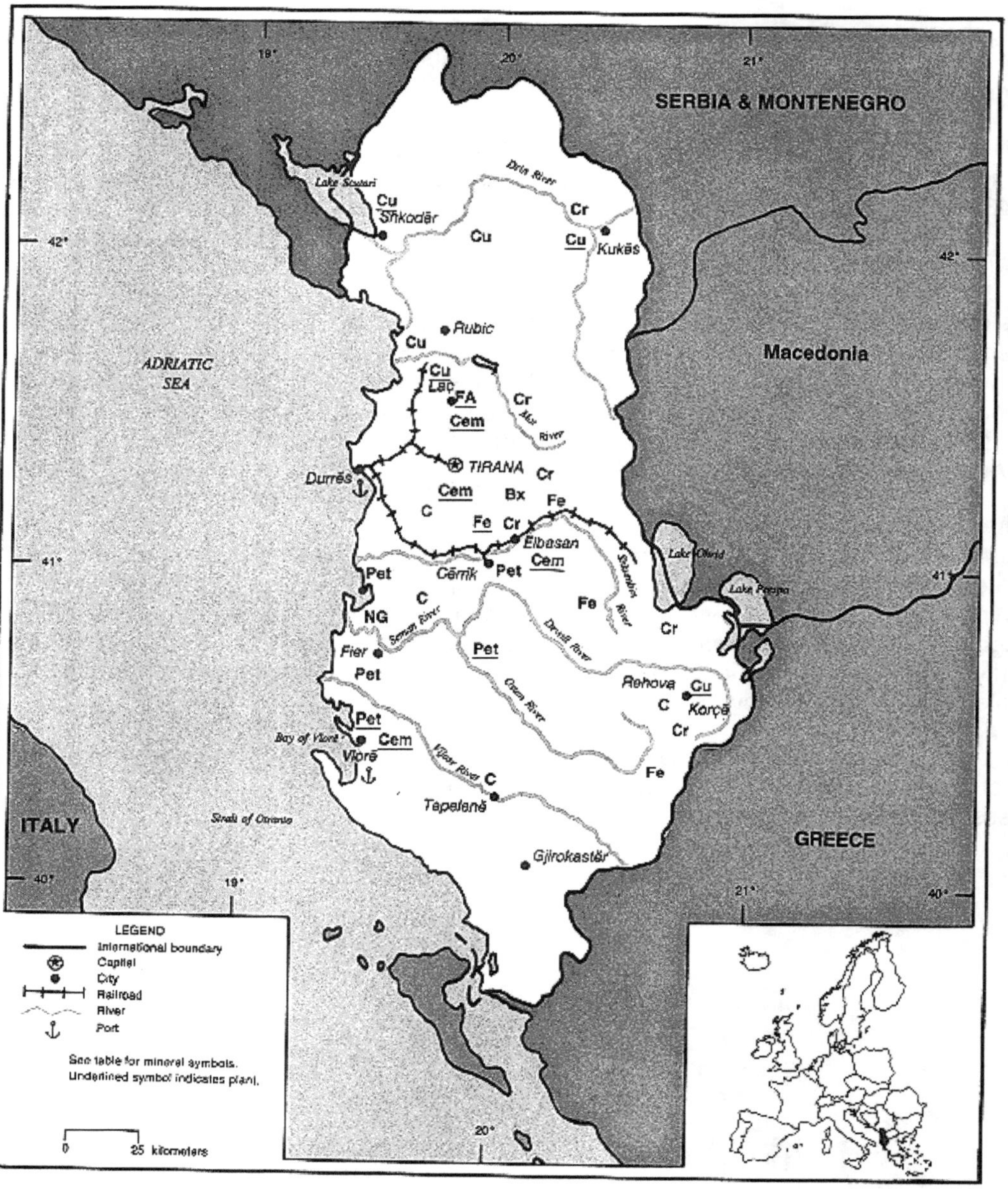

THE MINERAL INDUSTRY OF ALBANIA - BASIC DEVELOPMENTS

Albania is a country with rich mineral resources. Mineral exploration, exploitation and processing constitutes a key component of the Albanian economy, due to a traditional mining industry that has been a solid foundation to the country economic sector generating substantial revenues. The minerals mined and treated in the past which still remain in Albania include chrome, copper, iron-nickel and coal. Mining industry development in Albania has passed through three main stages:

The first stage includes the period before the World War II. It has been marked by two important events of the mining industry. In 1922 was compiled the first Geological Map of Albania, the first of its kind in the Balkans, whereas 1929 signs the approve of the Mining Law of the Albanian Kingdom, which paved the way to the exploration and exploitation of mineral resources.

The second stage (1944-1994) marks the period when the mining activity has been organized in state-owned enterprises.

The third stage includes the period from 1994 up to date. It is the most important period of the mining industry, during which it is enabled the transition from an economically centralized type of operation into one based on the free market. With the assistance of the World Bank, in 1994 it was composed and approved the Mining Law of Albania.

Albania's important mineral deposits included chromium, copper, limestone, and petroleum. Production of mineral commodities was limited, but the number of exploration projects increased as Albania continued to attract international exploration companies.

Albania has the potential to increase its production of metals and mineral fuels as exploration projects continue and as foreign companies increase investments in Albania. Further investment will depend on economic and social stability as well as on the improvement of infrastructure.

MINERALS IN THE NATIONAL ECONOMY

In 2009, Albania's gross domestic product (GDP) increased by 2.8% and the rate of inflation was 2.2%. In 2008 (the most recent year for which data were available), industrial production made up about 9% of the GDP, and the mineral extraction industry accounted for about 10% of the value of industrial production and almost 1% of the GDP (Institute of Statistics of the Republic of Albania, 2010; International Monetary Fund, 2010, p. 159, 165).

PRODUCTION

Production data for mineral commodities in 2009 were entirely estimated with the exception of ferrochromium, chromite, and crude steel production. Production of chromite and crude steel increased by 24%, and 16%, respectively, compared with that of 2008. Rolled steel production was estimated to have increased by about 16% and crude petroleum production was estimated to have increased by 5%. Production of ferrochromium decreased by about 37%. Revised figures for 2008 show that a number of significant production increases and decreases occurred between 2007 and 2008. In 2008, silica sand production increased by 174% compared with that of 2007; limestone production increased by 124%; gypsum production, by 68%; bitumen production, by 33%; crude steel production, by 44%; rolled steel production, by 43%; natural gas production, by 20%; and crude petroleum production, by 12%. Lignite production decreased by 63%; refined fuels production, by 30%; coke production, by 20%; and cement production, by 17% in 2008 compared with production in 2007 (table 1).

TABLE 1
ALBANIA: PRODUCTION OF MINERAL COMMODITIES[1]

(Metric tons unless otherwise specified)

Commodity[2]		2006	2007	2008	2009[e]
METALS					
Chromite, gross weight (18-42% Cr_2O_3)		212,581[r]	199,771[r]	207,104[r]	256,000[3]
Copper:					
Ore, gross weight		35,071[r]	98,000[r]	105,000[r]	105,000
Cu content or ore (1.3-2.5%)[e]		670	1,900	2,000[e]	2,000
Iron and steel:					
Metal, ferroalloys, ferrochromium		17,040	--	11,916	7,556[3]
Steel:					
Crude steel, secondary		205,534	263,271	380,000[r]	440,000[3]
Rolled steel		114,000	136,000	194,000[r]	226,000
Iron-nickel and nickel-silicate ores[4]		79,000	369,559	353,290	350,000
INDUSTRIAL MINERALS					
Cement, hydraulic	thousand metric tons	525	889	737	740
Clay, kaolin[e]	do.	300	300	300	300
Dolomite[e]		1,000,000	1,000,000	1,000,000	1,000,000
Gypsum		19,683	46,200	77,633	78,000
Limestone	cubic meters	1,339,440	1,716,122	3,837,529	3,800,000
Salt[e]		25,000	25,000	25,000	25,000
Silica sand	cubic meters	3,200	4,400	12,077	12,000
MINERAL FUELS AND RELATED MATERIALS					
Coal, lignite		3,800[r]	4,000[r]	1,500[r]	1,500
Gas, natural, gross production	thousand cubic meters	11,091	11,089	13,295	13,300
Petroleum:					
Crude, gross weight	thousand 42-gallon barrels	2,084	3,580[r, e]	4,000[r, e]	4,200
Refinery products:					
Bitumen		83,000	69,000	92,000	92,000
Coke		64,000	59,000	47,000	47,000
Fuels[e]	thousand 42-gallon barrels	2,060	2,010	1,400	1,400

[e]Estimated; estimated data are rounded to no more than three significant digits; may not add to totals shown. [r]Revised. do. Ditto. -- Zero.

[1]Table includes data available through May 19, 2010.

[2]In addition to the commodities listed, a variety of industrial minerals and construction materials (common clay, lime, olivinite, sand and gravel, and stone) were believed to have been produced, but output is not reported quantitatively, and available information is inadequate to make reliable estimates of output. Also, a small amount of bauxite for use in the cement industry was believed to have been produced.

[3]Reported figure.

[4]Iron-nickel and nickel-silicate ore production were not reported separately. Estimates of metal content of ores were not made owing to the significant variations of the iron and nickel content of the ores, which depend not only on the type of ore, but also on the region in which it was mined.

Iron-nickel ores were reported to contain from 37.22% to 44.72% Fe and from 0.97% to 1.07% Ni; nickel-silicate ores were reported to contain from 16.6% to 21.73% Fe and from 1.06% to 1.2% Ni.

STRUCTURE OF THE MINERAL INDUSTRY

Mining activities in Albania are regulated by the Mining Law of Albania, No. 7796, dated February 17, 1994. Privatization of Albanian mineral resources is accomplished through the granting of prospecting permits, exploration concessions, and mining concessions to Albanian and foreign companies. As of December 2009, 832 outstanding permits for prospecting, exploration, and mining were reported; 680 of these permits were for mining. Out of the 832 outstanding permits, the largest number were for limestone (282 permits), chromite (262 permits), and iron-nickel and nickel-silicate (37 permits). Table 2 is a list of major mineral industry facilities. Previously listed copper ore and metal production facilities, iron ore mines, and lignite mines were removed from table 2 owing to a lack of information about these facilities (Parliament of Albania, 1994, p. 6-12; National Agency of Natural Resources of Albania, 2010, p. 9).

METALS

Chromium.—In August, Albanian Chrome, Sh.p.k. (ACR) restarted production at its 1,500-metric-ton-per-month (t/mo)-capacity high-carbon ferrochromium smelter. ACR halted production in December 2008 owing to low demand and falling prices for ferrochromium. Total ferrochromium production capacity increased to 36,000 metric tons per year (t/yr) in October when ACR began production at its new 1,500-t/mo-capacity low-carbon ferrochromium smelter. Also, DCM Decometal obtained the 50% share of ACR that was formerly held by Tenwingo Ltd. of Russia. The date and details of the share exchange were unknown (Metal Bulletin, 2009a, p. 9; 2009b, p. 9).

Although the gross weight of chromite output is reported in table 1, figures for marketable chromite ore and concentrate that were reported in the the 2008 Minerals Yearbook were removed owing to a lack of information on production of these products. The National Agency of Natural Resources of Albania reported chromite ore reserves of 36.9 million metric tons (Mt) (National Agency of Natural Resources of Albania, 2010, p. 14).

In January, Empire Mining Corp. received exclusive exploration and development rights to four licenses located near Bulqiza. The area of the licenses covered 64.5 square kilometers (km^2) (24 square miles). JAB Resources Ltd. held three exploration permits that covered 120 km^2 in northeastern Albania. The company's target was to mine 22 Mt of ore containing an average of 14% chromium oxide during the life of the mine; the ore would be processed into concentrate consisting of greater than 40% chromium oxide. The company expected initial production to be about 700,000 t/yr of crude ore and 120,000 t/yr of concentrate. No dates were given for the expected start of production (Empire Mining Corp., 2009; JAB Resources Ltd., 2010).

INDUSTRIAL MINERALS

No data were available on the production of industrial minerals. Production is estimated to have remained near the 2008 production levels.

Cement.—Antea Cement Sh.a. (a subsidiary of Titan Cement Company S.A. of Greece) continued construction of a 1.5-million-metric-ton-per-year (Mt/yr)-capacity cement plant in the Kruje region. The plant was expected to begin operating in March 2010. Cementos Aquila sh.p.k. (a subsidiary of Grupo Empresarial Aricam S.L.) planned to construct a cement plant in Mamurras with an initial capacity of 1.3 Mt/yr and an eventual capacity of 2.6 Mt/yr. The company expected the plant to be operational in 2010.

The Spacelift Cement Group cement plant was removed from table 2 because it now appears that the plant has not yet been built. The unidentified cement plant located in Vlore that appeared in table 2 in the Albania report of the 2008 Minerals Yearbook has also been removed because the plant seems to have closed in 1994. Two other cement plants in Balldre and in Lezha were also thought to be in the construction stage, but details on these plants were unavailable (Grupo Empresarial Aricam, 2008; Titan Cement Company S.A., 2010, p. 31, 47).

MINERAL FUELS

Crude Petroleum.—Crude petroleum production was estimated to have increased by about 5% compared with production in 2008. The increase in production was attributed to an average daily output increase to 6,438 barrels per day (bbl/d) from 5,875 bbl/d in 2008 by Bankers Petroleum Ltd. at the Patos Marinza oilfield in southwestern Albania. Bankers Petroleum also reported an increase of proved reserves at its Patos Marinza license to 92.8 million barrels (Mbbl) from 69.4 Mbbl in 2008.

Proved and probable reserves increased to 213.9 Mbbl from 180 Mbbl in 2008 (Bankers Petroleum Ltd., 2010, p. 8). The state-owned company Albpetrol sh.a. was the only other producer of crude oil, but production data were not available for 2009, so production was estimated to have remained at about 1.9 Mbbl.

MINING INDUSTRY - GENERAL OVERVIEW

Albania is a country with rich mineral resources. Mineral exploration, exploitation and processing constitutes a key component of the Albanian economy, due to a traditional mining industry that has been a solid foundation to the country economic sector generating substantial revenues. The minerals mined and treated in the past which still remain in Albania include chrome, copper, iron-nickel and coal.

Mining industry development in Albania has passed through three main stages:

The first stage includes the period before the World War II. It has been marked by two important events of the mining industry. In 1922 was compiled the first Geological Map of Albania, the first of its kind in the Balkans, whereas 1929 signs the approve of the Mining Law of the Albanian Kingdom, which paved the way to the exploration and exploitation of mineral resources.

The second stage (1944-1994) marks the period when the mining activity has been organized in state-owned enterprises.

The third stage includes the period from 1994 up to date. It is the most important period of the mining industry, during which it is enabled the transition from an economically centralized type of operation into one based on the free market. With the assistance of the World Bank, in 1994 it was composed and approved the Mining Law of Albania.

No. of companies: 682 local and foreign companies equipped with mining exploitation
154 domestic and foreign companies equipped with mining, search and discovery or disclosure

Exports: 8.3% increase, the commercial balance +30% (2010/2011)

Contribution: 4,689 employees

Mineral trade volume reached 23.542 million Leke

Exported products: Chromium and construction materials (eg cement)

LICENSING

The licensing process initiated in 1994, upon approval of the Albanian Government. There were issued about 800 mining permits out of which were 590 exploitation permits. Out of a total of 800 mining permits, 220 permits have been issued for chrome, 30 permits for ironnickel and nickel-silicate, 259 permits for limestone, 15 permits for marble limestone, 17 permits for copper, 5 permits for coal, 2 permits for bauxite, 5 permits for quartz, 11 permits for gypsum alabaster, 35 permits for clay, 38 permits for limestone tiles, 26 permits for sandstone and 2 permits for plagiogranite. The rest of exploitation licenses include rock types, like as fractured limestones, quartz sands, sandstones, schistes, bituminous sands and gravels, basalts, ultra basic rocks, etc.

CONCESSIONS

In 1995 was approved the Law "On Concessions". With its approval determined parts of the Mining Industry i, chrome, copper, iron-nickel and bitumen were given on concession.The concession was applied for the determined parts of the mining industry that required overall investments in prospecting, exploration, exploitation or restructuration of the processing industry.

There are given on concession:

Chrome's mines of Bulqiza, Katjel, Pojska

Copper's mines of Lak Rosh dhe Karmë

Bitum's mine of Selenica

MINING POTENTIAL OF ALBANIA

No.	Minerals	Geologic Reserves	
		Q-ty (million tons)	Content, %
1	2	3	4
1.	Chromite	32,8	Cr_2O_3 (18-42)%
2.	Iron-Nickel Nickel-Silicate	230,29 81,4	Fe 42.3%; Ni 0.98%; SiO_2 12.8%; Co 0.063% Fe 18.3%; Ni 1.3%; SiO_2 36.9%; Co 0.043%
3.	Copper	53	Cu (1.3-2.5)%
4.	Coal	794	3200 kcal/kg
5.	Peats (Turfs)	156 mil. m^3	2907 kcal/kg, moisture 11.3%, ashes 30%, S 1.1%
6.	Natural Bitumen	0,864	(4.41-9.73)% rarely 11.94% bitumen
7.	Bituminous sands	>246	(8-10)% bitumen
8.	Bituminous coal	3-4	3500-7500 kcal/kg
9.	Pirobitumens	6,4	2000-3000 kcal/kg, C (78-80.6)%
10.	Titanomagnetites	137	TiO_2 6%; Fe_2O_3 18%; V_2O_5 0.2-0.5%
11.	Bauxite	12	Al_2O_3 (40-50)%; SiO_2 13%, Fe_2O_3 (7.8-18.6)%; TiO_2 2.1%, CaO 2.4%

Through studies and geologic exploration carried out in the course of the last 50 years have been concretised a lot of important mineral resources

1	2	3	4
12.	Barite	0,72	
13.	Mergele	>2,6	CaO (36-38)%, MgO (73-77)%, SiO_2 (1.9-2.6)%, Fe_2O_3 (2.1-3.5)%
14.	Trepele	6,4	CaO (0.03-0.35)%, MgO (18-28)%, SiO_2 (1.5-4.9)%, Fe_2O_3 (0.41-1.5)%
15	Polymetals	1,031	Cu 0.25-1.035, Zn 0.15-0.89%, Pb 0.15-0.29%, Au 0.39gr/t, Ag 6.5 gr/t, S 12%
16.	Feldspat + albitophyres	71,64	Al_2O_3 17.74%, SiO_2 71.2%, Na_2O 3.47%, K_2O 4.42%
17.	Fluorite	0,758	
18.	Sulphur	0.2	S - 2-51%
19.	Pyrophylite	6	CaO 0.37%, MgO 1.09%, SiO_2 68.4%, Al_2O_3 18.58%
20.	Talc	616	
21.	Chalk	2	MgO 62%, SiO_2 1.66%, Al_2O_3 .74%, TiO_2 0.23%, CaO 53.05%,HK 42.37%
22.	Limestones	>492	CaO (50-55)%, MgO (0.25-4)%, SiO_2 (0.1-3)%, Fe_2O_3 (0.1-0.8)%
23.	Dolomites	>190	CaO 30.34%; MgO 18.21%, Fe_2O_3 (0.14-0.43)%

The average content of these minerals, according to their deposits are given below on table 1.

24.	Carbonatic Decorat. Stones	370 mill.m³	CaO 50%
25.	Basalts	Huge quantity	SiO_2 47%, Fe_2O_3 10%, Al_2O_3 13%
26.	Magnesites	1	MgO 35-39%, SiO_2 11-13%, CaO 3.6%, Fe_2O_3 1.9-2.2%
27.	Phosphorites	23	P_2O_5 4-12%, CaO 48-50%, SiO_2 5-8.5%, U_3O_8 > 0.005
28.	Olivinites	108,6	Al_2O_3 (0.18-0.82)%, MgO (47-49)%, SiO_2 (37-39)%, Fe_2O_3 (0.2-5.2)%
29.	Gypsum-anhydrites	85	$CaSO_4 2H_2O$=88-98%
30.	Volcanic Glass	18,6	Al_2O_3 (9.8-10.7)%, MgO (0.4-0.9)%, SiO_2 63.4%, Fe_2O_3 (1.1-5)%, CaO 4.6-4.8%, TiO_2 (0.27-0.64)%, Na_2O (1.4-2)%, K_2O 0.27%
31.	Granites	71	
32.	Rock Salt	300	NaCl=76-82%
33.	Clays	262	Al_2O_3 (11-14)%, MgO (2.6-7)%, SiO_2 (43-51)%, Fe_2O_3 (0.4-11)%, CaO (0.7- 0.8)%, TiO_2 (0.3-0.7)%
34.	Kaolin	1,9	Al_2O_3 (29-35)%, MgO (2.8-8)%, SiO_2 (43-46.8)%, FeO 3.38%, CaO (1.4-1.9)%,
35.	Silica sands + quartzites	Over 200	Over 80% SiO_2, about 10% Al_2O_3 and up to 1.5% Fe_2O_3
36.	River-bed gravels	Over 270 mill. m³	Sand and gravel
37.	Ophiolitic decorative stones	Over 70 mill. m³	CaO (31-52)%, MgO (0.3-18.3)%, SiO_2 (0.25-0.96)%, Fe_2O_3 (0.1-0.8)%

No.	Sort of mineral	Unit		Production			
			2005	2006		2007	2008
1	Chrome	ton	162 772	212 581		199 771	207 104
2	Copper	ton	68 312	35 071		98 000	105 000
3	Iron-Nickel and Nickel-Silicate	ton	800	79 000		369 559	353 290
4	Coal	ton	2 640	3 800		4 000	1500
5	Bitum + bituminous sand	ton	13 955	9 000		6 785	23 968
6	Limestones	m3	1 337 373	1 339 440		1 716 122	3 837 529
7	limestones flags	m3	-	23 193		29 263	27 900
8	Marbled limestones	m3	-	11 620		2 805	4 264
9	Silica sands	m3	3 200	3 200		4 400	12 077
10	Clays	ton	315 085	562 469		855 675	724 282
11	Gypsum	ton	14 770	19 683		46 200	77 633

CHROME-CHROME'S DEPOSITS ALBANIA

Albania is known as a country with a high chrome potential, as compared to the other Mediterranean countries. The main deposits of this mineral are situated in the Ophiolites of the Eastern Belt area, along the direction Tropoja-Kukës-Bulqiza-Shebenik.

Least development is identified in the deposits of this mineral in the western belt of ophiolites.

From the geographic perspective, there are three main regions where chrome is located:

1. North-eastern Region (Tropoja and Kukës Ultrabisc Massifs)
2. Central Region (Bulqiza Ultrabasic Massif).
3. Southeastern Region (Shebenik-Pogradec Ultrabasic Massif)

The Ultrabasic Massif of Bulqiza is the massif with the biggest chrome potential. In this massif is explored and is being exploited the chrome mine "Northern Bulqiza".

The perspective areas for exploration-exploitation of chrome ore can probably be: the region of Shebenik- Pogradec, deepness of Northern Bulqiza deposit, Qafe-Buall deposit, Bater-Lugu i

Gjate-Fushe Lope area, Liqeni i Sopeve-Theker-Ternove and Thekna in deepness area, the area in the region of Kalimashi and deepness of Valna deposit and also the area around Zogaj deposits.

The Ultrabasic Massif of Bulqiza is the massif with the biggest chrome potential. In this massif is explored and is being exploited the chrome mine Northern Bulqiza.

Present Geologic Reserves of chrome in these regions are:

Category B+C1 21.8 million tons Category C2: 15.1 million tons Total: B+C1+C2: 36.9 million tons

•Tropoja Ultrabasic Massif

Geological reserves:

6.1 million tons x 26.48% Cr_2O_3 Perspective deposits: Zogaj, Vlahnë, Qaf-Perollaj

•Kukës Ultrabasic Massif

Geological reserves : 6.8 million tons x 21.4% Cr_2O_3 Perspective deposits : Kalimash, Përroi Batrës

• Bulqiza Ultrabasic Massif

Geological reserves : 12 million tons Geological reserves, more than 38% Cr_2O_3:

7.5 million tons Geological reserves: 1.2 million tons, more than 38% Cr_2O_3 Perspective regions: Katjel-Pojskë; Bushtricë-Përroi Govatës.

ALBANIA COPPER

Based on the geologic conditions, their morphology, genetic and mineralogical components, are distinguished four main types of copper deposits:

1. Hydrothermal-metasomatic and volcanogenic-sedimentary deposits, such as Munella, Qafë-Bari, Gurth, Rruga e Rinisë, etc.
2. Volcanogenic-hydrothermal-metasomatic vain deposits, such as Tuç, Spaç, Derven, Paluce, etc.
3. Volcanogenic-sedimentary deposits, such as Munella, Gjegjan, Palaj, Karma, Rubik.
4. Massif sulphide metasomatic deposits, such as Kurbnesh, Golaj, Thirra, Nikoliq, etc.

There are considerable sulphur deposits in the Western and Eastern Belt of Ophiolites.

Perspective areas for exploration and exploitation of copper reserves wealth can be alongside and in the deepness of Munella, Gurth, Perlat, Karmë and Rehova deposits.

ALBANIA – IRON-NICKEL AND NICKEL-SIL CATE

No	Region	Q-ty, 000/ton	Fe %	Ni %	SiO_2 %	Co %
1.	*Devolli*					
	Nickel-Silicate	52.179	16,60	1,20	35,12	0,0397
	Iron-Nickel	59.193	38,66	1,074	12.2	0,056
2.	*Kukësi*					
	Nickel-Silicate	29.221	21,73	1,057	40,12	0,053
	Iron-Nickel	65.504	37,22	1,029	26,93	0,0547
3.	*Librazhd Pogradec*					
	Iron-Nickel	105.592	44,72	1		
	Total Iron-Nickel	***230.289***				
	Total Nickel-Silicate	***81.400***				

Iron-nickel and nickel-silicate are mainly located in Devoll (Bilisht, Bitincka, etc), Pogradec (Guri Kuq, Çervenaka, etc), Librazhd (Prrenjas, Skroskë, Xixillas, Bushtrice), Kukes (Mamez, Trull Surroj, Nome).

The deposits are composed by the following mineral ores:

- Nickel-silicate ore of the remaining crust or primary crust,
- Iron-nickel ores,
- Re-deposited or secondary crust nickel-silicate ores.

Perspective areas for exploration and exploitation of iron-nickel and nickel-silicate ore can be: Bilisht- Kapshtice, Skroske-Bushtrice, deepness of Prrenjas deposit, Trull Surroj-Mamez and Kukes-Has region.

The average content of nickel – silicate and iron-nickel according to their regions are given below on table.

NICKEL MINERAL RESERVES ACCORDING TO THE REGIONS

Region Quantity Fe% Ni % SiO2% Co % 000/ton

Total Ni-Si	52 179
Total Fe-Ni	59 193
Kukësi	
Total Ni-Si	29 221
Total Fe-Ni	65 504
Librazhd-Pogradec	
Fe-Ni	105 592
Total Fe-Ni	230 000
Total Ni-Si	81 400
Coal	

Albania has considerable coal reserves . The reserves are estimated about 794 million tons and are mainly located in three coal reserves areas:

Tirana region, about 86% of reserves;

Korça-Pogradec region, 10% of reserves;

ALBANIA COAL

Albania has considerable coal reserves, which are mainly located in three coal reserves areas:

- Tirana region, about 86% of reserves
- Korçe- Pogradec region, 10% of reserves
- Memaliaj region, 4% of reserves

Albanian coal reserves are of the lignite type, with a calorific analytic power in the limits between 2000-5600 kcal/kg .

Peats (turfs)

Peats constitute another energetic resource and are located in the South-eastern part of Albania (Maliq) , with these qualificative indicators.

- Calorific power: 2200 kcal/kg
- Humidity: 11%
- Volatile particles: 39%
- Sulphur presence: 1.1%

NATURAL BITUMEN AND BITUMINOUS SUBSTANCES

Albania is characterised by a significant presence of natural bitumen, which results from the natural transformation of petroleum in the oil deposit areas, particularly near the major tectonic falls. They are mostly occurring between limestone and bituminous dolomites, in schistes and sands.

Natural Bitumen

The high-quality bitumen deposit is located in Selenica (Vlora region). From this mine is extracted a porous bitumen, which is plastic and polished. It is a high quality bitumen containing 15-17% ashes, with a melting point of 105-115° C.

Bituminous coal

Like the natural bitumen, this mineral is found in Selenica and contains free carbon at 70-92% and releases a calorific power of 3500-7500 KCal/Kg (or 14,7-31,5 MJ/kg). Bituminous sands

Considerable deposits of bituminous sands are discovered in the areas of Treblova, Kasnica and Visoka. Bituminous sands in Albania present the petroleum floating asphalt and the gas stratifications. The mode of forming is the same with that of tar sands formed in Venezuela, Canada (Alberta), etc.

Bituminous sands

Considerable deposits of bituminous sands are discovered in the areas of Treblove, Kasnice and Visoke

Bituminous sands in Albania present the petroleum floating asphalt and the gas stratifications. The mode of forming is the same with that of tar sands formed in Venezuela, Canada (Alberta), etc.

NON-METALLIFEROUS MINERALS

Albania is rich with non-metalliferous industrial minerals, which constitute an extraordinary asset for the country that needs to become a marketed component as their best use possible could have a significant impact on the economic consolidation.

Each of the non-metalliferous minerals has specific importance, but the most needed ones are those found in considerable amount and which have a broad scope of application, such as limestone and dolomites, clays, gypsums and anhydrites, all types of decorative stones, basalts, etc. without excluding olivinites, caolines, volcanic glass, granites, phosphorites, etc.

DEPOSITS OF NON-METALLIFEROUS MINERALS

Limestones

Limestones represent the carbonatic raw material, distributed from the oldest Triassic-Jurassic depositaries up to the youngest ages of Cretaceous and Eocene, in the form of massifs, layers and belts, in almost all districts of the country as, Tropoja, Kukesi, Shkodra, in the North up to Korça, Kolonja and Gjirokaster in the South.

There are recognised about 60 deposits of limestones objects calculated with huge quantities with an open perspective to enlarge. Limestones are used for the cement productions, lime and construction aggregates.

Dolomites

Dolomites as limestones are widely spread in Albania in the form of seams, packs and belts of considerable dimensions. Dukat deposit is the main deposit with an average content of MgO, 18-21 %. Dolomites seams are located in the Borsh, Kurbin and Kruja region with an average of 18%.

There are more than 33 deposits of dolomites, travertine, marls and trepel, with a huge quantities of reserves.

Carbonatic Decorative Stones

Carbonatic decorative stones are mainly located in the Korabi zone, in the peripheral parts of Mirdita tectonic zone. In the Alps regions, in Krasta-Cukali, Kruja and that Jonic, starting from Tropoja and Kukes in the North, continuing in the South with Dibra, Bulqiza, Mat, Librazhd, Pogradec, Korca, Kolonja and the zones of Lezha, Kruja, Tirana, Elbasan, Lushnja, Vlora, Tepelena, Gjirokaster and Saranda, in the South.

There are about 90 deposits of decorative carbonatic and ophiolitic stones in huge quantities, with opened perspective to be enlarged.

Actually, the usage of decorative stone in construction sector is low.

Phosphorites

The phosphorites deposits are located mainly in the carbonatic rocks of Jonic tectonic zone, in the regions of Tepelena (Gusmar), Gjirokaster (Fushe Bardha), Saranda, etc.

Actually 12 phosphorite deposits have been discovered, with a considerable quantity of reserves.

Clays

There are huge quantities of clay reserves. There are over 90 deposits of different kinds of clays as follows:

Porcelanous clays in Tamara and Burrel

Montmorillonite, atapulgite clays in Shëngjin and Burrel

Flysch Clays are deposited in over eight occurrences such as: Bradasheshi (Elbasan), Drisht and Tarabosh in Shkodra, Brar in Tirana, etc. A specific characteristic of these clays is the high CaO presence, making them appropriate for the cement production.

Silica Sands and Quartzites

Findings speak of almost 30 deposits of quartzes and silica sand with considerable mineral reserves. Silica sands are used in glass production, abrasive and metallurgy. The average contents of silica sand is above 80% SiO_2 , about 10% Al_2O_3 and Fe_2O_3

Gypsums Anhydrites

Thanks to the geological workings an important quantity of gypsum reserves has been discovered. The main gypsum deposits are located in Dumre, Kavaja, Vlora Saranda and Dibra regions.

Rock Salt

The main deposts of rock salt are located in Mengaj, Tile and Dhrovjan areas. The quantity of reserves estimated in these deposits is more than some hundred million tons with a content of NaCl =76-82%.

River-bed Gravels

Almost 52 deposits of river-bed aggregates (sand and gravel) have been studied and discovered throughout all the rivers of the country, with a huge quantity reserves estimated.

Olivinites

The olivinite deposits are mainly locate in the Eastern Belt of ultrabasic massifs. The most important deposits are located in Kukes and Tropoja-ultrabasic massifs. The olivinittes may be used as a refractory material, when they are fresh and the MgO content in them is at 46-48 %, but they may also be used as decorative stones.

Volcanic Glass

Volcanic glasses are represented by volcanic middle-acid lime rocks and acid aquiferous rocks, which, subjected to a technologic process at the temperature of 900-1200° C, may be expanded within 30-60 seconds, enlarging the volume with 5-20 times.

Volcanic glasses deposits are locatedin the volcanic complex of Central Mirëdita, mainly in the western part of Munella mountain, from Marshterkor in south up to Lak Roshi in the north.

Magnesites

Magnesites deposits are located in the ultrabasic rocks which are connected with moulder and serpentized peridotites in the massifs of our country (Gomsiqe, Levrushk, Korthpulë, Shahinaj, Shengjun, Lucanë, Devoll)

Granites

Albania has several massifs known as bearers of small granite occurrences (Trokuzë, Levrushk, Fierza, Radomir, Peladhi, etc.). The mineralization in Levrushk granite massif is represented by (feldspar quartz), which can be used in glass and ceramics production.

Ophiolitic Decorative Stones

These kind of stones can be found in Mirdita area, from Tropoja to Kukes in north, down to Korca and Kolonja in south.

There are 20 discovered deposits of ophiolitic decorative stones, which contain more than some million m^3 of reserves.

The further geological study of these deposits can be a source for the increase of its using direction and enlarge the quantity of reserves..

Basalts

Basalts arelocated in Mirëdita tectonic zone, in the northern part of Kukës region, Puka, Mirëdita, as well as in Korca and Kolonja.

By this huge quantity of reserves, located from North to South, can fulfil not only the requests of the country but to export them.

Mining Industry Development Trends and Priorities

- Production increase of the traditional, such as chrome, copper, nickel, as well as enhancement of their processing scale, in order to make them competitive in supplying the domestic and foreign market;
- Expansion of the production range and processing of other minerals, such as bituminous sands, olivinites, basalts, decorative stones, etc.;
- Promotion of all the existing reserves, enabling the exploitation, processing and marketing of the products, both for the domestic and foreign market;
- Application of updated technologies in mines and processing units (enriching plants, breaking-fractioning-grinding plants, metallurgic factories, etc.), enabling a complex mineral exploitation;
- Enhancement of management methods. Effective utilization of the existing mineral resources and of those to be found in the future, in order to introduce them in the market and eye an increase of revenues from their exportation, as well as raw or processed products.

LEGISLATION ON MINING ACTIVITY

The law no. 10304 dated 15.7.2010 "On the Mining Sector" (the "mining law") as amended, is the principal governing law of the entire mining sector in Albania. This law regulates the relationship between the Albanian state and entities that will conduct their business in the mining sector. It establishes the rules for the development of the mining and post-mining activities in Albania and aims to provide incentives to the mining sector through securing transparency and free competition for the development of such sector, maximising the public benefits from mining activity and protecting the environment and public health from mining risks and mining waste. All secondary legistation that regulates the Albanian mining sector (such as Council of Minister decisions, guidance, regulations, orders, etc.) is issued pursuant to the mining law.

The responsible governmental central authority that administers the entire mining industry is the Ministry of Energy and Industry of the Republic of Albania.

Mining activities are regulated through the award of mining licences, which are obtained through competitive procedures, under the open area principle and also through a concession procedure. Therefore, another law that affects the mining industry is law no. 125/2013 dated 25.4.2013 "On Concessions and Public Private Partnerships".

Other laws are:

- law no. 10448 dated 14.7.2011 "On Environmental Permits";
- law no. 10440 dated 7.7.2011 "On Environmental Impact Assessment";
- law no. 10431 dated 9.6.2011 "On Environmental Protection"; and
- law no. 8561 dated 22.12.1999 "On Expropriation and Temporary Taking Over of Private Property for Public Interest".

PERSPECTIVE ZONES

The estimated quantities of different kind of ores reserves in Albania are as below:

- Chrome - 36.9 min tons
- Copper-27 min tons
- Iron- Nickel and Nickel-Silicate -311 min tons
- Coal -794 min tons
- Decorative stones and ophiolitic – 230 min tons
- Basalts-1064 min tons
- Olivine- 108 min tons
- Gypsum – 170 min tons
- Lime stones and carbonatic decorative stones - 1335 min tons
- Sand stones - 860 min ton and other minerals. Some of the perspective zones for research, exploration and exploitation are:

CHROMIUM:

There are three main regions of Ultrabasic Massifs of chrome in Albania:

1. North-East Region (Ultrabasic Massif of Tropoja and Kukës)
2. Central Region (Ultrabasic Massif of Bulqiza).
3. South-East Region (Ultrabasic Massif of Shebenik-Pogradecit)

Present Geologic Reserves of chrome in these regions are:

- Category B+C1 21.8 million tons
- Category C2: 15.1 million tons

Total: B+C1+C2: 36.9 million

• Tropoja Ultrabasic Massif Geological reserves: 6.1 million tons x 26.48% Cr_2O_3

Perspective deposits:

Zogaj, Vlahnë, Qaf-Perollaj

• Kukës Ultrabasic Massif Geological reserves : 6.8 million tons x 21.4% Cr_2O_3

Perspective deposits :

Kalimash, Përroi Batrës

• Bulqiza Ultrabasic Massif Geological reserves : 12 million tons

Geological reserves, more than 3 % Cr_2O_3: 7.5 million tons

Perspective deposits: North Bulqiza, Qaf- Buall, Batër, Krasta in depth, Thekna in

depth, intermediate region of Batër-Liqeni

Sopeve-Thekën-Tërnovë

• Shebenik-Pogradec Ultrabasic Massif Geological reserves: 1.2 million tons, more than 38% Cr_2O_3

Perspective regions: Katjel - Pojskë; Bushtricë-Përroi Govatës.

• In Manazdren- Selishtë- Shtrungëz area;

• In Lura massif; Copper

• In Munellë area;

• Around Perlat area; 27

• Around Rehovë area. Iron- Nickel and Nickel- Silicate

• In the depth of Përrenjas mine and Bushtrica drift;

• In the area between Bitinckë and Kapshticë areas;

• In Kukës- Krumë area. Carbonatic decorative stones

• Bedded limestone In Rasfik, Rubik area;

• Decorative marble limestone in Kolosjan - Skavicë- Kovashicë of Kukës- Dibër- Bulqizë areas;

• Conglomerate In Bilisht- Kapshticë area;

• Decorative limestone ate locates in QafShtamë and Mat area. Silica sands decorative stones

- Leskovik- Përmet- Këlcyrë- Ballaban region;
- Corovodë- Polican- Berat region;
- Plovisht- Mesmal in Korça District;
- In Shushica river- bed, Vlora region.

OIL AND GAS RESOURCES

Albania is an oil and gas bearing country. It is almost one century that Albania is producing significant petroleum quantities. Petroleum operations in Albania started early 1800 when the first geological surveys have taken place. Later, early 1900 petroleum operations were intensified and a lot of oil and gas fields were discovered.

The cooperation with international petroleum industry has started around 1900, when some concessions were granted by Albanian government to the most known petroleum companies of the time. After 1990 several licensing rounds were organized and a number of petroleum agreements with foreign companies were approved. Petroleum operations carried on during these times produced also a great number of data that are used for evaluation and planning of the current petroleum operations.

AKBN is promoting the free areas. The conduct of petroleum operations is possible thanks to a specific and very effective legal framework in petroleum sector. A suitable institutional organization is in place in petroleum sector. There are specific licensing procedures issued by AKBN that are clear and make possible a time save in this process.

OPURTUNITIES FOR EXPLORATION

Based on the geological studies, old seismic acquired by Albpetrol and these performed in the recent years by the foreign companies it appears that Albania, in spite of the existing oil and gas fields, still has a very good potential and is very promising area for further exploration in both onshore and offshore.

ONSHORE

Thrusting westwards in the Albanides and especially in the External Albanides are associated with the masking of the separate anticline structures or anticline chains, which have potential for new oil and gas discoveries. In the cases when thrusting westward is associated with the back thrust tectonic faults, synclines of triangular type are formed which are not easily identified but generally hide potential structures for oil and gas discoveries. From this point of view, still there is enough room for further exploration for identifying the new possible sub thrust structures in onshore areas. Seismic lines below illustrate this model. The possible structures linked to Triassic salt diapirism must be taken into consideration for further exploration in the onshore areas, close to the region where salt diapirism is present. See the following example. Gas Potential discoveries could be found under the existing oil discoveries in the deeper

levels, but the seismic information it is not enough, to draw the prospects. New reprocessing and acquisition of new seismic field are necessary for this target.

OFFSHORE

Oil Potential in the offshore area is related to the Possible Ionian carbonate structures and morphological highs of Apulia platform. In the appropriate conditions and places in the offshore there are possibilities for finding of the new and potential oil accumulations both in the clastic section (charged by the underlying platform carbonate) as it was the case in A4-1x well, and/or in the platform carbonate reservoirs. See the following lines. Gas Potential is related to the Miocene–Pliocene folded structures, as identified in the offshore to be valid based on old seismic (1991) and confirmed by the new seismic recently acquired. Taking into consideration the fact

that, the dimensions of the prognosed structures in offshore are considerably larger than their analog structures in
the existing gas fields in onshore, big reserves of biogenic and /or termoogenic area expected to be found in the area.

ALBANIAN LEGAL FRAMEWORK FOR PETROLEUM EXPLORATION AND PRODUCTION

Petroleum Exploration, Development and Production in Albania is governed by the "Petroleum Law (Exploration and Production)", No.7746 dated 28 July 1993, amended by Law No.7853 dated 29 July 1994, the Law No.7811 dated 12 April 1994 "On Approval of the Decree No.782 date 22.02.1994, "On the Fiscal System in the Hydrocarbons Sector (Exploration and Production)", and the Law No. 9975, date 28.07.2008 "On the National Taxes". The legislative framework offers considerable flexibility to the Government in negotiating acceptable terms with oil companies. At the same time these laws give incentives and enough flexibility to attract international oil companies and thus stimulate oil exploration in the country.

All petroleum deposits existing in their natural condition in strata lying within the jurisdiction of Albania are the exclusive property of the Albanian State "The Petroleum Law (Exploration and Production)" expressly permits the Ministry of Industry and Energy to enter into a Petroleum Agreement under which an oil company may be granted exclusive rights to explore for and produce petroleum. The Government's objective is to negotiate terms with the oil industry, which are fair and balanced, bearing in mind the usual risk, associated with exploration and the State's legitimate right for revenues as owner of natural resources. At the same time based on the fiscal law the Albanian Government pursue to encourage the development of small and marginal discoveries. Exploration for hydrocarbons in Albania commenced before the Second World War and many important oil fields in limestone and sandstone's have been discovered. Albania has the favorable geological and geochemical conditions for the discovery of new fields, providing exploration and commercial opportunities for oil companies.

A. TERMS AND CONDITIONS OF PRODUCTION SHARING AGREEMENTS

A.1 According to "Petroleum Law", "Petroleum Operations" means all or any of the operations related to the exploration for development, extraction, production, separation and treatment, storage and transportation and sale or disposal of petroleum up to the point of export, or to the agreed delivery point in Albania or the point of entry into a refinery and includes natural gas processing operations but does not include petroleum refining operations.

A.2 Hydrocarbons existing in their natural state are the property of the Albanian State. The Government represented by the NATIONAL AGENCY OF NATURAL RESOURCES (Decision No. 445 dated 03.09.2006) authorizes the performance of

petroleum operations by the Nat ional Oil Company (ALBPETROL) in its exclusive areas, or a Contractor in remainder of the territory of Albania. The NATIONAL AGENCY OF NATURAL RESOURCES is authorized to make available to interested oil companies the existing geological and geophysical data on the free areas in order to give oil companies the opportunity to evaluate the data before submitting bids.

A.3 The contract type is the Production Sharing Agreement between the National

Petroleum Agency, acting on behalf of the Albanian Government, and the Contractor.

According to the "Petroleum Law", "Production Sharing Agreement" means a Petroleum Agreement which provides for the recovery of Contract Costs from Petroleum produced in the Contract Area or from a proportionate part thereof, and for the division between the State and the Contractor of the balance of petroleum remaining after the recovery of Contract Costs in accordance with a scale or formula specified in the Petroleum Agreement.

A.4 The Production Sharing Agreement includes provisions such as:

A.4.1 The performance of a minimum work program, backed by a performance guarantee.

A.4.2 The presentation of an annual work program and budget.

A.4.3 Preference given to local employment and supplies during petroleum operations, where these are competitive in terms of quality, availability and cost.

A.4.4 The opportunity for local service companies to bid and preference given to them when the offer is comparable or better than other third parties.

A.4.5 Indemnify the State or the Ministry against all claims made by third parties in respect of injury, loss or damage resulting from the conduct of any operation carried out by the Contractor or by any subcontractor.

A.4.6 "The Petroleum Law" deals with access to private land after giving the occupier and the owner a minimum time notice. However, the Contractor must pay fair, just and equitable compensation with regard to any disturbance or damage caused during the conduct of petroleum operations.

A.4.7 The P.S.A. provides for the establishment of a training and administration fund, which is used for the training of NATIONAL AGENCY OF NATURAL RESOURCES National Petroleum Agency employees, and for administrative purposes.

A.4.8 The Contractor shall conduct Petroleum operations in a safe and proper manner in accordance with generally accepted international petroleum industry practice and shall cause as less damage as is reasonably practicable to the general environment including (inter alias) the surface air, seas, lakes, rivers, marine life, animal life, plant life, crops, other natural resources and property, and shall forthwith repair any damage caused to the extent reparable, and shall pay reasonable compensation for all damage which is beyond repair.

B. TECHNICAL CLAUSES

B.1 Under the petroleum agreement the Contractor is authorized to conduct petroleum operations during an Initial Exploration period, which can be extended twice. It is preferred that the Exploration Period includes a drilling commitment by the Contractor. The duration of the exploration period is up to 5 years and can be prolonged up to 7 years according to the "Petroleum Law". The phases of Exploration Period are subject to negotiation.

B.2 If the Contractor declares a commercial discovery during the exploration period, it has the right to extend for a development/production period of twenty-five years, which can be prolonged according to the "Petroleum Law".

B.3 During the exploration period, the Contractor is subject to minimum work programs and expenditure obligations. In the case of either the Initial Exploration period or the additional Exploration period expiring and the Contractor not having fulfilled its obligations for the said period, the Contractor must pay to the Government the monetary equivalent in respect of the work not carried out. All monetary obligations are expressed in US Dollars.

B.4 Before the end of each Contract year, the Contractor must submit and present toNATIONAL AGENCY OF NATURAL RESOURCES the exploration program and budget for the next Contract year. NATIONAL AGENCY OF NATURAL RESOURCES may suggest modifications to the said work program and budget and the Contractor shall be implemented them when found in accordance with good international petroleum industry practice.

B.5 In the event of a discovery, the Contractor will notify NATIONAL AGENCY OF NATURAL RESOURCES and evaluation of this discovery will be carried out pursuant to an approved appraisal work program. After appraisal, the Contractor will declare to National Petroleum Agency the commercial implications of the discovery.

B.6 If the Contractor considers the discovery commercial, the area in respect of that commercial discovery is set apart from the Contract area as a Development Area. The Contractor prepares then a development plan, which is submitted for approval by NATIONAL AGENCY OF NATURAL RESOURCES.

B.7 For the exploitation of discovered marginal fields, or fields that have become marginal due to their exploitation, pursuant to Decree No.782 of 22.02.1994 "On the Fiscal System in the Petroleum Sector", the Council of Ministers may issue special decisions to alleviate the fiscal system in order to render possible the exploitation of the marginal fields.

B.8 In the case of an oil discovery together with the flow of associated gas, the Contract considers the utilization of such gas. (Provisions concerning the flare and use of such gas either in petroleum operations or in the local economy are open for negotiations).

B.9 Contractor has the right to develop and produce the natural gas discovered in the Contract Area. Preferably such gas will be utilized in the internal market or exported. In case of a commercial Natural Gas discovery, NATIONAL AGENCY OF NATURAL RESOURCES and the Contractor will negotiate additional terms in the P.S.A, which will endeavor to ensure that the proportion of economic returns for both parties is similar to that for an oil discovery. NATIONAL AGENCY OF NATURAL RESOURCES may process and utilize the natural gas with no compensation to the Contractor where the Contractor considers that either the natural gas is not required for use in petroleum operations, or there is no possibility of exporting it, or its utilization is not economical.

B.10 Unitization According to the "Petroleum Law", if a petroleum reservoir is located partly in the Contract Area and partly in an other Contract Area and where it appears to the Ministry that gains in efficiency may be achieved through the joint development and operation of that reservoir, the Ministry shall have the right to order the Contractors to develop and operate the reservoir jointly under an agreement entered into by them for that purpose. If at any time during the which a Petroleum Agreement is in force the petroleum bearing strata in the Contact Area, forming part of a single Commercial Discovery, overlap an area over which the Government of Albania has jurisdiction and in respect of which no contact or license has been entered into or is in force, the NATIONAL AGENCY OF NATURAL RESOURCES and Contractor shall enter into an agreement to enlarge the Contact Area accordingly and to provide for the proper development of the Commercial Discovery.

C. COST OIL AND PROFIT OIL SHARING

C.1 Exploration expenditures and capital expenditures are recoverable only in the case of a commercial discovery but not before the start-up of production.

C.2 Operating expenditures are recoverable during the year in which they are incurred.

C.3 Reasonable and necessary administrative expenditures of the Contractor are recoverable.

C.4 A negotiable set of a sliding scale of daily production for the part of oil referred to as "profit oil" can be used to share the profit. Based on that model, the oil from which costs are recovered is referred to as "Cost Oil". The remaining part of production, which is referred to as "Profit Oil" is shared between NATIONAL AGENCY OF NATURAL RESOURCES and the Contractor according to the sliding scale (bbl/day); Or An "R" factor model can be also used to Profit Share. The "R" factor is defined as the ratio between the cumulative revenues of Contractor reduced by cumulative tax assessed on Contractor and the cumulative costs and expenses incurred in Petroleum Operations. Based on different negotiated "R"-factor values, after the Cost Oil is recovered, the remaining part of production, which in this case is referred to as "Excess Cost Oil", is shared between NATIONAL AGENCY OF NATURAL RESOURCES and the Contractor.

C.5 The Contractor is subject to tax on profit, according to the Law No.7811, date 12.04.1994, "On approval of Decree No.782, date 22.2.1994 "On the fiscal system in the hydrocarbons sector (Exploration-Production)", and the Royalty according to the Law No. 9975, date 28.07.2008 "On the National Taxes". The tax is at the rate of 50% of the realized profit and the Royalty is 10% of sales revenues.

C.6 In compliance with the above mentioned Law, The NATIONAL AGENCY OF NATURAL RESOURCES takes the Government's tax and/or its share of profit oil in cash.

C.7 The Contractor shall have the right to receive and retain abroad the proceeds from its export sales to the extent not required to meet on a current basis its local currency costs in Albania. The Contractor shall have the right to convert foreign currency into local currency at the generally applicable rate of exchange for commercial transactions.

D. MISCELLANEOUS

D.1 The Contractor and its sub-contractors are allowed to import into Albania all equipment and materials required for use in petroleum operations provided that NATIONAL AGENCY OF NATURAL RESOURCES has certified that equipment and materials are to be used solely in petroleum operations. By both, Law No.7811 dated 12.04.1994 and Presidential Decree No.1510 28.06.1996, the Contractor and his sub contractors are exempted from the customs and VAT duties and obligations either for the imported goods and services or services provided by the local market.

D.2 The Contractor may export the share of production to which he is entitled.

D.3 The Contractor may assign all or part of its interest under the contract to any affiliate or third party, which assignation is subject to a guarantee for the performance of Contractor's obligations to be submitted by the assignee, as well as subject to the consent of the NATIONAL AGENCY OF NATURAL RESOURCES.

D.4 The petroleum agreement and petroleum operations are governed by the laws of ALBANIA and the generally accepted practices of International Oil Industry.

D.5 Arbitration shall be in accordance with the UNCITRAL arbitration rules, preferably under Swiss Law.

D.6 All international oil industry investments are fully protected (as are all foreign investors) pursuant to Law No.7764, date 22.11.1993 "On Foreign Investments

MINING SECTOR REFORM

A matrix of thorough mining sector reform in Albania[1]

Reform	Principal Objective of Reform	Responsible Entity	Area of Focus
Preparation of a road map/strategy for sustainable development of the mining sector	Develop strategic actions for future development of the mining sector, including addressing mining legacy issues	Ministry of Ministry of Economy, Trade and Energy, Ministry of Environment	Nationwide Investors and communities
Strengthening Sector	Strong adherence to laws to	METE;	Nationwide
Governance	mitigate against nontransparent / discretionary authority; Implementation of EITI to improve transparency and accountability in the extractive industries sector		Investors in mineral license areas
Institutional	Improved sector administration	METE;	Nationwide
Strengthening and	of exploration and		Investors
Capacity Building	development; Clear-cut Terms of Reference to avoid both institutional overlap and gaps appearing in the minerals administration; Facilitate access for investors in Albanian Mining sector through "one stop shop"; Strengthening enforcement of mining	Independent Mining Licensing (Cadastral) Authority working in conjunction with Ministry of Economy, Trade and Energy; and Ministry of Environment	Non-performing license holders

[1] The World Bank Materials

	polices, laws and regulations. Revocation of licenses that do not perform according to contract agreements and/or regulations		
Addressing Environmental / Social Legacy Issues	Prioritize unaddressed environmental / social legacy issues to define a strategic long-range program through the preparation and implementation of a Strategic Environmental and Social Assessment	Ministry of Environment; Ministry of Labor	Nationwide; Former metallic mining operations, small-tomedium construction material operations, pensioned miners
Improving Sustainability at the Community Level and Benefit Sharing	Sustainable long-range sector development in which a broad stakeholder group participates in resource development planning and sharing of benefits; this also requires transparency with regard to payments between the companies and the Government	METE	Stakeholders and vulnerable groups in affected communities around resource development
Sustaining Sector Growth	Increased investment in exploration and development; Transform national geological database into an electronic format and make publicly accessible on an integrated basis via a dedicated website; Other forms of sector promotion (international exhibitions, features in respective magazines, websites etc...)	Geological Survey, oversight by the Independent Mining Licensing Authority; METE; sector promotion agencies	Prospective mineral areas for metals, cement and industrial minerals

Such an overall reform agenda would entail the following components:

I. Strengthening Sector Governance. Good sector governance is defined by a stable, transparent and efficient regulatory environment that enables private-sector led investments, facilitates sustained economic growth, and increases revenues to the Albanian government. Through commercialization and/or privatization of state-owned enterprises, the Ministry focuses on policy making and regulatory functions across four main areas:

Setting Sector Policy. Create and implement policies for solid and energy minerals, and take the lead in formulating policies and drafting laws, regulations, standards, and mode contracts.

Strengthening Laws. Define transparent, non-discretionary laws, regulations, licenses, contracts, and standards. Regulation should require that Ministry of Economy, Trade and Energy be able to measure or verify production; calculate royalties, fees, and inspect and make the necessary measurements to check compliance with health, safety, and environmental standards.

Improving Sector Revenue Management. Through (a) improved regulatory enforcement on surface fees and royalties for small and large-scale mining, and (b) strengthening assessment and collection of royalty payments. Transparency and accountability of the sector revenues will benefit from Albania's adoption of the Extractive Industries Transparency Initiative (EITI), a generic, proven program that could bring beneficial results in a comparatively brief time. EITI is currently implemented in around 30 countries worldwide. Through regular reporting of all payments to the government that spring from the mineral sector, and the parallel reporting of government receipts, transparency is credibly increased and shows the country's commitment to accountability. In addition, EITI can involve a full audit process, which enables civil society and the government to examine if the levels of payments received are equal to what the companies are supposed to pay according to the prevailing contracts. Due to the fact that these revenues will be scrutinized by an independent auditor on a regular basis, and thanks to the active involvement of civil society stakeholders, EITI has shown to create widely accepted accountability of the mineral sector, and is often an incentive for the administration to save or spend revenues more appropriately (see Annex E for additional information on EITI).

Building Strategic Planning and Technical Capacity. Formulating strategies for sector growth will challenge METE to develop a better understanding of factors that make sectors economic and efficient, and to adjust institutional, legal and contractual frameworks based on learning.

II. Institutional Strengthening and Capacity Building. Capacity building and institutional strengthening comes via exposure of personnel to best international practices in the mineral industries. Key tasks include:

Functional Management Review. To assess necessary capacities for administration, regulatory functions, and collection of geoscience for sector promotion.

Institutional Reform. To look at the demands placed on the METE, the type of agencies needed to respond, the long-range policy and legal planning capacity, the need for strong regulatory institutions, and the need to collect geoscience and produce ongoing production statistics in support of sector promotion. Attention is given to the specific needs of ministerial departments for sector policy, cadastre services, mines inspection, health and safety issues, environmental matters, commodity certification and quality control, and geological survey and laboratory services.

Strengthening of Mineral Rights Regime. Establishing an independent cadastre office for administration of all existing and future mineral licenses and improving monitoring and enforcement of health and safety, and environmental and social compliance.

III. Addressing Environmental and Social Legacy Issues. Another important factor to make the Albanian mineral sector (a) more attractive to new good practice investors and (b) improve its developmental outcome will be to address the environmental / social legacy issues. The most urgent *environmental problems* are[15]

decaying facilities and other structures of former mining- and processing plants, which occupy the sites (pictures 4 and 5);

pollution of water by shut-down copper mines, leaking of methane and carbonic gases form shut-down coal mines; soil contamination, dust collection and precipitation systems;

the subsidence of ground across all mines, especially in the Bulqiza and Mirdita areas, as well as the former major coal deposits;

insufficient spacial planning between use of space for mines, processing, living and other economic activities (e.g. agriculture)[16];

rehabilitation of mining surfaces.

The following list is drawn from the Government's own "Strategy for the Development of the Mining Industry" from 2005 [16] This can be of very negative consequences, as according to the AGS, housing is not seldom constructued on subsiding terrain and/or thin galleries

IMPORTANT LAWS AND REGULATIONS

BASIC REGULATIONS

LEGAL FRAMEWORK

• Law no.10081, dated 23.2.2009 "On Licensees, Authorizations and Permits in the Republic of Albania";

• Law no. 7796 dated 17.02.1994 "Albanian Mining Law" as amended;

• Guideline no. 1028, dated 10.12.2009 "On the content of the documentation to grant a mining permit" from the Minister of Economy, Trade and Energy According to the Albanian Mining Law the legal entities and individuals have the right to conduct mining activities.

These entities for acquiring mining permits for minerals of group 1,2,3,4 must present a request to the National Registration Centre according to the procedure predicted in Articles 17, 31, 32, and 33 of the Law " On licenses, Authorizations and Permits in the Republic of Albania. " According to Guideline No. 1028, dated 10.12.2009 "On the content of the documentation for granting mining permits" documentation should include:

• Request for granting a mining permission, defining exactly the coordinates of the area and the surface asked for exploitation. Brief description and a map of the mining area of scale 1: 25 000 (defined by its coordinates in plan and its surface).

• Verification Act conducted by the National Agency of Natural Resources (AKBN), according to the format prepared by the Agency for each type of required mining permit.

• The Decision of National Registration Centre as a legal entity, where the object of activity in registration form have to be approved as development of mining activities with work in surface or underground, according to the type of permit requested.

• Financial resources needed for investment that are predicted to be completed The juridical persons who apply for a mining permit, where they themselves declare that had not exercise before any business activity, must submit their financial sources through one of documents as below:

• A statement from the Bank to confirm that the legal entity has opened account

number, which should have deposited at least 30% of the projected investment. A declaree from the Bank that confirms that the legal person has an account and where are deposited at least 30% of the predicted investment value and/or:

• A document certifying that the legal person has secured a loan from a bank or any other financial entity with a value which covers the value of investments predicted to be completed, and/or

• A contract with an investor who provides financial support for implementation of

investment program. In this case the company must submit a notarized document, in which are expressed willingness of investors to support this investment, as well as documents to provide the financial resources of investors. (bank guarantee, or balance sheet of the company in which the investor is sole or majority shareholder).

For the legal persons that apply for mining permits, that have previously developed a mining activity or any other business activity, as documents for the accomplishment of financial sources will be considered:

• Accounting Investments done. Physical Inventory with main investments as

buildings, machinery, office equipments, etc. Financial balance sheet of the last year. Types of permits and the required documents

For Exploration Permits of minerals of group 1, 2, 3, the application must contain the conditions set out in Article 25 of the AlbanianMining Law :

The demand for an Exploration Permit must have:

a) Name and address of the applicant.

b) Specification of financial resources and technical skills that are needed to the license applicant, and his experience in the mining industry.

c) A description of the requested area, including a map.

d) Specifications of the proposed research program to be performed, the proposed working methods, an assessment of costs and terms of carrying out the program. "

The term of this Permit is defined by point 23 of this Law where is cited: "The maximum term will be a year and it is not an object to a time extension."

• For the Prospecting Permit of minerals in Group 1, 2 and 3, the request must contain the conditions set out in Article 31 of the Mining Law of Albania, where it is cited as below":

The demand for a Prospecting Permit shall include:

a) identity and address of applicant;

b) statement of relevant experience;

c) statement of financial and technical resources available to the applicant for purposes of the requested concession;

ç) proposed area of concession, including map;

d) mineral or minerals (Group 1, 2 or 3) for which the concession is sought;

dh) proposed method of explorations proposed work program and anticipated schedule and expenditure for carrying it out.

An exploration concession shall specify the minimum worse program to be undertaken by the concessionaire. Performance of produced minimum worse program shall be guarantied by a guarantor acceptable to the Minister. The form and substance of produced guarantee shall also be subject to the Minister's prior approval. According to Article 34 of Albanian Mining Law , the initial term of an exploration concession shall be for two years, subject to up to three extensions of one year each if requested by the end of the then current period.

For the Exploitation Permit for minerals in Groups 1, 2 or 3, the request must include the

conditions as predicted by Law in article 45 of Albanian mining Law, as it is cited below "The request for en exploitation Permit shall:

"The request for an Exploitation Permit shall include:

a) identity and address of applicant;

b) specify the area over which the mining concession is sought (including map);

c) specify the mineral or minerals in Groups 1, 2 or 3 for which the mining concession issought;

ç) give details of the mineral deposits in the area over which the mining concession is sought, including details of all known minerals proved, estimated or inferred, ore reserves and mining conditions;

d) be accompanied by a technical report on mining, treatment and value added possibilities within Albania and the intention of the applicant in relation thereto;

dh) provide a proposed development and investment program and schedule;

e) give particulars of the proposed mining operations, including:

(i) estimated capacity of production and scale of operations,

(ii) nature of the products,

(iii) proposals for the prevention of pollution, the treatment of wastes, the safeguarding of natural resources, the progressive reclamation and rehabilitation of land disturbed by mining and for the minimization of the effects of mining on surface water and ground water and on adjoining or neighbouring lands,

(iv) the anticipated residual effects on the environment of the mining operations and proposals for their minimization on and mitigation, and any particular risks (whether to health or otherwise) involved in mining the mineral and proposals for their control or elimination;

give a detailed forecast of capital investment, operating costs and revenues and the anticipated type and source of financing;

give particulars of the applicant's proposals with respect to the employment and training of citizens of Albania, and shall give particulars of expected infrastructure requirements and arrangements

According to Article 49 of Albanian Mining Law "The duration of a mining exploitation permit shall be till to twenty years from its effective date, subject to up to four renewals of till to five years each if requested by the Owner of the Permit not less than one year before the expiry of the previous term.

• To permit the prospecting and exploration of minerals in the 4th Group the request must contain the specified conditions according to Article 64 of the Albanian Mining Law as below:

The application for a prospecting and exploration permit for group 4 of minerals

shall include:

a) identity and address of applicant;

b) statement of financial and technical resources available to the applicant for purposes of the requested concession, statement of relevant experience in prospecting and exploration for group 4 of minerals;

c) proposed area of concession, including map;

ç) mineral or minerals (Group 4) for which the concession is sought;

d) proposed method of explorations and proposed worse program and anticipated schedule and expenditure for carrying it out.

The duration of a the Permit shall be till to two years from its effective date, the maximum area for a prospecting and exploration concession is thirty contiguous square kilometers.The extension of the permit depends on the specifics of the activity the person wants to accomplish" - The second paragraph of Article 63 of the Mining Law.

• To permit the exploitation of minerals in the 4th Group, the application must contain the conditions set out in Article 70 of the Albanian Mining Law, cited as below:

An application for quarry permit shall include:

a) name and address of the applicant;

b) indicate the minerals or materials of the 4th Group for which the permit is sought;

c) specify the initial duration for which the permit is sought;

ç) provide particulars of the financial resources available to the applicant to pay for the minerals and materials to be extracted;

d) In the case of a type 1 quarry permit, indicate the minimum and maximum quantities on an annual basis and the specifications of each mineral or material for which the permit is sought.

dh) in the case of a type 2 quarry permit,

(1) specify the exact location of the applicant's proposed quarry,

(2) give details of the deposit over which the quarry permit is sought,

(3) provide a proposed development and investment program and schedule,

(4) give a detailed forecast of capital investment, operating costs and revenues and the anticipated type and source of financing,

(5) give particulars of expected infrastructure requirements and arrangements for

provision,

(6) provide a detailed list of construction materials and minerals to be produced from the quarry, estimated capacity of production and scale of operations, and planned markets for the production,

(7) detail the experience of the applicant in operating quarries and in marketing

minerals and materials of the type to be produced from the quarry;

(8) give particulars on environmental aspects of the proposed quarry operation,

including:

i) proposals for the prevention of pollution, the treatment of wastes, and the safeguarding of natural resources,

ii) the anticipated residual effects on the environment of the quarry operations and proposals for their minimization, and

iii) any particular risks (whether to health or otherwise) involved in mining the materials and minerals and proposals for their control or eliminations and

9) give particulars of the applicant's proposals with respect to the employment and training of citizens of Albania.

Under Article 69 of this Law "Is authorized to provide two types of permits quarries":

a. Type 1 quarry permit, is a permit that permits the exploitation of minerals and construction from a public quarry on payment of produced fee as may be imposed by the Minister in the given permit and the value of this payment ispredicted in Regulation. The maximum initial duration of a type 1 quarry permit is one year, subject to renewal for successive periods of six months as requested by the holder.

b. Type 2 quarry permit, being an exclusive permit to develop and mine a quarry for minerals or construction materials in consideration of paying the fee specified in

permit as may be imposed by the Minister in the given permit and the value of this payment is predicted in Regulation

The maximum initial duration of a type 2 quarry permit is ten years, subject to renewal for successive one year periods if requested by the holder.

• In exceptional cases, when the term of the grant of permission required usage mining up to 99 years, the Relevant Ministry negotiates with the individual/subject who asks for a Permit , approval of which is done by Council of Ministers. This Agreement shall enter into power once approved by Parliament.

• To permit the exploitation of minerals in Group 1, 2, 3 and 4 the request must also contain:

• Local Government opinion of the Commune or the Municipality, for the permition of g mining activity development and mineral exploitation in the object that is required. In cases when the land is a private property owned by a legal person should be submitted the agreement with the owner of land for the exploitation permition.

• Opinion of the Forest Service Directorate of the District to allow the development of mining activity in the object sought to be used, for the case when the object is in the forest fund.

• Environmental Permit issued by the National Licence Centre. Environmental permit can also be given to an area smaller than that required for the mining permit, but that is part of it, provided that;The mine exploitation to be started from this area. Before the exploitation start outside this surface, must be taken the new environmental permit, which must be submitted to AKBN.

The contract with the technical director who shall be a mine engineer except when it is

not going to be used explosives could be an geologist engineer. The Albanian legal framework related to the mining industry is constituted by the following laws:

• The Law “Mining Law of Albania”, No.7796, date 17.02.1994, amended by Law No.9261, dated 22.07.2004 and Law No.9667, dated 29.12.2006;

• The Law “On civil using of explosives in the Republic of Albania”, No.9126, dates 29.07.2003;

• The Law “On Concessions”, No. 9663, dates 18.12.2006;

• The Law “On National Taxes”, No. 9975, dates 28.07.2008.

The draft of a new law on mining, after being consulted with all groups of interest, is already in pipe and soon it will be discussed and approved by the Albanian Parliament.

MINING LEGISLATION IN ALBANIA FAQS

Who can exercise mining activity?

• Every individual or company (Albanian or foreign) may exercise mining activity, after having obtained a mining permit.

Which body has the authority to license mining activity?

• METE (Ministry of Economy Trade and Energy) is the licensing body.

What is the mining permit?

• The mining permit is an intangible, visible and independent right from the right of the landowner.

What are the types of mining permit?

There are three types of mining permit:

• Permit for research purposes

• Permit for discovery

• Permit for exploitation.

The mining permits are specific depending on the classification of mines.

What are the criteria to obtain a mining permit?

• The interested subjects to obtain a mining permit should have sufficient financial resources for exercising the activity and also the necessary machinery and equipment for research, discovery and exploitation of minerals. Before beginning their activity, they should have the approval from the local government and forest service authorities.

What are the specific details related to the mining permits for different groups of minerals?

• The research permit for the first, second and third group of minerals (metal, non metal, coal and tar) gives the permit holder, individual or company, Albanian or foreigner, the exclusive right to search for minerals inside the allowed area.

• Access to the allowed area with necessary or indispensable employees, tools, machinery and equipment for research of minerals on and under the ground surface.

• Mineral research and other necessary work operations with the condition that the permit holder does not take part in the excavation, drilling or other underground techniques for which he is not authorized according to his research permit.

• Extraction and movement of non-commercial quantities of mineral samples from the allowed area only for study purposes.

How large an area is allowed for research purposes?

• The allowed area for research purposes should not exceed 400 km^2, should be one piece, and should not overlap with an area, which is object of another research permit.

What is the term of mining permit for research purposes?

• This permit is granted for one year and is not subject to extension.

What is the procedure for granting research and exploitation permit for mineral groups I, II and III?

• The minister, after the request of the person who is considered to have sufficient financial, technical resources and mining experience, can grant this person a discovery and exploitation permit, which gives him the exclusive right to discover and exploit the specific minerals inside allowed area. Before granting the permit for exploitation, the licensing authority (the minister) should make sure that the territory given for mining exploitation is properly guarded.

What are the rights that the holder gets from a discovery permit?

The *permit for discovery* gives the holder the following rights:

• To enter the allowed area with employees, tools, machinery and other equipment necessary for discovering minerals on and under the ground surface.

• To discover minerals and do other necessary work for this purpose, such as digging research wells, big and small holes and other research work on and under the ground surface.

The *exploitation permit* gives the holder the following rights:

• To undertake the necessary actions to complete mining operations effectively on the allowed area for exploitation.

• To extract and move from allowed area mineral or minerals specified in the exploitation permit.

• To install and put to work inside the allowed area any enrichment factories, foundries, refineries and other factories that increase the value of minerals extracted in his allowed area of exploitation. inside his area

What is the term of discovery permit?

• The initial term for the discovery permit is two years and is subject to three extensions of one year each, if this is requested by the permit holder. The request for extension should be presented at least 30 days before expiry of former permit. The exploitation permit is valid for 20 years and is subject to four extensions of five years each. The request for extension in this case should be presented no later than one year from the expiry date of former license.

How large a site is allowed for discovery?

• The maximum site allowed in discovery permits is 200 km^2, whereas in exploitation permits the site is 15vkm^2 and one piece. It should not overlap with areas which are object of research, discovery and exploitation of other people's permits.

How can one obtain a research-discovery permit for the fourth group of minerals ?

• The minister, after the request of a person who is considered to have sufficient financial resources and technical experience with the fourth group of minerals, can grant this person a permit, which gives him the exclusive right to research and discover minerals of the fourth group inside his area.

What is the term of research-discovery permit for the fourth group of minerals?

• This license is granted for two years and for a site up to 30 km^2. The extension of the permit depends on the specifics of the activity that the person wants to exercise.

Why is the exploitation permit for the fourth group of minerals needed?

• The exploitation permit for the fourth group minerals is requested and granted for the exploitation of minerals and building materials.

What types of exploitation permits are granted?

These permits are classified in two types:

• The first type of mining permit is a permit which allows the exploitation of minerals and building materials by a public mining, against a payment to be set by the Minister in the permit. The term of this license is one year, with the right of renewal for two six-month periods. The request for renewal should be presented at least 30 days before expiry of former period.

• The second type of mining permit is an exclusive permit to open and exploit a mine for minerals or building materials against a payment to be set by the Minister in the permit. The license is given for 10 years with the right of renewal up to one year. The request should be presented by the holder within 30 days from the day in which the initial license expires

What licenses are granted for the fifth and sixth group of minerals?

• Licenses for the fifth and sixth group of minerals are granted for research, discovery and exploitation of these minerals. Before requesting a mining permit for the fifth and sixth group of minerals, the applicant should define the site which he requests the mining permit for and through local government notify the owner or owners of this land, if it is not under his ownership. In relation with the research-discovery and exploitation of minerals group V and VI, the person who makes the request can:

1. Construct buildings and objects that serve the work for which the permit is obtained,

2. Exercise any right according to the permit obtained,

3. Perform inside the allowed area any activity for research, discovery and exploitation of minerals and materials for which the permit is obtained,

4. Extract from the allowed area all the minerals and materials for which the permit is obtained,

5. Sell the extracted minerals and materials only through persons licensed to trade minerals and in no other way.

What is the term of research-discovery and exploitation permit for the fifth and sixth group of minerals?

• This type of permit is valid for a maximum period of 5 years. The permits for the minerals of the fifth and sixth group can be obtained for a maximum area of 2 hectares and in one piece.

What is the required documentation to obtain a mining permit?

The procedure to obtain an exploitation permit follows the following steps:

Presentation of initial request to obtain an exploitation permit at METE (Ministry of Economy Trade and Energy)

This request contains:

A. Some brief information about the subject;

B. The border coordinates of the requested area;

C. A map in 1:25 000 scale, with the requested area.

After the presentation of this request, according to the article 47 and before granting the exploitation permit the Minister should make sure that the territory given for mining exploitation is properly guarded.

For this purpose, the Minister may advise the exploitation permit applicant to prepare surveillance on his own expenses, compliant with requests specified in the regulation approved by the Minister.

The surveillance act or verification of site bordering with the map of the site requested for mining exploitation permit is made by AKBN (National Agency of Natural Resources) or METE (Ministry of Economy, Trade and Energy). In the case when it is made by AKBN, the interested subject gets a response within 10 days.

After the verification act is made, the Minister, within 30 days, responds to the interested subject to continue or not further procedures to obtain the mining exploitation permit and invites him to present, within 90 days, the file with all the corresponding documents to obtain the mining exploitation permit.

The corresponding file to obtain the mining exploitation permit should contain the following documents:

1. The request to obtain the exploitation permit;

The form and content of such request to obtain the mining exploitation permit is defined with a regulation approved by the Minister.

2. The court decision for the registration of the company. The name of the subject (including the activity of exploitation, production, processing and export of minerals and hydrocarbons, and when indispensable, even the need to use explosive materials).

3. Registration certificate of the company for taxes (NIPT).

4. Certificate from the tax office, clearing the company from debts.

5. Bank certificate with the company's account number and financial resources for the exercising the activity.

6. Opinion from local government with jurisdiction over the site, which consents the exploitation of minerals therein.

7. Opinion from Forest Service Directory, with jurisdiction over the site, which consents the exploitation of minerals therein.

8. The environmental permit granted by the Ministry of Environment.

9. The labor contract with the technical director (mining engineer).

10. The technical-economical study and the project to exploit the site.

11. The assessment of the technical-economical study and project to exploit site, as well as the decision of the Technical Council in AKBN (National Agency of Natural Resources).

The procedure in AKBN described in point 11 takes 10 days from the effective date of the study and project delivery in AKBN.

After completion of file and its delivery in METE, according to the second paragraph of article 47 of the Mining Law in force, the Minister should notify the exploitation permit applicant about his decision regarding the request, within 90 days after it was received.

What are the criteria and procedures to obtain a professional license for design, evaluation, consulting, monitoring and technical management of mining activity?

• Based on the Albanian Mining Law Nr.7796, of the date 17.02.1994 amended, and on the Decision of the Council of Ministers No.54, date 28.01.2005, amended with the decision of the Council of Ministers No.271, date 10.05.2006, the Minister of Economy Trade and Energy has issued a regulation that defines the criteria and procedures to obtain a professional license.

How and where can the registration of professional licenses and companies be done?

The license is written in two original copies and it is registered in the Main Registration Book for Professional and Personal Licenses and in the Main Registration Book of the company, reflecting its content. The registrations should be accurate, clear, without rectifications, in a chronological order and without abbreviations.

Nothing can be erased from the Main Registration Book. The adjustments are made following a chronological fraction number.

An original copy of the license together with all documents brought by the applicant, are kept in the Protocol- Archive in AKBN.

COMPANY REGISTRATION

Any foreign and joint capital company which wants to exercise mining activity in the field of design, evaluation, consulting and monitoring, should register in the Main Registration Book of the Company, presenting the required documents for its licensing according to article 21 of this regulation.

Can disciplinary measures be taken against licensed subjects and on what grounds?

Revocation or temporary suspension of the right to exercise activity in design or implementation is made by the Commission in the cases when:

1. False declarations are made in the documents accompanying the request.

2. There are forgeries on the documentation handed over to the special commission.

3. Person exercises activity without a technical director fails to fulfill the obligations deriving from this regulation.

4. The technical director leaves the company without reasons.

5. There are motivated proposals from AKBN, METE, local government, tax office, customs office etc., for violating relevant laws in the mining activity.

6. Failure to pay tariffs specified in article 32. In each case there is an evaluation report which is discussed in the next meeting of the commission. Disciplinary measures for companies, technical directors and licensed individuals, according to the violations committed in the exercise of their activity include the revocation of the right to exercise the licensed activity for 6 months, 1 year, 2 years or forever, totally or partially depending on license class and category

A.dopted measures are notified to the corresponding subject, respective tax office and Ministry of Economy Trade and Energy.

The appeal

For every decision of the commission, according to the article 32 of this regulation, individuals and companies have the right to appeal to the Minister of Economy Trade and Energy within 40 days from the day of publication. The minister, after reviewing the appeal presented by the subject, within 10 days decides:

- Accept the verdict of the commission

- Turns the verdict back to the commission for review.

What are the tariffs for obtaining a professional license for albanians and foreigners?

• The following tariffs are applied for Albanian or foreign individuals and companies who obtain a professional license:

1. individuals: 6 000 (six thousand) leke, for every year of license validity,

2. accessories to the license for individuals: 4 000 (four thousand) leke,

3. renewal for individuals: 6 000 (six thousand) leke,

4. license conversion: 15 000 (fifteen thousand) leke,

5. companies: 60 000 (sixty thousand) leke,

6. accessories to the license for companies: 20 000 (twenty thousand) leke,

7. extension of license term for companies: 30 000 (thirty thousand) leke,

8. change and additional legal and technical director: 5 000 (five thousand) leke,

9. change of company name: 5 000 (five thousand) leke,

10. extraction of information from the Main Registration Book: 1 000 (one thousand) leke,

11. duplicate for individuals: 3 000 (three thousand) leke,

12. Duplicate for companies: 10 000 (ten thousand) leke.

WHAT DO YOU HAVE TO KNOW IN ORDER TO OPEN A BUSINESS?

Who should be registered in QKR (National Registration Office)?

All the subjects who belong to the following categories should register at the National Centre of Registration (QKR):

a. Individuals who exercise economical, commercial activity.

b. Simple companies, according to the Civil Code articles.

c. Commercial Companies.

d. Branches and offices of foreign representation companies.

e. Saving-Credit Companies and Unions.

f. Reciprocal Cooperation Companies.

For more information please contact the following:

• Ministry of Economy, Trade and Energy;www.mete.gov.al / (Policies and Legislation);

• Company Registration; National Registration Centre: www.qkr.gov.al;

• Mining Law Nr.7796, of the date 17.02.1994;

• Decision of Council of Ministers number 27, date 19.01.2007 "On the approval of evaluation rules and concessions";

• Decision of the Council of Ministers No.271, date 10.05.2006, "Issues the Regulation that defines the criteria and procedures to obtain a professional license";

• Public Procurement Agency www.app.gov.al;

MINING LAW OF ALBANIA

No. 7796, date 17.02.1994

CHAPTER I SHORT TITLE AND EXTENT

ART. 1

This Law shall be known as the Mining Law of Albania(1994).

ART. 2

It extends to the whole territory of the Republic of Albania including the seabed and subsurface of waters under its jurisdiction.

CHAPTER II GENERAL PRINCIPLES

ART. 3

In this Law, unless the context otherwise indicates:

"State" means the Republic of Albania.

"Minister" means the member of the Council of Minister for the time being responsible for mines and minerals.

"Ministry" means the ministry dependent on the Minister.

"Person" means a natural or juridical person.

"Mineral" means any substance, whether in solid, liquid or gaseous form, occurring naturally in or on the earth, in or under water or in tailing and having been formed by or subjected to a geological process, excluding petroleum that is in a liquid or gaseous state in situ and water, but including sand, stone, rock, gravel and clay, as well as soil, other than topsoil.

"Mine" means, when:

-(a) used as a noun, i) any excavation in the earth, including the portion under water or in any tailing, as well as any borehole, whether being WORKED or not, made for the purpose of searching for or winning a mineral, or ii) any other place where a mineral deposit is being exploited,including the mining area and all buildings, structures, machinery, mine dumps, access roads or objects situated on produced area and which are used or intended to be used in connection with produced searching,winning or exploitation or for the processing of produced

minerals and -(b) used as a verb, the making of any excavation or borehole referred in paragraph -(a)

i) or the exploitation of any mineral deposit in any other manner, for the purpose of

winning a mineral, including any prospecting or exploration in connection with the

winning of produced mineral.

"Underground" means, in relation to a mine, any place in a mine under the natural surface of the earth which is solely connected to the surface by means of a shaft, adit, raise, wince, tunnel or decline or a combination thereof.

"Quarry" means any place (not being a mine) where quarry material or quarry mineral has been removed or is being removed, whether by excavation or otherwise to supply material for construction, commercial, industrial or manufacturing purposes.

"Process" means, in relation to any mineral, the recovering extracting, concentrating, refining, calcining,classifying, crushing, screening, washing, reducing, smelting or gasification thereof.

"Mining right" means a permit, concession, license or other authorization granted pursuant to this Law to engage in activities related to prospecting, exploration or mining.

"Investment agreement" means an agreement entered into between a concessionaire and the Minister pursuant to "Art. 44".

"Public interest" means something in which the public, the community at large, has somepecuniary interest, by which their legal rights or liabilities are affected.

"Royalty" means the payment to the State of a percentage of the value of the delivered minerals.

"Effective date" means the date on which a permit or concession is signed by the Minister.

ART. 4

The present Law governs the relationship between the State and natural or juridical persons with respect to the obtaining of mining rights and the execution of mining activities. Excluded from the application of this Law are petroleum that is in a liquid or gaseous state in situ and waters.

ART. 5

All mining rights granted pursuant to this Law and the exercise of any mining activities shall be governed by and be subject to the laws of Albania.

Art. 6

Activities under a mining right are declared to be in the public interest for purposes of allowing access to and use of land.

ART. 7

The State encourages the ongoing development and modernization of the mining sector in Albania in a free market economy based on competition and open access to economic activitie.

CHAPTER III DOMINION OF THE STATE AND MINING RIGHTS

ART. 8

All minerals in situ existing in the territory, to which this Law extends,whatever be their origin, form or physical state,within or on the surface of the earth, in the depths or in the waters are the inalienable and inprescriptible property of the State represented by the proper Ministry.

ART. 9

The State may grant mining rights in accordance with this Law to persons, national or foreign, allowing the holder to carry out mining activities. No person may engage in mining activities except in accordance with rights granted under this Law.

ART. 10

Before granting any right pursuant to this law, the Minister or his delegate shall make produced consultations with the relevant local authorities as the Minister may deem appropriate in cases where the granting of produced rights may seriously and adversely affect the residents of produced locality.

Art. 11

Any rights to conduct mining activities granted prior to this Law must be affected in accordance with this law.

Art. 12

A mining concession is an intangible right, distinct and independent from that of the ownership of the land. Subject to the prior written consent of the Minister, the rights emanating from a mining concession may be transferred and may be pledged. The constructions and other installations that affect the permanent operations are considered as immovable accessories to the concession.

Art. 13

No mining right shall authorize the holder thereof to use the underground or any shafts, adits, tunnels or other access to the underground for any purpose other than that expressly specified in the concession or permit. The use of the underground or access thereto for storage or disposal of toxic, radioactive or other wastes is prohibited.very cultural, monetary, historical, archeological material, which should be found in the permit area are or other material are the inalienable and inprescriptible property of the State. The concessionaires who found these materials must be noticed immediately to General Mining Directorate.

CHAPTER IV GROUPING OF MINERALS

ART. 14

For purposes of this Law, minerals are divided into the following groups: a) Group 1 Metallic Elemental Minerals b) Group 2 Non-metallic Elemental Minerals c) Group 3 Coal and oil-shale d) Group 4 Quarry and construction

minerals / materials e) Group 5 Precious stones f) Group 6 Semi-precious stones

The minerals that fall within each Group are listed in Schedule A, which is a part of this Law.

CHAPTER V ADMINISTRATION

ART. 15

The Minister is designated as the competent authority to act on behalf of the State in the execution of this Law.

Art. 16

A General Mining Directorate is hereby created as a dependency of the Ministry to monitor mining activities in Albania. The research institutes on mining activities shall provide technical advice and assistance to the Minister and to the General Mining Directorate on the specific aspects of the mining industry that fall within their respective technical expertises.

Art. 17

The Minister may make Regulations as are necessary or convenient to be prescribed for carrying out or giving effect to the provisions of this Law.

CHAPTER VI STATE MINING ENTERPRISES

ART. 18

All State owned enterprises engaged in mining activities are to operate as autonomous, whose activities shall be treated in all respects in the same manner as private sector entities.

Art. 19

The State mandates that the areas and activities for which the State Mining Enterprises are granted rights be privatised.

Art. 20

The contribution of the State Mining Enterprise in privatisation shall be valued at the reasonable fair market value of the rights and assets assigned by the State Mining Enterprise at the time of transfer. The method of valuation of the contribution of the State Mining Enterprise shall be determined by regulations.

CHAPTER VII MINING RIGHTS FOR GROUP 1, 2 OR 3 MINERALS A) PROSPECTING PERMIT

Art. 21

The Minister may on the application of any person grant to that person a prospecting permit in the form prescribed by Regulation whereunder the permit shall have the exclusive right to search within the permit area for indications of minerals.

Art. 22

The area of a prospecting permit shall not exceed 400 contiguous, square kilometres and shall not cover any area that is subject to another prospecting permit or exploration concession or exploitation concession granted pursuant to this Law unless the holder of produced existing permit or concession specifically consents in writing.

Art. 23

The term shall be for maximum of one year, not subject to extension.

Art. 24

A person may hold more than one prospecting permit simultaneously.

Art. 25

An application for a prospecting permit shall: a) state name and address of applicant b) provide particulars of the financial and technical resources available to the applicant

for the permit as well as experience in the mining industry c) provide a description of the area over which the permit is sought,including a map, and d) provide particulars of the program of reconnaissance operations proposed to be

carried out, proposed methods of work,an estimate of the costs and of the period required for completion of the program

Art. 26

Within sixty days after receipt of an application, the Minister shall give notice to the applicant for the grant of a prospecting permit of his decision on the application.

Art. 27

A prospecting permit confers the following rights on the permit:

a) to enter the permit area with produced agents, employees,vehicles, machinery and equipment as may be necessary or expedient for the purpose of prospecting for minerals in, or under the land;

b) to prospect for minerals and to carry out produced operations and produced works as necessary, provided that the permitee may not engage in drilling, excavation or other subsurface techniques except where and to the extent he is authorized by his permit to use any of those techniques and

c) to extract and remove from produced land samples of minerals in non-commercial quantities for purposes of analysis.

Art. 28

In addition to other conditions imposed in the prospecting permit, every prospecting permit shall be subject to the following:

a) the permitee shall promptly report to the Minister in writing the discovery of any minerals of economic interest;

b) all disturbances to the surface of the land which are made while prospecting shall be filled in or otherwise made safe to the satisfaction of the Mining Directorates and c) the permit shall take all necessary steps to prevent damage to vegetation or other

property.

Art. 29

The permitee shall, at produced times and in produced a manner as may be prescribed by Regulation, file or cause to be filed with the General Mining Directorate reports on the worse done within the permit area, the money expended and the results. A representative portion of all geological samples extracted by the permitee shall be provided to the General Mining Directorate alongwith the results of all tests or treatments carried out on the samples.

B) EXPLORATION CONCESSION

ART. 30

The Minister may, on the application of any person considered to have the requisite financial and technical resources and mining experience, award to produced applicant an exploration concession granting the concessionaire the exclusive right to explore for specified minerals in the concession area. The exploration concession shall be in the form prescribed by Regulation.

Art. 31

The application shall include:

a) identity and address of applicant;

b) statement of relevant experience;

c) statement of financial and technical resources available to the applicant for purposes of the requested concession;

cc) proposed area of concession, including map;

d) mineral or minerals (Group 1, 2 and/or 3) for which the concession is sought;

dh) proposed method of explorations and

e) proposed worse program and anticipated schedule and expenditure for carrying it out.

An exploration concession shall specify the minimum worse program to be undertaken by the concessionaire. Performance of produced minimum worse program shall be guarantied by a guarantor acceptable to the Minister. The form and substance of produced guarantee shall also be subject to the Minister's prior approval.

Art. 32

The holder of a prospecting permit shall have a priority right over other applicants during the term of produced prospecting permit and for a period of thirty days hereafter to be granted one or more exploration concessions over the area covered by the prospecting permit provided that the Minister is satisfied with items (b), (c), (dh) and (e) of art 31, the application of the holder of the prospecting permit.

Art. 33

Within sixty days after receipt of an application, the Minister shall notify the applicant of his decision on produced application.

Art. 34

The initial term of an exploration concession shall be for two years, subject to up to three extensions of one year each if requested by the concessionaire at least thirty days before the end of the then current period provided that the concessionaire has fully complied with its accrued obligations under the concession and provided further that it offers a worse program for the requested extension that is satisfactory to the Minister.

Art. 35

Within ninety days after the effective date of the exploration concession the concessionaire shall commence field operations.

Art. 36

The maximum area of an exploration concession shall be 200 square kilometres which are contiguous and shall not cover any area that is subject to a prospecting permit or an exploration or mining concession held by another, unless the Minister and the other permitee or concessionaire agree that the new concession will not unreasonably affect the existing contractual rights.

Art. 37

An exploration concessionaire may hold more than one exploration concession simultaneously.

Art. 38

The exploration concessionaire shall relinquish portions of the concession area progressively during the term thereof in accordance with the following schedule: a) at least forty percent of the original concession area, not later than the end of the

initial term; b) at least fifty percent of the original concession area, not later than the end of the first one year extension; c) at least seventy five percent of the original concession area, not later than the end of the second one year extensions and d) all portions of the original concession area not covered by a mining concession, by the end of the third one year extension.

Art. 39

Every one year extension that the concessionaire requests shall be agreed by the Minister as a condition of the extension and once approved by the Minister shall be deemed a firm undertaking by the concessionaire.

Art. 40

The exploration concessionaire shall pay to the State an annual rental, payable on the effective date of the exploration concession and on each anniversary of produced effective date on the number of square kilometres comprising the concession area on the date payment is due. The annual rate of produced rental shall be ecuivalent in lek of 300 Swiss Francs in the moment of payment per square kilometre or fraction thereof.

Art. 41

An exploration concession confers on the exploration concessionaire the right: a) to enter the concession area with produced agents, employees, vehicles, machinery and equipment as necessary for the purpose of exploring for minerals in, on or under the land;

b) to explore for minerals and to carry out produced works and operations for that purpose as may be necessary including digging pits, trenches and holes, and sinking bores and tunnels in, on or under the lands and

c) to extract and remove from produced land and export samples of minerals in non-commercial quantities for the purpose of testing.

Art. 42

The exploration concessionaire shall keep complete and detailed records of the surveys and other operations conducted pursuant to the concession and shall make produced records available in Albania at all reasonable times for inspection by the Minister and the General Mining Directorate. The exploration concessionaire shall furnish the Mining Directorate with copies of produced information relating to surveys and other operations conducted by it as the General Mining Directorate may request. The obligations of Articles 28 and 29 shall also apply to an exploration concessionaire.

Art. 43

Provided that it has complied with its obligations under the exploration concession, the exploration concessionaire shall have the right during the term of the exploration concession to elect to convert to one or more mining concessions the portions of the exploration concession area that it commits to develop and exploit. The application for the mining concession shall be filed in accordance with Article 45.

C) MINING CONCESSION

ART. 44

The Minister may on the application of any person considered to have the requisite financial and technical resources and mining experience, award to produced applicant on behalf of the State a mining concession granting produced concessionaire the exclusive right to mine and exploit one or more specified minerals from the concession area. The document evidencing the mining concession shall be in the form prescribed by Regulation. The Minister is authorized to negotiate and, enter into on behalf of the State an investment agreement with the concessionaire.

Produced investment agreement shall require the prior approval of the Council of Ministers, and Parliament granting investment facilities, incentives and guarantees not included in the Albanian legislation.

Art. 45

The application for a mining concession shall:

a) provide identity and address of applicant; b) specify the area over which the mining concession is sought (including map); c) specify the mineral or minerals in Groups 1, 2 and/or 3 for which the mining concession is sought;

ç) give details of the mineral deposits in the area over which the mining concession is sought, including details of all known minerals proved, estimated or inferred, ore reserves and mining conditions;

d) be accompanied by a technical report on mining, treatment and value added possibilities within Albania and the intention of the applicant in relation thereto;

dh) provide a proposed development and investment program and schedule;

e) give particulars of the proposed mining operations, including:

(i) estimated capacity of production and scale of operations,

(ii) nature of the products,

(iii) proposals for the prevention of pollution, the treatment of wastes, the safeguarding of natural resources, the progressive reclamation and rehabilitation of land disturbed by mining and for the minimisation of the effects of mining on surface water and ground water and on adjoining or neighbouring lands,

(iv) the anticipated residual effects on the environment of the mining operations and proposals for their minimisati on and mitigation, and

(v) any particular risks (whether to health or otherwise) involved i n mining the mineral and proposals for their control or elimination;

e) give a detailed forecast of capital investment, operating costs and revenues and the anticipated type and source of financing; f) give particulars of the applicant's proposals with respect to the employment and training of citizens of Albania, and g) shall give particulars of expected infrastructure requirements and arrangements provision.

Art. 46

Where the applicant is not the holder of an exploration concession, the application shall also include full details of the financial and technical capacity of the applicant and information regarding his relevant experience in the mining sector.

Art. 47

The Minister shall notify the applicant for a mining concession of his decision on the application within ninety days after receipt thereof. With regard to applications from exploration concessionaires, produced decision shall be taken in accordance with Article 45. The Minister shall assure that the land over which a mining concession is granted has been properly surveyed before the mining concession is granted. For the purpose of doing so, the

Minister may direct the applicant for the mining concession to cause a survey to be prepared at the applicant's expense in accordance with produced requirements as may be specified in the direction. All mining rights must be publicated in the official papers or other manner of information.

Art. 48

The maximum area for a mining concession is fifteen contiguous square kilometres. The same concessionaire may hold more than one mining concession simultaneously.

Art. 49

The duration of a mining concession shall be till to twenty years from its effective date, subject to up to four renewals of till to five years each if requested by the concessionaire not less than one year before the expiry of the then current term.

Art. 50

The mining concessionaire shall pay to the State on the effective date of the mining concession and on each anniversary date of produced effective date an annual rental fee with respect to the concession area. The rate shall be determined by the Minister from time to time for the particular mining concession, subject to the criteria approved by the Council of Ministers. An annual rental fee with respect to the concession area have as minimum the ekuivalent in lek of 3 000 Swiss francs and as maximum the ecuivalent in lek of 10 000 Swiss Francs in the moment of payment for each square km^2 or fraction thereof.

Art. 51

Not later than fifteen days after the end of each calendar month, the mining concessionaire shall pay to the State in lek the ecuivalent of Swiss francs, a royalty of two per cent of the market value of the total volume of minerals from the concession area delivered to customers during produced calendar month. The procedure for determining the market value of the minerals shall be specified in Regulations.

Art. 52

A mining concession confers on the concessionaire the right:

(a) to do all acts and things that are necessary to carry out effectually mining operations

in, on or under the concession area;

(b) to take and remove from the land the mineral or minerals for which the mining concession is granted and to dispose of the; and

(c) to install and operate within the concession area plants for beneficiation, smelting, refining an otherwise adding value to the minerals extracted from the concession area.

Art. 53

A mining concessionaire has right to construct/install and operate within the concession area buildings, camps, storage facilities, pipelines, electric generation and transmission facilities, communications systems, railway lines, petroleum storage facilities and other infrastructure or facilities required for its operations

Art. 54

The State has no obligation to provide any infrastructure within or outside of the concession area. In the event that the concessionaire wishes to use facilities or infrastructure belonging to the State that are generally available to the public, it shall have the right to use produced infrastructure in accordance with legislation in force.

Art. 55

A mining concessionaire has the right without further license or authorization to sell in Albania or for export all minerals produced pursuant to the mining concession from the concession area, as well as finished products and by-products therefrom.

Art. 56

The mining concessionaire shall keep complete and detailed records of all operations conducted pursuant to the concession and shall make produced records available at all reasonable times for inspection by the Minister and the General Mining Directorate.

Art. 57

The mining concessionaire shall maintain in Albania full and complete books of account and produced other books and records as may be necessary to show the worse performed under the concession, the costs incurred and the quantity, quality and value of all minerals extracted from the concession area. All produced records and accounts shall be maintained in accordance with Albanian legislation and generally accepted accounting practices in the international mining industry.

Art. 58

The mining concessionaire shall furnish to the Mining Directorate technical, operational and production data in produced form,at produced intervals, in respect of produced periods and containing produced detail, as may be prescribed by Regulations.

Art. 59

The mining concessionaire shall present for the Minister's approval an annual worse program and budget and production schedule for the concession area. The first produced program shall cover the balance of the calendar year in which the effective date occurs and shall be presented within thirty days after produced effective date. For each subsequent year, the submittal shall be made at least ninety days prior to the calendar year to which the proposed program, budget and production schedule relate. The concessionaire's submittal shall be deemed approved if the Minister does not take written exception thereto within forty days after receipt.

Art. 60

Where the Minister considers that the holder of a mining concession is using wasteful mining or treatment practices or is conducting its operations contrary to the object of optimum exploitation of minerals, he may give notice to the concessionaire (giving in the notice particulars of produced practices) and require the concessionaire to show cause within produced period as the Minister shall specify in the notice why it should not cease to use those practices. Where within the period specified in the notice under subarticle (1), the concessionaire fails to satisfy the Minister that the practices specified in the notice are not wasteful or contrary to optimum exploitation or that the use of those practices is justified, the Minister may issue a direction ordering the concessionaire to take produced rectifying steps within a period specified in the direction as may be required by the Minister.

Art. 61

If any person in any manner uses or causes to be used or intends to use the surface of any land which may in the opinion of the Minister detrimentally affect the object of this Law in relation to optimum exploitation of any mineral which occurs or which may occur in economically exploitable quantities in or on produced land or in tailing on produced land, the Minister may cause to be held into the matter and may issue an order in accordance with the legislation in power.

Art. 62

The concessiona are shall give notice to the Minister:

(a) one year in advance if it proposes to cease production from a mine in the concession area concerned;

(b) 180 days in advance if it proposes to suspend production from any produced mine, and

(c) 90 days in advance if it proposes to curtail production from any mine by more than ten per cent of the volume anticipated in the approved production schedule.

Produced notice shall state in detail the reason or reasons for produced proposed cessation, suspension or curtailment.

CHAPTER VIII MINING RIGHTS FOR GROUP 4 MINERALS AND MATERIALS

A) PROSPECTING AND EXPLORATION PERMIT

Art. 63

The Minister may, on the application of any person considered to have the requisite financial and technical experience with group 4 of minerals, award to produced applicant an prospecting or exploration concession described in regulation, granting the concessionaire the exclusive right to prospect or explore for group 4 of minerals in the concession area which should be primarily minerals to open a quarry of type 2. The duration of a this concession shall be till to two years from its effective date, the maximum area for a prospecting and exploration concession is thirty contiguous square kilometres. The same concessionaire may hold more than one mining concession simultaneously. In case of the exploration permit the concessionaire must pay to the state an rental fee equal to the ecuivalent in lek of 100 Swiss Francs in the moment of payment for each square km^2 or fraction thereof for its concession area.

Art. 64

The application for a prospecting and exploration permit for group 4 of minerals shall include:

a) identity and address of applicant;

b) statement of financial and technical resources available to the applicant for purposes of the requested concession, statement of relevant experience in prospecting and exploration for group 4 of minerals;

c) proposed area of concession, including map; ç) mineral or minerals (Group 4) for which the concession is sought; d) proposed method of explorations and proposed worse program and anticipated schedule and expenditure for carrying it out.

Art. 65

Within sixty days after receipt of an application, the Minister shall notify the applicant of his decision on produced application.

B) MINING CONCESSION

Art. 66

A quarry permit is required for the mining of construction minerals and materials except in following instances:

a) the owner of the surface taking materials therefrom for use in construction on his own property;

b) local authorities or other persons engaged in the construction of public roads or other public works utilizing the spoil from necessary excavations or from borrowpits close to produced road or works;

c) the holder of a mining concession taking construction materials from within its concession area for use in its mining operations.

Art. 67

Any dispute as to whether a person qualifies for an exception under Art. 66 shall be decided by the Minister whose decision in the matter shall be final.

Art. 68

The Minister shall establish any public quarries by ministerial decree (type 1). A public quarry shall be under the operational jurisdiction of the director general of the General Mining Directorate.

Art. 69

Two types of quarry permits are authorized:

a) Type 1 quarry permit, being a permit to remove construction minerals and materials from a public quarry on payment of produced fee as may be imposed by the Minister in respect to the materials removed. The maximum initial duration of a type 1 quarry permit is one year, subject to renewal for successive periods of six months each if requested by the permitee at least thirty days before he expiry of the then current period.

b) Type 2 quarry permit, being an exclusive permit to develop and mine a quarry for specified Group 4 minerals or materials in consideration of paying the fee specified in permit in respect of the minerals or materials removed. The maximum initial duration of a type 2 quarry permit is ten years, subject to renewal for successive one year periods if requested by the permit at least thirty days before the expiry of the then current period.

Art. 70

An application for quarry permit shall:

a) state name and address of the applicant; b) indicate the Group 1 minerals or materials for which the permit is sought; c) specify the initial duration for which the permit is sought; ç) provide particulars of the financial resources available to the applicant to pay for the

minerals and materials to be extracted; d) in the case of a type 1 quarry permit, indicate the minimum and maximum quantities on an annual basis and the specifications of each mineral or material on which the permit is sought; dh) in the case of a type 2 quarry permit,

(1) specify the exact location of the applicant's proposed quarry,

(2) give details of the deposit over which the quarry permit is sought,

(3) provide a proposed development and investment program and schedule,

(4) give a detailed forecast of capital investment, operating costs and revenues and the anticipated type and source of financing,

(5) give particulars of expected infrastructure requirements and arrangements for provision,

(6) provide a detailed list of construction materials and minerals to be produced from the quarry, estimated capacity of production and scale of operations, and planned markets for the production,

(7) detail the experience of the applicant in operating quarries and in marketing minerals and materials of the type to be produced from the quarry;

(8) give particulars on environmental aspects of the proposed quarry operation, including: i) proposals for the prevention of pollution, the treatment of wastes, and the safeguarding of natural resources, ii) the anticipated residual effects on the environment of the quarry operations and proposals for their minimisation, and iii) any particular risks (whether to health or otherwise) involved in mining the materials and minerals and proposals for their control or eliminations and

(9) give particulars of the applicant's proposals with respect to the employment and training of citizens of Albania.

Art. 71

Within thirty days after receipt of an application, the Minister shall notify the applicant of his decision on produced application. The Minister may accept, accept with conditions or reject any application for a quarry permit. In any event, he shall communicate his decision on the application within thirty days after receipt thereof. The permit shall be in the form prescribed by the Regulation. The permit shall contain produced additional conditions as the Minister shall impose as a condition thereof.

Art. 72

With respect to a type 2 quarry permit involving an export oriented project, the Minister is authorized to negotiate and enter into on behalf of the State an investment agreement of the type referred to in Art. 44.

Art. 73

The mining concessionaire shall pay to the State on the effective date of the mining concession and on each anniversary date of produced effective date an annual rental fee with respect to the concession area. The rate shall be the ecuivalent in lek of 1 500 Swiss Francs in the moment of payment for each square km^2 or fraction thereof.

Art. 74

Not later than fifteen days after the end of each calendar month, the mining concessionaire shall pay to the State in lek the ecuivalent of Swiss francs, a royalty of two per cent of the

market value of the total volume of minerals from the concession area delivered to customers during produced calendar month. The procedure for determining the market value of the minerals shall be specified in Regulations.

Art. 75

The Minister have the right to give at local authorities with a particular decree the administration of the minerals and materials of group 4 minerals.

CHAPTER IX GROUPS 5 AND 6 MINERALS

ART. 76

No person may prospect for or mine Group 5 or Group 6 minerals without a mineral claim granted by the Minister.

Art. 77

Before applying for a mineral claim the applicant must stake out the area of land over which the person wishes the mineral claim to be granted and must notify the owner or owners of produced land, if not the State, through local authorities of the applicant's intention to seek a mineral claim over the respective property.

Art. 78

Any person, including a person who has previously held a mining claim on some or all of the same area, may apply to the Minister for a mineral claim covering specified Group 5 or Group 6 minerals.

The application shall:

a) provide the name and address of the applicant,

b) identify the land to which the application relates and specify whether produced land is owned by the State or by third parties,

c) where produced land is not owned by the State, give the name and address of each registered owner of the land to which the mineral claim application relates, provide a consent from the registered land owner, executed before a notary, to the granting of the mineral claim over his property, and

d) specify the Group 5 and Group 6 mineral or minerals in respect of which the mineral claim is sought.

Art. 79

Within thirty days after receipt of the complete application the Minister shall notify the applicant of his decision on the application. If Minister is willing to grant the mining right, he shall include in the notice the rate or rates of royalty payable as well as special conditions, if any, that are to apply to the mineral claim and the amount and type of bond or other security that the applicant must post with the Minister and maintain to guarantee

(i) correct reporting of all minerals extracted from the mineral claim area and

(ii) their value as well as

(iii) proper and timely payment of royalty thereon concerning his mineral claim.

Art. 80

A mining claim may be granted over a maximum area of two contiguous hectares. The same person may hold more than one mining claim simultaneously. A mining claim may not be granted over any area over which another mining right has been granted pursuant to this Law unless the holder of produced other mining right gives an irrevocable consent in writing thereto.

Art. 81

A mining claim shall have a maximum validity of five years from the date of the Minister's notice to the applicant accepting the application.

Art. 82

The holder of a mining claim may, in accordance with the conditions prescribed by the Minister in respect of produced claim, prospect, explorer and mine the Group 5 and 6 mineral or minerals in respect of which the claim is granted and may in connection with any produced prospecting, exploration or mining:

(a) erect buildings and structures,

(b) exercise any rights in the nature of easements,

(c) carry out within the mining claim area any activities of prospecting, exploration and mining, (ç) extract from the claim area all minerals authorized by the mining claim, and

(d) dispose of the minerals extracted through a licensed mineral dealer, but not otherwise.

Art. 81

The holder of a mining claim shall pay to the State within five days after the end of each calendar month in lek the ecuivalent of Swiss francs, a royalty of two per cent of the market value of all minerals from the claim area sold during produced month.

Art. 84

The holder of a mining right shall comply with produced rules and procedures as may be prescribed by Regulation in relation to the registration and sale of minerals extracted by the mining claim holder.

Art. 85

No person may make commerce in Group 5 or Group 6 minerals unless he holds a mineral dealer's license issued by the Minister.

ART. 86

An application for a mineral dealer's license shall:

a) state the name and address of the applicant, b) detail the experience of the applicant in the commerce of Group 5 and Group 6

minerals, c) indicate the mineral or minerals for which the mineral dealer's license is sought, and d) provide evidence of the source of financial sources available to the applicant for conduct of the proposed commerce in minerals.

Art. 87

The Minister shall notify the applicant under Art. 86 of his decision on the application within thirty days after receipt thereof.

CHAPTER X RELATIONSHIP BETWEEN THE HOLDERS OF MINING RIGHTS AND THE OWNERS OF THE SURFACE

Art. 88

The relationship between holders of mining rights and the owners of the surface shall be regulated in accordance with the Albanian legislation in power.

CHAPTER XI GENERAL OBLIGATIONS OF HOLDERS OF MINING RIGHTS

Art. 89

Every holder of a mining right shall give preference in selecting employees at all levels to applicants of Albanian nationality who possess the requisite expertise and experience.

Art. 90

Every holder of a mining right shall undertake development and training of its personnel.

Art. 91

The holder of a mining right shall conduct all mining operations in a safe, prudent and responsible manner and shall take reasonable measures to protect all persons against potential dangers from produced operations in accordance with mine safety regulation.

Art. 92

The holder of a mining right shall provide basic medical facilities and staff.

Art. 93

The holder of a mining right must maintain in force and effect at all times produced insurance as may be required by applicable law. Any insurance which it or its shareholders obtain must be in accordance with Albanian Insurance Legislation.

Art. 94

The holder of a mining right shall facilitate the inspection and audit of its operations by duly authorized representatives of the State.

Art. 95

The holder of a mining right shall assure that all activities related to its mining right are carried out in an environmentally responsible manner. The holder of the mining right shall take necessary precautions to prevent pollution or damage to the environment including the undertaking of remedial measures within a reasonable period to repair or offset damage to the environment in cases where is determined that any works or installations of the holder of the mining right or any operations conducted by or on behalf of produced holder endanger property of others or cause pollution or harm flora or fauna or the ecosystem. Where pollution occurs the holder of the mining right must promptly treat or disburse it in an environmentally acceptable manner.

Art. 96

The holder of a mining right shall prepare an implement an environmental management plan to prevent the environment for the Minister of Health and Environmental approval and, once approved, this plan which will, among other elements, address the handling and acceptable disposal of all solid, gaseous and liquid wastes from the holder's operations.

Art. 97

The holder of a mining right that uses water in its operations must return the water to the river, lake or other source from which taken, free from contamination that could adversely affect human health or the development of flora and fauna.

Art. 98

The rehabilitation of the surface of land concerned in a mining activity shall be carried out by the holder of the mining right in accordance with a specific rehabilitation program proposed by the holder and approved by the Minister.

Art. 99

Whenever a mining right is terminated or lapses or an area covered by a mining right is surrendered, the person who was the holder of the mining right immediately prior to produced

termination, lapse or surrender shall demolish all buildings, structures or any other thing which was erected or constructed in connection with produced mining right on the surface of the land concerned and shall remove all debris and, as far as practicable, restore within a reasonable time any produced surface to its natural state to the satisfaction of the Minister. Produced demolition or removal shall not be applicable in respect of structures, buildings or objects

a) which the State may elect, by notice from the Minister, to succeed to the ownership free of charge or

b) which the owner of the land wishes to retain and which has been agreed upon between produced former holder of the mining right and the owner of the land in a writing lodged with a notary.

CHAPTER XII SPECIAL BENEFITS TO PROMOTE PRIVATE INVESTME

Art. 100

With the object of promoting investment in the mining sector, the following benefits are guarantied to holders of mining concessions for types 1, 2 or 3 minerals and their shareholders, and may at the discretion of the Minister be extended in accordance with article 44 as he considers justified to the holders of any other type of mining right for an activity that is primarily export oriented: a) right to import directly goods and equipment required for operations; b) right to maintain books of account in US dollars or other foreign exchange acceptable

to the Albanian National Bank; c) right to exchange foreign exchange into local currency at the generally prevailing rate

for commercial transactions at time of the exchange; d) right to receive and retain abroad proceeds from export sales and to cover local costs; e) right to convert local currency income into foreign exchange at the

generally prevailing exchange rate for commercial transactions as required for purposes of paying for imports, and remitting abroad debt service, profits and dividends;

f) right to open foreign trust accounts in connection with project financing; g) right to maintain and operate bans accounts both in Albania and abroad; h) undertaking that the mining sector in relation to other sectors of economic activity will not be discriminated against fiscal package consisting of:

(i) land and property rental at the applicable rate specified in Albanian legislation;

(ii) import duties at generally applicable rates under Albanian legislation;

(iii) royalty or fee as applicable specified in this Law;

(iv) corporate profits tax at rates under Albanian legislation in effect on date ofgranting of the mining concession, permit or authorization, as applicable, calculated in accordance with rules under Albanian legislation in effect on produced date.

(v) taxes or fees on locally formed companies with rules under Albanian legislation,

i) exemption from turnover tax under Albanian legislation and from other taxes which may substitute this for the holder of the mining right or its shareholders which profit from this law writings and

j) guarantee of stability of the fiscal package set forth in

i) above for the full term of produced mining right;

k) guarantee that the legal regime under which the mining right is granted shall apply to the holder of the mining right and its shareholders for the full term of the mining right and that changes in produced legal regime, including enactment of new laws, shall not be applicable unless the Minister and the holder of produced mining right agree in

l) right to have any disputes between the State and the holder of the mining right settled by arbitration in accordance with the rules of the International Chamber of Commerce, Paris, France or Competent Albanian Court.

Art. 101

In cases where the Minister extends some or all of the benefits under Art. 100 to the holder of a qualifying other type of mining right, the benefits so granted shall be specified in the document granting the mining right or in an investment agreement.

CHAPTER XIII REGISTRY OF MINING RIGHTS

ART. 102

The General Mining Directorate shall maintain a registry of all mining rights granted, renewed, transferred or cancelled. It shall be the sole responsibility of the holder of the mining right to register its mining right and any renewal,transfer or cancellation thereof and to pay a fee in lek equivalent to 100 Swiss francs for each registration or change thereto. The register shall be kept available for inspection.

Art. 103

For purposes of any legal proceeding concerning a mining right that is registered: a) a registered interest has priority over an interest that is not registered, and b) an earlier registered interest has priority over a later registered interest.

Art. 104

No transfer of a mining right or an interest therein shall be effective unless approved in writing by the Minister and until both the transfer and the Minister's approval thereto are recorded in the register.

CHAPTER XIV PENALTY FOR CONDUCT OF MINING ACTIVITIES WITHOUT VALID MINING RIGHTS; RIGHT OF MINISTER TO TERMINATE MINING RIGHTS

Art. 105

An person who carries out mining activities without a valid mining right issued under this Law shall be guilty of an offence and liable for payment of a fine imposed by the Minister not less than ecuivalent in lek of 50000 and not more than ecuivalent in lek of 500000 Swiss francs in the moment of payment for each such violation.

Art. 106

The Minister shall have a right to terminate any mining right where the holder thereof: a) is found to have made material misrepresentations in its application for the mining right especially for the material and financial resources; b) commits a material breach of this Law; c) commits a material breach of obligations under the document granting its mining right; d) closes down or ceases to operate a mine for 180 consecutive days, or e) unreasonably curtails production from a concession area.

Art. 107

The following procedure shall be followed in giving effect to a termination under Art. 106: a) the Minister shall give notice to the holder of the mining right specifying his intention to terminate the mining right and the reason for produced termination, b) the holder of the mining right shall have a period of ninety days after receipt of the

notice to: i) appeal to the tribunal having jurisdiction over disputes between the State and the holder of the particular mining right (international arbitration or the courts in Albania, as applicable) if it disputes the validity of the Minister's reason for the termination or ii) remedy to the Minister's satisfaction the reason for the termination where produced reason falls within Art. 106 b), c) or e);

c) if the holder of the mining right appeals the pursuant to b) i) above the validity of the reason for termination, the Minister may not proceed with the termination until a final decision is rendered by the tribunal having jurisdiction, provided that the holder of the mining right is diligent in pursuing its claim in produced proceedings and

d) if the holder of the mining right fails to pursue either of the rights listed in b) above, the mining right shall terminate effective ninety days after the holder's receipt of the Minister's notice under a) above.

Art. 108

In the event of a termination for a reason specified in Art. 10610, the Minister shall have the right to take without paying any compensation therefore any and all property of the holder of the mining right related to the terminated mining right. In addition the Minister shall have a right to execute any outstanding bonds or other guarantees given by or on behalf of produced holder and to pursue without limitation any other legal rights it may have to collect compensation and damages from produced person.

CHAPTER XV MISCELLANEOUS

ART. 109

All notifications required or permitted under this Law shall be in writing.

Art. 110

Technical data and samples provided by the holder of a mining right to the Mining Directorate shall be maintained by the State as confidential, unless otherwise agreed by the provider of produced data or samples, until the first to occur of the following:

a) the termination or expiry of the mining right, b) the relinquishing of the area to which the data or samples relate c) the elapse of two years from the date on which the General Mining Directorate received the particular information or samples

d) the publication of produced data; provided however that nothing in this Article shall be construed as limiting the right of the State to use produced information in the preparation of economical-financial reports and returns required of or by the State.

Art. 111

The holder of a mining concession for Group 1, 2 or 3 minerals shall have the right to import minerals into Albania for processing and then re-export,with both the import and export being exempt from all taxes, duties or other impositions by the State.

Art. 112

Under no circumstances shall the State, or any person acting on its behalf, be liable to third parties as a result of injury to persons or damage to property resulting from the grant of or exercise of rights or the performance of any duty or function conferred or imposed by this Law. The holder of a mining right shall indemnify and hold harmless the State and any produced person acting on behalf of the State from any such person claim by third parties.

Art. 113

This law become in power 15 days after the publication in official newspaper.

TABLE A GROUPS OF MINERALS ********************************

GROUP (1) METALLICS Antimony Molybdenum Silver Monazite Gold Nickel Arsenic Oxide of iron Copper Osmiridium Bismuth Pyrites of arsenic Caesium Platinum Cinnabar Lead Fluorspar Rubidium Galena Rutile Garnet Selenium Germanium Sulphur Iron Scheelite Ilmenite Tantalus Indium Titanium Tin Thorium Cadmium Tungsten and its ores Cobalt Vanadium Chromium Wolfram Columbium Wulfenite Lithium Zinc Manganese Zircon Iron ore Zircon Platinoid minerals Mercury Rare earth minerals **********************************

GROUP (2) NON-METALLICS

Alumina Cryolite Alunite Rock salt Apatite Quartzite Asbestos Laterite Barytes Magnezite Bauxite Mica Beryllium and its ores Ores of silicon Borates Perlite Ceolite Mineral pigments Diatomaceous earth Pyrophyllite Feldspar Reef quartz Phosphates Chert Graphite Steatite Graphite clays Emerald Emery Iceland spar Soapstone Talc Halite Peat Shale ash Topaz Calcite Vermiculite Chloride Wollastonite ************************************** GROUP (3) COAL AND OIL SHALE

Coal Oil shale Bituminous Pyrobituminous Bituminous sands
** **

GROUP (4) MINERALS AND CONSTRUCTION MATERIALS

Marine aggregate Gyps Anhidritet Gabroide Bentonite clay Kaolin Brick clay Marble Pipeclay Ophiocalcite Pottery clay Slate Fire clay Plagigranite clay and clay shale Sands (for construction) Serpentine Bentonite Syenite Brecsious Clay shale Dolomite Travertine Fuller's earth Tufts Granite Gravel Limestone Zhuret ***

GROUP (5) PRECIOUS ROCKS

Diamond Ruby Corundum Sapphire **

GROUP (6) SEMI PRECIOUS ROCKS AND OPAL

Agate Rhodonite Chalcedony Torquoise Quartz crystal Tourmaline Nephrite Jade Opal

ON SOME SUPPLEMENTS AND AMANDMENTS OF THE MINING LAW OF ALBANIA

No. 7796, DATE 17th FEBRUARY 1994

Based on articles 78 and 83 of principle 1 of the Constitution, with the proposal of the Council of Ministers.

THE PARLIAMENT OF THE REPUBLIC OF ALBANIA DECIDED:

In the Law nr.7796, date 17.02.1994

Mining Law of Albania, these supplements and amendments take place:

ARTICLE 1

The title of Law changes in ▫ALBANIA MINING LAW▫.

ARTICLE 2

In the article 3 these changes take place:

1. Mineral stand for every valuable substance, in solid, liquid or gas form, that is found naturally under or above the earth surface, under or above the water, in the waste of the worked mines or sterile of processing plants, slugs of black and coloured metallurgy, formed from geological processes, expect liquid oil, natural gas in gas form and water, but including sand, stones, rocks, gravel and clay. Sands, and gravel□s are administrated by this law in case they are not included in definitions of ▫the Law on water reserves nr.8093, date 21.03.1996.

2. After the term

Mineral is added the paragraph: Mining Activities stands for all the works concerning searching, exploration, opening exploitation, treatment and marketing of mineral products, as well as maintenance, monitoring or closing of mines, having in consideration the rehabilitation of the ambient.

ARTICLE 3

At the end of article 10, is added a paragraph:

▫In areas declared from Council of Minister s as The second paragraph of article 16 is changed as follow: The Mining and Processing Technology Institute, is the specialised scientific institution that provide for the concerning Ministry and General Mining Department technical assistance through projects, monitoring and other activities related to mining policies and works concerning this law▫.

ARTICLE 5

The title of capture VI State Mining Enterprises ▫is changed as ▫Companies that act in Mining Activities .

ARTICLE 6

Article 18 is changed as follows: Article 18 ▫. Mining Activities concerning designs, administrating, search, exploration and exploitation of minerals in the territory of Albanian Republic in according with Albania legislation, are executed from trade companies, juridical persons expect the cases for seen in articles 66 and 69 of this law.

ARTICLE 7

Article 19 is changed as follows:

Concessionaire companies included in mining activities, act according to dispositions of this Law

ARTICLE 8

Article 20 is changed as follows: Article 20 Mining Activities, in general, concerning designs, valuation ▫consultancy, monitoring and

technique administration of the companies are realised from specialists licensed from the proper Minister according to criteria approved from the Council of Ministers.

Article 9

In the article 40 expressions

equivalent in lek of value of 300 Swiss francs is done 30000 lek

At the end of second paragraph of the article 47, after the word specified are cancelled the words from him and are added in the regulation approved from him .

In the article 48, after the words as a whole is added the expression defined in space according to three co-ordinates .

ARTICLE 12

In the article 50, expression

equivalent in lek of the 3.000 and in maximum value, equivalent in lek of 10.000 Swiss francs per km^2 , is done 300.000 lek and maximum value, 1.000.000 lek per km^2 (square km).

Article 13

At the end of the letter the words legislation.

after having c of the been article 52, after the licensed for such words for exploitation activities, according to are added Albanian

ARTICLE 14

In the article 63 the expression equivalent in lek of the value of 100 Swiss francs is substituted from 10.000 lek .

ARTICLE 15

In the letter b of the article 69 the expression which should be presented al least 30 days before the ending of period ahead is cancelled.

ARTICLE 16

In the article 73 the expression in lek equal the value of 1500 Swiss francs is substituted from 150.000 lek .

ARTICLE 17

After the article 74, is added article 74/1 as follows:

Article 74/1 The paragraphs 2 and 3 of the article 47, the articles 53, 54, 55, 56, 57, 58, 60, 61 and 62 are applied also for the minerals of group 4, but article 59 is applied for a period at least of 30 days .

ARTICLE 18

In the article 102, the expressions In the article 105 the expression

> not less than the equivalent in lek of 50.000 Swiss francs for every violation (of law) is substituted with not less than 500.000 lek and not more than 5.000.000 lek for every violation ▫.

ARTICLE 20

The article 106 is changed as follows:

Article 106

1. The violations (of law) are administrative ones, and General Mining Directory has the right to fine as follows: a) When, after giving the permit, it is verified that in the application for mining permit,

there are doubtful financing information, the fine is 100.000 lek b) When there are violations of the obligations defined in the mining permit, the fine is 50.000 lek c) When, in an unjustified way, it is decreased the production in a mining licensed

area, the fine is from 10.000 lek up to 50.000 lek d) When other violation of the mining law are committed, the fine is 50.000 lek up to

100.000 lek.

2. In case the violations defined in letters a

are repeated, and when the company cuts down the work in mine for 180 days continuously, the mining permit in cancelled.

▫

The violator has the right to complain to proper Minister within 1 mouth from the date of being fined.

ARTICLE 21

After the article 106, is added the article 106/1 as follows:

□Article 106/2 Against the decision of the Minister, the subject has the right to complain according to

the law on administrative violations □.

Article 22

In the table □Group 4

Minerals and constructing materials are added too the words sands, conglomerates, tractolities and basalt s □.

□

ARTICLE 23

This law enter in power 15 days after being published in the official paper. Declared with the decree nr.4290, date 2.08.2004 of the president of the Republic of Albania, Alfred Moisiu.

THE DOCUMENTS AND PROCEDURES FOR OBTAINING AN EXPLOITATION MINING PERMIT

ACCORDING TO THE LAW NO.7796, DATE 17.02.1994, MODIFIED BY LAW NO. 9261, DATE 22.7.2004 AND THE LAW NO.9667, DATE 29.12.2006:

I. The presentation at the Ministry of Economy, Trade and Energy (METE) of a preliminary demand for obtaining an exploitation permit:

a. This demand must provide some general data about the company;

b. The topogeodezical coordinates which determinate the perimeter of area demanded;

c. A map in scale 1:25 000 with the area demanded (concerned) and around it;

II. After the presentation of this demand the Minister, according to the article 47 of Mining Law of Albania, before to give an exploitation permit, must by sure that the surface is well surveyed.

III. For this purpose the Minister, according the rules specified in an regulation approved by him self can demand the titleholder to carry out the survey with his expanses.

IV. The survey process of land surface included in the area of demand for obtaining an exploitation mining permit might by carried out by the National Agency of Natural Resources (AKBN) or METE.

V. When the survey process of land surface is carried out the Minister, after 30 days from the date of presentation of demand, give the answer to the company in order to continue or not the procedures and invite the company to present at the METE the dossier with all the necessary documents for obtaining of the exploitation mining permit

VI. In the case when the survey process of land surface is carried out by AKBN the company can have the answer after 10 days.

The dossier for obtaining an exploitation mining permit must contain the follows documents:

1. Demand for obtaining an Exploitation Mining Permit;
2. The form and the contain of the demand for obtaining an Exploitation Mining Permit are determinate in the regulation approved by Minster;
3. The Tirana Court Decision for the registration of the company

▫Name of Company ▫Ltd. (with a description of activities such as mineral production, mineral and material treatment, miner import and export and if it is necessary the explosives using);

1. The fiscal certificate certifying that the company is registered at list as a Ltd;
2. The fiscal certificate certifying that the Title holder of license has no due obligations to the state budget;
3. Bank statement proof of establishing the financial guarantee for successful mining activity;
4. Regional State opinion about the future exploitation mining activity in the demanded area;
5. Frostier Service Directorate opinion about the future exploitation mining activity in the demanded area;
6. The environmental permit (agreement) given by Environmental Ministry;

10.Contrat with tecnical responsibel;

Feasibility study and exploitation project for deposit exploitation

11.Reviewer of Feasibility study and exploitation project for deposit exploitation and the AKBN Technical Council Decision about this study.

The whole duration of the procedure provided in the point 11, in AKBN from the date when the dossier is presented in AKBN is 10 days. From the moment when the dossier is completed and registered at the METE protocol, according the second paragraph of the article 47 of Mining Law of Albania, the Minister within 90 days, must give the answer the demander about his decision concerning the exploitation mining permit.

An such decision, related with demand for a discover permit is taken according the article 45.

FOR APPROVAL OF ENVIRONMENTAL PERMIT APPLICATIONS FOR THE ELEMENTS AND ENVIRONMENTAL PERMIT

Pursuant to Article 100 of the Constitution and paragraph 1 of article 37 of Law No. 8934 , dated 05.09.2002 " On Environmental Protection " , with the proposal of the Minister of Environment , the Council of Ministers

THE DOCUMENTS AND PROCEDURES FOR OBTAINING ENVIRONMENTAL PERMIT REGULATIONS

1 . Natural and legal persons , domestic or foreign , to obtain an environmental permit must submit a request for approval of the project or activity that will exercise and documentation, as defined in Annex 1 attached to this decision .

2 . Application is submitted to the regional environmental agency of the county , where the activity will take place .

3 . Environmental permit contains the elements, requirements and conditions described in Annex 2 attached to this decision .

4 . The Ministry of Environment to implement this decision .

This decision shall enter into force after its publication in the Official Journal .

PRIME

ANNEX 1 COMPULSORY DOCUMENTS REQUIRED FOR ENVIRONMENTAL PERMIT

1 . Request a natural or legal person to the Ministry of Environment for approval of the project and to obtain environmental permits .

2 . Description of project or activity that addresses :

a) Characteristics of the project :

i) description of main processes , technology, capacity , raw materials , auxiliary materials , intermediate products and finished products;

ii) work program for construction and operation ;

iii) other activities that may be required as a result of the project (eg new roads , provision of drinking water etc. .) .

b) Location of the project :

i) The boundaries of the project blueprint ;

ii) maps and photographs showing the location of the project ;

iii) existing plans to use the area where the project takes place .

c) Potential impacts on health and the environment :

i) impacts on human health , flora and fauna , soil , water and air, climate and landscape , cultural and historical heritage ;

ii) the nature of the impact (direct , indirect, permanent , temporary , positive, negative) ;

iii) measures to mitigate impacts on the environment ;

iv) impacts of transboundary nature .

3.Vendimi court for registration of the applicant as a natural or legal person .

4 . Report on environmental impact assessment prepared by legal and natural persons certified by the applicant 's environmental permit .

ANNEX 2 ELEMENTS of the environmental permit

1 . Name of the Ministry of Environment as the authority to issue environmental permits for activities that affect the environment .

2 . Name and address of the natural person or legal entity obtaining the environmental permit .

3 . Legal references supporting the environmental permit .

4 . Details on the compliance of emission norms in every discharging joint and in total emission rates quoted .

5 . Requirements for implementation of the monitoring program including health indicators , impact , sampling stations and their frequency of measurement , method of measurement or calculation , presentation formats and data entry .

6 . Defining measures to reduce the consumption of raw materials , water and energy and to improve the technology under a program .

7 . The obligation to submit a quarterly monitoring data on regional environmental agencies, county and publish them once a year .

8 . Defining measures and deadlines for environmental rehabilitation of damaged or contaminated .

9th . Measures for waste treatment and hazardous waste by the activity .

10 . Restoration measures required in the event of closure of business.

11 . Deadlines for environmental renewal , and its expiration , when the activity begins to be exercised .

12 . The obligation to perform environmental assessment .

13 . The obligation to implement the requirements of the permit when the activity goes in the ownership or use of another person .

14 . Sanctions for failure to comply with environmental permit conditions .

15 . Environmental permit fee .

16 . Effective date of the permit .

IMPORTANT REGULATIONS

ORDER FOR APPROVAL OF FORM AND CONTENT OF INFORMATION MANDATORY

PREPARED BY HOLDERS OF MINING PERMITS

Nr.312 , dated 04/13/2011

Pursuant to Article 102 paragraph 4 of the Constitution of the Republic of Albania , Article 36 paragraph 23 and Article 56, paragraph 2 of Law No. 10 304 , dated 15.07.2010 "On the mining sector in the Republic of Albania "

ORDER :

1 . Any holder of a mining permit search and discovery shall prepare and submit to the institution of the Albanian Geological Survey (AGS) required information according to the format , content and definitions of the terms specified in the Mining Law No. 10 304 , dated 15/07/2010 " For the mining sector in the Republic of Albania " and bylaws for its implementation .

These information are required :

a) The financial guarantee for the implementation of the minimum work program , no later than 30 (thirty) calendar days from the date that corresponds to the effective date of the permit ;

b) financial guarantee document for the implementation of environmental remediation of the mining area that appears in every year , not later than 30 (thirty) calendar days from the date that corresponds to the effective date of the permit , for each following year ;

c) Information 3 (quarterly) on realization of investments , mining and realized all operations performed for environmental rehabilitation and management of mining waste , in accordance with its obligations mining permit and plan, not later than the date 15 of the following month for each quarter ;

d) Information on the annual financial and technical analysis and all operations carried out in accordance with the obligations specified in his permit and the annual work plan , including all measures taken to protect the health and safety at work , training of employees , not later than 30 (thirty) days from the end of the relevant year ;

e) Annual Appraisal values guarantee for the implementation of the minimum work program and financial guarantee for the implementation of environmental remediation of the mining area , which appears in every year , not later than 30 (thirty) calendar days from the date that corresponds to the effective date of the permit for each following year for approval ;

f) Final Report on the development of mining activities by giving in detail the investments made during search - detection work done in his permitted area (coupled with engineering drawings) and the results of all tests taken ;

g) Report on payments to local and national taxes , under the initiative for transparency in the extractive industries ;

h) Information on storage , handling and management of mining waste and wastewater treatment facilities arising from mining and waste disposal ;

i) Information on licenses , authorizations or permissions , obtained by the holder of the permit if the performance of its activities, an action or the use of a public good in the area allowed , that , according to the permit is not part of the rights the holder of the mining permit , required prior approval from state authorities ;

j) To hold the offices of the company available for inspection by the AGS and shall give such information and explanations as required by the institution .

2 . Any holder of a mining exploitation and / or exploration- discovery - exploitation shall prepare and submit to the institution of the National Agency of Natural Resources (AKBN) required information according to the format , content and definitions of the terms specified in the Mining Law No. .10 304 , dated 15.07.2010 "On the mining sector in the Republic of Albania " and regulations adopted pursuant to it . These information are required :

a) The financial guarantee for the implementation of the investment program , not later than 30 (thirty) calendar days from the date that corresponds to the effective date of the permit ;

b) financial guarantee document for the implementation of environmental remediation of the mining area that appear every year , not later than 30 (thirty) calendar days from the date that corresponds to the effective date of the permit for each following year ;

c) Information on payment of royalty , by type of mining permit , the terms set forth in the legislation on taxes and fees ;

d) Information 3 (quarterly) on realization of investments , mining and realized all operations performed for environmental rehabilitation and management of mining waste , in accordance with its obligations mining permit and plan, not later than the date 15 of the following month for each quarter ;

e) Information on the annual financial and technical analysis and all operations carried out in accordance with the obligations specified in his permit and the annual work plan , including all measures taken to protect the health and safety at work , hospi training seekers , not later than 30 (thirty) days from the end of the year concerned;

f) Annual Appraisal values guarantee for the implementation of the investment plan and financial guarantee for the implementation of environmental remediation of the mining area that appear every year , not later than 30 (thirty) calendar days from the date the corresponding entry in effect permit every year following the approval ;

g) The final report for the development of mining activities , giving in detail the investments made during mining activities , work done in his permitted area (coupled with engineering drawings) and the results of the closure plan , rehabilitation plan , plan waste management and post-mining monitoring plan ;

h) Report on payments to local and national taxes , under the initiative for transparency in the extractive industries ;

i) Information on storage , handling and management of mining waste and wastewater treatment facilities arising from mining and waste disposal ;

j) Information on licenses , authorizations or permissions , obtained by the holder of the permit if his performing an action or the use of a public good in the area allowed , that , according to the permit is not part of the rights the holder of the mining permit , required prior approval from state authorities ;

k) To hold the offices of the company available for inspection by the AGS and shall give such information and explanations as required by the institution .

This order is effective immediately .

ORDER FOR APPROVAL OF FORM AND CONTENTS OF PLAN OF ACTIVITIES FOR CLOSURE OF A MINING ACTIVITIES

Nr.383 , dated 20/05/2011

Pursuant to Article 102 paragraph 4 of the Constitution of the Republic of Albania , Article 53 , paragraph 7 , and Article 56 , paragraph 2 of Law No. 10 304 , dated 15.07.2010 "On the mining sector in the Republic of Albania " ,

ORDER :

1 . Plan to close the mining activity is part of the rehabilitation plan of the mining area , as his special chapter includes the entirety of the documentation and technical , economic and environmental .

2 . Plan to close the mining activity prepared by the applicant for obtaining a mining permit and drawn by natural or legal persons licensed in the field of design research activities in the mining area . This plan is drawn up in accordance with the basic principles for drafting the rehabilitation of the mining activity that rely on mining and environmental legislation in force , as well as international best practices and submitted along with documentation to obtain mining rights .

3 . The plan for the closure of mining activity abandoned mine , used by the former state-owned enterprises , or an object mining research and discovery with the drilling of wells conducted by the state , drawn from relevant structures Albanian Geological Survey (AGS) for areas search and discovery , and the National Agency of Natural Resources (AKBN) for areas of use .

4 . All of abandoned mines that are considered as such , pursuant to Law No. 10 304 , dated 15.07.2010 "On the mining sector in the Republic of Albania " , pass post-mining monitoring regime after closing and evaluation studies of the National Agency of Natural Resources (NANR) and together with the financial costs for the closure , which are covered by the state budget approved by the Council of Ministers .

5 . AKBN proposes the closure of mining areas mining activity , according to a plan for the closure of mining activity . This plan should argue and justify the closure of mining activity and should include the necessary actions by the deadlines , ensuring financing for effective measures for closing the mine , according to the requirements of mining and environmental legislation in force ,

6 . All mines abandoned by holders of mining permits , pass post-mining monitoring regime after closing and evaluation studies of the National Agency of Natural Resources (AKBN) and approved by the Council of Ministers . Financial guarantee for environmental rehabilitation used for the realization of this plan .

7 . The closure plan for the mining activity permits mining areas abandoned by the holder of the mining permit and mining used by the state implemented by specialized state entities , or private , selected according to procurement procedures , in accordance with the legislation in force , controlled and AGS has monitored the search and discovery areas and areas AKBN exploitation and exploration- discovery - exploitation .

8 . Procedures for the closure of mining activity done by a mining facility closure plan approved mining activities , pursuant to the provisions of Article 53 of Law No. 10 304 , dated 15.07.2010 "On the mining sector in the Republic of Albania " .

9 . Plan to close the mining activity should be based on the principles of :

a) Ensuring the elimination of harmful effects of mining activity in the life and health of the community in the future mining areas for a much longer period ;

b) Ensuring the elimination of mining activity harmful effects of pollution on land , in water , flora and fauna and the ecosystem in general discharges and emissions in the future for a period as long as the observance of standards and minimum , approved by the legislation on mining and the environment ;

c) Closing progressive mining activity , eliminating the effects of this activity during the period of the mining permit ;

d) Ensuring the safe closure of mining activities ;

e) Ensuring the safe demolition of buildings of the mining activity , which can not be used further , after the completion of this activity , as defined in the applicable legislation ;

f) Implementation of the completion of the process of closing the mining facilities of the former state-owned mining enterprises ;

g) cooperation and joint actions between central authorities and local government ;

h) Coordination between environmental protection and economic development .

10 . Plan to close mining activities should include:

a) Project termination of mining activities to be implemented , taking into account:

i) general description of the area , flora and fauna ;

ii) description of the mining facility exploit, reached during the talks pun capital and ancillary surface facilities , processing plants and recycling and waste disposal Square , used reserves or remaining ;

iii) the mineral composition of the waste and physico-chemical characteristics thereof;

iv) the movement of surface and underground waters ;

v) infrastructure and proximity to residential areas ;

vi) the impact of the mining facility closed in the life and health of the local mining community ;

vii) the impact on the ecosystem of the mining area and its surrounding her ;

viii) the impact on the ecosystem in general ;

ix) the level of emissions into the environment and causing pollution to surface and underground waters , flora and fauna , future mining facility after closure ;

x) treatment in the future after the close of water and gases , which emerge from the mine ;

xi) protective pillars that are part of the resource / mining stocks or the surrounding rocks , which are not used for the protection of underground and surface mining area ;

xii) the manner of protection or river embankments and other areas included in the danger zone of a mining right .

b) Forecast for procedures and deadlines realizing the mine closure process , careers , processing plants , recycling plants and the disposal site .

c) the progressive realization of the process of termination of mining activities , when it is projected in the development of mining activities .

d) Options risk of accidents and mining facility after closing .

e) For mining , remains of which result from processes which use toxic and hazardous , such as cyanide, acids , harmful chemical substances , plan termination of mining activities should also include and eliminate these toxic substances and dangerous .

11 . Informational documents held by structures or entities responsible for implementation of the plan selected for closure of mining activities must be in accordance with the requirements of the mining and environmental legislation in force and shall include also :

a) Gent plan works for closing the facility mining permitted mining area and the tailing disposal site , according to the approved project ;

b) works Gent closure plan for the processing and recycling plant ;

12 . Form and content type of " closure plan for the mining activity " for search and discovery permits will be under Annex 1 , attached to this order .

13 . Form and content type of " closure plan for the mining activity " for licenses and permits use of search and discovery - use will be as specified in Annex 2 attached to this order .

14 . To implement this order institutions tasked the National Agency of Natural Resources (AKBN) , Albanian Geological Survey (AGS) and the National Licensing Center (NLC) .

This order is effective immediately .

Minister of Economy , Trade and Energy

Naco Nasip

Annex 1

TIP FORM AND CONTENTS OF " THE CLOSING PLAN OF ACTIVITIES

MINING ACTIVITY " PERMITS FOR SEARCH AND DISCOVERY

I. CONTENTS OF TEXT

1 . General considerations

2 . Information on the subject when the plan drawn up for a new mining area :

i) Name of the entity according to the NRC registration :

ii) the mining area with no identification number , to which the mining permit and included in the annual plan approved for mining

iii) Type of ore / minerals for which the issuance of the permit :

iv) Name and surname of the administrator of the subject mining permit application for registration by the NRC :

v) Address of the headquarters of the entity according to the NRC registration :

vi) no. Phone / fax :

vii) The name of the local government / local units required areas including :

viii) Name and surname of technical leaders :

ix) Date of completion of the professional license of technical leaders : / /

3 . Information on mining facility

A. when the object is abandoned mining mining permit holder :

i) mining area with no identification number , included in the approved annual plan for the year mining license and mining permit No. dated .... / /

ii) Name of the subject mining permit holder under NRC registration :

iii) Type of ore / minerals :

iv) Name and surname of the subject under registration administrator at NRC :

v) Address of the headquarters of the entity according to the NRC registration :

vi) no. Phone / fax :

vii) The name of the local government / local units required areas including :

B. When the object mining is an abandoned mine and used by the former state-owned enterprises :

i) mining area with no identification number ,

ii) state the name of the entity owns mining assets Facility

iii) Type of ore / minerals :

iv) Nr . Telephone / Fax state subject :

v) The name of the local government / local units required areas including :

4 . The legal basis on which drafted the project :

Decision of the Council of Ministers to approve the transfer in the mining facility closure regime .

5 . General data mining shorter object (according to the project usage) :

a) Location of the facility administrative and topographical .

b) The geography of the area , landscape , flora , fauna and the ecosystem in general etc. .

c) Building and deposit geology of the region .

d) hydrographic and hydrogeological conditions of deposit . Types of water and their kimizimi .

e) Description of the method of carrying out the search and discovery , key works , wells , trenches , galleries , quantity and type of water that flows from mineral operations , the amount of sterols and mineralogical composition , location of storage sites .

f) Description of surface facilities , such as roads , wells , offices , showers and toilets , cloakroom , dormitory , canteen , warehouse materials , compressor room , electrical cabinets , pumping station , workshops , warehouses of explosive material and other environments .

6 . Inventory investment made in the mining facility :

a) approved the actual physical inventory ;

b) Inventory of basic works , board and search and discovery ;

c) Inventory Accounting (enacted by the balance sheet) .

7 . Forecast method and mine closure operations :

a.1 . Locking comprehensive that includes :

- Closing of the canyons and geological galleries of pusëzave wells .

- Complete filling of spaces created by the surface thickens .

- The implementation of the rehabilitation plan , the order no .... date , ...

a.2 . Partial closure :

- Closing of the gorges of galleries ,

- Implementation of progressive rehabilitation plan , under Order No. .... date , ...

8 . Selection and detailed description of the method of closure .

9 . The estimates are detailed and specified for each operation mode selected for closure .

10 . Draft final estimate of closing .

11 . Draft schedule of implementation of the action plan of closing .

12 . Conclusions and recommendations .

II. PART GRAPHIC

No. Denomination rate

1 Topographic Map 1:25000 area required

2 General layout with geologic (updated with final state) 1:5000 or 1:2000 , 1:500 or 1:1000 or

3 Geological transverse topographic profiles (updated with final condition , traces of the mineralized body) 1:1000 or 1:2000 , 1:500 or 1:200

4 gjeometrizimin vertical projection of the body and / or body or mineralized zone (updated with final state) 1:1000 or 1:2000 , 1:500 or 1:200

5 passports closure of geological

Scheme 6 enclosures if required as necessary and preventive deployment of 1:500 or 1:200 signage

ANNEX No. 2

TIP FORM AND CONTENTS OF " THE PLAN OF ACTIVITIES termination of mining activities " USE PERMITS FOR LEAVE OF - USE SEARCH AND INTELLIGENCE

I. CONTENTS OF TEXT

1 . General considerations

2 . Information on the subject when the plan drawn up for a new mining area :

i) Name of the entity according to the NRC registration :

ii) the mining area with no identification number , to which the mining permit and included in the annual plan approved for mining

iii) Type of ore / minerals for which the issuance of the permit :

iv) Name and surname of the administrator of the subject mining permit application for registration by the NRC :

v) Address of the headquarters of the entity according to the NRC registration :

vi) no. Phone / fax :

vii) The name of the local government / local units required areas including :

viii) Name and surname of technical leaders :

ix) Date of completion of professional technical managers license : / /

3 . Information on mining facility

A. When the object is abandoned mining mining permit holder :

i) mining area with no identification number , included in the annual plan approved for mining and mining permit licensed with no date ... / /

ii) Name of the subject mining permit holder under NRC registration :

iii) Type of ore / minerals :

iv) Name and surname of the subject under registration administrator at NRC :

v) Address of the headquarters of the entity according to the NRC registration :

vi) no. Phone / fax :

vii) The name of the local government / local units required areas including :

B. When the object mining is an abandoned mine and used by the former state-owned enterprise :

i) mining area with no identification number ,

ii) state the name of the entity owns mining assets Facility

iii) Type of ore / minerals :

iv) Nr . Telephone / Fax state subject :

v) The name of the local government / local units required areas including :

4 . The legal basis on which drafted the project :

Decision of the Council of Ministers , which approves the transition to the mining facility shutdown mode .

5 . Ing general information about the object mining short (under utilization project) :

a) Location of the facility administrative and topographical ;

b) The geography of the area , landscape , flora , fauna and the ecosystem in general etc. . ;

c) Building and deposit geology of the region ;

d) The type and thickness of land cover in mining area ;

e) Tectonics of the deposit ;

g) hydrographic and hydrogeological conditions of deposit . Types of water and their kimizimi ;

h) On the morphology and composition of ores and / or useful ores . Add to short on the type of ore , physico - chemical him.

A. For the case of using underground deposit

a) Description of the way the opening of the mine , the opening main proceedings , the amount and type of water flowing from the mining works , the amount of sterols and mineralogical composition , location of storage sites , processing and recycling plants ;

b) utilization system using economic and technical indicators to realize the quantity and quality of reserves that can be exploited or utilized divided by horizons and profiles ;

c) Description of surface facilities , such as roads , wells , offices , showers and toilets , cloakroom , dormitory , canteen , warehouse materials , compressor room , electrical cabinets , pumping station , workshops , warehouses of explosive material and other environments .

B. For the case of exploitation of the deposit career :

a) Description of options and gjysmëtrasheve opening roads , their length and section . Determining the actual boundaries career , its real dimensions , determining the coordinates of Vertex , the amount and type of water flowing in career and emerging from it , the location of waste disposal sites , the location of processing and recycling plants ;

b) use system that is used and the technical- economic indicators achieved , quantity and quality of resources used , or that can be used divided by horizons and profiles ;

c) Description of surface facilities , such as roads , wells , offices , showers and toilets , cloakroom , dormitory , canteen , warehouse materials , compressor room , electrical cabinets , pumping station , workshops , warehouses of explosive material and other environments .

6 . Inventory investment made in the mining facility :

a) approved the actual physical inventory ;

b) Inventory of basic work , preparation and exploitation ;

c) Inventory Accounting (enacted by the balance sheet) ;

d) List of machinery and technological equipment :

7 . Forecast manner and closing operations of the mine :

a) In case of groundwater exploitation :

a.1 . Comprehensive mine closure means :

- Closing of the gorges of the opening of the mine workings ;

- Complete filling of spaces created by the use and Mulde (funnel) to the surface ;

- Encirclement of hazardous areas ;

- Setting the warning signs and stop ;

- The implementation of the rehabilitation plan , under Order No. .... dated .....

a.2 . Partial closure of the mine :

- Closing of the gorges of the works of opening ;

- Encirclement of hazardous areas ;

- Setting the warning signs and stop ;

The implementation of the rehabilitation plan , the order no .... dated .....

b) In case of using the career :

- Closure and / or blocking of roads , thick or gjysmëtrasheve career entry ;

- Siege of space and / or spaces created by the use of career ;

- Setting the warning signs and stop ;

- The implementation of the rehabilitation plan , under Order No. .... dated ...

8 . Selection and detailed description of the method of closure .

9 . The estimates are detailed and specified for each operation mode selected for closure .

a. For the case of underground mining :

- On closing of major works gorges ;

- For the filling of underground spaces ;

- For filling the Mulde (hopper on the surface) ;

- For the siege of hazardous areas ;

- For signage ;

- To implement the rehabilitation plan ;

- For disassembling various mechanical and electrical ;

- To perform other ancillary processes , such as removal of water , transport workers materials , machinery and equipment etc. . ;

- Disassembling machinery and electrical and mechanical equipment in underground and surface ;

- Projektorganizimi for dismantling the machinery and plant equipment enrichment or enrichment plant (if any) ;

- Other expenses for the liquidation of the mine ;

- Problems and tasks influence on surface for field use ;

- Liquidation of surface facilities ;

- Monitoring the liquidation of the mine ;

- Technical security measures for carrying out the liquidation proceedings and other auxiliary processes .

b) In the case of careers :

- For the closing and / or blocking of roads , thick or gjysmëtrasheve career entry ;

- For the siege of space and / or spaces created by the use of career ;

- For setting the warning signs of prohibitive f ;

- To implement the rehabilitation plan ;

- For disassembling various mechanical and electrical ;

- To perform other ancillary processes , such as removal of water , transport workers materials , machinery and equipment etc. . ;

- Disassembling machinery and mechanical appliances and electrical surface;

- Projektorganizimi for dismantling the machinery and plant equipment enrichment or enrichment plant (if any) ;

- Other expenses for the liquidation of the mine ;

- Problems and tasks influence on surface for field use ;

- Liquidation of surface facilities ;

- Monitoring the liquidation of the mine ;

- Technical security measures for carrying out the liquidation proceedings and other auxiliary processes .

10 . Draft final estimate of closing .

11 . Draft schedule of implementation of the action plan of closing .

12 . Conclusions and recommendations .

II. PART GRAPHIC

No. Denomination rate

A. For underground mines

1 Topographic Map 1:25000 area required

2 . General layout of the works of opening (updated with final state) 1:5000 or 1:2000 or 1:1000 , or 1:500

3 . Plans related horizons (up to date with the final condition of the body and harness tracks) 1:1000 or 1:2000 1:500 or 1:200

4 Geological transverse topographic profiles (updated with final condition , body harness tracks and space utilization) 1:1000 or 1:2000 , 1:500 or 1:200

5 gjeometrizimin vertical projection of the body and / or body or mineralized zone (updated with final condition , body harness tracks and space utilization) 1:1000 or 1:2000 , 1:500 or 1:200

6 topographic map of the area used to document and update infrastructure collapsed area or areas that are under the influence or exploitation (updated) 1:5000 or 1:2000 , or : 1000, or 1:500

7 Table of establishing administrative facilities , socio- cultural and industrial (updated with final state) 1:500 or 1:200

8 passports closure of mining

9 Passport filling spaces underground and / or Mulde (funnel to the surface)

10 scheme and placement of signage enclosures preventive

B. careers

1 Topographic Map 1:25000 area required

2 General layout of career finally updated using the final state 1:1000 or 1:2000 or 1:500

3 Transverse profile development career ladder updated with final state 1:1000 or 1:2000 , or 1:500

4 Geological topographic object of opening roads and landfill sites sterols or derivatives , the final state 1:5000 or 1:2000 or 1:1000 , or 1:500

5 Table of establishing administrative facilities , socio - cultural and industrial placement scheme of machinery and equipment working in the square 1:100 , 1:200 or schematic with parameters

6 passports closing roads career 1:500 or 1:200

7 Scheme of surrounding space and placement of signage career preventive

ORDER FOR APPROVAL OF REGISTRATION PROCEDURES AND DOCUMENTATION CADASTRE REGISTER

WITH MINING AND MINING REGISTER , AND FORM AND REPORTING PROCEDURES OF THIS DOCUMENTATION BY MINING PERMITS POSSESSOR

Nr.384 , dated 20/05/2011

Pursuant to Article 102 , paragraph 4 of the Constitution of the Republic of Albania , Article 44 , paragraph 2, and Article 56 , paragraph 2 of Law No. 10 304 , dated 15.07.2010 "On the mining sector in the Republic of Albania " ,

ORDER :

1 . Mining registry includes all data for the legal regime of surface mining areas and neighboring areas , ownership , topographical situation of the mining areas of work supporting mining activities , reserves and mineral production , as well as data on the holder of the permit mining , as follows:

A. The data on the legal regime of surface mining areas and neighboring areas :

a) mining area with no identification number , which was approved mining permit and included in the annual plan approved for mining and mining permit licensed with no date ... / /

b) Type of ore / minerals , for which the permit is granted :

c) allowing surface area in km2 mining permit :

d) map of the mining permit allowing the state coordinates plans , its legal regime under the act of verifying the relevant structure (a copy of her original) .

e) allowing map of the mining permit in the state coordinates plans , approved by the authorities responsible under the decision of the technical committee (a copy of her original) .

f) Map of the area adjacent areas to allow mining permit , their legal regime under the act of verifying the relevant structure (a copy of her original) .

g) Act of approving mining permit prepared by the directorate responsible MoETE covering mining activity and approved by the Minister ;

h) format which is published by permission of the NLC institution ;

i) The name of the local unit / local units permitted areas including mining permit : ..

B. Information on ownership of land surface mining areas and neighboring areas :

a) The ownership of the land surface mining permit area or change this property after approvals from the relevant structures under Albanian law .

b) The title deed of the land area adjacent to the permitted mining area or change their properties after approvals from the relevant structures under Albanian law .

c) The act of changing the land use designation after approval by the relevant structures under Albanian law .

C. The data for topographic situation of the mining areas mining activities supporting works , according to project development and mining activities approved updated :

Mining permits search and discovery :

a) Administrative Location ;

b) The geography of the area , relief , climate , vegetation ;

c) Buildings and infrastructure facilities in the area allowed ;

d) Hydrography , Hydrogeology ;

e) demographics ;

f) The economy of the area and the main activities ;

g) Description of search and discovery works h) water supply scheme

i) The scheme of power supply ;

j) general transport scheme ;

k) Statement of comprehensive equipment and mechanisms used in underground and surface ;

l) Summary table of investment ;

m) topographic map of the area with the documentation required infrastructure update (updated) ;

n) Geological map with topographic work done for exploration and ore (canals , wells , drilling gallery) ;

o) General layout of the mine workings of search and discovery , roads , disposition , placement of surface facilities and landfill sites, sterols , designed .

Exploration permits and exploitation - use search and discovery :

a) Administrative Location ;

b) The geography of the area , relief , climate , vegetation ;

c) Buildings and infrastructure facilities in the area allowed ;

d) Hydrography , Hydrogeology ;

e) demographics ;

f) The economy of the area and the main activities ;

g) description of the operating system ;

h) description of the selection process , breakage, Factiousness , enrichment or other methods that will be used for ore processing and realization of products provided . with appropriate technological schemes and indicators ;

i) The work of opening the facility and ancillary mining capital , their parameters ;

j) works mining facility utilization , their parameters ;

k) - blast drilling passports ;

1) ventilation scheme ;

m) scheme compressed air supply ;

n) water supply scheme ;

o) scheme of power supply ;

p) the total transport scheme ;

q) Statement of comprehensive equipment and mechanisms used in underground and surface ;

r) Summary table of investment ;

s) topographic map of the area with the documentation required infrastructure update (updated) ;

t) with topographic map geological work done on the use of ore (wells , galleries etc. .) ;

u) General layout of the mine workings opening. Topographic map of the surface of the mine with roads , disposition , placement of objects surface and landfill sites sterols or derivatives , designed ;

v) deposit topographic map with contours of dangerous areas from the influence of exploitation ;

w) General layout of the ore processing facilities .

D. Data on reserves and mineral production under the project development of the mining activity , approved and updated :

Mining permits search and discovery :

a) Reserves according to fields and facilities, their quantity and quality ;

b) The method of calculating reserves and calculating tables mineral reserves , geological reserves of extractable ore in quantity and quality ;

c) Information on the characteristics of mineralization and ore bodies ;

d) The content of useful elements .

Exploration permits and exploitation - use search and discovery :

a) Reserves according to fields and facilities, their quantity and quality ;

b) The method of calculating reserves and calculating tables mineral reserves , geological reserves of extractable ore in quantity and quality ;

c) Information on the characteristics of mineralization and ore bodies ;

d) The content of useful elements ;

e) Reserves used , and readily detected .

E. The data on the holder of the mining permits :

a) Name of the entity that holds mineral mining permit registration by the NRC :

(a copy of the extract of NRC society at the time of granting the permit , which must be updated to reflect the changes in this extract during the term of the mining permit and the completion of the period) .

b) the name / names of the owners of the mining company , possessing the mining permit , according to their percentages in the company according to the NRC registration :

(percentages of the shareholders in the company at the time of granting the permit , which must be updated to reflect the changes in this extract during the term of the mining permit and the completion of the period) . When the owner / holder of the shares of the company leading change , changes in mining registry act should reflect the transfer of the permit .

c) Name and surname of the administrator of the subject mining permit holder under NRC registration :

d) Address of the headquarters of the entity according to the NRC registration :

e) Nr . Phone / fax :

f) Name and surname of technical leaders :

g) Data for professional drivers license Technical date of issue / ,

institution that issued the license

h) Name of person and no. phone for emergencies and accidents :

2 . The data included in the mining registry dealing with :

i) topographical situation of the mining areas of work supporting mining activities ;

ii) reserves for mineral production submitted by the holder of the permit at the time of application for a mining permit and deposited with the National Licensing Center (NLC) .

3 . The data on the holder of the mining license after the act of approval of the Minister , submitted to the NLC institution , the department responsible for mining activities MoETE is held by this institution .

4 . The data included in the mining registry dealing with the legal regime of surface mining areas and neighboring areas , ownership , assessed in the act of verification and decision of the Technical Council of the Albanian Geological Survey (AGS) for search and discovery areas and National Agency of Natural Resources (AKBN) for areas of exploitation and exploration-discovery - exploitation , and sent to NLC .

5 . Department responsible for mining activities MoETE Albanian Geological Survey (AGS) and the National Agency of Natural Resources (AKBN) have the right to dispose of online data related to the object of their work activity .

6 . Register for any mining permit mining also includes data for administrative violations of the holder of the mining permit , mining permit status , suspension or revocation proceedings .

7 . In the mining registry includes also all mining areas that are closed or are in the process of closing or conservation .

8 . Institution NLC holds the mining registry , linking all the data for a mining area with data mining permit holder and realizes management of these data structures responsible for mining activities under the laws of the functioning of this center .

9 . Changes to the mining permit holder that realized from the transfer of the permit , should be

reflected in the mining registry within a period not exceeding thirty (30) calendar days from the date of the act of tr ansferimit .

10 . Changes the administrator and technical managers realized in the National Registration Center (NRC) by the subject reflected in the mining and mineral extract subject to NRC , should be reflected automatically in the registry NLC mining .

11 . Mining cadastre inventory includes systematic data on immovable property , supporting mining activities , land , buildings and installations of the surface or underground , in the technical, economic and other data for the permitted mining areas as follows :

A. Data on land surface area allowing a mining permit :

a) Agricultural land with the level of prolificacy ;

b) of forest land and pasture ;

c) Land owned by local authorities ;

d) State Land ;

's) private land ;

f) Land owned by the mining permit holder subject .

B. Add to immovable property of the mining permit holder :

a) The basic works , auxiliary and exploitation , the development of underground mining activity or career .

b) Surface , such as automobile road opening and exploitation of the mining facility , column wells , schedules, offices , showers and toilets , cloakroom , dormitory , canteen , warehouse materials , compressor room , electrical cabinets , pumping station , workshops , warehouse explosive material and other environments .

c) Land area permit allowing mining entity owned mining permit holders .

d) Machinery and equipment used underground or surface mining activity to develop .

e) mineral processing plants .

f) recycling plants and waste water .

g) Equipment for monitoring of mining activities and mining risk .

h) dams or structures constructed for waste disposal .

i) Financial Value of real estate valued at the time of registration .

C. Information for real estate in the area allowing existing mining permit :

a) The basic works , ancillary exploitation , mining conducted on the premises of the former state-owned mining enterprises or previous holder of the mining permit for that object mining .

b) Surface mining facility constructed by the former state mining enterprises or previous holder of the mining permit for that facility mining , such as automobile road opening and exploitation of the mining facility , column wells , schedules, offices , showers and toilets , wardrobe , dormitory , canteen , warehouse materials , compressor room , electrical cabinets , pumping station , workshops , warehouses of explosive material and other environments .

c) Land area allowed to permit state-owned mining and / or local authorities and / or private and / or offset .

d) Machinery and equipment used underground or surface mining activities for development , which have been owned by the former state-owned mining enterprises .

e) mineral processing plants , recycling plants and waste water , equipment for monitoring of mining activities and mining risk , dumps or structures built for storage of waste that have been owned by the former state-owned mining enterprises .

f) Financial Value of real estate , valued at the time of registration .

D. Information on real estate and other realized by the holder of the mining permit mining activity under , but not related to the event that may or may not be owned by the holder of the mining permit :

a) socio - cultural facilities , education , health facilities for community protection mining area .

b) infrastructure facilities like roads etc. . , to serve the community of the mining area .

12 . The data relating to real estate created by the mining permit holder involved in the mining cadastre recorded in the cadastre upon the request of the holder of the mining permit certifying their ownership in accordance with the requirements of the legislation on immovable property .

13 . The data included in the mining cadastre and dealing with real estates created by former state mining enterprises , registered in the mining cadastre estimates after mining institutions and presentation of these estimates in the NLC , where their registration is subject to any mining or mining area .

14 . Information on ownership of land taken by the respective institutions and proof of this property recorded in the mining cadastre NLC , where their registration is subject to any mining or mining area .

15 . Institution NLC holds mining cadastre , linking all data to a data mining area of real estate , land ownership of the mining area and realizes management of these data structures responsible for mining activities under legal operation of this center .

16 . Both documents mining registry and cadastre mining related to each other through the mining area which is the first element identification of these two registers .

17 . Registries in electronic form in the institution of NLC . The level of data confidentiality realized in respect of the requirements of the mining legislation and Albanian legislation .

18 . To implement this order institutions charged NLC , NRC 's AGS NANR and MoETE directorate responsible in addressing the problems of mining permits .

This order is effective immediately .

ORDER FOR APPROVAL OF RULES FOR USE OF MINING PERMISSION

Nr.386 , dated 20/05/2011

Pursuant to Article 102 , paragraph 4 of the Constitution of the Republic of Albania , Article 50 , paragraph 6 and Article 56 , paragraph 2 of Law No. 10 304 , dated 15.07.2010 "On the mining sector in the Republic of Albania " ,

ORDER :

1 . All data for mineral resources in the Republic of Albania , irrespective of their conservation , belonging Albanian state and made available to the relevant structure , with the latter's request , and in accordance with the provisions of Law No. 10 304 , dated 15.07.2010 "On the mining sector in the Republic of Albania " .

2 . Technical data and study samples , which are owned by responsible structures as the result of these structures , which belong to the Albanian state available and used in accordance with the Albanian legislation in force .

3 . Technical data and research evidence relevant structures owned by information obtained from binding mining license holders are confidential .

4 . Technical data and research evidence that the holder of the mining permit creates the realization of his mining activities and are part of the mandatory information that a holder of the mining permit realizes responsible structures are confidential . The mining permit holder may use the above data only on behalf of itself and only during the term of validity of the mining permit . Transfer of these data by the holder or former holder of a license to third parties can be made only after prior approval from the authorities responsible and respected Albanian legislation to copyright .

5 . Data on local tax payments and national not considered confidential. Data on tax payments are published in local and national public transparency within the mining .

6 . Each applicant for a mining right may use data obtained from the relevant structures or previous holder of mining permits , while maintaining their confidentiality and stating their source at the time of application .

7 . Use of technical data and research evidence , that the holder of the mining permit creates the realization of his mining activities that are confidential and may be used when the owner of the data agrees to follow the order , as follows :

a) completion of the term of the mining right ;

b) the permit holder performs search and discovery application for mining exploitation;

c) leaving the area in which technical data are taken , and study samples ;

d) two years after the date of receipt of such data and evidence from the relevant structure ;

e) the publication of such data .

Can not be performed before the next execution of that previous paragraph .

8 . 6 point settings can not restrict the right of the state to use such information for preparing

reports or economic- financial and technical- scientific needs him .

9 . Study results of tests involving chemical analysis , mineralogical , petrographic , technological studies etc. . , Within the final report with the closure of the mining permit expires AGS submitted to the institution for the search and discovery licenses and permits use NANR . Sampling for results consist of :

a) incurred in drilling permits search and discovery , the permit holder shall submit to AGS : graphically geological drilling columns , duplicates of samples of chemical analysis , where it caught the mineral body , and anshlife SHLIF representative mineralogical and petrographic studies , and the description thereof.

b) evidence of ore treatment , the permit holder search and discovery , exploitation and exploration- discovery - use scheme delivers graphically realized technological parameters for each product of the scheme include : quantity, quality , recoverability , the contents of the rigidity , the duplication of the final product chemical analysis and description of the parameters of the equipment used in the technological scheme .

10 . Responsible structure and other state authorities that perform state functions in the mining area , are required to maintain the confidentiality of data received by holders of mining permits or data to which they have learned during their exercise of that function constitute a trade secret in accordance with the legislation in force . Violation of this provision is punishable under the laws in force .

11 . For the implementation of this order are charged AGS 's institutions . and NANR directorate responsible in bugs that treats problems of mining permits . This order is effective immediately

DECISION FOR SOME CHANGES IN THE DECISION NR.1203

DATED 27/08/2008 THE COUNCIL OF MINISTERS " FOR DETERMINING THE VALUE OF EXACT , PERCENT, TO royalty , ACCORDING TO THE MARKET , OR FOR ANY GROUP MINERAL MINIERALESH "

Nr.1306 , dated 24/09/2008

Pursuant to Article 100 of the Constitution and paragraph 4 of Article 4 of Law No. 9975 , dated 28.07.2008 " On national taxes " on the proposal of the Minister of Economy , Trade and Energy and the Minister of Finance , the Council of Ministers

DECIDED :

In nr.1203 decision dated 08.27.2008 of the Council of Ministers , made the following changes :

1.Pika 3 is changed as follows:

" 3 . Where the minerals used in the manufacture of by-products (concentrate ore or metallurgical products) , which are exported , mineral endowment will apply to customs , the value of the mineral used in the production of by-product . This value shall be calculated on the basis of sales invoices quantity of ore , used in the production of by-product . where exporter fallout

(ore or concentrate, metallurgical products) is also producer of ore , the royalty rate will be calculated on the cost of production (extraction) of ore used . This value is determined according to the quantity of final product (concentrate or metallurgical products) , declared at customs , norms and corresponding ore used . Standards are sent periodically by the Ministry of Economy , Trade and Energy , the Ministry of Finance , and published in uebsaitin the Directorate General of Customs . " .

2 . Point 4 is amended as follows:

" 4 . For all other categories of mineral byproducts , which can be derived from minerals specified in Appendix No. 1 , attached nr.1203 decision dated 08.27.2008 of the Council of Ministers , and for which the Ministry of Economy , Trade and Energy has not determined the corresponding norms of the minerals , which are components of this by-product when the permit holder

exploitation of mineral processing is also , mineral endowment will be applied on the cost of production (extraction) of ore , the cost , which is declared by the manufacturer and is paid with the tax authorities , according to the procedures provided in the instruction of the Minister of Finance . "

DECISION FOR APPROVAL OF RULES , PROCEDURES AND CRITERIA FOR ISSUANCE OF CERTIFICATE OF SPECIALIST ASSESSMENT AND ENVIRONMENTAL AUDITING

Pursuant to Article 100 of the Constitution and Section 3 of Article 31 of Law No. 8934 , dated 05.09.2002 " On Environmental Protection " , as amended , the proposal of the Minister of Environment , Forestry and Water Management , the Council of Ministers

DECIDED :

1 . Adoption of rules , procedures and criteria for issuing the certificate of specialist impact assessment and environmental auditing , as follows .

2 . The right to have a certificate of graduate specialists in the field of environment or agromjedisit , Polytechnic University of Tirana , Agricultural University of Tirana , in private universities or university abroad . Certificate of specialist impact assessment and environmental auditing given by the Minister of Environment , Forestry and Water Management .

3 . Certificates for the device as a specialist for impact assessment and environmental auditing , the graduate , according to paragraph 2 of this decision , submit to the Ministry of Environment , Forestry and Water Administration an application , accompanied by self-declaration which , among other things , degree and proven experience working in the environmental field , no less than five years .

4 . Graduates , according to paragraph 2 of this decision , seeking to be certified , subject to examination at the Polytechnic University of Tirana or the Agricultural University of Tirana .

5 . Programs and procedures development and evaluation of examinations set by the Ministry of Environment , Forestry and Water Management , in cooperation with the Ministry of Education and Science .

6 . Exams for issuing a certificate as a specialist for impact assessment and environmental auditing conducted two times a year .

7 . Exam evaluation committee submits for signature , within 5 days from the date of the exam , the summary of the exam results of all competitors to the Dean of the faculty , which is developed exam . Results are displayed in the premises of the respective faculties and a copy is sent to the Ministry of Environment , Forestry and Water Management .

8 . Based on the results of the examination , the Minister of Environment , Forests and Water Administration issues a certificate , within 10 days from the date of receipt of the final results of the exam .

9 . Legal persons certified under personal certificates that were given at least two of their specialists .

10 . Legal persons to obtain a certificate , submit to the Minister :

a) the application ;

b) notarized copies of certificates of no less than two of their specialists ;

c) employment contract with certified specialists ;

d) the certificate of registration from the National Registration Center (NRC) .

11 . Specialists to identify a certificate , the Ministry of Environment , Forestry and Water Administration created the national registry of certified specialists , according to rules adopted by the Minister .

12 . Registry is disponueshën to the public, according to the rules defined in the regulations of his administration .

13 . Certificate declared invalid by special order of the Minister , it is proved that the specialist has cheated with the data presented in the documents . The order , which invalidated certificate published .

14 . Against refusal of application for a certificate , and to order the invalidation of specialist may appeal administratively and in court within one month from the date of refusal or the issuance of the order .

15 . When appointed certified specialist in public administration , in a task which involves a conflict of interest , the certificate is not used by him for as long as it is in that position .

16 . For examining the application , the applicant pays the service fee , in the amount of 10 000 (ten thousand) , which is paid upon submission of application and is non-refundable even if the application is not approved . Revenue from fees paid into the State Budgeting .

17 . Certificates issued before the entry into force of this decision remain valid .

18 . Decision No.268 , dated 24.04.2003 of the Council of Ministers "On certification of specialists , for impact assessment and environmental auditing " is repealed .

19 . The Ministry of Environment , Forestry and Water Management and the Ministry of Education and Science for the implementation of this decision .

This decision shall enter into force after its publication in the Official Journal .

INSTRUCTION FOR THE CONTENT OF DOCUMENTS FOR MINING EQUIPMENT

Nr.1028, dated 10.12.2009

In the context of institutional reform, based on Articles 15 and 17 of the 7796 Mining Law of Albania, dated 02.17.1994, amended by Law No.9261, dated 07.22.2004, pursuant to Sections 25,26,31,33, 45,47,64,65,70 and 71 of this Law,

GUIDE:

Approval of documentation that legal person shall submit to permit mining of minerals of group 1, 2, 3 and 4. The application, along with supporting documentation, submitted to the NLC counters. According to the procedure laid down in Articles 17, 31, 32 and 33 of Law 10,081, dated 23.02.2009 "On licenses, authorizations and permits in the Republic of Albania".

The documentation should include:

1. Demand for mining equipment, determining exactly the coordinates required to use the area and its surface. Short description and a map of shk.1: 25,000 mining area:

- Determining exactly her plan coordinates (X, Y) and Z cases necessary);

- Its surface.

2. Verification Act, conducted by the National Agency of Natural Resources (AKBN), according to the form prepared by it, for each of the types of mining permit required. In this form the data are also reflected whether or not harmful to the monuments and archeology.

3. NRC's decision to register as a legal entity, where the object of the activity have approved the development of mining activities in surface or underground works upon request.

4. Financial resources needed to cover the investment envisaged performed during mining activity.

4.1 For legal entities applying for mining permits and to explain the self-declaration that they have not exercised earlier mining activity, or any other business activity, financial resources must present one of the following documents:

- A statement by the bank, to confirm that the legal person has opened the account number, which must be stored at least 30% of the investment of the investment program is presented, and / or;

- A document certifying that the legal person has secured a loan from a bank or other financial entity worth, which covers investments that are expected to be performed, and / or

- A contract with an investor, which provides financial support for the realization of the investment program. In this case, the legal entity must submit a notarized document, in which the expressed willingness of investors to support this investment, as well as documents proving the financial resources of the latter (bank guarantee or economic balances of society, in which the investor is the sole owner or majority shareholder).

4.2 For legal entities applying for mining permits, who have previously developed mining activities, or other business activity, as a document for completion of financial resources will be considered:

- Investment accounting are performed;

- Physical inventory with its main items such as plant and key equipment etc..;

- Financial balance last year.

5. For permission to search minerals group 1, 2 and 3, the application must contain the conditions specified in Section 25 of the Mining Law of Albania.

6. To permit the detection of group minerals 1,2 and 3, the application must contain the conditions specified in Section 31 of the Mining Law of Albania.

7. To permit search and discovery of minerals group 4, the application must contain the conditions specified in Section 64 of the Mining Law of Albania.

8. To permit the exploitation of minerals of the group 1, 2 and 3, the application must contain the conditions specified in Section 45 of the Mining Law of Albania.

9. To permit the exploitation of minerals group 4, the application must contain the conditions specified in Section 70 of the Mining Law of Albania.

10. To permit the exploitation of minerals of the group 1, 2, 3 and 4, the application must also contain:

10.1 Opinion local commune or municipality, to allow for development of mining activity in the mineral exploitation of the object being sought. In cases where the land is private property, the legal entity shall submit the agreement with the landowner to allow exploitation.

10.2 Opinion of the Directorate of Forest Service district to allow development of mining activity in the object sought to be used, for the case when the object is in forests.

10.3 Environmental Permit issued by the NLC. The environmental permit may be issued for an area smaller than that required for the mining permit, but that's part of it, provided that:

- Exploitation of the mine to start from this area;

- Before you start using outside this area, the new environmental permit is obtained, which submitted NANR.

10.4 Contract with the technical director of the works, which should be mining engineer, except when explosives not used, can also be a geologist engineer.

10.5-economic and technical study for the case of exploitation permits, facility utilization project designed by specialists certified by NANR, geological-mining field and markshderike.

The decision of the technical committee on NANR be clearly stated in relation to economic and technical study of the project mining facility utilization, presented by the subject, which confirmed ensuring normal development work program and completion of all technical insurance claims mine.

For monitoring and implementation of this policy, loaded NLC, AKBN and Coordination Directorate and Contract Management in the General Regulatory.

ALBANIA: LAW ON PETROLEUM.

(Exploration and production)

Since the policy of the Republic of Albania for order:

(I) to promote research and production of oil and natural gas or;

(Ii) to rehabilitate existing equipment and increase extraction of oil and gas reserves already discovered;

(Iii) ensure that the development of these reserves become irrevocable in accordance with national interests, in orderly manner, in accordance with applicable standardtet International;

(Iv) ensure that petroleum operations are not endanger human life or cause environmental damage, pursuant to article 16 of Law No.7491, dated 29.4.1991 "For main constitutional provisions ", upon proposal of the Council of Ministers,

Article I Quote

This law stated hydrocarbons law (research and production), 1993.

Article 2 Definitions

In this law, unless the context requires otherwise, "Albpetrol" means the Oil and Economic Union Gas.

"Natural gas" means all hydrocarbons which are gaseous state at normal atmospheric conditions including liquid gas, dry gas, gas in the space loops and residual gas that remains after the extraction or separation of liquid hydrocarbons from gas and gas liquid johidrokarbur produced jointly with liquid hydrocarbons and gaseous.

"Hydrocarbons" means crude oil or natural gas.

"Research" means the search for hydrocarbons by means geological, geophysical and other, and includes the drilling of wells research and evaluation.

"Contractor" means any person or persons who Ministry enters into hydrocarbons, and can include Albpetroltin or any other state agency.

"Ministry" means Ministry of Industry, Resources Minerals and Energy.

"Petroleum Agreement" means an agreement

connected by the Ministry in accordance with paragraph I of Article 5 of this law, which authorizes the Contractor to conduct operations in Contract area and can take the form of an Agreement with Production division or any other form agreed between Ministry and the Contractor which is not inconsistent with this law.

"Production Sharing Agreement" means an agreement Hydrocarbon, which provides coverage of Contract Costs Hydrocarbons produced from the Contract Area or from part proportional to its partition between the State and Contractor the quantity of hydrocarbons remaining after the cost recovery Contract in accordance with a formula to determine the degree or Petroleum Agreement.

"Crude oil" means oil, asfalte, ozokerite, and All kinds of hydrocarbons and bitumen, and solid liquid, in their natural state or obtained by gas natural through condensation or extraction, but not prifshin coal or any other substance that can be downloaded from coal.

"Petroleum Operations" means all or any

operation related to the research, development, extraction, production, separation and processing, collection, transportation and sale or disposal of Hydrocarbons to the point of export or to a delivery point in Albania which is agreed upon or at the point of entry into a refinery, and includes operations in natural gas processing, but does not include petroleum refining operations.

"Development plan" means a plan for development and production of hydrocarbons found in a contract area, the prepared in accordance with the benchmarks of Section 6 of this law and relevant provisions of this Agreement Hydrocarbon contract area.

"Pratik good oil deposits" means All those practices generally accepted in the industry international oil companies as good, safe, economical and efficient research and production of hydrocarbons.

"Person" means a natural person or legal partnership, corporation or other entity other association.

"Manufacturing" means the issuance and availability of hydrocarbons.

"Reservoir" means a collection of separate hydrocarbon.

"Albania" means the Republic of Albania.

"Disclosure" means a discovery of hydrocarbons encountered First piercing the well in a structure that can be downloaded at surface with a debit measurable by conventional measurement testing of the hydrocarbon industry.

"Contract Area" means the area within which the Contractor authorized to seek, develop and produce hydrocarbons under a Petroleum Agreement.

"Development" means construction and installation of equipment Petroleum production and drilling of wells exploitation.

Article 3 Ownership of Hydrocarbons

All deposits hydrocarbons that exist in their natural state layer, which lie within the jurisdiction of Albania, including marine areas, are the exclusive property of the Albanian state which is represented by the relevant ministry and all these resources will be used to benefit the Albanian people.

Article 4

Petroleum operations

In accordance with Section I2. (2) and except as evaluation of facility operations conducted under and in accordance with a permit issued to the facility assessment accordance with Article 8, no person shall seek, develop or produce hidokarbure in Albania without being authorized by Ministry to do so under the terms and conditions of a Marrëeshjeje hydrocarbon

Article 5

Petroleum Agreement

(L) The Ministry may, subject to paragraph (2) of this article, enter the Petroleum Agreement with any person, by the person authorized under the terms and conditions defined in this Agreement, seek, develop and produce hydrocarbons in the Contract Area.

(2) Ministry will not connect to the Petroleum Agreement any person if the Ministry is satisfied that the person with which will be linked Hidrokarburve Agreement has or may provide financial resources and technical competence required to the Contractor's obligations under the Agreement Hydrocarbons.

(3) A Petroleum Agreement may:

(A) Provide a contractor under the terms and conditions defined in:

(1) The exclusive right to conduct research within Contract Area for a period other than any additional time required to complete work undertaken to evaluate an invention, will not exceed 5 years total, except when Contractor convince the Ministry that there are conditions which require a specific period of long, the Contractor may be given a period not exceeding 7 years total.

(2) The exclusive right for a period not exceeding 25 years, to develop and produce hydrocarbon reserves in the Contract Area, in accordance with the terms of the Development Plan approved by the Ministry, and to renew this right and to the extent it provides Hydrocarbon Agreement.

(3) The right to build, extend and operate pipes in Albania, subject to requirements to allow the use of excess capacity by third parties on commercial terms and you subject to the conditions applicable to any treaty to which Albania is party to connect them with pipes and fittings of countries other.

(B) give the Contractor right of ownership to the its hydrocarbons produced in the area of contract in a point specified in the Petroleum Agreement.

(C) The Contractor guarantees the right to sell or export trade or anything else for Hydrocarbons which he has taken possession under the Petroleum Agreement, unless the law is subject to terms of order emergency and any obligation contained Agreement Hydrocarbons to supply or contribute to supplying the local market.

d) A Petroleum Agreement, in which a party a foreign investor, may contain clauses regarding stability of fiscal regime.

(E) Subject to these safeguards and reservations as may be included in the Agreement Hydrocarbons, this Agreement may recognize contractor right:

(1) to obtain and retain the proceeds abroad foreign currency sales of hydrocarbons which has taken owned by Petroleum Agreement and to use such benefits as it deems appropriate, you subject to payment of income tax and liabilities Other in Albania.

(2) to send abroad, in foreign currency convertible, the profits achieved by the contractor from the sale of Hydrocarbon in Bangladesh.

(3) to open and use a foreign bank account order to pay for goods, services and personnel required to conduct Petroleum Operations under Hydrocarbon Agreement.

(4) to convert foreign currency into domestic currency by favroshëm exchange rate on the authorized agencies,

to meet local currency obligations arising from

Petroleum operations.

(F) When a foreign investor is a party to a Marrëeshje

Hydrocarbon, to settle by arbitration clauses to resolve international disputes arising from or related to Agreement.

(G) Includes other provisions that may appear necessary and desirable in connection with the performance of Operations Hydrocarbons.

Article 6

Obligations of Contractor Any agreement related hydrocarbons mnga Ministry will contain an appropriate form agreed between parties, commitments by the Contractor:

(A) to conduct operations in accordance with hydrocarbon this law, the legal provisions in force "On Environmental Protection" and in accordance with regulations issued by the law and best practices of the oil industry;

(B) to report the discovery of Hydrocarbons Minister in the Contract Area

(C) to prepare and submit to the Ministry for approval, in case of a commercial discovery, the development plan who:

(1) shall ensure the efficient use and benefit Hydrocarbon reserves of unified by the Contractor;

(2) will properly care for environmental preservation and welfare of the people who live in areas where operations are performed Hydrocarbons under the agreement; (D) to reimburse the State or the Ministry to all third party claims related to injuries, losses or damage resulting from any opercion conducted by Contractor or any subcontractor;

(E) to give priority to employment and training Albanian citizens, as well as domestic goods and services, in accordance with the provisions to be included in Plan Development. to the extent that they are competitive in terms of comparable price and quality terms.

Article 7

Contractor Authorization

When a contractor has signed Petroleum Agreement with Ministry, the State will give the Contractor or to ensure that Contactor to be given all permits, licenses, approvals or Other legal powers which the contractor may reasonably require to enable them to conduct Petroleum Operations in accordance with the Agreement Hydrocarbons.

Article 8

Permits for building assessment

(L) The Minister may give permission for any building rating person, under terms and conditions set out in it,

License holder authorized to undertake research in the area allowed through the air studies, geophysical, geochemical, paleontological, geological, topographical, survey studies and their seismic interpretation.

(2) Unless shown otherwise not permit evaluation, that permit:

(A) shall expire at the end of a period of 2 years;

(B) shall not be exclusive;

(C) shall not authorize the drilling of wells Search

(D) will not recognize any permit holder preference right to enter the Petroleum Agreement with the Ministry.

Article 9

Regulations and Model Contracts

(L) Pursuant to this law, the Ministry can issue regulations for or in connection with:

(A) Registration of Contractors;

(B) The manner in which must be submitted by Contractor reports, data, information and accounts.

(C) Measures related to natural resource conservation hydrocarbons, safety, health, environmental protection and avoidance of leakage, waste, pollution and accidents;

(D) Segregation of areas with hydrocarbon potential in the area or blocks of numbers;

(E) The right to use public lands and private operations related to hydrocarbons;

(F) € will issue about which the Ministry considers that the regulations should be drafted to make it effective this law.

(2) The Ministry may occasionally publish Agreement Hydrocarbon model.

Article 10

Access to land

(L) Subject to the conditions specified in regulations designed in accordance with Article 9.l (e), shall be deemed a The contractor is given according to law " Earth ", the right to access and use of public land or Private Petroleum operations conducted under the Agreement Hydrocarbons where the Contractor is a party.

(2) If the contractor does not pay compensation when required, he will be subject to penalties specified in regulations relevant.

(3) For purposes of this section "private land" means privately owned land and leased land or in use by the State.

Article II Unification

When a hydrocarbon reservoir is located partly in a Contract Area and partly in another Contract Area and the Ministry of looks that can increase the efficiency achieved through joint development and operation in the reservoir, The Ministry shall have the r ght to order the contractors to develop and operate together as a reservoir agreement entered into by them for this purpose.

Article 12

Transitional Provisions and Exceptions.

1) In terms of the agreements described in Appendix attached to this law (agreements on the sea), the date on which this Act comes into force:

a) € will one of these deals will be considered is lawfully connected by the Ministry under section 5 of this law and under section I2. (I) will continue to be valid and enforceable in accordance with its terms.

b) € will one of these agreements is considered that references to DPNG (here and below will be understood as Directorate General of Oil and Gas) or to any successor rights DPNG, refer to the Ministry.

c) Without the participation interests in mind from here

on can be obtained from any successor rights DPNG, under agreements between the Contractor and the Ministry, DPNG nd its followers will not be owned by a party or not have any right, property or interest in any of these agreement.

2) As regards the areas where Albpetrol is performed operations research, development and exploitation of hydrocarbon will be considered that the Ministry has entered into agreements with Albetrolin, dsuke authorized him to perform these operations in accordance with this Agreement

Article 13

Entry into Force of the Petroleum Agreement.

1) A hydrocarbon agreement, pursuant to Article 5 of this law, shall be signed by the Minister of Industry, Mineral Resources and Energy or by a person authorized in writing by him.

2) A hydrocarbon agreement enters into force after approval Council of Ministers.

Article 14

All legal provisions which are inconsistent with this law repealed.

Article 15

This law enters into force 15 days after publication in the Official Journal.

Promulgated by Decree no., Date, the President of the Republic of Albania, Sali Berisha.

Appendix

l) agreement "for research development and production of hydrocarbons ", between DPNG and Deminex New Petroleum OMV GmbH, the Council of Ministers No. 152 dated 20.4.199l.

2) The "For research, development and production of hydrocarbons ", between DPNG and Chevron International (South Africa) zlimited, the Council of Ministers nr.334, dated 10.9.1991.

3) The "For research, development and production of hydrocarbons ", between DPNG and Occidental of Albania Inc.., with Council of Ministers decision nr.360, dated 21.9.1991.

4) The "For research, development and production of hydrocarbons ", between DPNG and Agip (Overseas) Limited, with Council of Ministers decision nr.376, dated ll.10.1991.

5) The "For research, development and production of hydrocarbons ", between DPNG and Hamilton Oil (South Africa), with Council of Ministers decision nr.476, dated 23.12.1991.

LAW ON SOME AMENDMENTS ON LAW NO. 7746, DATE 1993 ON PETROLEUM (EXPLORATION AND PRODUCTION)

No.7853, date 29.07.1994

Based on Article 16 of Law No.7491, date 29.04.1991, "On the main constitution provisions", upon proposal of the Council of Ministers,

PEOPLE 'S ASSEMBLY OF THE REPUBLIC OF ALBANIA DECIDED:

Article 1

In Law No.7746, date 28.07.1993, Article 12, following item 2, the following paragraphs are added:

In connection with the above agreement, this shall be called “Agreement Albpetrol",

a. The Agreement Albpetrol shall be valid and obligatory pursuant to its items and conditions and the Ministry of Energy and Mineral Resources supplies Albpetrol with a license as it is anticipated in the Agreement.

The license should authorize Albpetrol, based on the terms and conditions stipulated in the Agreement, to explore for, develop and produce hydrocarbons in the contract area or to continue the hydrocarbon operations in the contract area. All the provisions of this Law, applied or in relation to the Hydrocarbon Agreement , will be implemented in or in relation to any license, which shall have force as a contract.

b. Notwithstanding the general character of the above paragraph (a), any licenses may allow Albpetrol, by approval of the Ministry, to assign all or part of its rights, title or interest to a juridical person, foreign or local to an international financial institution, which it wishes to cooperate with the purposes anticipated in the Agreement Albpetrol.

c. Agreement Albpetrol authorizes Albpetrol to enter into Hydrocarbon Agreements, authorizing the respective person or institution , based on stipulated terms and conditions therein, to explore for, to develop and to produce hydrocarbons in the contract area or to continue the hydrocarbon operations in the contract area. Such a Hydrocarbon agreement, which shall not run contrary to the relevant license terms, shall be the Hydrocarbon Agreement bound to this Law".

Article 2

In the annex attached to the Petroleum Law, following item 5, the following paragraph is added:

"Agreement for authorizing hydrocarbon operations, signed on July 26, 1993, by and between the Ministry of Industry, Mineral Resources and Energy (Actually Ministry of Energy and

Mineral Resources) and Albpetrol (Oil and Gas Economical Corporation)".

Article 3

This law enters into effect immediately.

Promulgated by Decree No.900, date 04.08.1994 of the President of the Republic of Albania, Sail Berisha.

TERMS AND CONDITIONS FOR APPLICATION UNDER P.S.A.

The Ministry of Economy, Trade and Energy through the National Agency of Natural Resources (AKBN) has declared free onshore and offshore areas open for petroleum operation and invites applications for Production Sharing Agreements.

In accordance with the "Petroleum Law" No.7746, date 28.07.1993, which authorizes the Ministry to enter into a Petroleum Agreement with foreign and local companies, in order to promote petroleum exploration and production on-shore Albania, the Ministry of Economy, Trade and Energy offers free areas for exploration.

Beginning in 1991 the Albanian Government has entered several agreements with oil companies for exploration and production of oil and gas.

I. SPECIFIC TERMS AND CONDITIONS

1. Form of Agreement

Petroleum agreements will be in the form of Production Sharing Agreements signed between the Ministry of Economy, Trade and Energy represented by the National Agency of Natural Resources (AKBN) and the Contractor. The most important items of PSA are given in the "Petroleum Law", No.7746, date 28.07.1993 and the document "Albanian Legislation and the Framework for Petroleum Exploration and Production" attached.

II. TERMS OF THE AGREEMENT

2.A. Duration of Exploration Period

An initial exploration period is planned, followed by two additional exploration periods to be negotiated with AKBN, subject to satisfactory completion of work program obligations of the previous period. The duration of the exploration period is up to 5 years and can be extended up to 7 years in conformity with the "Petroleum Law". The Exploration Periods are subject to negotiation.

2.B. Duration of the Development and Production Period

In the case of a commercial discovery, the period for development and production of the development area shall be twenty-five years and can be further extended as provided for in the "Petroleum Law".

2.C. Mandatory Relinquishment

The preferred portion to be relinquished is:

i) Twenty five percent (25%) of the original contract area at the end of the initial exploration period.

ii) Twenty five percent (25%) of the original contract area at the end of first extension of the initial exploration period. (The area upon which a Contractor has reported a Commercial Discovery is excluded from the above).

Both of the above provisions are subject to negotiations.

2.D. Minimum Work and Expenditure Obligations

These obligations will be defined by the Contractor in its application to AKBN and are subject to negotiations before entering the agreement.

2.E. Natural Gas

In the case of a commercial Natural Gas discovery, AKBN and the Contractor will negotiate additional terms in the P.S.A, which will endeavor to ensure that the proportion of economic returns for both parties is similar to that for an oil discovery.

2.F. Training and Administration Funds.

The amount will be specified by the Contractor in its application and is subject to negotiations.

2.G. Cost Recovery and Petroleum Sharing

The terms for cost recovery and petroleum sharing will be specified by the contractor in its application, subject to negotiations with AKBN before the signing of the Agreement.

2.H. The Contractor shall have the right to receive and retain abroad the proceeds from its export sales to the extent that they are not required to meet on a current basis its local currency costs in Albania. The Contractor shall have the right to convert foreign currency into local currency at the generally applicable rate of exchange for commercial transactions.

2.I. Bonus

Under the P.S.A., the Bonus is payable in various stages, including the signature bonus. The production bonus and the signature bonus per square kilometer are subject to negotiation.

APPLICATION PROCEDURE

1. There is no deadline for the submission of applications. Discussions will commence directly thereafter with all companies that submitted offers provided that the Area is still available.

    1. Address for Delivery
    2. National Agency of Natural Resources, Blloku Vasil Shanto, ish Instituti Minierave, Tirana, Albania
    3. Method of Delivery:
    4. 3.A By sealed envelope delivered by registered mail, or by hand.
    5. 3.B The envelope must be clearly marked: Petroleum Exploration Project CONFIDENTIAL
    6. 3.C There is no application fee.

2. Presentation of applications shall be in accordance with the provisions of Item III below, taking into account the specific terms and conditions specified in the "Petroleum Law", No.7746, date 28.07.1993, the Decree of the President No. 782, date 22.02.1994 as well as the document "The Albanian Legislation and the Framework for Petroleum Exploration and Production" attached.

3. Any information or clarification for the submission of an application may be obtained from:

National Agency of Natural Resources, Blloku Vasil Shanto, ish Instituti Minierave, Tirana, Albania

Tel.& Fax. +355 42 34 031 Att. Milo Kuneshka Chairman

6. After having examined the application received, AKBN will invite for negotiation the applicant in due time. It is the intention of AKBN that once contracts are negotiated and agreed upon by both parties, they will be entered into as soon as possible.

III. FORM OF PRESENTATION OF APPLICATIONS

An application will be presented in a sealed envelope.

An applicant may present applications for more than one Area, but each application will be made in a separate envelope.

A company or a group of companies may apply for a contract

An application shall contain the following:

4.1. The contract area to which the application applies.

4.2. IN RESPECT OF EACH APPLICANT:

4.2.A. The name of the applicant in full.

4.2.B. The nature of its business.

4.2.C. The place of incorporation.

4.2.D. The countries in which the applicant or applicants operate.

4.2.E. Evidence of the financial standing and technical qualifications of the applicant, including the most recent audited accounts, and those for the previous three years, of the applicant and of any corporate body having control of such applicant

4.3. The main terms proposed by the applicant in respect of the major aspects of the model Production Sharing Agreement i.e.

4.3.A. Duration of exploration periods.

4.3.B. Minimum exploration work and expenditure obligations.

4.3.C. Training.

4.3.D. Cost recovery and the net profit oil for Contractor.

4.4. Each application may contain the applicants technical evaluation of the area and an explanation of the adequacy of the proposed minimum work commitment in support of the Contractor's exploration concepts for the area.

OPEN BLOCKS

The open areas for bidding are all the areas where at the time of application there are no contract signed or no negotiations carried out on exclusive basis.

ALBANIAN LEGISLATION AND FRAMEWORK FOR PETROLEUM EXPLORATION AND PRODUCTION

I. INTRODUCTION

Petroleum Exploration, Development and Production in Albania is governed by "The Petroleum (Exploration and Production) Law", No.7746 dated 28 July 1993, amended by Law No.7853 dated 29 July 1994 and Law No.7811 dated 12 Apri11994 On Approval of Decree No.782 date 22.02.1994, "On the Fiscal System in the Hydrocarbons Sector (Exploration and Production)". The legislative framework offers considerable flexibility to the Government in negotiating acceptable terms with oil companies. At the same time these laws give incentives and enough flexibility to attract international oil companies and thus stimulate oil exploration in the country.

All petroleum deposits existing in their natural condition in strata lying within the jurisdiction of Albania are the exclusive property of the Albanian State

"The Petroleum (Exploration and Production) Law" expressly permits the Ministry to enter into a Petroleum Agreement under which an oil company may be granted exclusive rights to explore for and produce petroleum.

The Government's objective is to negotiate terms with the oil industry which are fair and balanced, bearing in mind the usual risk associated with exploration and the State's legitimate right for revenues as owner of natural resources. At the same time Government seeks to encourage the development of small and marginal discoveries.

Exploration for hydrocarbons in Albania commenced before the Second World War and many important oil fields in limestone and sandstone's have been discovered.

Albania has the favorable geological and geochemical conditions for the discovery of new fields, providing exploration and commercial opportunities for oil companies.

II. LEGISLATION

A. Terms and Conditions of Production Sharing Agreements

A.l According to "Petroleum Law", "Petroleum Operations" means all or any of the operations related to the exploration for development, extraction, production, separation and treatment, storage and transportation and sale or disposal of petroleum up to the point of export, or to the agreed delivery point in Albania or the point of entry into a refinery and includes natural gas processing operations but does not include petroleum refining operations. A.2 Hydrocarbons existing in their natural state are the property of the Albanian State. The Government represented by the National Agency of Natural Resources authorizes the performance of petroleum operations by the National Oil Company (ALBPETROL) in its exclusive areas, or a Contractor in remainder of the territory of Albania. The National Agency of Natural Resources (AKBN) is authorized to make available to interested oil companies the existing geological and geophysical data in the open areas in order to give oil companies the opportunity to evaluate the data before submitting bids. A.3 The contract type is the Production Sharing Agreement between the National Agency of Natural Resources, acting on behalf of the Albanian Government, and the Contractor. According to the "Petroleum Law", "Production Sharing Agreement" means a Petroleum Agreement which provides for the recovery of Contract Costs from Petroleum produced in the Contract Area or from a proportionate part thereof, and for the division between the State and the Contractor of the balance of petroleum remaining after the recovery of Contract Costs in accordance with a scale or formula specified in the Petroleum Agreement A.4 The Production Sharing Agreement includes provisions such as:

A.4.1 The performance of a minimum work program, backed by a performance guarantee.

A.4.2 The presentation of an annual work program and budget A.4.3 Preference given to local employment and supplies during petroleum operations, where these are competitive in terms of quality, availability and cost A.4.4 The opportunity for local service companies to bid and preference given to them when the offer is comparable or better than other third parties. A.4.5 Indemnify the State or the Ministry against all claims made by third parties in respect of injury, loss or damage resulting from the conduct of any operation carried out by the Contractor or by any subcontractor.

A.4.6 "The Petroleum Law" deals with access to private land after giving the occupier and the owner a minimum time notice. However, the Contractor must pay fair, just and equitable compensation with regard to any disturbance or damage caused during the conduct of petroleum operations.

A.4.7 The P.S.A. provides for the establishment of a training and administration fund, which is used for the training of National Agency of Natural Resources employees, and for administrative purposes.

A.4.8 The Contractor shall conduct Petroleum operations in a safe and proper manner in accordance with generally accepted international petroleum industry practice and shall cause as little damage as is reasonably practicable to the general environment including (inter alia) the surface air, seas, lakes, rivers, marine life, anima1life, plant life, crops, other natural resources and property, and shall forthwith repair any damage caused to the extent reparable, and shall pay reasonable compensation for all damage which is beyond repair.

B. Technical Clauses

B.1 Under the model agreement the Contractor is authorized to conduct petroleum operations during an Initial Exploration period, which can be extended twice.

It is preferred that the Exploration Period includes a drilling commitment by the Contractor.

The duration of the exploration period is up to 5 years and can be prolonged up to 7 years according to the "Petroleum Law". The phases of Exploration Period are subject to negotiation.

B.2 If the Contractor declares a commercial discovery during the exploration period, it has the right to extend for a development/production period of twenty-five years, which can be prolonged according to the "Petroleum Law".

B.3 During the exploration period, the Contractor is subject to minimum work obligations. In the case of either the Initial Exploration period or the additional Exploration period expiring and the Contractor not having fulfilled its obligations for the said period, the Contractor must pay to the Government the monetary equivalent in respect of the work not carried out.

All monetary obligations are expressed in US Dollars.

B.4 Before the end of each Contract year, the Contractor must submit and present to National Agency of Natural Resources the exploration program and budget for the next Contract year. National Agency of Natural Resources may suggest some modifications to this work program and budget, which shall be implemented by the Contractor when in accordance with good international petroleum industry practice.

B.5 In the event of a discovery, the Contractor will notify National Agency of Natural Resources and evaluation of this discovery will be carried out pursuant to an approved appraisal work program. After evaluation, the Contractor will declare to National Agency of Natural Resources the commercial implications of the discovery.

B.6 if the Contractor considers the discovery commercial, the area in respect of that commercial discovery is set apart from the Contract area as a Development area. The Contractor prepares a development plan, which is submitted for approval by National Agency of Natural Resources.

B.7 For the exploitation of discovered marginal fields, or fields that have become marginal due to their exploitation, pursuant to Decree No.782 of 22.02.1994 "On the Fiscal System in the Petroleum Sector", the Council of Ministers may issue special decisions to alleviate the fiscal system in order to render possible the exploitation of the marginal fields.

B.8 In the case of an oil discovery together with the flow of associated gas, the Contract considers the utilization of such gas. (Provisions concerning the flare and use of such gas either in petroleum operations or in the local economy are open for negotiations).

B.9 Contractor has the right to develop and produce the natural gas discovered in the Contract Area. Preferably such gas will be utilized in the internal market or exported.

In case of a commercial Natural Gas discovery, National Agency of Natural Resources and the Contractor will negotiate additional terms in the P.S.A, which will endeavor to ensure that the proportion of economic returns for both parties is similar to that for an oil discovery.

National Agency of Natural Resources may process and utilize the natural gas with no compensation to the Contractor where the Contractor considers that the natural gas is not required for use in petroleum operations; there is no possibility of exporting it; or its utilization is not economical.

B.10 Unitization

According to the "Petroleum Law", if a petroleum reservoir is located partly in one Contract Area and partly in an other Contract Area and where it appears to the Ministry that gains in efficiency may be achieved through the joint development and operation of that reservoir, the Ministry shall have the right to order the Contractors to develop and operate the reservoir jointly under an agreement entered into by them for that purpose.

If at any time in which the Petroleum Agreement is in force the petroleum bearing strata in the Contact Area, forming part of a single Commercial Discovery, overlap an area over which the Government of Albania has jurisdiction and in respect of which no contact or license has been entered into or is in force, the National Agency of Natural Resources and Contactor shall enter into an agreement to enlarge the Contact Area accordingly and to provide for the proper development of the Commercial Discovery.

C. Cost Oil and Profit Oil Sharing

C.l Exploration expenditures and capital expenditures are recoverable only in the case of a commercial discovery but not before the start-up of production.

C.2 Operating expenditures are recoverable during the year in which they are incurred.

C.3 Reasonable and necessary administrative expenditures of the Contractor are recoverable.

C.4 The oil from which costs are recovered is referred to as "Cost Oil". The remaining part of production which is referred to as "Profit Oil" is shared between National Agency of Natural Resources and the Contactor according to a sliding scale, which is subject to negotiations.

"R” factor model can be used in Profit Sharing. "R” factor is defined as the ratio between the cumulative revenues of Contactor reduced by cumulative tax assessed on Contractor and the cumulative costs and expenses incurred in Petroleum Operations.

C.5 The Contactor is subject to income tax law. According to the Decree No.782 date 22.02.1994, "On the Fiscal System in the Petroleum Sector", the Contractor is obligated to pay each fiscal year only the impost on the profit realized during that fiscal year.

The tax is at the rate of 50% of the realized profit.

C.6 The Contractor shall pay a Royalty Tax of 10% of the revenues from the sales of petrolum according to the Law No. 9975, date 28.07.2008 “On National taxes”.

C.7 According to the Decree No.782 date 22.02.1994, "On the Fiscal System in the Petroleum Sector", The National Agency of Natural Resources may elect to take the Government's tax and/or its share of profit oil in cash or in kind or in both forms. (According to the international market prices in case the National Agency of Natural Resources elects cash).

C.8 The Contractor shall have the right to receive and retain abroad the proceeds from its export sales to the extent not required to meet on a current basis its local currency costs in Albania. The Contractor shall have the right to convert foreign currency into local currency at the generally applicable rate of exchange for commercial transactions.

D. Miscellaneous

D.1 The Contractor and its sub-contractors are allowed to import into Albania all equipment and materials required for use in petroleum operations provided that National Agency of Natural Resources has certified that equipment and materials are to be used solely in petroleum operations.

The Contractor and his sub-contractors are exempted from the customs obligations as for the equipment, machinery, materials etc.

D.2 The Contractor may export the share of production to which he is entitled.

D.3 The Contractor may assign all or part of its interest under the contract to any affiliate or third party, which assignation is subject to a guarantee for the performance of Contractor's obligations to be submitted by the assignee, as well as subject to the consent of the National Agency of Natural Resources.

D.4 The petroleum agreement and petroleum operations are governed by the laws of ALBANIA and the generally accepted practices of International Oil Industry.

D.5 Arbitration shall be in accordance with the UNCITRAL arbitration rules, preferably under Swiss Law.

D.6 All international oil industry investments are fully protected (as are all foreign investors) pursuant to Law No.7764 of 22.11.1993 "On Foreign Investments"

LAW ON FOREIGN INVESTMENT

ARTICLE 1 GENERAL DISPOSITIONS

For the purpose of this law:

1. "Territory" is understood to mean the territory under the sovereignty of the Republic of Albania, including water courses, sea zones and the continental shelf, upon which the Republic of Albania, in accordance with international norms, exercises its rights of legal sovereignty.

2. "Foreign investor" is understood to mean:

a)every physical person that is a citizen of a foreign country; or
b)every physical person that is a citizen of the Republic of Albania but who has always resided outside the country; or
c)every legal entity founded according to the laws of a foreign country, which directly or indirectly seeks to carry Out or is carrying out an investment in the territory of the Republic of Albania in accordance with its law; or has carried out investment in accordance with laws that have taken effect since 31.7.1990 to the present.

3. "Foreign investment" is understood to mean every kind of investment in the territory of the Republic of Albania under the direct or indirect ownership of the foreign investor, which consists of:

a) movable or immovable assets, tangible or intangible assets or any other kind of possession;
b) a company, stock shares in a company and any form of participation in a company;
c) loans, financial obligations or obligations in an activity that has economic value and that is connected with an investment;
c) intellectual property, including literary, artistic, scientific, technological, audio recording, invention, industrial designs, semiconductor mask works, know-how.
d) every right given by law or contract, and every license or authorization given in accordance with the laws.

4. "Foreign dispute investment" is understood to mean every disagreement or pretense that is caused by a foreign investment or that is associated with one.

5. "Revenue" is understood to mean the amount of money that arises from or related to an investment, including profit, dividends, interest, recapitalization, management fees, technical assistance fees, or other fees or contributions in-kind.

ARTICLE 2 AUTHORITY AND TREATMENT

1. Foreign investment in the Republic of Albania is not subject to prior authorization. It is permitted and treated based on conditions not less favorable than those that apply to domestic investment in similar circumstances, excluding ownership of land, which is regulated by a special law.

2. In all cases and at all times investments have equal and impartial treatment, and full security.

3. In all cases foreign investment is treated no less favorably than that secured by general norms, accepted by international law.

ARTICLE 3 THE RIGHT TO EMPLOY

A company with foreign investment, has the right to employ Albanian and foreign citizens.

ARTICLE 4 EXPROPRIATION AND NATIONALIZATION

Foreign investments will not be expropriated or nationalized neither directly nor indirectly and will not be subject to any measure or similar action, except for public purposes determined by law. Foreign investments will be treated in a nondiscriminatory manner and paid immediately, in a fair and effective manner, and in accordance with due process of law.

ARTICLE 5 COMPENSATION FOR EXPROPRIATION AND NATIONALIZATION

1. The compensation will be equivalent to the fair market value of the expropriated investors.

2. The compensation will be paid without delay and include interest at the commercial market rate from the date of the expropriation; the compensation is fully transferable and convertible at the market rate of exchange on the date of the expropriation.

3. A foreign investor has the right to request an immediate review of an expropriated action or compensation, through the appropriate legal or administrative institutions, according to article 8 of this law.

ARTICLE 6 WAR AND ARMED CONFLICTS

Foreign investors, whose investments suffer losses due to war, armed conflicts, state of national emergency or other similar events, will be treated no less favorable than the treatment accorded to Albanian investors regarding measures adopted in relation to such losses.

ARTICLE 7 TRANSFERS

1. Foreign investors have the right to transfer out of the territory of the Republic of Albania all assets related to a foreign investment, including as follows:

a) revenues
b) compensation
c) payments as a consequence of an investment disagreement;
c) payments made under a contract, including loan and interest payments according to a loan agreement;
d) revenues stemming from the sale or the payment of any or all part of an investment;
dh) return of shareholders' equity, resulting from the reduction of capital when the company has decreased its capital according to Albanian legislation.

2. Foreign investors will have the right to make transfers out the territory of the Republic of Albania to a freely convertible currency calculated at the prevailing market rate on the date of the transfer, with respect to spot transactions in the currency to be transferred.

3. The Republic of Albania may limit the right of transfer through the equal and nondiscriminatory manner of the laws of general application, including laws regarding the payment of taxes and the satisfaction of claims and court decisions.

ARTICLE 8 DISPUTE SETTLEMENT

1. If a foreign investment dispute arises between a foreign investor and either an Albanian private party or an Albanian state enterprise or organization, which cannot be settled amicably, then a foreign investor may choose to submit the dispute for resolution to any applicable, previously agreed upon dispute settlement procedure. If no dispute settlement procedure has been agreed upon, then a foreign investor may submit the dispute for resolution to an authorized court or arbitrator of the Republic of Albania, according to laws of Albania.

2. If a foreign investment dispute arises between a foreign investor and the state administration of the Republic of Albania, and this disagreement cannot be settled amicably, then a foreign investor may choose to submit the dispute for resolution to an authorized court or arbitrator of the Republic of Albania according to the laws of Albania. In cases when the dispute arises out of, or relates to expropriation, compensation for expropriation, discrimination or transfers according to article 7 of this law, then a foreign investor may submit the dispute for resolution and the Republic of Albania hereby consents to the submission thereof, to the International Center for Settlement of Investment Disputes ("Center"). established by the Convention on the Settlement of Investment Dispute between States and Citizens of Other States, approved in Washington. D.C., in March 1965.

3. Any award of international arbitration according to this article is final and binding on the parties to the dispute. The Republic of Albania must carry out, without delay, dispositions of any such award and provide for its enforcement within the territory of Albania.

ARTICLE 9 THE STATUS OF THIS LAW

1. Law no.7549, date 4.8.1992 "On foreign investments" and all other clauses within laws or decisions of the Council of Ministers contrary to this law are repealed.

2. In the event that this law does not conform with any other international agreement or treaty ratified by the Parliament to which the Republic of Albania or the Government of Albania is member, the latter will prevail, to the extent that they provide greater rights or protection to a foreign investor than those provided by this law.

ARTICLE 10 NATIONAL SECURITY

There is nothing in this law that will prevent the application by the Republic of Albania of measures necessary for preserving public order, satisfaction of international obligations of Albania relating to preservation and restoration of international peace or security, protection of its own national security or defense interests.

ARTICLE 11 PUBLICATION OF LAWS

The Republic of Albania will publish all laws, rules and procedures concerning foreign investment.

ARTICLE 12 COMING INTO FORCE

This law comes into force 15 days after publication in Fletorja Zyrtare.

Proclaimed with decree no.687, date 10.11.1993 of the President of the Republic of Albania, Sali Berisha.

LAW ON CONCESSIONS

CHAPTER 1 GENERAL PROVISIONS

Article 1 PURPOSE OF LAW

The purpose of this law is to create a favorable framework for promoting and facilitating the implementation of privately financed Concession Projects enhancing transparency, fairness, efficiency and long-term sustainability, in development of infrastructure and public service projects.

It aims at further developing the general principles in the award of contracts by public authorities through the establishment of specific procedures for the award of Concession Projects.

Article 2 DEFINITIONS

In this law, the following terms shall mean:

1. "Bidder" or "Bidders", means legal entities, including groups thereof, that intend to

participate or participate in a selection procedure concerning a Concession.

2. “Competitive Selection Procedure”, means the procedure for the selection of the Concessionaire in accordance with Articles 10 to 21 of this law.

3. “Concession”, means the agreement, not withstanding the term, between the Contracting Authority and the concessionaire which provides for requirements and conditions in terms of which the Concessionaire:

(a) Carries out an economic activity which would otherwise be carried out by Contracting Authority related to a concession project, management contract or other public services;

(b) Assumes all or substantial part of risks related to such economic activity;

(c) Receives a benefit by way of:

(i) Direct payments paid by or on behalf of contracting authority;

(ii) Tariffs or fees collected from users or customers;

(iii) A combination of such direct payments and tariffs.

1. “Concessionaire” is a legal person, Albanian or foreign, with or without local or foreign participation, that enters into a concession contract with the contracting authority.

2. “Concession register”, means the appropriate record of information pertaining to the Concession selection and award procedure to be kept by the contracting authority and which at the end of the process is filed with the Public Procurement Agency. Form and method of filing shall be determined by this Agency.

3. “Contracting Authority”, means a public authority that has the power to enter into a Concession Contract.

4. “Infrastructure Facility”, means physical assets and systems that directly or indirectly provide services to the public.

5. “Concession project”, means each of the following activities or any combination such as: the design, construction and development of new infrastructure facilities, rehabilitation, modernization, expansion of existing infrastructure facilities; administration, expansion or other services pertaining to new or existing infrastructure facilities.

6. “License” means an administrative act which is issued by a relevant public authority to exercise an activity based on objective qualification criteria.

7. “Local Concessions” are concessions for those economic activities which according to the legislation in effect in the Republic of Albania fall under the competence of local government units.

8. “State Concessions”, means Concessions for those economic activities, which based on the legislation in effect in the Republic of Albania, fall under the competence of the central government.

9. “Unsolicited Proposal” means any proposal undertaking concession projects that is not

submitted in response to a request issued by the Contracting Authority within the context of a Competitive Selection Procedure.

10. "Private Investment" means the proposal, financed and implemented fully by private sector where the public sector does not participate directly or indirectly. For the purpose of this law, any kind of guarantees, financial or other guarantees, given by public sector, will be considered as participation of public sector in private investment.

11. "Public Procurement Agency is the agency created and operating according to Law no. 9643, dated 20.11.2006 "On Public Procurement".

12. "Procurement Advocate" is the institution established and operating according to law no 9643, dated 20.11.2006 "On Public Procurement.

13. Temporary union of companies" is an agreement in writing between two or more legal entities, the scope of which is the accomplishment of a certain activity, whereby the role of each party is defined and where one party is the main company that represents the union in signing the contract and in each initiative.

14. Value for money, is a term, which is used to determine whether a contractual authority has gained the maximum profit from goods or services, which it receives and/or provides for use within the limits of resources it possesses. This term is not only used to measure the value of goods or services, but assesses the quality, cost and utilization of resources, compliance with the purpose, time and possibility to decide that all of these together constitute the best economic value.

Article 3 SCOPE OF LAW

This law defines conditions, modalities, criteria and procedures for granting concession in the Republic of Albania.

Article 4 SECTORS FOR APPLICATION OF CONCESSIONS

1. This law is implemented for granting of concessions by contractual authorities for the economic activities in the following sectors:

a) transport (railway system, rail transport, ports, airports, roads, tunnels, bridges, parking, public transport);

b) generation and distribution of electricity and heating;

c) production and distribution of water, treatment, collection distribution and administration of waste water, irrigation, drainage, cleaning of canals, dams;

ç) collection, transfer, processing and administration of solid waste;

d) telecommunication;

dh) education and sport;

e) health;

ë) tourism and culture;

f) prison infrastructure;

g) recycling projects, rehabilitation of land and forests, in industrial parks, housing, governmental buildings, service of maintenance of IT and data base infrastructure;

gj) natural gas distribution;

h) management contract or provision of public services including those related to sectors specified above.

1. Council of Ministers, upon the proposal of the Minister responsible for economy, authorizes Concessions to be implemented in other sectors.
2. In particular instances, for the promotion of investments pointed out in point 1 of this Article or for other priority sectors for the economic development of the country, in line with the strategic objectives, Council of Ministers may offer to local or international investors concessions for the symbolic price of 1 EURO. Council of Ministers, upon the proposal of the Minister responsible for economy, approves the list of assets that will be given on concession, to the effect of applying this point.
3. This Law shall not apply to grant of licenses, except to the extent that a license is issued within the framework of a Concession Contract.
4. This Law shall not apply to public procurement of services, goods and constructions, as well as for private investments.

Article 5 CONTRACTING AUTHORITY

1. The contracting authority is the ministry or the local government unit, which in compliance with the legislation in effect is responsible for the economic activity for which the concession is granted.
2. The contracting authority for local concessions is the responsible authority of the local government units.
3. Council of Ministers shall identify the contracting authority for each concession after the identification of potential concessions, according to Article 11 of this law.
4. Council of Ministers approves the evaluation regulations and granting of concessions, to the effect of achieving the purpose and applying the provisions of this law, as well as standard documents in concession field.

Article 6 SUPERVISION OF APPLICATION OF CONCESSIONARY PROCEDURES

1. Supervision of application of the concession procedures and administrative review of complaints against them shall be performed by the Public Procurement Agency.
2. Exercising the concession functions, Public Procurement Agency has the following competencies:

a) it requires from the contracting authorities periodic reporting, once in 6 months regarding the concessions situation;

b) it verifies the application of concessionary procedures, in compliance with this law and other acts stemming from its implementation, while requesting from the concession authorities all the necessary information;

c) it proposes disciplinary measures and imposes penalties to the extent defined in the procurement legislation, in the instances when it observes violation of the procedures of this law.

ç) it conducts the administrative review of complaints from bidders regarding concession procedures.

d) it decides and announces the debarment from concession procedures of bidders who have, during a concessionary procedure, deposited forged documents or declared false information;

dh) it provides to Council of Ministers its opinion regarding the procedure followed for concessions.

Article 7 REPRESENTATION OF LEGAL INTERESTS OF BIDDERS

1. Monitoring of the implementation of this law and the bylaw acts, stemming from it and for its implementation, during the conduct of the concessionary procedures, in protection of the legitimate interests of the bidders, is done by the Procurement Advocate.
2. Exercising the functions under this law, the Procurement Advocate has the following competencies:

a) reviews complaints of interested persons relating to acts or omissions on the side of the contracting authority;

b) institutes administrative investigation upon finding out that the cases consists a violation of this law;

c) upon completion of the administrative investigation, informs the contracting authority and Public Procurement Agency about the results of the investigation.

1. The Procurement Advocate notifies, within 5 days from the beginning of the investigations, the interested parties and the Public Procurement Agency about this fact.
2. In the course of exercising his functions for the investigation of administrative procedure, the Procurement Advocate may:

a) inspect on the spot acts and documents relating to the investigation case;

b) seek information and explanation from public administration or interview any person with regard to the case under investigation, as well ask for expertise from third parties.

c) recommend changes in the law and the acts issued for its implementation, upon observing that the content of these acts possibly causes the violation of concessionary procedures.

Article 8 CONCESSION TRATMENT UNIT

The Concession Treatment Unit shall be under the Minister responsible for economy, to promote and assist the contracting authority in evaluation and negotiation of concessions.

CHAPTER II IDENTIFICATION OF POTENTIAL CONCESSIONS AND SELECTION OF THE CONCESSIONNAIRE

Article 9 IDENTIFICATION OF POTENTIAL CONCESSIONS

1. Identification of Potential Concessions shall be done by competent ministries or local government authorities, in cooperation with the Concession Treatment Agency.

2. Potential Concessions may also be identified by a proponent through unsolicited proposals, in compliance with the procedures set forth in Article 23 of this law.

2. Competent ministries or the Local Government units, in cooperation with the Concession Treatment Unit, shall carry out a viability and bankability analysis to decide whether a potential concession should be implemented. This analysis shall be based upon the principles of value for money, alignment of potential Concessions with the national strategic objectives, as well as with sector strategic objectives, the technical and commercial feasibility of the potential Concession and its ability to attract potential Concessionaires and private financing.

Article 10 SELECTION STAGES

1. The Concessionaires are selected through a pre-qualification procedure, accompanied by a request for proposal foreseen in Articles 11 through 21 of this law. An exception to this rule shall constitute concessions granted according to point 2 of this Article and Article 23 of this law.

2. Notwithstanding the definition contained in point 1 of this Article, the Contracting Authority shall be entitled to request proposals from all potential bidders, without a pre-qualification procedure, if it deems that in this case the conduct of prequalification procedure is not necessary.

Article 11 PRE-QUALIFICATION PROCEDURE

1. The Contracting Authority shall prepare the invitation for participation in the pre-selection procedure and the pre-qualification documents with a view to identifying bidders that are suitably qualified to implement the concession.

2. The invitation to participate in the pre-qualification procedure shall be published in the Public Announcements Bulletin, as well as in the international and local press.

3. The invitation to participate in the pre-selection procedure shall include the following data:

a) A brief description of the infrastructure facility;

b) indicators of other essential elements of the concession, such as the services to be delivered by the concessionaire, ways of financing the concession envisaged by the contracting authority (for example, funds to be used, whether they will be entirely financed by user fees or payments or whether public funds shall be provided to the concessionaire, such as direct payments, loans or guarantees);

c) where appropriate, a summary of the main terms of the concession contract to be entered into;

ç) manner and place for the submission of applications for pre-qualification and the legal deadline for the submission, expressed as a specific date and time, allowing sufficient time for bidders to prepare and submit their applications;

d) manner and place of receiving the pre-qualification documents.

Article 12 PRE-QUALIFICATION DOCUMENTS

In the pre-qualification criteria, there are at least included: a) pre-qualification criteria in accordance with Article 13 of this law; b) participation of the temporary union of companies, in line with Article 12 of this law; c) any requirement for the necessity to create a legal entity for the wining bidder, according to the legislation in effect.

Article 13 PRE- QUALIFICATION CRITERIA

1. In order to participate in the selection procedure, interested bidders must meet some objective criteria, which the Contracting Authority considers appropriate in the particular procedure.

The criteria shall at least include:

(a) professional and technical qualifications, human resources, equipment and other physical facilities as necessary to carry out all the phases of the concession project, including design, construction, operation and, where appropriate, maintenance;

(b) Sufficient ability to manage the financial funds of the project and capability to finance the project;

(c) Appropriate managerial and organizational capability, reliability and experience in operating similar projects.

2. Interested qualified bidders are qualified to participate in a selection procedure when:

(a) they are not subject to proceedings of bankruptcy, liquidation or controlled administration or termination of activity or of any other related situation, which according to the effective laws, brings about proceedings of the same character;

(b) they have not been found guilty of producing false documents.

Article 14 PARTICIPATION OF TEMPORARY UNION OC COMPANIES

1. The contracting authority shall, prior to inviting the bidders into the selection phases, allow them to form temporary bidding unions of companies. Unless otherwise stated in the pre-qualification documents, the information required from members of temporary bidding unions of companies to demonstrate their qualifications in accordance with provisions of this article, shall relate to the temporary union of companies as a whole as well as to its individual members in particular.

2. Each member of a temporary union of companies may participate, either directly or indirectly, in only one temporary union of companies at a time. A violation of this rule shall cause the disqualification of the temporary union of companies and of the individual member of this union of companies.

Article 15 PRE-QUALIFICATION DECISION

The contracting authority performs the qualification of each bidder that has submitted an application for pre-qualification, in accordance with the criteria set forth in the pre-qualification documents. The contracting authority shall publish the list of pre-qualified bidders in the Public Announcements Bulletin within 30 days from taking the decision. All pre-selected bidders shall be invited to submit proposals in accordance with provisions of Articles 16 through 21 of this law.

Article 16 PROCEDURES FOR SOLICITED PROPOSALS

1. The procedures for solicited proposal shall take place in 1 or 2 stages.
    1. The contracting authority provides, against payment of a fee that might be applied, the pre-qualified bidders with the request for proposal and related documents, in compliance with Article 5 of this law, or any other document if deemed necessary. If the pre-qualification
    2. procedures are not implemented, the request for proposal shall be issued to all potential bidders.
2. Notwithstanding the above, the contracting authority may use a two-staged procedure to request proposals from Bidders, if elements of the concession project such as project specifications, performance indicators, financial arrangements or contractual terms can not be described in the request for proposal in a manner that detailed or accurate that would allow the bidders to submit their final proposals.
3. Where a two-staged procedure is used, the following provisions apply:

a) The initial request for proposals shall call upon the bidders to submit, in the first stage of the procedure, initial proposals relating to project specifications, performance indicators, financing requirements or other characteristics of the project, as well as to the main contractual terms proposed by the contracting authority;

b) The contracting authority may convene meetings and hold discussions with any of the bidders to clarify questions concerning the initial request for proposals or the initial proposals and accompanying documents submitted by the bidders. The contracting authority shall prepare minutes of any such meeting or discussion on this issue. (The minutes contain the questions raised and the clarifications provided by the contracting authority.)

c) Following examination of the proposals, the contracting authority may review and revise the initial request for proposals by deleting or modifying any aspect of the initial project specifications, performance indicators, financing requirements or other characteristics of the project, including the main contractual terms, and any criterion for evaluating and comparing proposals and for ascertaining the successful bidder, as well as by adding characteristics or criteria to it. The contracting authority shall indicate in the concession register, the justification for any revision to the request for proposals. Any such deletion, modification or addition shall be contained in the invitation to submit final proposals;

ç) In the second stage of the procedure, the contracting authority shall invite the bidders to submit final proposals with respect to a single set of project specifications, performance indicators or contractual terms in accordance with Articles 17 through 21 of this law.

Article 17 CONTENT OF THE REQUEST FOR PROPOSALS

The request for proposals, prepared by the contracting authority, shall include in the least the following data:

a) general information as may be required by the bidders in order to prepare and submit their proposals;

b) project specifications and performance indicators, as appropriate, including the contracting authority's requirements regarding safety and security standards and environmental protection;

c) contractual terms proposed by the contracting authority, including an indication of non-negotiable terms;

ç) criteria for evaluating proposals and the thresholds, if any, for evaluating the proposals, the relative importance of each criterion and the manner in which the criteria and thresholds are to be applied in the evaluation and disqualification of proposals;

d) requirements pertaining to bid security.

Article 18 CLARIFICATIONS AND MODIFICATIONS

1. The contracting authority may, whether on its own initiative or upon a request for clarification by a bidder, review and, as appropriate, revise any element of the request for proposals in compliance with article 17 of this law.
2. Each change shall be communicated promptly to all candidates having purchased the documents. If the contracting authority deems it necessary to change the documents, and when this is done within less than 1/3 of the number of days defined for the preparation of bids, it shall postpone the deadline for bid submission by the same period.

2. The contracting authority shall, in the case set forth in point 1, indicate in the concession register the justification for any revision to the request for proposals. Any such deletion, modification or addition shall be communicated to the bidders in the same manner as the request for proposals.

Article 19 EVALUATION CRITERIA

1. The criteria for the evaluation and comparison of the technical proposals shall include at least:

a) technical soundness;

b) compliance with environmental standards;

c) operational efficiency;

ç) quality of services and measures to ensure their continuity;

d) social and economic development potential offered by the proposals.

2. The criteria for the evaluation and comparison of the financial and commercial proposals shall at least include, as appropriate:

a) present value of the proposed tolls, unit prices and other charges over the concession period;

b) present value of the proposed direct payments by the contracting authority, if any;

c) costs for design and construction activities, annual operation and maintenance costs, present value of investments and operating and maintenance costs;

ç) extent of financial support, if any, expected from a public authority of the Republic of Albania; and

d) soundness and viability of the proposed financial arrangements.

3. Council of Ministers determines, in line with implementation of point 3 of Article 4 of this law, additional criteria which will be taken into account in the bid evaluation process. These criteria are based on the sector importance of the development of economy, investment amount, and employment level, priorities for the development of particular areas of the country, other sector specific indicators, as well as the proposed price or fee. Council of Ministers determines in this case the weight of each criterion in the bid evaluation.

Article 20 COMPARISON AND EVALUATION OF PROPOSALS

1. The contracting authority shall compare and evaluate each proposal in accordance with the evaluation criteria, the relative weight accorded to each such criterion and the evaluation process set forth in the request for proposals.
2. For the purposes of point 1 of this Article, the contracting authority may establish minimum thresholds with respect to quality, technical, financial and commercial aspects. Proposals that fail to achieve these minimum thresholds shall be regarded as non responsive and disqualified.

Article 21 DETERMINATION OF THE SUCCESSFUL BIDDER AND FINAL NEGOTIATIONS

1. The contracting authority shall rank all responsive proposals on the basis of the evaluation criteria and notify about this the bidders. Upon notification, all bidders have the right to present any claims in compliance with provisions of CHAPTER III of this law. Upon expiry of the complaining period, the contracting authority shall invite for final negotiations the bidder that has attained the best rating.
2. Final negotiations shall not concern those contractual terms that were stated as nonnegotiable in the final request for proposals.
3. If it becomes clear to the contracting authority, within a time period set by Council of Ministers, that the negotiations with the bidder invited will not result in a concession contract, the contracting authority shall terminate the negotiations with such bidder and invite for negotiations the other bidders in the order of their ranking until it signs a concession contract or rejects all remaining proposals. The contracting authority shall not resume negotiations with a bidder with which negotiations have been terminated pursuant to this point.
4. Following completion of concession contract negotiations, the Concession Treatment Agency shall, within 45 days, issue an opinion on the terms thereof. Following such opinion and the signature of the Concession Contract, it shall be submitted to Council of Ministers for approval.
5. The contracting authority shall publish in the Public Notification Bulletin the name of the concessionaire and essential terms of the concession contract within 30 days after the

approval in line with the provision of point 4 of this Article.

Article 22 NEGOTIATION OF CONCESSION CONTRACTS WITHOUT SELECTION PROCEDURES

1. Contracting authority may conduct the negotiation of concession contracts without using the selection procedure, only with the approval of Council of Ministers, where:

(a) the project affects national security. The cases where national security is affected as a consequence of implementation of selection procedure, shall be approved upon the decision of National Security Council;

(b) the concession contract has been terminated due to a serious violation by the concessionaire and where there a selection procedure is not possible to be implemented, due to the urgent need to ensure continuation of activity.

1. The duration of a concession contract signed according to letter (b), point 1 of this Article shall not exceed 12 months.
2. No concession contract shall be concluded pursuant to letter (b), point 1 of this Article, unless the contracting authority has initiated a competitive selection procedure for the selection of a concessionaire, in accordance with the contract terms set forth in point 2 of this Article or when it has decided not to grant a concession following expiry of such contract term.
3. When a concession contract is negotiated pursuant to this article without using the Selection Procedure, the contracting authority shall determine reasonable evaluation criteria for the requirements of the projects, based on which there shall be evaluated and ranked the proposals.
4. The contracting authority shall publish in the Public Announcements Bulletin the name of the concessionaire and essential terms of the concession contract within 30 days after the

approval of the Concession Contract by the Council of Ministers, excluding the cases determined in letter "a", point 1 of this Article.

Article 23 UNSOLICITED PROPOSALS

1. The contracting authority is authorized to review and accept unsolicited proposals pursuant to the procedures set forth in this article, provided that such proposals do not relate to a project for which selection procedures have been initiated or announced.
2. Procedures for determining the admissibility of unsolicited proposals are the following:

a) within 90 days of receipt and review of such unsolicited proposal, the contracting authority shall determine whether the project is considered to be in the public interest, and to this end informs the proponent.

b) if the concession project is considered to be in the public interest, the contracting authority shall invite the proponent to submit additional data, to make an evaluation of the proponent's qualifications and the technical and financial feasibility of the project;

c) within 120 days of the invitation from the contracting authority, the proponent has to submit a technical and financial feasibility study (including but not limited to a financial model and a project financing plan), an environmental impact study and satisfactory information regarding the concept or technology contemplated in the proposal.

ç) in course of reviewing the unsolicited proposal, the contracting authority shall respect the intellectual property, trade secrets or other exclusive rights contained in, arising from or referred to in the proposal. The contracting authority shall not make use of information provided by or on behalf of the proponent in connection with its unsolicited proposal without the consent of the proponent, for a period of 12 month from its receipt.

3. Initiation of a Selection Procedure shall be done as follows:

(a)the contracting authority shall, within 6 months of receipt of the documentation in compliance with letter "b" of point 2 of this Article, decide to accept or reject the potential concession project derived from the unsolicited proposal. If the unsolicited proposal is accepted by the contracting authority, the contracting authority shall initiate a competitive selection procedure in accordance with Articles 11 through 21 of this law, while when the proposal is refused and the parties do not agree differently, the contracting authority shall return to the proponent the original documents and the submitted copies of documents;

(b)the proponent shall be invited to participate in the competitive selection procedure initiated pursuant to letter (a) of point 3 of this Article, and upon decision of the Council of Ministers, it shall be awarded a bonus on its technical and/or financial score during the competitive selection procedure up to a maximum of 10% of the points. The identity of the

proponent and the existence and amount of the bonus shall be indicated in the competitive selection procedure documents.

Article 24 CONFIDENTIALITY

The contracting authority shall preserve the confidentiality of all the technical, economic, financial and other data of the proposals done by the bidders. Unless provided for by law or court decision or request for proposals, no party to the negotiations shall disclose to any other person any technical, price or other elements with regard to discussions, communications and negotiations, pursuant to the aforementioned provisions without the consent of the other party.

CHAPTER III ADMINISTRATIVE REVIEW PROCEDURES

Article 25 COMPLIANT PROCEDURES

1. Each bidder may request an administrative review of the selection processes, when he deems that an action undertaken by the contracting authority is in violation of the provisions of this law or other legal or bylegal acts on the concession procedures.
2. The complaint shall be submitted to the Public Procurement Agency within 5 calendar days from the date of the publication of the announcement of the pre-qualified candidates or announcement of the ranking of the bidders by the contracting authority.
3. Upon receipt of the complaint, the Public Procurement Agency notifies within 5 days the contracting authority regarding suspension of concession procedures and institution of administrative review procedures.

1. Public Procurement Agency does not suspend the concession procedure when: a) from the preliminary review it results that the complaint has no legal grounds.

2. b) suspension would be in conflict with the public interest or would be to the detriment of the contracting authority or other bidders.

4. During the review of the complaint, until the moment of entering into the contract, Public Procurement Agency shall be entitled to:

a) cancel partially or wholly decisions or acts of the contracting authority.

b) guide the contracting authority to rectify the violation prior to proceeding with the concession procedures.

1. The Public Procurement Agency shall, during the procedures of administrative investigation, have all competencies set forth in the law no 9643, dated 20.11.2006 "On public procurement" and in the bylaw acts issued for its implementation.

2. The complaint with the Public Procurement Agency is done by the relevant form, which includes the name and address of the petitioner, the reference to the concrete procedure, the legal basis and the description of the violation. The above mentioned elements are indispensable for the review of the complaint. The Public Procurement Agency reviews the complaint, in compliance with this legislation, bylaw acts issued for its implementation, as well as with the Administrative Procedures Code.

3. Public Procurement Agency concludes the administrative review within 20 calendar days from the submission of the complaint and notifies the contracting authority and the petitioner about the decision.

9. The decision of Public Procurement Agency constitutes a final administrative act.

Article 26 COMPLAINT IN THE COURT

The petitioner is entitled to take an appeal against the decision of the Public Procurement Agency within 30 days since the notification to the effect of having the administrative conflict tried at the Court of Tirana Judicial circle (Administrative Section).

The court shall carry out the judicial review in line with the procedures and time periods established in the provisions of the Civil Procedures Code, chapter II, "Adjudication of administrative disputes".

The review of such a complaint in the court does not suspend continuation of the concession procedures.

CHAPTER IV CONCESSION CONTRACTS

Article 27 CONTENT

Concession contracts shall provide for such issues as the parties deem appropriate, such as:

a) nature and scope of works to be performed and services to be provided by the concessionaire;

b) concession contract duration, which shall be adjusted to the specific requirement of the relevant concession and shall not exceed 35 years, and conditions, if any, to its extension;

c) assistance that the contracting authority and the concession treatment agency may provide to the concessionaire in obtaining licenses and permits necessary for the concession;

ç) any requirements relating to the establishment and minimum capital of a legal entity to be established by the successful bidder in accordance with the effective laws, and prohibition of transfer of shares or part of the capital of this company without prior consent of the contracting authority;

d) ownership on assets related to the concession project and the obligations of the parties, as appropriate, concerning the acquisition of the concession project site and any necessary facility;

dh) remuneration of the concessionaire, regardless whether it consists of tariffs or fees for the use of the infrastructure facility or the provision of services; the methods and formulas for the establishment or adjustment of any such tariffs or fees; payments, if any, that may be made by the contracting authority or other public authority; as well as whether there is any obligation of the concessionaire to make payments to the contracting authority;

e) procedures for the review and approval of engineering designs, construction plans and specifications by the contracting authority, as well as the procedures for testing and final inspection, approval and acceptance of the infrastructure facility, rules and standards based on which the concession projects are designed, which should ensure the application of best practice, developing the market through sensible risks allocation;

ë) extent of the concessionaire's obligations to ensure, as appropriate, the modification of the service so as to meet the actual demand for the service, its continuation and its provision under essentially the same conditions for all users; mechanisms to deal with eventual costs related thereto;

f) right of contracting authority, or of another public authority to monitor the works to be performed and services to be provided by the concessionaire and the conditions and extent to which the contracting authority may order variations in respect of the works and conditions of service. The right of contracting authority to take such other reasonable actions as they may find appropriate to ensure that the infrastructure facility is properly operated and the services are provided in accordance with the applicable legal and contractual requirements, as well as the right to monitor mechanisms to deal with eventual costs related thereto;

g) concessionaire's obligation to provide the contracting authority, or other public authority, as appropriate, with reports and other information on its activity;

gj) any restrictions or conditions applicable to the assignment of rights and obligations of the concessionaire under the concession contract;

h) Any restrictions or conditions related to the transfer of a controlling interest at the concessionaire;

i) definition and consequence of force majeure, change in law and other changes in circumstances (including any right of the parties to seek compensation or revision of concession contract);

j) eventual liabilities, if any, of the relevant public authorities or contracting authority;

k) circumstances under which the contracting authority has the right to temporarily take over the operation of the infrastructure facility for the purpose of ensuring the effective and uninterrupted delivery of the service in the event of failure by the Concessionaire to perform its obligations and to rectify the breach of contract;

l) any rights of the contracting authority to review and approve the main contracts to be entered into by the concessionaire, in particular with the concessionaire's own shareholders or other legal entities where the concessionaire is participating or vice versa;

ll) guarantees of performance to be provided and insurance policies to be maintained by the concessionaire in connection with the implementation of the concession;

m) remedy procedures available in the event of breach of contract by any of the parties;

n) conditions and procedure for amendment and/or termination of contract; rights and obligations of the parties upon the expiry of time period or termination of contract (including mechanism of transfer of assets, technology, compensation, training and support services to be provided by the concessionaire);

nj) applicable law and the mechanisms for the settlement of disputes that may arise between the contracting authority and the concessionaire;

o) rights and obligations of the parties with regard to confidential information.

Article 28 TERMINATION OF THE CONCESSION CONTRACT

1. Unless otherwise provided for in the concession contract, the contracting authority may terminate the concession contract when:

(a) tt has a reason to believe that the concessionaire can no longer be expected to perform its obligations, owing to insolvency, serious breach or other cases which hinder or do not allow the continuation of concession contract;

(b) concessionaire fails to ensure the financing of the project within 12 months as of signing the concession contract.

2. Either party shall, unless otherwise provided for in the concession contract, have the right to terminate the Concession Contract, when:

(a) performance of its obligations is rendered impossible by circumstances beyond either party's reasonable control;

(b) there is serious breach by the other party, and that party fails to rectify such breach within the time period and in the manner established in the concession contract.

3. The parties shall also have the right to terminate the concession contract upon mutual consent.

CHAPTER V FINANCING

Article 29 FINANCIAL ARRANGEMENTS

1. The Concessionaire shall have the right to charge, receive or collect tariffs or other incomes for the use of the facility or the services provided by it, in accordance with the concession contract, which shall provide for methods and formulas for the establishment and adjustment of those tariffs or payments.

2. The contracting authority shall have the power to make direct payments to the concessionaire as a substitute for, or in addition to, tariffs or payments for the use of the facility or services provided by it.

CHAPTER VI SETTLEMENT OF DISPUTES AND APPLICABLE LAW

Article 30 APPLICABLE LAW

1. The concession contract shall be governed by the laws of the Republic of Albania.

2. The concessionaire, its shareholders and other business partners shall be free to choose the law governing their relations.

Article 31

DISPUTES BETWEEN THE CONTRACTING AUTHORITY AND THE CONCESSIONAIRE

1. Any disputes between the contracting authority and the concessionaire shall be settled through the dispute settlement mechanisms agreed by the parties in the concession contract, including procedures of international arbitration.

2. The concessionaire, its shareholders and other business partners shall be free to choose the appropriate mechanisms for settling disputes among themselves.

CHAPTER VII FINAL PROVISIONS

Article 32 REPEAL

The Law No .7973, dated 26.7.1995 "On concessions and the participation of the private sector in public and infrastructure services" as amended, shall be repealed.

Article 33 TRANSITION PERIOD UNTIL THE ESTABLISHMENT OF THE CONCESSION TREATMENT AGENCY

Until the establishment of the Concession Treatment Agency in accordance with Article 8 of this law and it becoming fully operational, its responsibilities and powers shall be exercised by the ministry responsible for economy.

Article 34 EXISTING AND SECTOR SPECIFIC LAWS

1. In case of incompatibility with the existing laws, this law shall prevail over all other existing laws on concessions.

2. All sector specific laws shall regulate concessions in accordance with this law.

Article 35 CONCESSION CONTRACTS ALREADY SIGNED

This law shall not apply to the concession contracts already signed prior to the date of this law. The contracts may never be renewed or extended, except in compliance with this law.

Article 36 ENTRY INTO FORCE

This law shall enter into force 15 days after its publication in the Official Gazette.

Promulgated by the Decree no 5179, dated 12.01.2007 of the President of the Republic of Albania. Alfred Moisiu

LAW NO. 9572, DATE 3.7.2006 ON THE FINANCIAL SUPERVISORY AUTHORITY

In line with articles 78 and 83 paragraph 1 of the Constitution of the Republic of Albania, with the proposal of the Council of Ministers,

THE PEOPLE'S ASSEMBLY OF THE REPUBLIC OF ALBANIA

DECIDED:

CHAPTER I GENERAL PROVISIONS

ARTICLE 1 SCOPE OF LAW

The scope of this law is to define the rules concerning the establishment, tasks and functions of the Financial Supervisory Authority, which hence is going to be referred to as the Authority

Article 2 Scope of activity of the Authority

The scope of activity of the Authority is the regulation and supervision of:

a. the securities market and the activity of the securities market, including the activities of other subjects included in this market;

b. The insurance market and the activities of the insurance market, which includes all activities of insurance, re-insurance, brokerage and operations that derive from these activities;

c. The supplementary pensions market and the activity of supplementary pensions market, which includes all activities of insurance of supplementary pensions offered by private supplementary pensions institutions;

ç. and other activities related to financial leasing, factoring, mortgage and other non-banking financial activities according to the definitions provided by the relevant legislation, which are going to be referred to as "non-banking financial markets".

CHAPTER II THE STATUS, STRUCTURE AND ADMINISTRATION OF THE AUTHORITY

ARTICLE 3 THE STATUS OF THE AUTHORITY

The Authority is a public legal person independent with the residence in Tirana specialized in the regulation and supervision of the activity of the subjects engaged in one or more of the activities mentioned in article 2 of this Law.

The Authority for the activity it exercises in line with this law reports to the Assembly.

Article 4 The Board of the Authority

The Board is the decision-making body of the Authority. The Board comprises of 7 members, namely: one Chairman, two Vice Chairmen, and four other members.

Article 5 Requirements for appointment of members of the Board

Members of the Board are:

1. Albanian citizens;
2. university degree in economics, or law, or actuarial science;
    1. at least 3 years professional experience in at least one of the following fields:
        1. finance -accounting;
        2. administration of trade companies
        3. legal counseling of trade companies;

ç. drafting of legislation;

d. Actuarial science

e. Social insurance and pensions

1. enjoy moral and professional integrity;
2. do not exercise any high ranking functions in a political party.
3. Have not been found criminally indicted through a court decision of final verdict
4. Meet the legal provision requirements regarding the conflict of interest.

The Chairman and the vice chairmen of the Board do not exercise other paid activities, except for lecturing, research and scientific activities or participation in local or international organizations related to the activity of the Authority.

The four other members of the Board may be full time employee in other institutions, but can not be members of more than one The Board or decision-making body of any other supervisory Authority.

Each member of the Board has the obligation to declare to the Speaker of the Parliament related to the circumstances anticipated in this article.

Article 6 Appointment of the members of the Board

The members of the Board get appointed by the Parliament.

The chairman, two Vice chairmen, and two of the members of the Board are appointed by the Parliament with the proposal of the Council of Ministers.

One member of the Board is appointed by the Parliament with the proposal of the Laws, Public Administration and Human Rights Parliamentary Commission.

One member of the Board is appointed by the Parliament with the proposal of the Economy and Finance Parliamentary Commission.

The Minister of Finance, Supervisory Board of the Bank of Albania, anc the National Accounting Council each are entitled to propose to the Council of Ministers one candidate as member of the Board of the Supervisory Authority. The candidate proposed by the BoA, should not be a member of BoA's Board. The candidate proposed by the NAC should not be a member of the NAC Board. The Council of Ministers based on its two candidates and the candidates proposed by the Minister of Finance, the Supervisory Board of the Bank of Albania, and the National Accounting Council drafts the proposals for the Parliament.

The proposal defines the functions that candidates will have/exercise in the Board of the Authority. In the case of the Vice Chairmen, the proposal also defines which will be the department that each will run.

The Parliament, in the decision for the appointment of each of the Vice Chairmen also determines the department that will be run by each of them.

Article 7 The mandate of the Members of the Board

The mandates of the Chairman, Vice Chairmen and other members of the Board are 5 years. In the instances, when the mandate of the chairman, vice chairmen or The Board's member has terminated, each will continue to exercise their duties until the appointment of the new members. One month before the termination of the mandate of each of the members, the Authority notify in a written form the Parliament, which starts the procedure for the appointment of the new member.

The individuals that have been once appointed as members of the Board of the Authority are entitled to be re-appointed only once. The individual who has been appointed once as Chairman of the Board of the Financial Supervisory Authority can not be re-appointed as Chairman.

At the end of his/her mandate, the member of the Board can not be employed for a period up to two years or be directly or indirectly paid from any of the subjects supervised by the Authority.

Individuals who held the position of either the chairman or of the Vice Chairmen of the Board, after their release from office, when is unemployed are entitled to one year of remuneration in the amount of the salary that they have had while in their position. The individual who has been re-appointed as member of the Board and the individual that is released from the duty based on article 8 of this Law are not entitled to this right.

Article 8 Release from duty of the members of the Board

The Parliament decides on the release from duty of any of the members of the Board, before the termination of the mandate provided for in the first paragraph of article 7 of this Law in the following cases:

a. the individual resigns;

b. the individual becomes physically incapacitated to accomplish the assigned task for more than 3 months;

c. due to new circumstances the provisions envisaged in points 5 and 6 of the first paragraph of article 5, and the conditions foreseen in paragraphs 2, 3, and 4 of article 5 of this law are no longer respected;

d. in case of absence, without proper ground, in more than three consecutive meetings;

e. during exercise of his/her functions acts in violation of the obligation for maintaining confidentiality;

f. Because of professional incapacity or negligence causes damages/detriment to the Authority or to the image of the Authority as an independent institution

g. Lost of Albanian citizenship

The proposal for the release from duty for any of members of the Board is submitted to the assembly from each of the institutions that enjoy the right for the proposal of members of the Board and from other public institutions, whose function is related to that of the Authority. The proposal also should define the reason thereof and evidence related to the case. The Parliament may decide suspension from office of a given member until the end of the process of verification and until decision making. The Parliament, after the review takes a decision regarding the proposal for the release from duty, while approving or refuting the proposal.

In case of release from office before the deadline of any of the members of the Board, the other member is appointed via the same procedure as the member who is being released for the period until the completion of the deadline of the member who is released.

Article 9

Competencies for the approval of the structure and salaries of the Authority

The monthly salary of the chairman of the Board, of the vice chairmen and remuneration for the other members who do not carry out executive functions in the Authority are approved by the assembly, with the proposal of the Board of the Authority.

The structure of the Authority is approved by the Parliament with the proposal of the Board of the Authority.

The Authority, in addition to other units is composed of two main Departments. The name of these departments and other units of the Authority are determined related to the structure of the Authority.

The Board approves its regulation, related to the structure, specific functions and responsibilities of the departments and directorates, procedures for communication among them, and the duties of the civil servants and other employees.

Article 10 Meetings of the Board

The meetings of the Board are summoned with the initiative of the chairman of the Board or upon the request of each of its members sent to the Chairman. The Board meets at least once a month to discuss and decide regarding the agenda.

The meetings of the Board are chaired by the chairman, and in his absence according to his delegation of Authority, by one of the vice chairmen.

The meetings of the Board are considered valid when have participated at least 4 members of the Board.

The decisions of the Board are considered valid when at least four members of the Board have voted “in favor”.

Abstention in not allowed in voting.

Minutes are kept for each meeting. The minutes are signed by all the members who have been present. The decisions of the Board are signed by the chairman and the responsible vice chairman for the issue for which the decision has been taken. In case the decision is of general nature, it is signed by the chairman and by both Vice chairmen.

The Board approves the regulation regarding the operation and maintenance of minutes of the meeting.

Article 11 Transparency in the activity of the Authority

The Board publicly announces the policies and practice it follows in the implementation of the legal and by-legal provisions, as well as the ground for their change/amendment.

The policies that the Board follows for the implementation of provisions according to the first paragraph of this article include also the means selected by the Authority and used independently from it in the course of fulfillment of the objectives of this law.

The Authority approves the regulations for the procedures of making available to the public its documentation and the deadlines and terms for maintaining/keeping certified copies of this documentation.

The Board approves regulations regarding the type of publications, deadlines for their publication, and formulation and operation of the web page of the Authority.

CHAPTER III THE OBJECTIVES, THE COMPETENCIES OF THE AUTHORITY AND THE RIGHTS OF THE BOARD

Article 12

THE OBJECTIVES OF THE AUTHORITY

In carrying out its functions and competencies foreseen in this law, the Authority has the following objectives:

1. To protect the interests of investors and insured persons;
2. To promote sustainability and enhance transparency and credibility of non-banking financial markets;
3. To ensure respect of law.

Article 13

The aim of the Authority's activity

The Authority and its structures aim to:

1. to regulate the activity of the supervised subjects via drafting of by laws foreseen by this law, as well as to publish guidelines and explanatory notes/materials;
2. To ensure public supervision on the securities market, insurance market, and supplementary pensions schemes, which are regulated and function in line with the relevant legislation

In the exercise of the competencies foreseen in article 2 of this law, the Authority, enjoy full rights regarding:

a) approval, issuing or rejection of licenses for subjects that wish to exercise activities in one of the non-banking financial markets;

b) oversight and organization of the supervision of subjects that request to exercise activities in one of the non-banking financial markets; The subjects, either individuals or physical or legal persons, that exercise the activities mentioned in Article 2 of this law, are called " supervised subjects".

c) Follow up the implementation of this law and its by-laws issued on its base and sectoral laws and their by-laws, and enforcement of the restringing measures.

Article 14 The competencies of the Board

The Board has the following competencies:

1. in line with the structure, the Board drafts rules regarding the job descriptions and the scope of work;
2. drafts and approves the basic principles of its activity;
3. drafts and approves rules and instructions envisaged in the law;
4. disseminates written instructions regarding interpretation and enforcement of laws that regulate the area of activity, and the by-laws for their implementation;
5. approves the format of licenses issued for the exercise of activities supervised by the Authority;

6. Issues, rejects, bring to a close, or revoke the licenses or permits to exercise activities in one of the non-bank financial markets supervised by the Authority. In line with this competency, the Board: a) in compliance with the deadlines, terms and procedures foreseen in the Albanian legislation for securities approves or refutes the prospects for public offers or for the registration of new emissions for sale according to the rules of the regulated securities market; b) supervise the enforcement of temporary or final decisions regarding publication of public bids of shares;

c) approves licenses for individuals or companies that wish to exercise activities in the securities market, including activities as security markets, registrars, depositories, brokers or investment advisors and other subjects involved in the market;

ç) approves licenses of companies that wish to exercise activities as administrators of investment funds, as well as licenses for the exercise of activities as investment companies;

d) endorse the statute and changes/amendments to the statute of the companies that wish to exercise activities in the securities market;

dh) in line with the legislation that regulates that the activity of insurance, reinsurance and brokerage in insurance and re-insurance approves licenses for the exercise of the activity of insurance, and for the exercise of the activity of insurance brokerage and operations that directly stem from these activities;

e) reviews requests for expansion of the activities from subjects that exercise activities in the insurance market;

ë) reviews requests for exercise of activities outside the territory of the Republic of Albania, as well as for opening representation offices of foreign companies that exercise related activities with the objective of Authority's function;

f) reviews requests for the transfer of portfolio, and for undertaking some of the functions of the insurance company;

g) approves the merger or split of insurance companies (licensed);

gj) approves high management bodies, approves the statute of the insurance companies (licensed), and the changes to the statute before they are submitted for approval to the general assembly of shareholders;

h) reviews the requests for influential participation in the insurance companies, and the capital investments of the insurance companies;

i) approves volunteer liquidation, and decides on the start of procedures for bankruptcy of the insurance company;

j) approves high management bodies, approves the statute and the changes to the statute of the companies that wish to exercise activities as private pensions institutions prior to court registration;

k) undertakes appropriate corrective measures and on time when the insurance or re-insurance companies do not reach the required level of payment capacity or in case there is an observation of cases of failure to meet the payment capacity as determined in the legislation in effect in the area of insurance and re-insurance;

l) approves methodological guidelines, the format of the insurance contracts, lists, types of notes and other documents related to the activities of private pensions institutions;

ll) approves the regulations of private supplementary pensions, as well as the changes to these regulations, and controls their implementation;

m) approves the type, format and content of the reports submitted to the Board by the licensed subjects;

n) approves the transfer of the takeover of the supervised subjects.

1. restricts or suspends investments of the insurance and re-insurance company when it is certified that these investments are not in compliance with the established regulatory and when they put at stake the financial position of the company;
2. within a month from the submission of the request, reviews the general and specific terms of the insurance contract, that the insurance company wants to put in the market;
3. approves the financial statements of the insurance and re-insurance companies;
4. approves and disseminates accounting standards, and the financial reporting formats mandatory for implementation by the licensees;

11.approves the list of the accounting experts who may exercise this function for the companies that operate in the non-banking financial markets;

12.in the instances spelled out in the legislation takes a decision for the start of the bankruptcy procedures for the supervised subjects, and when spelled out in the law, it also appoints the liquidator;

13.approves the policy for wages and remuneration of staff and other employers of the Authority;

14.in line with the activity of the Authority, it takes decisions for signing memorandums of understanding and exchange of information with authorities within and outside the country;

15.it discusses on periodical terms the reports related to the main activity of the

main departments of the Authority; 16.approves the draft budget and the Annual Report of the Authority; 17.within June of each year, it approves the Industry Report regarding the status

and perspective of the market supervised by the Authority; 18.in the regulations for internal administrative procedures, it approves the

deadlines for submission of issues/cases for review; 19.approves the inspection manuals; 20.defines the policies on supervising and control of supervised subjects and the

development of non-banking financial market; 21.decides on purchase of the counseling service from experts of the area; 22.approves rules on employment and resignation of the employees of the Authority

23. other competencies spelled out in this law or in other legislation of the area.

The decisions are reasoned and are subject of appeal to a court.

The administrative decisions of the Board are published in the forms decided by the Board for the publication of official notifications.

Article 15

The competencies of the Chairman of the Board

The chairman of the Board is also the general executive director. The chairman runs and administers the activities of the Authority and its administration, except for the activities which are the competencies of the vice chairmen of the Board or of the other members spelled out in this law or in any other act.

The chairman of the Board is in charge of:

1. representing the Authority;
2. calling and chair the meetings of the Board;
3. to coordinate the work of the two vice chairmen;
4. propose the ratio of salaries of staff and other employees of the administration;
5. organizing, run and control the activities of the administration;

6. organizing the work for the preparation and submission for approval by the Board of the draft budget;

7. organizing the work for the implementation of the budget, closure of the financial year, and of the financial report, and submit them for approval by the Board.

8. signs for criminal investigation in the instances of discovery of actions or failure of action that constitute a criminal act.

9. exchanging information with the Bank of Albania, other governmental institutions and agencies, local authorities and administration, NGOs that exercise their activity in the financial non-bank markets supervised by the Authority, and with the supervised subjects;

10. in cooperation with the Bank of Albania, through a joint order instructs and orders carrying out of inspections in the depository banks regarding the activities of the subjects licensed by the Authority, and which exercise activities in one of the financial non-banking financial markets supervised by the Authority.

11. requesting the Bank of Albania to exercise inspections within a given scope in the banks of this level, in compliance with the law "On second tier (commercial) banks in the Republic of Albania", and to be informed about the results of the control.

12. establishing advisory committees that support him in the exercise of his functions.

Article 16 The competencies of the Vice Chairmen

The competencies of the Vice Chairmen are determined in the rules of the job description prepared by the Board.

The Vice chairmen of the Board, according to the definition of the decision for their appointment are each managers of one of the two main departments of the Financial Supervisory Authority. Within the legal competencies, the vice chairmen organize, run and are responsible for the work of the relevant departments.

Article 17

Competencies of the members that do not hold executive functions

The four members of the Board, who do not have managerial functions in the Authority, in cases of a request for the review of a special case related to deficiencies or law violations during the Authority's activity operate as the Audit Committee. The Members of the Board review the documentation and prepare detailed reports which they submit to the Board. In case of observation of violations or gaps, the report contains recommendations for the measures that need to be taken.

The audit committee appoints one of its members as a reporter who reviews the appeals and claims against the decisions of the Board and its bodies.

The rapporteur enjoys all rights to carry out a full-fledged inspection regarding the matter. For the appealed decisions, the rapporteur prepares detailed reports and submits them to the Board. In case of observation of violations or gaps, the report contains recommendations regarding the measures that need to be taken regarding the improvement of the situation.

The Board reviews the submitted report and decides regarding the proposed measures, if any.

The Parliament decides, if it is necessary the external auditing of the Authority.

Article 18

The procedures for the execution of the rights of the Board and of the structures of the Authority

In the exercise of the rights of the Board and all other structures of the Authority, members of the Board and the appointed employees with supervisory functions enjoy these rights in compliance with the procedures spelled out in this law, and with the duty that they are in charge of delivering:

1. to request from the supervised subjects and other subjects as well who have been acting in violation of the provisions of this law or other legislation that regulate the markets of the area, written explanation, documentation, including certified copies of documents, data, information and other data, and verify the documentation and the reporting. The documentation and written information shall be in Albanian;

2. to obtain data regarding funds, assets, including securities and other assets in the ownership of supervised subjects;

3. to inspect the accounts, trade/commercial documents, and other documentation related to the performed transactions;

4. to lead the third party inspections, which will include the review of that part of the documentation of the third party's activity, related to the issue that the supervised subject is inspected.

5. request from third parties information, and documentation including certified copies of documents, statement of accounts, and other necessary data for the process of verification;

6. to attend the meetings organized by the managerial and control structure of the supervised entities.

In order of the implementation of the exercise of the supervisory procedures, the vice chairman in charge can for a supervised subject ask from the Board the appointment of external experts, in compliance with the specific requests approved by the Board. In this particular instance, the incurred expenses shall be paid by the supervised subject.

Upon the request of the chairman of the Board, the banks for the supervised subjects by the Authority must provide information regarding the existing or closed account numbers and codes alongside with the data of the latest transaction.

All data and documents related to violation of this law, which contain the name of the individual in charge of their drafting, are submitted to the third parties by the chairman of the Board, only with the preliminary approval/consent of the above mentioned individual, except when the law foresees otherwise.

The police authorities, prosecutor's offices and all other state authorities shall within their competencies assist the work of the Authority and of its staff during the course of the exercise of their supervisory functions.

In the context of the exercise of the competencies of this law, the Authority may carry out general inspections, in cooperation with the tax authorities.

The members of the Board of the Authority and the other staff of the administration are not financially liable for damages caused in the course of the exercise of their inspection activity, except when they have committed a crime or have been acting wrongly on purpose.

Article 19

The Inspection

The inspection is exercised by the staff of the Authority according to the definition of the Order signed by the chairman or one of the Vice chairmen. The inspection takes place with prior notification or without.

The staff appointed according to paragraph 1 of this article inspects the following:

1. respect of the legal and by-legal provisions of the legislation that regulates the activities of the non-banking financial markets;

2. prevention and identification of violations.

In the course of the exercise of the inspection, the supervised subject shall have to ensure normal working conditions, and provide documentation or any other written information in Albanian.

The staff of the administration of the Authority shall have to introduce themselves at the outset of the inspection procedures, by presenting the order spelled out in the first paragraph of this article.

The supervised subject shall assist the Authority and its administration, and to this end it:

a) provides them with the necessary means for inspection if so requested, and responds to the questions in the facilities of the Authority; b) from its staff appoints the contact persons that will help out in the process of inspection; c) ensures free access in the building;

ç) makes available all the accounts, commercial documentation, and any other necessary documentation to determine the facts and circumstances related to the case for which the inspection is taking place;

d) after a preliminary request, ensures and makes available photocopies of the accounts and other documents, putting in writing in capital letters: "the same with the original' and the date and signature of the person authorized by the inspected subject.

The final report for each inspection is prepared in two copies, and is signed by the staff of the Authority in charge with the inspection, and is submitted for countersignature to the person that represents the supervised subject.

CHAPTER IV THE ADMINISTRATION OF THE SUPERVISORY AUTHORITY

ARTICLE 20 ORGANIZATION AND OBLIGATIONS

The activity of the Authority is supported by an administration which operates in compliance with the internal regulation of the job description of the administration of the Authority, and the other regulations related to the operation of the administration, which are approve by the Board in line with the proposal of the chairman.

The working relations with the personnel of this administration are regulated according to the Labor Code. The following individuals can not be employed in the structures of the Authority: a) have been criminally charged with a decision of the court of the final instance; b). they are shareholders in supervised subjects; c) have been members of executive or control entities of the supervised subjects during the last 2 years;

ç) have family links with the individuals spelled out in letter "c" of this article, with members of the Board, or with other staff of the administration who have hierarchical relations;

d) work part-time or full time in the supervised subjects;

dh) do not have a good reputation and have violated previously the ethics.

Article 21 Remuneration of the administration

The internal rules regarding the level of salaries, monthly salary of staff of the Authority, and remuneration are established by the Board with the proposal of the chairman, in accordance with the regulatory framework of the field.

CHAPTER V DECLRATION OF CONFLICT OF INTEREST

Article 22

Conflict of interest

The Members of the Board and the staff of the Authority shall declare their assets at the moment of the start of their duty, and further on in line with the legal provision in effect.

The Members of the Board do not participate in the procedures of discussion, voting and decision making in the cases when they have a direct or vested interest in the matter in discussion, which makes him/her bias in the official position.

The staff of the Authority does not participate in inspections of the supervised subjects if they have direct or vested interests in the matter for which the inspection is taking place, and which makes him/her biased in the official positions.

The Members e The Board and the staff of the Authority, in case they observe that they are in a situation spelled out in the second and third paragraphs of this article they declare this in written and withdraw from the review of the case.

In case there is an observation that even though they have been faced with a case spelled out in the second and third paragraphs of this article, and have not made the relevant declaration and consequently have not withdrawn from the review of the case, the individuals are either released from duty or fired. This measure does not have an impact on the decisions taken up until that moment.

CHAPTER VI CODE OF ETHICS, PROFESSIONALISM AND CONFIDENTIALITY

ARTICLE 23 CODE OF ETHICS AND PROFESSIONALISM

The members of the Board and the other employees of the Authority in the exercise of their activity implement the code of ethics and the professional standards approved by the Board, according to the proposal of the chairman.

In those instances when there is an observation of the violation of the code of ethics disciplinary measures are taken up to release from duty or firing.

Article 24 Confidentiality

The information which is made available to the Authority, in the course of the exercise of the supervisory activity of the institution, and the dissemination of which might infringe the commercial interest or the good name of the supervised subject is classified under confidential information.

Commercial information which has been obtained by the supervised subject, and the obligation for the publication of which is spelled out in this law or other legislation is not considered confidential information. Classification of information is done through internal regulations approved by the Board.

Members of the Board, the staff and the other employees of the Authority shall preserve and not distribute confidential information.

In those instances when there is a verification of the violation of the terms spelled out in this article, administrative measures are taken up to the release from duty of the members of the Board, or firing of other staff of the Authority.

Article 25 Termination of treatment as confidential information

Information which falls under the confidential category is no longer regarded as such 3 years from the moment it has become available to the Authority. This deadline may be prolonged with a decision of the Board.

Exceptions regarding the respecting of the deadline spelled out in the first paragraph of this article are the cases when:

1. it is requested by the court authorities according to legal requirements ;
2. requested by the bank supervisory authorities or intelligent services according to the criteria and conditions spelled out in joint agreements;
3. requested by the supervisory authorities of other countries who have equal or similar activity with that of the Authority, based on joint agreements with the scope of exchange of information, and when these authorities ensure:

a) at least the same level of confidentiality for the information being forwarded; b) have the authority and agree, that with the request of the Authority to make available the same type of information; c) have justified reason for the request for information

In the provision of this information shall apply the legal provisions regarding personal data.

The information obtained by the supervised subject may be given back to it any time.

CHAPTER VII FINANCING AND THE BUDGET OF THE AUTHORITY

ARTICLE 26 FINANCING AND THE BUDGET

The Authority is an independent institution which is financed mainly by its own resources. Any differences that arise between the funds sources and the expenditures for the activity, the

Financial Supervisory Authority is financed from the state budget until the moment when the income of the Authority are sufficient to ensure its normal functioning. The part of the financing from the state budget for the Authority is approved by the Albanian parliament as an independent part of the state budget. The surplus of the budget for the financial year, goes to the state budget revenues within 4 months after the end of financial year, except the funds for ongoing investments.

The revenues of the budget of the Authority are generated from:

1. tariffs according to article 27;
2. revenues from sanctions in line with the legislation in effect in the area of non-banking financial markets,
3. sale of periodical publications;
4. financings from the state budget;
5. other resources and activities permitted by law, and the legislation in effect for the non-banking financial markets.

The tables of income and expenditures are drafted in compliance with the legal provisions in effect.

Article 27 Tariffs

The Authority applies tariffs for:

1. issuing of licenses for the exercise of activities stipulated in the Law "On Securities", Law "On Activities of Insurance, re-insurance and intermediaries in insurance and re-insurance", and the Law "On supplementary pensions and private pensions' institutions".
2. approval of the public offerings' prospectus;
3. approval of the decision of the General Meeting of Shareholders for liquidation of a company that exercises activities as a pension institution.
4. Approval of additional permit for the exercise of activities, which include a new type or a new insurance package;
5. insurance companies as contributions of 1,5% of gross premium collected from the insurance and re-insurance non-life activities, and the quota obtained from the activities of life insurance and re-insurance. Gross premium collected from the activities of non-life insurance and re-insurance, and the quota obtained from the activities of life insurance and re-insurance shall be certified by an independent external auditor of the insurance company. The reconciliation of contributions of this point according to the figures certifies by the independent external auditor shall take place within 30 days from the signing of the audit certificate.
6. The companies of supplementary pensions as annual premium, which must be not more than 1.5% of the contributions.
7. Review of the documentation for the publication of declarations or announcements/notifications regarding the issues spelled out in points 1, 2, 3, and 4 of

this paragraph.

The list of the tariffs is subject of approval by the Parliament.

The tariffs for taxation purposes are reported as an expenses account of the supervised subject.

The chairman of the Board issues the order for the collection of tariffs whose liquication deadline has expired, and which should be paid to the Authority. The appeal against the decision of the Board through the court does not suspend its execution.

Payments which according to the decision of a court of final instance are considered that are in excess are returned to the supervised subject.

CHAPTER VIII ACCOUNTING AND CONTROL OF THE AUTHORITY

Article 28

Reporting and control

Within April of the next year, the Authority submits to the parliament:

1. the annual report of its activities ;
2. declaration of the annual financial position, and
3. the report on the realization of the budget plan.

The annual report of the Authority regarding its activities, in addition to other information that may be requested by the parliament shall contain the following information:

1. The suitability of the legal infrastructure of the financial market supervised by the Authority;
2. decisions regarding the licenses, approvals and other individual administrative acts issued in compliance with this law, refusal of issuing licenses or other requests that have been submitted to the Authority, registrations in the records, decisions appealed by the Board and in detail the claims supported by the decisions of the court;
3. result of the inspections carried on the supervised subjects;
4. public information policies, and those of domestic and international cooperation;
5. organization, financing and policies regarding the selection of the staff of the Authority;
6. other data in line with the decision of the Board.

The Authority submits to the Parliament any type of information and documents upon the request of the latter regarding its activities.

CHAPTER IX RECORDS OF THE AUTHORITY

Article 29 Records

The Authority keeps open records with the public regarding:

1. companies that exercise activities in the securities market (stock exchange);
2. public companies and other companies issuing securities;
3. investment companies;
4. companies that administer investment funds; and private institutions of pensions
5. investment funds
6. investment brokers; investment advisors
7. insurance companies
8. insurance agencies;
9. companies that exercise activities as private pensions institutions

The Board, in line with the proposal of the chairman, approves other records and procedures regarding initial recording, maintaining and keeping of records, as well as the procedures that ensure the proper functioning of the registry as a full-fledged information system.

CHAPTER X CONSULTATIVE GROUP OF FINANCIAL STABILITY (GKSF)

Article 30

Mode of operation of GKSF

The consultative group of financial stability, to which we shall hence refer as GKSF is established as a consultative entity to:

1. provides assistance in the development of joint policies, and coordination of the actions of the members of the council when it becomes necessary to carry out inspections over the supervised subjects;
2. ensures exchange of information among the members of the group;
3. assists in maintenance, stability and development of the financial markets in the Republic of Albania;
4. assists in improving and increasing the efficiency of the control over the participants in the financial markets.

Members of GKSF are:

-the Minister of Finance;

-The chairman of the Board of the Authority;

-The Governor of the Bank of Albania.

With the invitation of the GKSF, in its meetings may also participate the chairman of the Parliamentary Economic Commission, and other persons.

The GKSF makes to each of the representatives recommendations, and proposals that aim at improving practices of filling in and expanding the legal infrastructure of the financial markets.

Every member of GKSF enjoys the right to convene e meeting of the GKSF.

The meetings of the GKSF are chaired by the Minister of Finance. The first meeting of the GKSF is convened by the Minister of Finance within 3 months from the date of effectiveness of this law.

CHAPTER XI ADMINISTRATIVE SANCTIONS

ARTICLE 31

Any individual who prevents the Financial Supervisory Authority and its structures or the authorized staff of its administration in the exercise of their supervisory competencies established in this law or any other act, if the violation does not constitute a crime are penalized with a fine ranging from Albanian Lek 50.000 75.000 In case of a repeat of the violation the amount is increase from Albanian Lek 80.000 to Albanian Lek100.000

Any violation according to the first paragraph of this article by individuals who are shareholders or partners of the legal entity and have managerial functions of the legal entity or are partners of the commercial company receive a fine from100.000 to125.000, and in case of a repeat of the violation the fine ranges from Albanian Lek 130.000 to Albanian Lek 150.000.

Administrative sanctions placed by the Board according to this article and the notification for the taken decisions are signed by the chairman of the Board. Appealing the decision via court does not hinder the execution of the decision of the Board

CHAPTER XII COMPETENCIES E AUTHORITY PER ZBATIMIN E MASAVE ADMINISTRATIVE

Article 32

UTILIZATION OF ADMINISTRATIVE MEASURES

The Board in order to prevent or suspend the violations of the law and the by-laws, to prevent or stop severe consequences of the violations of the law, and in case of hindrances in the exercise of the supervisory activity of the Authority may take decisions for the supervised subject. The orders shall contain the method that needs to be pursued by the supervised subject to correct the situation or to prevent the damage. The order contains the deadlines for these changes to take place or for the correction of actions as well as may put the obligation of changing of the administrators or managers when are cases of breaching of the law.

The Authority may inform the public regarding the measures it has taken in implementation of the first paragraph of this article.

CHAPTER XIII TEMPORARY PROVISIONS

Article 33

Termination and transfer of the Competencies

On the date of effectiveness of this law, the decision-making competencies of the following terminate:

1. the Albanian Securities Commission established by Law no. 8080 dated 01.03.1996 "On securities", amended;

2. the Insurance Supervisory Authority established by Law no. 9268 "On the organization and functioning of the Insurance Supervisory Authority", amended.

3. the Inspectorate for the Supervision of Supplementary Private Pensions' Institutions established by Law no. 7943, dated 1.6.1995 "On supplementary pensions and private pensions institutions", amended.

The means, income sources, archives, liabilities and other competencies of the Albanian Securities Commission, Insurance Supervisory Authority, and Inspectorate of the Supervision of Supplementary Private Pension's Institutions are included in the assets, archives, liabilities, and the competencies of the Financial Supervisory Authority. This process is closed at the moment of the merger of the administration of the Albanian Securities Commission, Insurance Supervisory Authority, and Inspectorate of Supervision of Supplementary Private Pensions' Institutions.

The tariffs exercised from the three authorities remain in power and are implemented by the Authority until the approval of tariffs according to article 27 of this Law.

Article 34 Appointment of the first members of the Board

Within 5 days from entering into power of this Law, the institutions submit to the Parliament proposals for the members of the Board.

Within 10 days from receiving proposals, the parliament appoints members of the Board,

First time appointment of the members of the Board takes place according to the following deadlines:

1. the chairman – 5 years

   1. One of the Vice Chairmen – 5 years, and the other 4 years according to the definition in the appointment decisions;

   2. the other members respectively; the first – 5 years; the second – 4 years, and the other two – 3 years, in line with the definition in the decisions for their appointments.

The chairman of the Board convenes the first meeting of the Board within 7 days from this law's effectiveness. The first meeting of the Board is organized with the call of the Chairman in a defined place.

Article 35

Termination of functions and merges of administrations of the Albanian Securities Commission, Insurance Supervisory Authority, and of the Inspectorate of the Supplementary Private Pensions' Institutions

With the effectiveness of this Law cease to exist the decision-making bodies of the Albanian Securities Commission, Insurance Supervisory Authority, and Inspectorate of Supplementary Private Pensions' Institutions. With the effectiveness of this Law terminates the mandate of the selected or appointed members in the decision-making bodies of these institutions.

Licenses and other individual administrative orders issued until this Law has entered into force from the institutions mentioned in the paragraph 1 of this article, remains into force.

Within 2 (two) months from the entering into force of this law are merged the administrations of the Albanian Securities Commission, Insurance Supervisory Authority, and Inspectorate of Supplementary Private Pensions' Institutions. In the course of this period, the chairman, according to the procedures approved by the Board starts recruitment of staff and other employees of the Authority, giving priority to the individuals already employed in these institutions. During this period, the persons that in these administrations exercise Executive functions have no decision-making competencies. They are responsibly for the delivery to the chairman of the Authority, the means, income sources, archives and other liabilities spelled out in the last paragraph of article 33 of this law.

The staff employed in the administration of the Albanian Securities Commission, Insurance Supervisory Authority, and Inspectorate of Supplementary Private Pensions' Institutions, who are not recruited by the Authority, are eligible to benefit from the rights spelled out in the Law "On the status of the civil servants".

Article 36

Establishment of salaries, remuneration and structure for the first financial year

For the first year of the activity, the structure of the Authority, the salary of the chairman, vice chairmen and remuneration of the other members of the board for the year 2006 shall be decided by the Council of Ministers, within 7 days from entering into power of this Law.

Article 37

The budget of the Authority for the first financial year

The budget of the Authority for 2006 is drafted based on the budgets of the Albanian Securities Commission, Insurance Supervisory Authority, and Inspectorate of Supplementary Private Pensions' Institutions.

The Minister of Finance is in charge of making the changes regarding the preparation of the budget of the Financial Supervisory Authority for 2006.

CHAPTER XIV FINAL PROVISIONS

ARTICLE 38 TERMINOLOGY

In this law the terms have the same meaning as the laws that regulate each of the non-banking financial markets, which are the subject of supervision by the Authority.

In this law titles means securities.

Article 39 Drafting of the regulations of the Authority

The Board within two months from the date of the beginning of its first meeting, drafts and approves the rule anticipated in the fourth paragraph of article 9 of this Law.

The Board within 6 months from the date of the beginning of the work drafts and approves other rules regarding the daily running of the institution.

Article 40 Cancellation

Law no. 9268 dated 29.07.2004 "On the organization and functioning of the Insurance Supervisory Authority" is cancelled.

The by-laws in line with Law no. 8080 dated 01.03.1996 "On securities", amended; Law no. 9267 dated 29.07.2004 "On activities of insurance, re-insurance and intermediaries in insurance and re-insurance", amended; and Law no. 7943, dated 01.06.1995 "On supplementary pensions and private pensions' institutions", amended by the Council of Ministers and which fall against this law are canceled.

The by-laws approved by the authorities regulated by the laws spelled out in the paragraph 2, within 6 months from entering into force of this Law are cancelled.

The Board of the Authority, within 6 months from entering into force of this law, review and approves all by laws which were approved before from the regulatory authorities of the laws mentioned in paragraph 2 of this article.

Article 41

Changes to Law no. 8080 dated 1.03.1996 "On securities"

In the law 8080, dated 1.3.1996 "On Securities" should make the following changes:

1. All over the law the word "Commission" is substitute with "Authority"
2. Chapter II and X are canceled
3. Points 2, 3 and 4 of article 64 are canceled.
4. Article 67 is cancelled.

Article 42

Changes to Law no. 7943, dated 1.6.1995 "On Supplementary Pensions and Private Pensions' Institutions"

In the Law no. 7943, dated 1.6.1995 "On Supplementary Pensions and Private Pensions Institutions" should be made the following changes:

1. Points 4 and 5 of article 1 are cancelled.
2. In point 10 of article 1 of Law no. 7943, dated 1.6.1995 "On supplementary pensions and private pensions' institutions", and anywhere used, the term receiving deposits shall be replaced with depository.
3. In article 19 the word inspectors is replaced with the appointed staff.
4. In Law no. 7943, the word permit is used shall be replaced with the word license.
5. The word Inspectorate to be replaced by the Authority.
6. Chapter XI is cancelled.

Article 43

STRATEGIC ECONOMIC AND LEGAL INFORMATION

INVESTMENT, LEGAL AND BUSINESS CLIMATE - STRATEGIC INFORMATION AND CONTACTS FOR STARTING BUSINESS

Albania is a relatively small country located in the Western Balkans with a population of approximately 3 million people and a landmass the size of Maryland. Although the country was largely spared from the severe fallout of the 2008 financial crisis, economic output has slowed since 2009, reflecting the prolonged European crisis in neighboring Italy and Greece where close to 1.2 million Albanians live and work and 66 percent of Albanian trade occurs. Faced with public debt ballooning to 70 percent of GDP and large arrears to the private sector, the government began an ambitious fiscal consolidation program and signed a EUR 330 million euro, three-year program with the IMF in February 2014. Albania's GDP grew by an estimated 2 percent in 2014, up from 1.4 percent in 2013 and the government estimates approximately 3 percent growth in 2015. Low petroleum and mineral prices and the ongoing economic crises in Italy and Greece are the two biggest obstacles that may keep Albania from meeting its 2015 growth targets.

With low domestic demand, low bank lending rates, and limited government spending, the Albanian government has been focused on promoting foreign direct investment (FDI) as the driver of growth in the economy by implementing a liberal foreign investment regime. In recent years, the government has enacted reforms to improve the overall business climate in the country by streamlining business procedures through e-government reforms and improved legislation in a variety of sectors. The government currently is drafting a new Law on Investment that will provide investment incentives and fast-track registration and licensing procedures for strategic foreign investors.

According to the 2015 World Bank Doing Business Report, Albania made progress in regulatory reforms, moving up 40 slots from 108 in 2014 to 68 out of 189 economies in 2015. Albania became an EU candidate country in June 2014 and currently is working to fulfill the criteria that would pave the way for the start of accession negotiations. The EU integration process may serve as a strong incentive for the country to push forward on structural reforms and improve the business climate as the country aligns its legislation with the EU.

The Albanian legal system does not discriminate against foreign investors. The Law on Foreign Investment allows 100 percent foreign ownership of companies and outlines specific protections for foreign investors. Albanian tax policy also does not distinguish between domestic and foreign investments. The U.S. - Albania bilateral investment treaty entered into force in 1998 and ensures that U.S. investors receive most-favored-nation treatment.

Foreign Direct Investment annual inflows in Albania have increased significantly since 2008, averaging close to USD 1 billion per year for the period 2008-2014. Greece and Canada are the largest source of Albanian FDI, representing 45 percent of Albania's USD 5.5 billion foreign investment stock in 2013, mostly in the telecommunications, financial intermediation, manufacturing, hydrocarbon, and mining sectors.

Investment opportunities for U.S. investors likely will increase in the coming years, focusing mostly in oil, gas, energy, infrastructure, financial intermediation, and manufacturing. The government plans to issue 13 oil and gas exploration licenses in the near future and construction on the Trans-Adriatic Pipeline is slated to begin in mid-2015. Upgrades to the electricity distribution and transmission grids also may create significant investment opportunities. The government also has announced plans to grant many public services to the private sector as public-private partnerships (PPPs) across a wide range of sectors.

Despite progress in these reforms, major challenges remain, with investors citing endemic corruption, weak law enforcement, insufficiently defined property rights, government red tape, lack of developed infrastructure, and frequent changes in the legal framework as major challenges to conducting business in Albania. Changes in political leadership also have raised questions about the legal certainty of licensing and concession agreements signed by previous governments.

1. OPENNESS TO, AND RESTRICTIONS UPON, FOREIGN INVESTMENT

Attitude toward Foreign Direct Investment

Albania has implemented a liberal foreign investment regime with the goal of increasing foreign direct investment. The Law on Foreign Investment allows 100 percent foreign ownership of companies and outlines specific protections for foreign investors. In addition, Albanian tax policy does not distinguish between domestic and foreign investments. The U.S. - Albania bilateral investment treaty entered into force in 1998 and ensures that U.S. investors receive most-favored-nation treatment. The government has taken measures to improve the overall business climate in the country by streamlining business procedures through e-government reforms and improved legislation in a variety of sectors.

Other Investment Policy Reviews

In 2010, the World Trade Organization conducted an Investment Policy Review of Albania, more information about this review can be found at:

https://www.wto.org/english/tratop_e/tpr_e/tp329_e.htm

Laws/Regulations of Foreign Direct Investment

The Law on Foreign Investment attempts to create a hospitable climate for foreign investors and stipulates the following:

No prior government authorization is needed for an initial investment and no sector is closed to foreign investment;

100 percent foreign ownership of companies is permissible;

Foreign investment may not be expropriated or nationalized directly or indirectly, except for designated special cases, in the interest of public use and as defined by law;

Foreign investors enjoy the right to expatriate all funds and contributions in kind from their investments; and

Foreign investors receive 'most favored nation' treatment according to international agreements and Albanian law.

The government of Albania (GOA) is in the process of drafting a new law on investments in strategic sectors, aiming to introduce guarantees to foreign investors. In an attempt to attract the much needed foreign direct investment, especially in manufacturing, the GOA recently approved a 500 hectare free economic zone in Spitalle near the major port of Durres and soon will announce a tender to select the developer of the zone. The fiscal incentives for the zone are not defined yet.

There are limited exceptions to this liberal investment regime, most of which apply to the purchase of real estate: agricultural land cannot be purchased by foreigners and foreign entities, but may be rented for up to 99 years; and commercial property may be purchased, but only if the proposed investment is worth three times the price of the land. There are no restrictions on the purchase of private residential property.

Investors in Albania are entitled to judicial protection of legal rights related to their investments. Foreign investors have the right to submit disputes to an Albanian court. In addition, parties to a dispute may agree to arbitration. Albania is signatory of the New York Convention and foreign arbitration awards are recognized by Albania. The Albanian Civil Procedure Code outlines provisions regarding domestic and international commercial arbitration. However, many companies complain that endemic corruption and inefficient court procedures undermine judicial protection in Albania and therefore choose to seek international arbitration as a means for dispute resolution.

Albania's tax system does not distinguish between foreign and domestic investors. Reforms are aimed at increasing the efficiency of tax administration and reducing corruption, informality in the economy (as high as 50 percent) makes tax administration a challenge. In an effort to address the sharp decline in government revenues during 2012-2013 and growing public debt, the government, in consultation with the International Monetary Fund, passed a new fiscal package in December 2013. The new fiscal package increased corporate income tax from 10 to 15 percent for medium and large companies and reduced the tax rate to 7.5 percent for companies with less than USD 80,000 in annual turnover. The package also implemented a progressive personal income tax and removed the cap for health insurance contributions and eliminated many tax breaks and incentives in the oil and gas sector. The government introduced improvements to the Value-Added Tax (VAT) law in January 2015, easing the VAT reimbursement process.

U.S. exporters often complain about the unequal application of base pricing, used by local customs to assess taxes and duties on goods imported into Albania.

Visa requirements to obtain residence or work permits are straightforward and do not pose an undue burden on potential investors. The only potential complication to obtaining a work permit is the requirement that a foreign employer maintain a mandated number of local employees. The Law on Foreigners states that a foreign employer will be granted a work permit if the number of foreign employees in the company does not exceed 10 percent of the total number of employees on the payroll for the 12 proceeding months.

The Law on Entrepreneurs and Commercial Companies sets guidelines on the activities of companies and the legal structure under which they may operate. The government adopted the law in 2008 to conform Albanian legislation to the European Union's Acquis Communitaire. The most common type of organization for foreign investors is a limited liability company.

The National Business Registration Center serves as a one-stop-shop for business registration. Starting a business is now easier with online publishing of forms and procedures, reduction of registration costs, and the consolidation of tax, health insurance, and labor registration into a single application. The Business Licensing Center streamlines the licensing process by abolishing many licensing requirements and simplifying other licensing procedures. The business registration page can be found at: www.qkr.gov.al and the business, licensing center is www.qkl.gov.al

Albania improved public procurement procedures by introducing an e-procurement law in 2006, which has been amended over the years to improve the public procurement processes. The legal framework on public procurement is governed by the following general principles: non-discrimination and equality of treatment of actual and potential bidders, transparency of procurement procedures, and, proportionality of requirements and obligations imposed on bidders. The legislation covers public entities' procurement of public goods, public services, and, public works with a few exceptions including, defense procurement, secret contracts, and contracts requiring special security measures, international obligations, service contracts awarded on the basis of an exclusive right, and other specific exclusions specified in the law.

The law stipulates the following procurement procedures: open procedures, restricted procedures, negotiated procedures, request for proposals and design contests.

The Public Procurement Advocate performs functions similar to an ombudsman by safeguarding the rights and interests of bidders against acts or omissions by contracting authorities. Despite improvements to the laws and regulations, companies continue to complain of nontransparent processes when competing for public tenders, whether it is 'fixed' technical specifications designed to lock out a potential bidder or a lack of clear communication with the relevant ministries. Public procurement opportunities are published on the website of the Public Procurement Agency www.app.gov.al.

In 2013, Albania approved a new law on concessions and public-private partnerships. All contracts signed or negotiated prior to the new law remain subject to the provisions of the previous law. The new law aims to better align Albanian policy with EU legislation and clarify the distinction between concession contracts and public-private partnerships. The law establishes the framework for promoting and facilitating the implementation of privately financed concessionary projects and aims to enhance transparency, fairness, efficiency, and long-term sustainability in the development of infrastructure and public service projects. Concessions may be identified by central or local governments or through third party unsolicited proposals. The law applies to the following sectors:

Electricity and heating: generation and distribution;
Health;
Natural gas distribution;
IT and database infrastructure: service and maintenance;
Urban and suburban rehabilitation and development
Prison and judicial infrastructure;
Recycling projects, rehabilitation of land and forests;
Industrial parks and mining;
Housing, governmental buildings;
Solid waste: collection, transfer, processing, depositing, and administration;
Telecommunication;
Tourism, leisure and hotels;
Culture and sports;
Science and education;
Transport (railway system, rail transport, ports, airports, roads, tunnels, bridges, parking facilities, public transport);
Social Services
Public lighting in the local government units

Water: production and distribution, treatment, collection distribution and administration of waste water, irrigation, drainage, cleaning of canals, dams;

Public services: management contracts, including those related to sectors specified above.

In order to promote investment in priority sectors, the government has announced that it may offer concessions to local or international investors for the symbolic price of one euro, but has not yet detailed specific concessions that will receive this treatment. The Government may, with the proposal of other central government agencies or local government, authorize concessions in other sectors other than those listed above. The law does not apply to concessions that require a separate operating license, unless that is included in the framework of the concession agreement.

Industrial Promotion

The GOA is eager to attract foreign investment across all sectors, particularly in job creating industries that will help the government address high unemployment rates.

Please see a detailed list of incentives under subchapter five. Interested investors should contact the Albanian Investment Development Agency (AIDA) (www.aida.gov.al), to learn more about specific sectors. The GOA is currently drafting a law on investments in strategic sectors that will outline incentives for investors in various sectors.

Limits on Foreign Control

There are no restrictions on foreign ownership or control in domestic corporations. According to the Albanian legislation 100 percent foreign ownership of companies is allowed. There also are no sector-specific restrictions that discriminate against market access applicable to foreign investment.

Privatization Program

The privatization process in Albania is nearing a conclusion, with only a few major privatizations remaining. These few opportunities include electricity distribution company, the state owned insurance company INSIG, 16 percent of the fixed line telephone company Albtelekom, the state owned oil company Albpetrol, and, 25 percent of oil refiner ARMO. SOEs operate in the energy generation, electricity transmission and distribution, water supply, ports, railway, insurance, postal services, and hydrocarbon sectors.

In recent years, the government has granted as PPPs a large number of services, previously performed by public administration and is in the process of granting a wider range of services under the same model. The Ministry of Economy announced at the end of 2014 a very aggressive program of granting more than 65 services as PPPs across all sectors. The tendering procedures are published online and bidding also can be done on line at the Public Procurement Agency website: www.app.gov.al

Screening of FDI

The government does not screen foreign direct investment.

Competition Law

The Law on Protection of Competition governs incoming foreign investment whether it is through mergers, acquisitions, takeovers, or green field investments, irrespective of the industry or sector. In the case of particular share transfers in insurance and banking industries, additional regulatory approvals are needed. Also, transactions between parties outside Albania – foreign to foreign transactions – are covered by the competition law, which explicitly states that it applies to all undertakings, whether domestic or foreign, whose activities have a direct or indirect effect on the Albanian market.

Investment Trends

The legal framework to promote investment has been improving and the country offers significant emerging opportunities across all sectors, especially in natural resources. Corruption and transparency remain a significant concern, however, especially in the natural resources sector, with many foreign companies reporting pressure to hire specific employees or sub-contractors affiliated with public officials. In June 2014, Albania became a European Union (EU) candidate country and now is working to fulfill the necessary criteria that would pave the way for the start of accession negotiations. The EU integration process likely will provide an incentive for Albania to continue on its reform path and to improve the business climate.

According to the 2015 World Bank's Doing Business Report, Albania made progress in regulatory reforms, moving up 40 slots from 108 in 2014 to 68 out of 189 in 2015.

Foreign Direct Investment annual inflows in Albania have increased significantly since 2008, averaging close to USD 1 billion per year for the period 2008-2014. The largest recipients of FDI inflows are extractive industries (primarily oil and gas), telecommunication, financial intermediation, and wholesale and retail sales. The government recently announced plans to license 13 oil and gas exploration blocks in 2015, which also may drive an increase in FDI in the coming years.

Foreign investors cite Albania's strategic location in the Balkans, vicinity with major European markets, free trade agreements with key markets (European Union, Turkey, CEFTA and EFTA countries), opportunities for investments in a wide range of sectors, and inexpensive and skilled labor force as major reasons for investing in Albania.

Table 1

Measure	Year	Index or Rank	Website Address
TI Corruption Perceptions index	2014	110 of 174	transparency.org/cpi2014/results
World Bank's Doing Business Report "Ease of Doing Business"	2015	68 of 189	doingbusiness.org/rankings
Global Innovation Index	2014	94 of 143	globalinnovationindex.org/content.aspx?page=data-analysis
World Bank GNI per capita	2013	USD 4,710	data.worldbank.org/indicator/NY.GNP.PCAP.CD

2. CONVERSION AND TRANSFER POLICIES

Foreign Exchange

The Central Bank of Albania (BOA) formulates, adopts, and implements foreign exchange policies and maintains a supervisory role in foreign exchange activities in accordance with the

Law on the Bank of Albania No. 8269 and the Banking Law No. 9662. Foreign exchange is regulated by the 2009 Regulation on Foreign Exchange Activities no. 70 (FX Regulation).

The BOA maintains a floating free exchange rate regime for its domestic currency, the Lek (ALL). Foreign exchange is readily available at banks and exchange bureaus. However, when exchanging large amounts, preliminary notification may be necessary as the exchange market in Albania remains small. The ALL has remained stable compared to the Euro, but depreciated by approximately 25 percent compared to the dollar over the past year (largely due to Euro depreciation). Albanian authorities do not engage in currency arbitrage and do not view it as an efficient instrument to achieve competitive advantage.

Remittance Policies

The Banking Law does not impose any restrictions on the purchase, sale, holding, or transfer of monetary foreign exchanges. However, the Law on the Bank of Albania authorizes the bank to temporarily restrict the purchase, sale, holding, or transfer of foreign exchanges in order to preserve the foreign exchange rate or its official reserves. In practice, the Bank of Albania rarely uses such measures. The last time was in 2009 when the Bank temporarily tightened supervision rules over liquidity transfers by domestic banks to their foreign mother banks due to the widespread lack of liquidity in international financial markets. It also asked banks to not distribute dividends and to use them to increase shareholders' capital instead. The Bank lifted these restrictions in 2010.

The Law on Foreign Investment guarantees the right to transfer and repatriate any funds associated with an investment from Albania into a freely usable currency at a market-clearing rate. Only licensed entities (banks) may conduct foreign exchange transfers and waiting periods depend on office procedures adopted by the banks. Both Albanian and foreign citizens entering or leaving the country must declare assets in excess of ALL 1,000,000 (USD 8,000) in hard currency and/or precious items. Failure to declare such assets is considered a criminal act and punishable by confiscation of the assets and imprisonment. Legal parallel markets are not in place in Albania as the financial sector does not make use of convertible or negotiable instruments.

Although the Foreign Exchange Regulation provides that residents and non-residents may transfer capital within and into Albania without any restrictions, capital transfers out of Albania are subject to certain documentation requirements. Physical persons must submit a request indicating the reasons for the capital transfer, the amount of capital transferred outside the territory of Albania, and the address to which the capital will be transferred. Such persons also must submit a declaration on the source of the funds to be transferred. In January 2015, The FX Regulation was amended and the requirement to present the documentation showing the preliminary payment of taxes related to the transaction was removed.

Albania is a member of the Council of Europe Committee of Experts on the Evaluation of Anti-Money Laundering Measures and the Financing of Terrorism (MONEYVAL), a Financial Action Task Force-style regional body.

3. EXPROPRIATION AND COMPENSATION

The Albanian Constitution guarantees the right of private property. According to Article 41, the expropriation or limitation in the exercise of a property right only can occur in the public interest and with fair compensation. In the post-communist period, expropriation has been limited to land needed for the public interest, mainly infrastructure projects such as roads, energy infrastructure, water works, airports, etc. Compensation has generally been below market value and owners have complained that the compensation process is slow and unfair. Civil courts are responsible for resolving such complains.

Political change also can be of concern to foreign investors. Following 2013 elections and a peaceful transition of power, the new government revoked or attempted to renegotiate numerous concession agreements, licenses, and contracts signed by the previous government with both domestic and international investors. This has occurred in years past, as well.

There are many ongoing disputes regarding properties confiscated during the communist regime. Identifying land titles and ownership in Albania is a perpetual problem that makes restitution for expropriated properties extremely difficult. The restitution and compensation process started in 1993, but has been slow and marred by corruption. Many U.S. citizens of Albanian origin have long-running restitution disputes. Court cases tend to drag on for years without a final decision, forcing many to take their case to the European Court of Human Rights in Strasburg, France. The Court has so far issued 18 decisions in favor of Albanian citizens in civil cases involving protection of property with an assessed financial cost of approximately USD 12 million. Reportedly there are in total 379 applications pending for consideration. Even once a case is settled in Strasburg, enforcement of the decision is often slow or nonexistent.

The GOA has presented three methods of compensation for confiscation claims: restitution; compensation of property with similarly valued land in a different location; and cash settlement/financial compensation. In practice however, a lack of funding and the large amount of claimants has significantly slowed the restitution process.

Albanian governments have not engaged in expropriation actions against U.S. investments, companies or representatives. There have been limited cases when the government has revoked licenses, especially in the mining and energy sectors, based on contract violation claims.

4. DISPUTE SETTLEMENT

Legal System, Specialized Courts, Judicial Independence, Judgments of Foreign Courts

Albania has a civil law system similar to that of most other European countries. The Albanian Constitution provides for the separation of legislative, executive, and judicial branches; thus supporting the independence of the judiciary. The Civil Procedure Code enacted in 1996 governs civil procedure in Albania. The civil court system consists of district courts, appellate courts, and the Supreme Court. The district courts are organized in specialized sections according to the subject of the claim: civil disputes; family disputes; and commercial disputes.

In 2012, Albania approved the law on administrative courts, and these courts began operation in late 2013. The administrative courts of first instance, the Administrative Court of Appeal, and the Administrative College of the High Court now adjudicate administrative disputes. Administrative courts aim to enable fast adjudication of administrative cases. The Constitutional Court reviews whether laws or subsidiary legislation comply with the Constitution and in limited cases protects and enforces the constitutional rights of citizens and legal entities.

Parties may appeal the judgment of the first instance courts within 15 days, while Appellate Court judgments must be appealed to the Supreme Court within 30 days. A lawsuit against an administrative action is submitted to the administrative court within 45 days from notification and the law stipulates short procedural timeframes enabling faster adjudication of administrative disputes.

Albania does not have a specific commercial code, but defines commercial legislation through a series of commercial laws. Relevant laws include: Foreign Investment Law; Commercial Companies Law; Bankruptcy Law; Environmental Law; Corporate and Municipal Bonds; Transport Law; Maritime Code; Secured Transactions Law; Employment Law; Taxation Procedures Law; Banking Law; Insurance and Reinsurance Law; Concessions Law; Mining Law; Energy Law; Water Resources Law; Waste Management Law; Excise Law; Oil and Gas Law; Gambling Law; Telecommunications Law; Value Added Law; Sports Law; etc.

Albania is signatory of the New York Convention and foreign arbitration awards may be enforced in local courts. Investors often cite corruption and inefficiency in the judiciary as a serious impediment to conducting business in Albania and often seek out international arbitration as an alternative means for dispute resolution.

Bankruptcy

The Bankruptcy Law governs the reorganization or liquidation of insolvent businesses. It sets out non-discriminatory and mandatory rules for the repayment of the obligations by a debtor in a bankruptcy procedure. The law establishes statutory time limits for insolvency procedures, professional qualifications for insolvency administrators, and an Agency of Insolvency Supervision to regulate the profession of insolvency administrators. A simplified insolvency procedure for small businesses is also in place.

A bankruptcy procedure can be initiated by debtors, creditors, as well as by tax authorities. Tax authorities can request a bankruptcy procedure when the subject reports financial losses three years in a row. The bankruptcy proceedings can initiate when the debtor is unable to pay the obligations at the maturity date. In addition, the inability to pay the obligations in the near future shall also be a reason for the debtor to file for bankruptcy.

According to the provisions of the Bankruptcy Law the initiation of the bankruptcy proceeding would suspend the enforcement of the claims of all the creditors against the debtor subject to bankruptcy. Creditors of all categories should submit their claims to the bankruptcy administrator in order to be treated under the bankruptcy proceeding. The Bankruptcy Law provides specific treatment for different categories, dividing them into: secured creditors; unsecured creditors; and unsecured creditors of lower ranking (i.e. those whose claims would be paid after all the secured and unsecured creditors are satisfied). The claims of the secured creditors will be satisfied by the assets of the debtor, which secure such claims under security agreements. The claims of the unsecured creditors will be paid out of bankruptcy estate excluding the assets used for payment of the secured creditors, following the priority ranking described under the Albanian Civil Code.

Pursuant to the provisions of the Bankruptcy Law, the creditors have the right to establish a creditors committee and the creditors' assembly. The creditors' committee is appointed by the Commercial Section Courts, before the first meeting of the creditors' assembly. The creditors' committee represents the secured creditors, the unsecured creditors with the larger claims, and creditors with the small claims. The committee has the right: (i) to support and supervise the activities of the insolvency administrator; (b) to request and receive information about the insolvency proceedings; c) to inspect the books and records; and d) to order an examination of the revenues and cash balances.

In the event that the creditors and administrator agree that reorganizing the company is the best option, the administrator of the bankruptcy shall prepare a reorganization plan and submit it to the court for authorizing implementation.

According to the law on bankruptcy, foreign creditors have the same rights as domestic creditors with respect to the commencement of, and participation in, a bankruptcy proceeding. The claim is valued as of the date the insolvency proceeding is opened. Claims expressed in foreign currency are converted into Albanian currency according to the official exchange value applicable to the place of payment at the time of the opening of the proceeding.

The Albanian Criminal Code provides for several criminal offences in bankruptcy such as: (i) the bankruptcy provoked intentionally; (ii) concealment of bankruptcy status; (iii) concealment of assets after bankruptcy; and (iv) failure to comply with the obligations arising under bankruptcy proceeding.

According to 2015 Doing Business Report of the World Bank, Albania ranks 44 out of 189 countries in the insolvency index. A reference analysis of the 'resolving insolvency' can be found here: http://www.doingbusiness.org/data/exploreeconomies/albania/resolving-insolvency/

The number of bankruptcy cases in Albania is limited, with only a handful of bankruptcy proceedings filed during 2014.

Investment Disputes

In the past ten years, there have been two major investment disputes between the Albanian government and U.S. companies. Both disputes were settled in International Arbitration, one in favor of the U.S. company and the other in favor of the Albanian government. In both instances, both parties respected and enforced the findings of the arbitration.

The recent dispute between the GOA and the Czech power group, CEZ, following its failed privatization of the Albanian Electricity Distribution company was settled outside of court.

International Arbitration

Under the Albanian Constitution, ratified international agreements prevail over domestic legislation. Albania is a member state to the International Centre for the Settlement of Investment Disputes (ICSID Convention). It is also a signatory to the convention on the Recognition and Enforcement of Foreign Arbitral Awards (1958 New York Convention). They have ratified the 1927 Convention and the European Convention on Arbitration (Geneva Convention).

In order for an arbitration award locally recognized the claimant must enforce the award before the Court of Appeals.

The procedure for the recognition of a foreign arbitral award typically last around one month and either party may appeal the Court's decision to the Supreme Court. The appeal must be filed within 30 days from the date of decision or notification of the other party (if absent).

The possibility of bringing an action before the local court in order to avoid arbitration proceedings is remote. According to explicit provisions in the Albanian Code of Civil Procedure, if a party brings actions before local courts despite the parties' agreement to arbitrate, the court would, upon motion of the other party, dismiss the case without entertaining the merits of the case. The decision of the court to dismiss the case can be appealed to the Supreme Court, which has 30 days to consider the appeal.

An alternative to dispute settlement via the courts is private arbitration or mediation. Parties can engage in arbitration when they have agreed to such a provision in the original agreement, when there is a separate arbitration agreement, or by mutual agreement at any time when the dispute arises. Legislation distinguishes arbitration of international disputes from arbitration of domestic disputes in that the parties involved in an international dispute may agree to settle through either a domestic or foreign arbitration tribunal. Mediation also is applicable in resolving all civil, commercial, and, family disputes and is regulated by the law "On Dispute Resolution through Mediation." Arbitral awards are final and enforceable and can be appealed only in cases foreseen in the Code of Civil Procedure. Mediation is final and enforceable in the same way.

There are no consolidated institutions for dispute resolution through arbitration and arbiters are appointed ad hoc in compliance with the provisions of the Code of Civil Procedure. While for the mediation process, the law provides for the establishment of the National Chamber of Mediators and Chambers of Mediators as institutions to perform mediation. Mediators are licensed and registered at the Mediators Register at the Ministry of Justice, which maintains a list of mediators from which the parties can choose.

The provisions with respect to arbitration procedures and the recognition and enforcement of the foreign awards are stipulated in the Albanian Code of Civil Procedure. Albania does not have a separate law on arbitration. Although the arbitration chapter of the Code of Civil procedure stipulates only the rules for domestic arbitration, the country is signatory of the 1958 New York Convention and as such, recognizes the validity of the written arbitration agreements and arbitral awards in a contracting state.

ICSID Convention and New York Convention

.Albania is a member state to the International Centre for the Settlement of Investment Disputes (ICSID Convention). It is also a signatory to the convention on the Recognition and Enforcement of Foreign Arbitral Awards (1958 New York Convention).

Duration of Dispute Resolution

The Albanian Code of Civil Procedure requires the courts to reach a judgment within a reasonable amount of time, but it does not provide for a specific deadline when referring to commercial disputes. Reaching a final judgment in a commercial litigation may take up to several years if all the stages of the process are exhausted.

The procedure for the recognition of a foreign arbitral award should take on average approximately one month, however in certain cases this decision may be appealable. An appeal against a court decision that recognizes a foreign arbitral award does not automatically suspend the effects of the enforcement.

5. PERFORMANCE REQUIREMENTS AND INVESTMENT INCENTIVES

WTO/TRIMS

Albania does not have any performance requirements that are inconsistent with the World Trade Organization (WTO) Trade-Related Investment Measures (TRIMs) obligations. Albanian law does not impose performance requirements on foreign or domestic investors. Furthermore, the bilateral investment treaty between the two countries prohibits either party from mandating or enforcing performance requirements as a condition for the establishment, acquisition, expansion, management, conduct, or operation of a covered investment.

Investment Incentives

The Albanian Investment Development Agency (www.aida.gov.al) is the best source to find incentives offered across a variety of sectors. Distinct from the incentives listed below, individual parties may negotiate additional incentives directly through AIDA or with the Ministry of Economy, Trade, Tourism and Entrepreneurship.

The hydrocarbons sector, exploration and exploitation: Companies operating in the oil and gas extraction industry pay profit tax at the rate of 50 percent (different from the flat 15 percent corporate income tax applicable for all other taxpayers) after deduction of all capital expenditure and operating and administrative expenses, in accordance with the respective petroleum sharing agreement signed with the government (PSA are negotiated on a case by case basis).

The import of goods or services relating to the performance of exploration/research phase of petroleum operations, carried out by contractors who work for these operations, is VAT exempt.

Energy sector: Cement and iron imported for the construction of HPPs is VAT exempt.

Foreign tax credit: Albania applies foreign tax credits rights even in case there is no double tax treaty in place with the country where the tax is paid. If a double taxation treaty is in force, double taxation is avoided either through an exemption or by granting tax credit up to the amount of the applicable Albanian corporate income tax rate (currently 15 percent).

Corporate income tax exemption: Film studios and cinematographic productions, licensed and funded by the National Cinematographic Centre are exempted from paying corporate income tax.

Loss carry forward for corporate income tax purposes: Fiscal losses can be carried forward for three consecutive years (the first losses are used the first). However, they can't be carried forward if more than 50 percent of direct or indirect ownership of the share capital or voting rights of the taxpayer is transferred (changed) during the tax year.

Tax exemption of dividends designated for investments: Dividends and profit share paid by a resident or non-resident company to a resident taxpayer will not be subject to corporate income tax for the resident taxpayer. This applies, despite the participation quote, in amounts or number of shares, in shareholder capital of the voting rights or participation in initial capital of the beneficiary.

Incentives for manufacturing sector

Lease of public property: Government of Albania can lease public property of more than 500 m2, or grant a concession for the symbolic price of 1 euro if the properties will be used for manufacturing activities with an investment exceeding 10 million euro, or for inward processing activities. The GOA can also lease public property or grant a concession for the symbolic price of 1 euro for investments of more than 2 million euro on activities that address social and economic issues in a certain area, as well as activities related to sport, culture, tourism and cultural heritage. Criteria and terms are decided on a by case basis by the Council of Ministers.

Manufacturing activities are exempt from VAT on machinery and equipment.

The employer is exempt from the social security tax payment for 1 year for all new employees.

The state pays the salaries for 4 months for the new employees and offers various financing incentives for job training.

VAT credit for fuel: Taxpayers whose main business activity is the production of bricks and tiles and the transport of goods with technological means are allowed to credit VAT on the purchase of fuel used wholly and exclusively for their business activities, up to the limit of a certain percentage of the taxpayer's total annual turnover.

Manufacturing sector obtains VAT refunds immediately in the case of zero risk exporters, within 30 days if the taxpayer is an exporter, and within 60 days in the case of other taxpayers.

Apparel and footwear producers are exempt from 20 percent VAT on raw materials as long as the finished product is exported. In 2011, the GOA also removed customs tariffs for imported apparel and raw materials in the textile and shoe industries (e.g. leather used for clothes, cotton, viscose, velvet, sewing accessories, etc.)

Research and Development

The Agency for Research, Technology and Innovation (ARTI), is a public, legal institution whose mission is to evaluate, finance, monitor and manage programs and projects in the fields of science, technology and innovation in Albania. ARTI (http://www.akti.gov.al/) aims to fund projects in the field of Small and Medium Business as well as transfer, modernization and renewal of their technologies. The Agency is funded by the state budget donations by both domestic and foreign individuals and private sector, EU programs and projects, from specific countries and partner organizations. There are no restrictions to apply for research and development projects for foreign firms operating in Albania.

Performance Requirements

Although visa, residence, and work permit requirements are straightforward and do not pose an undue burden on potential investors, the Law on Foreigners requires foreign investors to prove that foreign employees are less than 10 percent of total workforce before granting a work permit.

Data Storage

According to the current legislation in force, companies that have sensitive data (mostly in telecommunications, banking, energy sector, etc.) are not authorized to transfer data abroad. In order to do so, they need to get approvals and fulfill certain security criteria. As such, many companies operating in Albania are returning their data inside Albania. The two large private datacenters in Albania belong to the telecom operator Albtelecom and Albanian Telecommunication Union.

6. RIGHT TO PRIVATE OWNERSHIP AND ESTABLISHMENT

Albanian law permits private ownership and establishment of enterprises and property. Foreign investors do not need additional permission or authorization beyond that required of domestic investors. The government applies restrictions only on the purchase of real estate: agricultural land cannot be purchased by foreign individuals or foreign companies, but may be rented for up to 99 years. Commercial property may be purchased, but only if the proposed investment is worth three times the price of the land. There are no restrictions on the purchase of private residential property.

Both foreign and domestic investors continue to experience significant issues in resolving property disputes arising from unclear or incomplete documentation.

Foreigners can acquire concession rights on natural resources and on resources of the common interest, as defined by the Law on Concessions and Public Private Partnerships The National Licensing Center (NLC) serves as a one-stop-shop for business licenses. More information on the types of licenses and application procedures is outlined at www.qkl.gov.al

The 2007 'Law Establishing the National Registration Center' (NRC) allows business entities to register in a single place, in one day, for one euro. More information on the NRC can be found at www.qkr.gov.al.

Foreign and domestic investors have numerous options available for organizing business operations in Albania. The 2008 'Law on Entrepreneurs and Commercial Companies,' and 'Law Establishing the National Registration Center' (NRC) allows for the following legal types of business entities to be established through the NRC: Sole Entrepreneur; Unlimited Partnership; Limited Partnership; Limited Liability Company; Joint Stock Company; Branches and Representative Offices; and Joint Ventures.

7. PROTECTION OF PROPERTY RIGHTS

Real Property

Real Estate is registered at the Immovable Property Registration Office (IPRO). The procedures are cumbersome and registrants have complained of corruption within the process. Recent changes in legislation allow a notary public to have access to real estate registers and confirm the legal ownership of property. For large transactions, it is still advisable to hire an attorney to check documents and procedures for property registration.

Property legislation has developed in a piecemeal and uncoordinated way. Immovable property rights enforcement is not efficient and is a common source of corruption allegations and lengthy legal procedures. Through the use of international donor assistance the recording system has improved. The initial property registration process has also seen progress because the GOA is committed to identifying property owners and properly registering land titles.

The process of registering property remains cumbersome and difficult to navigate. Approximately 13 percent of properties nationwide are not yet registered, mostly in urban and high value coastal areas. Illegal construction is a major impediment to securing property titles. The legalization process to address large-scale illegal construction started in 2006 and is still ongoing. There are an estimated 350,000 illegal buildings in Albania. In an attempt to legalize property and punish illegal construction, the government's National Urban Construction Inspectorate (INUK) began a campaign of building demolition in late 2013. There were credible reports that the government demolished some homes without due legal process as part of a wider campaign to demolish illegally constructed buildings. Citizens also submitted complaints that INUK ignored citizens' requests to demolish some illegal buildings while choosing to demolish other buildings about which citizens had not complained. Unresolved property issues continue to undermine efforts to develop a functional land market.

The civil court system manages property rights disputes. Decisions from civil courts often take many years and authorities often do not enforce court decisions. In 2010 there were amendments to the law on foreign investments, which granted special protection to foreign investors on property disputes. However, the new law on strategic investments aims to fill in the gap and provide to foreign investors assistance on a large variety of issues including property title.

According to the 2015 World Bank's Doing Business Report, Albania performed poorly in the registering property category, ranking 118 out of 189 economies. It takes 22 days and 6 procedures to register a property and the associated cost can reach 10 percent of the total property value.

Intellectual Property Rights

Copyright

Albania is not and never has been on the Special 301 Watch List or Priority Watch List. However, IPR infringement and theft are common due to weak legal structures and poor enforcement. Counterfeit goods are present in the local market ranging from software to garments and machines. Albanian law protects copyrights, patents, trademarks, stamps marks of origin, and industrial designs, but there remains a significant gap between the law's intent and its enforcement. Regulators are ineffective at collecting fines and prosecutors rarely press charges for IP theft. U.S. companies should consult an attorney experienced in IPR issues and avoid potential risk by establishing solid commercial relationships and drafting strong contracts.

The Albanian government persists in failing to enact key legislation that would strengthen IPR enforcement and address shortcomings in existing legislation.

The main institutions responsible for IPR enforcement include the Albanian Copyright Office (ACO), Audiovisual Media Authority (AMA), the General Directorate of Patents and Trademarks (GDPT), the General Directorate for Customs, Tax Inspectorate, Prosecutor's Office, police, and the courts. Most IP-related fines are never collected and the few cases that the regulatory agencies refer to prosecutors are rarely enforced.

The AMA, which regulates broadcast and cable television, has been ineffective in fighting content theft in the broadcast sector due to political disputes over the composition of the Board of Directors. In November 2014, all vacancies were filled but challenges persist. The Albanian Copyright Office (ACO), established in 2006, is the main institution responsible for monitoring and implementing Albanian copyright law, but the ACO lacks administrative and institutional capacity. Law enforcement on copyrights remains virtually nonexistent and copyright violations are rampant.

The number of copyright violation cases brought to court remains low. ACO sanctions are not effective and the low fines it levies are rarely collected and do not serve as an adequate deterrent. In 2010, a 'Law on Administrative Contraventions' was adopted to improve collection of fines for infringement of copyrights, but enforcement of this law remains weak to non-existent. The ACO, along with the customs, tax and police authorities, are responsible to report on the seizure of counterfeit goods. While official figures are not available, Customs does report the quantity of counterfeit goods destroyed annually. In case of seizure, the rights holder has the burden of proof and must first inspect the goods before any further action takes place. The rights holder is also responsible for the storage and destruction of the counterfeit goods.

Patents and Trademarks

The General Directorate for Patents and Trademarks (GDPT) is responsible for the registration and administration of patents, commercial trademarks and service marks, industrial designs, and geographical indications. The 2008 law on Industrial Property was amended in 2014 to reflect EU legislation on this matter. Despite adequate legislation, the GDPT still needs further capacity building and additional human resources to be effective. Specifically, examination procedures are lengthy due to the very limited number of examiners for patents and trademarks.

Albania became a contracting party to the WIPO Patent Law Treaty and a full member of the European Patent Organization in 2010. The government became party to the London Agreement on the implementation of article 65 of the European Convention for the Patents in 2013.

For additional information about treaty obligations and points of contact at local IP offices, please see WIPO's country profiles at http://www.wipo.int/directory/en/.

Resources for Rights Holders

Contact at mission on IP issues:
Donald A. Brown
Economic and Commercial Officer
Phone: + 355 (0) 4229 3115
E-mail: BrownDA8@state.gov
Country resources:
American Chamber of Commerce: www.amcham.com.al
Address: Rr. Deshmoret e 4 shkurtit, Sky Tower, kati 11 Ap 3 Tirana, Albania
Email: info@amcham.com.al
Phone: +355 (0) 4225 9779
Fax: +355 (0) 4223 5350

8. TRANSPARENCY OF THE REGULATORY SYSTEM

Albania's regulatory system has improved in recent years but still faces challenges. Uneven enforcement of legislation, cumbersome bureaucracy, and lack of transparency are all hindrances to the business community.

Albania has adopted legislation and established agencies that superficially provide transparent rules and regulations to foster competition and attract investment. The government has amended the 2003 'Law on Protection of Competition' several times and created the Agency for the Protection of Competition in 2004. The law seeks to promote clear rules of the game. However, the legislation's uneven enforcement is one of the major reasons for distorting competition in the market. The operational independence and administrative capacity of the Competition Authority also needs to be strengthened so it can serve as an able watchdog.

Other independent agencies and bodies, including the Energy Regulator, Telecom Regulator, and other major institutions operate to ensure transparency in specific sectors. New legislation on public procurement introduced e-procurement and resulted in improved transparency in public procurements. However, as in many other areas, the proper enforcement of the law remains a challenge and problems with tender procedures are frequent. Business registration and licensing are streamlined through the one-stop-shop centers for registration and licensing. Although business registration is an easy step, licensing still remains cumbersome in some sectors. Albanian legislation includes rules on disclosure requirements, formation, maintenance and alteration of capital, mergers and divisions, takeover bids, shareholders' rights, as well as corporate governance principles. The 'Law on Accounting and Financial Statements' includes reporting provisions that stipulate large companies will apply International Financial Reporting Standards, while small and medium businesses will apply National Financial Reporting Standards.

In an effort to improve the dialogue between the public and private sector and to increase transparency in the process of drafting and approving new laws and regulations, the government established the National Economic Council (NEC) in 2014. According to the law, the NEC serves as an institution to guarantee institutional cooperation between the private and public sector. The law regulating the Council's activity clearly stipulates the principles and timeline of the consultation process. Although the participation of the business community in the consultation process has increased, issues of concern remain. Oftentimes, laws are rushed into the approval process without providing ample time for business community to comment, while at other times stakeholder input is not incorporated into the final version. Many representatives of the business community complain that the NEC has not become a forum for effective private sector consultation as it was intended to be.

9. EFFICIENT CAPITAL MARKETS AND PORTFOLIO INVESTMENT

In the absence of a stock market, the country's banking sector remains the main channel for business financing. It is sound, profitable, and well-capitalized, although the high rate of non-performing loans remains a concern. At the end of 2014, non-performing loans reached 22.8 percent of all private loans, marking the first reduction compared to their peak level of 25 percent throughout most of the 2014. However, capital adequacy at 16.8 percent -- far above Basel requirements -- indicates the sector currently has sufficient assets, which totaled USD 12 billion in 2014. The banking sector is fully private and consists of 16 banks, most of which are subsidiaries of foreign banks. The Turkish National Commercial Bank is the largest bank, with 23.5 percent of the market, followed by Austrian Raiffeisen Bank with 20.5 percent market share. The market share of Greek banks has decreased significantly in recent years, with French and Italian banks filling the void. The two main Albanian banks possess approximately 12.5 percent of sector assets.

Money and Banking System, Hostile Takeovers

Albania's banking sector weathered the financial crisis better than many of its neighbors, largely due to a lack of exposure to international capital markets and domestic housing bubbles. There is sufficient liquidity in the market to enter and exit sizeable positions. The sector remained profitable even during the peak of the financial crisis when it suffered a reduction of deposits of about 15 percent. In 2014, profits reached approximately USD 100 million with a 0.9 percent return on assets and 10.5 percent return on equities. Market concentration remains high, as the five largest banks dominate the market with about 73 percent of total assets. The Bank of Albania has the flexibility to intervene in the currency market to protect exchange rates and official reserves, but only for a period not exceeding 12 months. In 2009, following the global financial crisis, the central bank restricted the distribution of domestic banking sector profits in order to maintain sufficient liquidity in the sector but lifted the restriction in July 2010. The Bank of Albania further loosened monetary policy in 2014 and again in March 2015, with official central bank interest rates reaching a historical low of 2 percent.

Foreigners are not required to prove a residency status to establish a bank account other than the normal know your client procedures. However, in the case of U.S. citizens, they are required to fill a form accepting the disclosure of their banking data to IRS authorities in the framework of U.S. Foreign Account Tax Compliance Act requirements.

Commercial Credit

The GOA has adopted policies promoting the free flow of financial resources as a mechanism to promote any type of foreign investment in Albania. The government and Central Bank refrain from restrictions on payments and transfers for international transactions. While being a shallow FX market, banks enjoy enough liquidity to support sizeable positions. Furthermore, portfolio investments remain limited mostly to company shares, government bonds, and real estate.

The credit market is quite competitive but interest rates can be high, currently between 7 and 11.5 percent. Most mortgage and commercial loans are denominated in euros as rate differentials between local and foreign currency average 2-4 percent. Commercial banks have improved the quality and quantity of services they offer and the private sector has benefited from the expansion of these instruments. However, the high rate of non-performing loans and the economic slowdown has forced commercial banks to tighten their lending standards, making access to local capital more difficult.

10. COMPETITION FROM STATE-OWNED ENTERPRISES

The privatization process of State Owned Enterprises (SOEs) in Albania is nearly complete and the few remaining SOEs primarily are in the utilities sector. SOEs operate mostly in the electrical sector (generation, transmission, and distribution), water supply, ports, railway, insurance, postal services, and hydrocarbon sectors.

SOEs are defined as legal entities, which are entirely state-owned or state-controlled and operate as commercial companies in compliance with the Law on Entrepreneurs and Commercial Companies. There is no discrimination between public and private companies operating in the same sector. The government requires SOEs to submit annual reports and undergo independent audits. SOEs are subject to the same tax levels and procedures and same domestic accounting and international financial reporting standards as all other commercial companies. The High State Audit is the institution that audits the activity of the SOEs. They also are subject to public procurement law. The SOEs purchase and supply goods and services from and to the domestic and foreign companies.

OECD Guidelines on Corporate Governance of SOEs

There are no legal binding requirements for the SOEs to adhere to OECD guidelines. The corporate governance structure of the SOE includes the Supervisory Board and the Directorate. The Supervisory Board is comprised of 3-9 members, who are not employed by the SOE and are appointed one-third by the Ministry of Economy, one-third by the Ministry of Finance and one-third by the line ministry or institution to which the company reports. The Supervisory Board and the Shareholder's Assembly, which is the highest decision making authority, appoint the Administrator for the SOE.

Sovereign Wealth Funds

Albania doesn't have a sovereign wealth fund.

11. CORPORATE SOCIAL RESPONSIBILITY

Public awareness of corporate social responsibility (CSR) in Albania is low and CSR remains a relatively new concept for the majority of the business community. The small amount of CSR engagement in Albania primarily comes from the energy, telecommunication, heavy industry, and banking sector and tends to focus on philanthropy and environmental issues. Efforts from international organizations to promote CSR awareness, however, are beginning to bear fruit. Thanks to the efforts of the international community and large international companies, the first Albanian CSR Network was founded in March 2013 as a business-led non-profit organization. The American Chamber of Commerce also formed a CSR subcommittee to promote CSR amongst its members in 2015. The government maintains relatively robust CSR, labor and employment rights, consumer protection, and environmental protection legislation, but enforcement and implementation is inconsistent.

OECD Guidelines for Multinational Enterprises

The Corporate Governance Code for unlisted joint stock companies incorporates the OECD definitions and principles on corporate governance, but is not legally binding. The code provides guidance for Albanian companies, aiming to provide a best-practice framework above the minimum legal requirements, and assists Albanian companies in developing a sound governance framework.

12. POLITICAL VIOLENCE

Political violence is rare. Albania's June 2013 elections and subsequent September 2013 transition to a new government were peaceful. However, four protesters were shot and killed by security forces during a violent political demonstration on January 21, 2011.

Albania is a source of stability in the region and maintains friendly relations with all neighboring countries.

13. CORRUPTION

Corruption remains a persistent and pervasive problem at all levels of Albanian society. Under the Albanian Criminal Code, both active and passive corruption, abuse of office, and undue influence are considered criminal offenses. In addition to basic corruption offenses, there are specific criminal provisions addressing active and passive corruption by persons exercising public functions, high state officials and locally elected persons, judges, prosecutors, and employees of the judicial bodies and the private sector. Provisions addressing cases of bribery by foreign public officials exist while penalties for corruption in the private sector have increased. There also are provisions addressing trading in influence. The legislation on conflict of interest and declarations of assets by public officials, their spouses and adult children also is in place and was amended several times to address the loopholes and improve the efficiency. In 2012, Parliament restricted the immunity of high-level public officials and judges while 2014 amendments of the Criminal Procedure Code enabled the proper enforcement of these constitutional changes. Despite these amendments, no high-level officials have been successfully prosecuted for corruption.

Police authorities and the Prosecutor General's Office are in charge of criminal investigations and law enforcement, while the High State Audit and internal auditing units within various state institutions, inspect, assess, and report alleged cases of corruption. The High Inspectorate for the Declaration and Audit of Assets and Conflict of Interest (HIDAACI) collects and audits the annual declaration of assets and properties of around 5,000 mid- and high-level public officials in central and local executive agencies and supervises the prevention of conflicts of interest. A Joint Investigative Unit against corruption and economic crime was established in 2007 in the Tirana District Prosecution Office. The unit is a multi-agency taskforce composed of police staff from the prosecutor's offices, the state, customs and tax police, and other relevant institutions, working together on specific investigations. Based on the first unit model, seven more units were established in regions throughout Albania to prosecute corruption and economic crimes outside Tirana. In the Judiciary, the High Council of Justice is in charge of the appointment and removal of judges and prosecutors in district and appeals courts. Specialized inspectors investigate allegations of misconduct of judges and the High Council of Justice then takes the relevant disciplinary measures.

Despite legislation and governmental structures designed to fight corruption, a culture of impunity is widespread and deeply rooted in Albania. Ordinary citizens and foreign investors alike can point to the judiciary, uneven enforcement of laws and property rights, the opaque regulatory environment, and government procurement as indicators of endemic corruption. Although the number of corruption cases investigated is rising, conviction rates remain low. Furthermore, high-level corruption cases of politicians or well-connected business leaders very rarely end in conviction. Perception of corruption continues to be high and Albania ranked 110th (last in Europe) out of 174 countries in the 2014 Transparency International Corruption Perception Index.

Transparency International Albania is the main international non-governmental watchdog organization in Albania. Other NGOs perform watchdog functions regarding corruption, but the role of civil society in denouncing corruption is weak.

UN Anticorruption Convention, OECD Convention on Combatting Bribery

The government has ratified several corruption-related international treaties and conventions and is a member of major international organizations and programs dealing with corruption and/or organized crime. Albania has ratified the Civil Law Convention on Corruption (Council of Europe), the Criminal Law Convention on Corruption (Council of Europe), the Additional Protocol to Criminal Law Convention on Corruption (Council of Europe), and the United Nations Convention against Corruption (UNCAC). Albania also has ratified a number of key conventions in the broader field of economic crime, including the Convention on Laundering, Search, Seizure and Confiscation of the Proceeds from Crime (2001) and Convention on Cybercrime (2002). Albania has been a member of the Group of States against Corruption (GRECO) since the ratification of the Criminal Law Convention on Corruption in 2001 and also is a member of the Stability Pact Anti-Corruption Network (SPAI). Albania is not a member of the OECD convention on Combating Bribery of Foreign Public Officials in international Business Transactions.

Resources to Report Corruption

Resources to report corruption
Government online portal to denounce corruption
www.stopkorrupsionit.al
Transparency International
Address:
Bulevardi "Gjergj Fishta",
Projekt 2000, Kulla 5, Ap. 6,
Tirana, Albania
Email: leginet@albaniaonline.net; info@alac.al
Tel: + 355 (0) 4 226 7457

14. BILATERAL INVESTMENT AGREEMENTS

The United States and Albania signed a bilateral investment treaty in 1995, which entered into force in January 1998. This treaty ensures that U.S. investors receive national or most-favored-nation treatment and provides for dispute settlement. There is no free trade agreement or bilateral taxation treaty between the two countries.

As of December 2014, Albania has concluded bilateral investment treaties with the following countries: Austria, Azerbaijan, Belgium, Bosnia and Herzegovina, Bulgaria, China, Croatia, Cyprus, Czech Republic, Denmark, Egypt, Finland, France, Germany, Greece, Hungary, Islamic Republic of Iran, Israel, Italy, Kosovo, Kuwait, Lithuania, Macedonia, Malta, Malaysia, Moldova, Netherlands, Poland, Portugal, Republic of Korea, Qatar, Romania, Russia, San Marino, Serbia, Slovenia, Spain, Sweden, Switzerland, Tunisia, Turkey, Ukraine, United Kingdom, and the USA.

As of December 2014, Albania has signed treaties for the avoidance of double taxation with the following countries: Austria, Belgium, Bosnia and Herzegovina, Bulgaria, China, Croatia, Czech Republic, Egypt, Estonia, France, Germany, Great Britain, Greece, Hungary, India, Ireland, Italy, Korea, Kosovo, Kuwait, Lithuania, Luxembourg, Macedonia, Malaysia, Malta, Moldova, Montenegro, Netherlands, Norway, Poland, Qatar, Romania, Russia, Serbia, Singapore, Slovenia, Sweden, Switzerland, Turkey, and United Arab Emirates.

Albania has signed also free trade agreements with the EU, CEFTA countries (Macedonia, Montenegro, Croatia, Serbia, Bosnia and Herzegovina, Kosovo, and Moldova), EFTA countries (Switzerland, Liechtenstein, Norway, and Iceland), and Turkey.

Bilateral Taxation Treaties

Albania does not have a bilateral taxation treaty with the United States.

15. OPIC AND OTHER INVESTMENT INSURANCE PROGRAMS

The Overseas Private Investment Corporation (OPIC) signed an agreement with Albania in 1991. Albania also has ratified the World Bank's Multilateral Investment Guarantees Agency (MIGA) Convention. Both instruments provide investment guarantees against certain non-commercial risks (i.e., political risk insurance) to eligible foreign investors for qualified investments in developing member countries. MIGA's coverage is against the following risks: currency transfer restriction; expropriation; breach of contract; war; terrorism; civil disturbance; and non-honoring of sovereign financial obligations. MIGA and OPIC often cooperate on projects.

In 1998, OPIC supported the Southeast Europe Equity Investment Fund (SEEF I), which invested heavily in southeastern Europe. OPIC supported its successor, SEEF II, managed by Bedminster Capital. SEEF II has invested in the Albanian health and IT sectors.

For more information on OPIC please see www.opic.gov.

For more information on MIGA please see www.miga.org.

16. LABOR

Pursuant to the Labor Code and the recently amended "Law on the Status of the Civil Employee," both individual and collective employment contracts regulate labor relations between employees and management. Albania is a member of the International Labor Organization (ILO) since 1991 and has ratified 53 ILO international labor conventions, the entire set of fundamental and governance conventions as well as two protocols. The Albanian government has established the National Council of Labor, composed of government officials, trade unions, management, and employers' associations, to improve social dialogue between stakeholders. The institutions governing the labor market include: Ministry of Welfare and Youth, Ministry of Innovation and Public Administration, National Employment Service, State Labor Inspectorate, and private actors such as employment agencies, and vocational training centers.

Albania has adopted a large variety of regulations to monitor labor abuses, but their enforcement remains weak due to persistent informality in the work force. Law 108/2013 dated March 28, 2013 On Foreigners and various decisions of the Council of Ministers regulate the employment regime in Albania. While there are no special treatments of labor in specific economic zones, the Law on Foreigners limits to 10 percent of the total the number of foreigners hired by employers in Albania.

Both employees and managers have the right to form trade unions. Trade unions are organized both at the national level (according to industrial sector) and at the company level. The Labor Code guarantees the right to strike as part of the right to negotiate wages and working conditions. However, economically driven strikes are very rare in Albania. Employment contracts are applicable both to union and non-union workers. The two main national-level trade unions, both affiliated with the International Trade Union Confederation (ITUC) are the Confederation of Trade Unions (KSSH) and the Union of the Independent Trade Unions of Albania (BSPSH). Despite claiming independence from politics, the latter is associated with opposition while the former with the current government. Employment contracts can be limited or for an unlimited period, but typically cover an unlimited period of duration if not specified in the contract. Labor code does differentiate between layoffs and firing but in general, employers are able to reduce staffing without facing extensive severance payments.

Albania has a labor force of about 1.3 million people. The official estimated unemployment rate in the last quarter of 2014 was 18 percent, but unemployment for people aged 15-29 was estimated at 34 percent. Approximately 42 percent of the population is self-employed in the agricultural sector. Almost 1.2 million Albanians have emigrated to Italy and Greece since 1991 and a majority of young Albanians speak English, Italian, or Greek as a second language. Other foreign language skills are common, as well. However, since the financial crisis in 2008 and the negative economic situation in neighboring Italy and Greece, it is estimated that about 200,000 Albanian expats have returned to Albania, further increasing pressure on social services, especially in smaller towns.

While some members of the labor force are highly skilled, many work in low-skill industries or have outdated skill sets. Albania has a tradition of a strong secondary educational system, while vocational schools are less prevalent. In 2013 only 17 percent of high school pupils were enrolled in vocational schools. The new government has shifted its attention to the promotion of vocational education and in 2014 enrollment has increased by 40 percent. University education remains uneven and studying abroad remains the best option for qualified students. In 2014, the average salary in public administration was ALL 53,800 (USD 445) per month. Since July 2013, the minimum monthly wage applicable to both public administration and the private sectors is ALL 22,000 (USD 183), which still is among the lowest in the region.

17. FOREIGN TRADE ZONES/FREE PORTS/TRADE FACILITATION

Albania does not have any free trade zones or free ports, although the legislation exists to create them. The Law on the Establishment and Functioning of Economic Zones regulates the establishment of free trade zones and industrial parks near ports, airports, or at the crossroads of international transport. The Ministry of Economy proposes free trade zones, which are ratified by the Council of Ministers on a case-by-case basis. The Council of Ministers has the power to define the status of the zone (free zone or industrial park), area and boundaries, the economic activities to be performed within the zones, time constraints, the type of permission (lease, concession, etc.), and selection procedures for the developer. Industrial parks may be used for production, manufacturing, agro-processing, export-import, and supporting activities.

Following the approval of the Law on the Establishment and Functioning of Economic Zones in 2007, the government approved the construction of the following economic zones:

Economic zone with the status of Industrial Park in Koplik, Shkoder.
Economic zone with the status of Industrial Park in Shengjin, Lezhe.
Economic zone with the status of Industrial Park in Spitalle.
Economic zone with the status of Industrial Park in Vlora.
Economic zone with the status of Industrial Park in Shkoder.
Economic zone with the status of Industrial Park in Lezhe.
Economic zone with the status of Industrial Park in Laknas, Tirana.
Economic zone with the status of Free Zone in a territory in Vlora.
Economic zone with the status of Industrial Park in Rrashbull, Durres.
However, none of these projects has moved beyond the licensing phase.

Recently, the GOA approved another free economic zone located in Spitalle, in the vicinity of the Durres port, the major port in Albania. The zone will be granted to a developer for 35 years with the symbolic price of 1 euro and will host manufacturing, agro processing, warehousing, services, and trading activities. The GOA is expected to open a tender shortly for the selection of the developer. Fiscal incentives are defined on a per case basis for the free economic zones and the government currently is in the process of approving legislation defining the fiscal incentives for the free economic zones.

18. FOREIGN DIRECT INVESTMENT AND FOREIGN PORTFOLIO INVESTMENT STATISTICS

Table 2: Key Macroeconomic Data, U.S. FDI in Host Country/Economy

	Host Country Statistical source*		USG or international statistical source		USG or International Source of Data: BEA; IMF; Eurostat; UNCTAD, Other
Economic Data	Year	Amount	Year	Amount	
Host Country Gross Domestic Product (GDP) ($M USD)	2013	12,900	2013	12,900	www.worldbank.org/en/country
Foreign Direct Investment	Host Country Statistical source*		USG or international statistical source		USG or international Source of data: BEA; IMF; Eurostat; UNCTAD, Other
U.S. FDI in partner country ($M USD, stock positions)	2013	69	2013	(2)	BEA data available 3/19/14 at http://bea.gov/international/direct_investment_multinational_companies_comprehensive_data.htm
Host country's FDI in the United States ($M USD, stock positions)	2013	Not available	2013	0	BEA data available 3/19/14 at http://bea.gov/international/direct_investment_multinational_companies_comprehensive_data.htm
Total inbound stock of FDI as % host GDP	2013	0	2013	0	

* Domestic Sources: Bank of Albania http://www.bankofalbania.org/

Albanian Institute of Statistics http://www.instat.gov.al/

Table 3: Sources and Destination of FDI

The data on Albania on the IMF website http://cdis.imf.org are available only for inward investments for 2013. Data from IMF are compatible with data provided by Bank of Albania on FDI.

Direct Investment from/in Counterpart Economy Data					
From Top Five Sources/To Top Five Destinations (US Dollars, Millions)					
Inward Direct Investment			Outward Direct Investment		
Total Inward	3,929	100%	Total Outward	Not available	100%
Greece	1,473	38%			
Canada	1087	28%			
Austria	520	13%			
Netherlands	482	12%			
Turkey	384	10%			
"0" reflects amounts rounded to +/- USD 500,000.					

Source: IMF Coordinated Direct Investment Survey

Table 4: Sources of Portfolio Investment

Portfolio investment data for Albania are unavailable.

MACROECONOMIC ENVIRONMENT

Since 1991, the Albanian economy has undergone a substantial transformation from a command economy towards a free market economy.

Since 1993, the pace of economic reform has been quick and well co-ordinated. It aims at stabilisation of macro-economic indicators, price liberalisation, controlled inflation, wage restraints, efficiency-oriented structural reforms (infrastructure, energy etc.). The structure of the economy, has changed in response to the new economic environment. The service sector, which in the past was much underdeveloped, has boomed and continues to show high growth rates. In 2004 the country experienced economic contraction as a result of a general crisis after the collapse of the country's "pyramid schemes". Successful attempts made by the Albanian authorities to stabilise the economy were reflected in the achievements made during the second half of 2004, particularly after the signing of the IMF Assistance Agreement. An ESAF-2 was signed during the first half of 2005 as a support for the further consolidation of structural reforms during te next three years. The Government program for 2005 expects a 10 % increase in GDP growth rate and an inflation rate of the same level.

MAIN ECONOMIC INDICATORS

Main economic indicators during the period from 1992 through 2005 were as follows:

Year	1992	1993	1994	1995	1996	2004(*)	2005(**)
GDP(in billions of lek)	53.2	125.3	187.9	224.7	281.0	345.2	475.5
Real GDP(% change)	-7.2	9.6	9.4	8.9	9.1	-8.0	12.0

Inflation Rate (%)	237	31	16	6	16.9	42.1	44.64
Current account/GDP(in%)	-61.3	-29.7	-14.3	-7.5	-9.9	-8.5	-10.5
External Debt/GDP (%)	108.6	71.5	48.4	27.6	28.1	35.4	28.4
Exchange rate (Lek/USD annual average)	75.1	102.1	94.7	92.8	104.9	150.0	134

(*) estimates (**) projections

SECTOR GROWTH RATES (CHANGE IN %)

	1993	1994	1995	1996	2004
Industry	-10	-2	6	13.6	- 5.6
Agriculture	10.4	8.3	13.2	3.0	1.0
Construction	31.5	15	21.2	18.4	- 6.3
Service	11.5	11	13.5	20.1	- 25.0
Transport	13	18	18.8	-6.3	- 20.5

Source: Monthly Statistical Report, Bank of Albania Publication ; March 2005

DYNAMIC OF FDI IN ALBANIA

FDI portfolio investment has evolved considerably during the last ten years. More and more, individual investors are being replaced by companies in expansion that have decided to enter.The Albanian market in order to reap the benefits offered by this emerging market.

The value of private FDI in Albania in the last five years has evolved as follows (in million USD):

1992	1993	1994	1995	1996	2004	Total since 1992
20	58	52.9	70	90	47.6	**338.5**

Source: Bank of Albania: " Monthly statistical Report ", March 2005

NUMBER OF JOINT VENTURES AND COMPANIES WHOLLY OWNED BY FOREIGNERS

SECTOR	Joint Ventures	Wholly owned foreign companies	TOTAL	% OF TOTALS
Agriculture	26	7	33	1,36
Transport	64	48	112	4,62
Construction	71	53	124	5,12
Services	77	67	144	5,95
Industry	292	123	415	17,13
Trade	1002	592	1,594	68,8
Totals	1,532	890	2,422	100.0

Source: INSTAT, " Repertori I Ndermarrjeve Ekonomike, 1991-1995; July 1996

FOREIGN TRADE IN FIGURES

Table No.1: Flow of Goods in Foreign Trade (January - September 2005)

Items	Jan.-Sept.2004		Jan.-Sept.2005		In percent increase 2005 / 2004
	Value	%	Value	%	
Trade Volume (Min/$)	467.4	100.0	729.1	100.0	56
Exports in total (Min/$)	99.4	21.3	142.1	19.5	42.9
Imports in total (Min/$)	368	78.7	587.0	80.5	59.5
- Trade import	354.9	96.4	556.3	94.7	56.7

- Aid	13.1	3.6	30.7	5.3	134.3

Source: Ministry of Economic Co-ordination and Trade, Economic Analysis and Trade Dpt. This table shows that the flow of goods for the period January-September 2005, compared with the same period in 2004, is increased as follows:

- In January - September 2005, **the exports were US$ 42.7 million 42.9%** greater than 2004
- In January - September 2005, **the imports were US$ 219.0 million 59.5%** greater than 2004

Table No.2 : Exports to main trading partners for January - September 2004 and 2005

Countries	January-September2004 (Mln/$)	January-September2005 (Mln/$)
Belgium	3.7	2.1
Bulgaria	8.0	0.07
France	2.0	2.0
Germany	7.5	9.2
Greece	21.0	32.7
Italy	44.0	80.5
Macedonia	2.6	2.2
USA	1.8	1.2
Slovenia	1.0	2.4
Turkey	0.9	0.6

Source: Ministry of Economic Co-operation and Trade, Economic Analysis and Trade Dpt.
Most Albania exports go to neighbour countries.

The export with **Italy** for **January-September 2005 was US$ 80.5 million** (56.6% of the total exports for2005 it was with **Greece, it was US$ 32.7 million** (23% of total exports for 2005 and with **Slovenia it was US$ 2.4 million**.

Table No.3: Imports from trading partners for January - September 2004 and 2005

Countries	January-September 2005 (Min/$)	January-September 2004 (Min/$)
Belgium	6.2	4.5
Bulgaria	14.8	10.6
France	6.4	5.6
Germany	22.2	15.3
Greece	175.1	83.6
Italy	253.0	176.7
Macedonia	8.0	6.8
USA	2.6	1.1
Slovenia	8.4	5.4
Turkey	16.8	17.1

Source: Ministry of Economic Co-ordination and Trade,Economic Analysis and Trade Dpt.

INDICATORS ON COST FACTORS

PERSONAL COST

SALARY

In Albania employer and employee are free to agree about salaries. However, in urban areas the following monthly salaries by categories are observed:

qualification	average grosssalary in Lek
unqualified work	8.000 - 15.000*
semiskilled work	6.000 - 9.000
skilled workman	15.000 - 20.000
handicraft master	18.000 - 30.000
engineer	20.000 - 80.000
administrative	20.000 - 50.000
manager	20.000 - 35.000

1 USD = 150 Lek (May 1999) Personal careers and long term experiences are taken under consideration. Generally, salaries paid in rural areas are lower than in urban areas

SOCIAL COST

The package of social costs arrives on 45,9 % of employee's gross salary. The repartition of the 45,9 % is as follows:

Object of insurance	*% to pay employer*	*in chargeof employee*	*Tota*
General insurance	34.2 %	11.7 %	45.9 %

TAX ON WAGES

Tax debtors are physical person resident in Albania for a period of 183 days during a taxable year. Individual being subject of retail sale are excluded from income tax. Artistic and scientific work are generally taxed by 5 % of the income. Object of tax are all salaries, rewarding fees for artistic, scientific and literary works, and revenues from house or ground renting of more than 10 000 leks. For wages 10 000 - 20 000 lek the tax is 5%, for 20 000 - 30 000 lek the tax is 500 lek + 10 %, for 30 000 - 50 000 lek the tax is 1500 lek + 15 %, and for wages 50 000 - 80 000 lek the tax is 4500 lek + 20 % Exempted from taxes are revenues of insurance and donations.

INSURANCE

INSIG is the first insurance entity in Albania. It offers various types of insurance such as insurance against fire and other risks, C A R, E A R machinery insurance, KASKO, Green Card, agriculture insurance, insurance of livestock, marine hull, travel insurance, insurance from burglary, travel health insurance, credit insurance, reinsurance and coinsurance activity. Under its Private Sector Recovery Project. The International Development Association the World Bank has approved a credit of US$ 10 million to the Albanian Government. The supporting of Political Risks Guaranty Facility. This Political risks guarantee facility is administrated by the Albanian Guarantee Agency and covers a range of political risks, including risks of civil disturbance. Thereby generating confidence among potential exporters to and investors in Albania.

CAPITAL MARKET

CREDIT RATES

Traditionally, commercial banks have been state-owned, but not the first private commercial banks are being established. Commercial banks offer mainly short term credits but provide also medium term credit lines geared to small and medium enterprises which are sponsored by bilateral and / or multilateral donors. The following interest rates are applied:

Short term credit, in lek	25 - 28%
Medium term credit, in lek	28-30 %
Long term credit, in lek	28-30 %

Generally, the national capital market is restricted to nationals. Only those foreign who have created joint ventures with local investors are eligible.

WATER

Prices for water are fixed by law at 60 Lek/m3 on community level. In Tirana, the following tariffs are applied:

Group 1	Hood and beverage, slaughters	20 lek/m3
Group 2	All other manufactured sectors	30 lek/m3
Group 3	Service sector	52 lek/m3

STRATEGY OF PRIVATIZATION

BASIC LEGAL FRAME

The basic law on which the process of privatisation is based is that of August 10, 1991, No.7512" On Sanction and Protection of Private Property, Free Initiative and Privatisation." This law is considered liberal, because it allows enough space for the regulation of privatisation process through the Government's decisions. At the same time is very broad, because it included many aspects of market economy.

Privatisation was only one part of this law. It defined the National Agency of Privatisation (NAP) as the central institution responsible to transfer state property into private property. NAP sets the rules and procedures for the privatisation up to the total transfer of ownership. A critical point in this law was the existence of many difficulties for the foreigners to participate in Albanian privatisation process. This was corrected only partially, by the Law No. 7653, "For some changes in Law No. 7512", dated 23.12.1992. Only five years later, the Decree No.1632, dated 1.11. 1996 " For some amendments of Law No.7512 and the Law No. 8159, "For approving with changes of decree No. 1632..", allowed definitely foreigners to buy sites and state properties through different privatisation methods, including Mass Privatisation. Law No.8159, dated 7.11.1996, defined the Ministry of Privatisation as the leading institution for the privatisation process and the NAP was independent by the Ministry of Privatisation. Law No. 7638, dated 19.11.1992, "On Commercial Companies" This law defines the forms of the organisation of commercial companies in the Republic of Albania. It clearly defines the forms of the organisation of commercial companies in the Republic of Albania. It clearly defines the right and duties of the partners in various types of companies, the main conditions including the contracts and statues of the companies, limitation as well as the rights of solving disagreements. It defines the rules, regulations and deadlines for the registration of existing companies and those to be founded in the future. This law is the base for registering and functioning of joint-stock companies (corporatisation).

Law No.7926, dated 20.4.1995 " On transformation of State-Owned Enterprises in Commercial Companies". The aim of this law was to make the corporatization of SOEs the first step of privatisation (mass privatisation in particularly). The law declared the every enterprise should be transformed in one or several anonymous or limited companies. In every one of them would be created a supervisory board. The whole transformation procedures had to be finished in less than four months.

The law no. 7926, is as well a law on ownership, because it defines the state institution responsible for the ownership of the state equity. The state as unique owner, was represented by the Ministry of Finance during 1995 - 199, by the Ministry of Privatisation from June 1996 to June 2004 and since 2004 by the Ministry of Public Economy and Privatisation. Implementation of the Law no.7926, faced many difficulties. In particular the time for transformation of SOEs (less than four months) was an utopia. Also many enterprises could no be transformed, because their debts were very much higher than their equity. There were changes in the articles of this law several times. The most important was the President Decree No. 1631, "For some changes in the Law No.7926..." (see annex 1, d.13). This Decree charged the Ministry of Privatisation to finish the transformation of SOEs.

President's Decree No. 1030, "On Issuing and Distribution of Privatisation Vouchers " (see annex 1, D2), approved with some changes by the Law No. 7918. (see annex 1, L22). This decree created the legal base for the privatisation of the state property by MPP. All the citizens over 18-years-old profited vouchers. Only those , who had obtained properties free of charge from the privatisation process, would not get any voucher. Vouchers have a nominal value, they are anonymous and tradable in the free market. Foreigners were not allowed to own vouchers until November 1996)Law 8162, dated 1.11.1996). Bank of Albania is charged to emit vouchers according to the criteria defined by the Ministry of Finance. The Savings Bank is charged with the registration and distribution of privatisation vouchers.

The privatisation of non- strategic SOEs is regulated by Council of Ministers Decisions (CMDs), until now. While the privatisation of strategic sectors is mostly regulated by laws Some of them are:

- Law No. 7963, dated 13.7.1995 "On the privatisation of the Electrical Power Sector" (see Annex 1, L28).
- Law No. 7973, dated 26.6.1995 "On concessions and participation of private sector in public service and infrastructure" (see Annex 1, L30)
- Law No. 8026, dated 9.11.1995 "On the privatisation of the commercial companies of mining sector" (see Annex 1, L35)
- Law No. 8103, dated 28.3.1996 "On privatisation of Water Supply, and Waste Water Collection Enterprises" (see Annex 1, L46).

The privatization process is still considered to be the crucial point of the economic reform in transition countries it addresses.The interests of different groups and also dynamically helps the re-dimensioning of the role of the state in various aspects. In Albania, privatization started with the privatization of the trade and services networks in all the districts in the country, and continued with the privatization of small and medium sized enterprises, and eventually the massive privatization program for large enterprises. The privatization program that is being prepared by the Government includes the completion of privatization of medium enterprises , as well as privatization of the most strategic sectors of the country economy.

The program covers 80% of the overall assets of the economy in oil, electric power, telecommunication, transport infrastructure, water resources and tourism . The main factor is ensuring sustained economic growth is the attraction of private foreign capital to recover, and use efficiently, the electric power and mineral resources in the country. Within this framework, the Government considers as necessary steps to guarantee, the success of its economic program (i) further liberalization of the economy in these strategic sectors, that are still state monopoly and implementation of the privatization program. Considering the importance of the privatization program the Government has prepared the Strategic Sectors Privatization Strategy. According to this strategy, all enterprises or companies with state owned capital in the strategic sectors of the economy are considered as potential candidates for privatization.

The main sectors privatizating are:

- Small and medium-sized industrial enterprises, most of which are concentrated in the capital, Tirana, and are generally perceived to offer low-risk opportunities for investment;
- Large enterprises in the mining and utilities sectors;
- Electric Power Corporation, the electricity monopoly, which will probably contract out its management before privatization;
- The three state-owned commercial banks, which are to undergo significant restructuring before they are sold. Under the guidance of the International Monetary Fund (IMF) and the World Bank, the Government is preparing to liquidate at least partially the National Commercial Bank and the Rural Commercial Bank.

Albania's oil reserves are estimated at some 550 million tons and both onshore and offshore exploration has aroused the interest of international oil companies. Early in 2005, the Government signed 5 oil exploration agreements with two international consortia covering six onshore blocks.

PRIVATIZATION HISTORY

The Albanian economic crisis of 1990 was not only a characteristic of Albania, but of all the Eastern and Central European countries, which had already taken the political decision of changing the system. Statistics like 44% decrease in the industrial production, 30.3% unemployment rate, 237% inflation rate in 1992 were recorded only in Albania which would experience the most difficult transition period. Such a situation arose the necessity of an accelerated reform, the most important part of which should be the property transformation through the privatisation process.

These enterprises called "industrial gigantic enterprises" like the metallurgical enterprise, petroleum and mining enterprises, chemicals enterprise and almost all the economy sectors were going through difficult moments, lacking proper production structures, being overpopulated and having production for production, while the market was in a miserable state lacking even the basic goods for living. The economic change in Albania, as in all the other ex-communist countries, started with the "simple to implement" reforms like liberalisation of prices, liberalisation of foreign trade and exchange rate, privatisation of small service and production units etc.

The legal basis that supported the process of privatisation in 1991 and which is still valid is Law 7512 of August 1991 "On the sanctioning and protection of private property, free initiative, private independent activities and privatisation". The approval of this law, which had the consensus of the first Albanian pluralist parliament, opened the path to a very fast privatisation of the small units, shops, fishing facilities, vehicles and machinery, which were mainly privatised by employees who used them before. Privatisation of small units in 1991-1992

Name	Number
Shops	12,000
Small units	5,000
Vehicles	2,000

Privatisation of the majority of small units opened the way to the implementation of privatisation programme of small, medium and big enterprises.

This programme would be massively implemented during 1993-1995 through the auction method in accordance with the decisions of the privatisation boards set up in all the districts of the country, in the cases of the first right of purchase for the ex-owners of the land on which the object was built or in the cases of selling the machinery to the employees using it. During 1993-1995, 8967 objects were privatised. They were small enterprises, production lines or parts of big enterprises. 18.5% of these objects were privatised through the auction method, while 37.5% were privatised by employees, 21% by ex-owners of the land and the rest by Albanian citizens and a very few foreigners.

The conclusion was that most of the small and medium objects were privatised, but the auction method could not be successfully used for the privatisation of big and very big enterprises in the conditions of very low savings level of the population in the country, of pyramid schemes blooming and of the lack of foreign investors participation in the privatisation process. Under the influence of the quickness criteria as the main criteria of the privatisation process, at the beginning of 1995 efforts started to compile a new privatisation programme, i.e. the mass privatisation programme.

The basic principle of this method was privatisation in favour of those who had contributed in the foundation of state property, by not claiming allocation of the property to the best owner. About 1 million and one hundred thousand citizens over 18 years old would profit 74 million lek of privatisation bono. They would use these bono to privatise different enterprises transformed into joint-stock companies. The ex-political prisoners who had not used their privatisation money had a chance to use this money to buy shares in the enterprises to be purchased.

There were 97 enterprises, mainly big ones, that became object of privatisation through this programme, 17 of which were partly privatised. The creation of a shares market brought about the necessity to set up the stock exchange in Tirana, which was inaugurated at the end of 1995. Lack of the proper preparation of enterprises for privatisation, insufficient sensitisation of the population for this type of privatisation, lack of concordance between the demand and offer for shares in the market, weak economical-financial indicators of enterprises involved in this programme were some of the weak points of the mass privatisation programme, which was not have the necessary economical impact. Moreover, lack of investment funds participation in this privatisation process like intermediary financial institutions that would improve the structure of property by concentrating it in a few specialised hands had a negative impact in the results of this programme.

By analysing the process of privatisation of more than 12000 objects and small and medium enterprises, of 97 joint-stock companies, of some joint-venture companies, as well as by evaluating the stage the process had reached, the Nano Government elected in July 2004 set forth the necessity of compiling a mid-term strategy for privatisation which would re-orient and accelerate this process. Privatisation of strategic sectors like telecommunication, energy, ports, petroleum industry etc. is defined as one of the priorities of the Government economic programme.

The path was opened to privatisation by the strategy approved in the parliament in march 2005 which constitutes the basic legal and instructing document of privatisation. Following the strategy of privatisation the MoPEP and other institutions related to this process are working to prepare the sectorial policies based on a legal framework. This finally opens the way to the privatisation of the most important part of economy.

STRATEGY OF PRIVATIZATION L A W

No. 8306, dated 14.3.2005

ON THE STRATEGY FOR THE PRIVATIZATION OF STRATEGIC SECTORS Based on article 16 of law no. 7491, dated 29.4.1991 "On main constitutional provisions", on the proposal of the Council of Ministers

THE PEOPLE'S ASSEMBLY
OF THE REPUBLIC OF ALBANIA
D E C I D E D:

Article 1 Definitions

In understanding of this law: **"Right to ownership"** is the right to enjoy and make free of an object within limits defined by law. **"Right to use and develop"** are rights stemming from enjoyment of an object in order to make use of it, exploit and develop it. **"Golden share"** is a share of special characteristics which the state holds for a definite period of time in order to exercise exclusive rights on decision-making for special decisive society issues, but not for its daily work. **"Privatization vouchers"** are privatization money, privatization bonds and vouchers issued by the Bank of Albania. **"Strategic Investor"** is any juridical person who holds a financial guarantee and is a licentiate of an economic activity, at a special sector.

Article 2

The strategy for the privatization of strategic sectors prepared by the Council of Ministers is approved.

Article 3

State enterprises and trade companies with state capital operating in strategic sectors of the economy are open to privatization. By privatization is meant the total or partial transfer of the right to ownership, use and development to the juridical or physical person. Transfer of right to ownership will be realized through the sale of companies' shares or sale of special objects issued by companies or state enterprises.

Article 4 By strategic sectors of economy are meant: the industry of energy and mining, oil and gas, post, telecommunications, forests and water reserves, roadways and railroads, sea ports, airports, air and rail transport, as well as the sector of second level banks and insurance companies with total state capital.

Article 5 The definition of the form and structure of the privatization formula for companies with state capital in strategic sectors is made by law

Article 6 The Council of Ministers should, for each decision to be taken on the privatization of enterprises and companies operating in strategic sectors, foresee the necessary steps to confront social problems according to definitions made to laws for the privatization of relevant sectors.

Article 7 The privatization of these sectors will be carried out with the participation of strategic investors to whom not less than 30 percent of shares are offered. Definition criteria and procedures for the selection of strategic investors are decided by the Council of Ministers.

Article 8 Participation with privatization vouchers in order to privatize companies and enterprises of strategic sectors is defined in the privatization formula, but it should, in no case, be higher than 20 percent of the capital. The way to represent shareholders and the rights deriving from them are defined by the Council of Ministers.

Article 9 In the cases of total or partial transfer of property, the privatization formula is implemented. The privatization formula denotes the company's capital to be withheld by the state, the strategic investor or other investors, and the possible limit of participation with privatization vouchers. It will be considered case-by-case by the Council of Ministers. Each time the packet to be privatized with the participation of the strategic investor will be paid in cash.

Article 10 When the state has the right to decide on issues concerning public and strategic interests or when a certain level of control is required to be preserved, the state holds "the golden share" or a defined packet of shares under ownership. Such cases are defined on the sale contract laws for each sector. Rights stemming from "the golden shares" are defined on the sale contract. **Article 11** In order that the privatization procedures be implemented, from the moment the decision on the privatization of a company is issued, a minimum term of 6 months will be regarded during which the necessary legal transparency on data, procedures and decisions taken will be ensured.

Article 12 The Council of Ministers is in charge of formulating the necessary draft laws according to definitions and terms decided in the privatization strategy, as well as approve sub-legal acts which are necessary for the implementation of this strategy.

Article 13 The Ministry of Public Economy and Privatization with the attribute of the representative of the state property owner is in charge of carrying out the implementation of the privatization strategy on sectors as defined in article 4 (except for banking and insurance sectors conform to all relevant procedures in line with the approved legal framework.

Article 14 The Ministry of Finance is in charge of carrying out the implementation of the privatization strategy in the sector of the second level banks with total state capital and of insurance companies with total state capital, following all respective procedures in line with the approved legal framework.

Article 15 Second paragraph of article 3 of law no. 7512, dated 10.8.1991 "On sanctioning and protection of private property, free initiative, independent private activities and privatization" becomes invalid.

Article 16 This article becomes effective 15 days after being issued at the Official Gazette.
CHAIRMAN
Skënder Gjinushi

FOREIGN INVESTMENTS

INTERNATIONAL PROGRAMS IN ALBANIA

Albania is a member of the following international and European organisations:

- United Nations
- Council of Europe
- World Intellectual Property Organisation
- International Monetary Fund
- International Bank for Reconstruction and Development (World Bank)
- European Bank for Reconstruction and Development
- Islamic Development Bank

Some of the most important international aid programs in Albania are: World Bank /IDA, EC/PHARE, USA/ USAID, United Nations/ UNDP, Italy/ Project Co-financing, EC/Cross Border, Germany/GTZ, EBRD, Switzerland/ Swiss Trust Fund, Japan/OECF. Other countries that have aid throughout in Albania are: Austria, Greece, Netherland, Norway, Sweden end others.

The Albanian Economic Development Agency AEDA -operation of AEDA with international organisations and institutions-operation of AEDA with international organisations and institutions-operation of AEDA with international organisations and institutions-operation of AEDA with international organisations and institutions in its work to create a favourable investment environment in Albania, co-operates with its counterpart organisations in other countries and is an active partner in the organisations and institutions like UNIDO, UNDP, EBRD, MIGA, WAIPA, SIMEST, FINEST, etc. Growth of co-operation with counterpart bodies in other countries and exchange of experience with these bodies are indispensable for the better use of human and natural resources in Albania, and of the financial instruments and mechanisms offered to Albania by the United States and EU Throughout.

FOREIGN INVESTMENT PROTECTION AND AGREEMENTS CONCERNING AVOIDANCE OF DOUBLE TAXATION

The foreigners, either juridical or physical persons, enjoy the right of exercising different economic activities in the Republic of Albania and to invest their capital in different sectors of the Albanian economy. They are allowed to participate in economic activity and carry out investments in Albania, generally enjoying no less favorable conditions than those given to local subjects, aside from the right of landownership.

The most important law, which in reality provide a number of basic guarantees and protections for foreign investors is Law No. 7764, dated November 2,1994 " On Foreign Investments". According to this Law, all foreigners, either physical or legal persons, who intend to invest in Albania have no need to ask for permission or authorization, they shall not be expropriated or nationalized or be subject to any other equivalent measure.

The foreign investor enjoys the right to transfer all funds in currency and in kind related to his investment out of the Republic of Albania. The investor enjoys legal protection of his rights related to an investment made in Albania. Such protection is guaranteed for a dispute that arise between a foreign investor and an Albanian party. It is up to the disputing parties to define the procedures for the resolution of the dispute through arbitration.

In the event of the failure of such provision, the foreign investor has the right to submit the matter to an Albanian court or to an Arbitration Court in Tirana. In the event of a dispute involving discrimination, transfer of assets, or indirect expropriation of a foreign investment by the Albanian Government, the investor may submit the dispute to the International Center for the Settlement of Investment Disputes ("ICSID"). Special protection is guaranteed to foreign investments in Albania and to foreign investors from the states with which the Republic of Albania has signed agreements the concerning avoidance of double taxation and mutual guarantee of investments.

To provide security and protection against lost arising from political risks (thereby providing confidence to potential exporters and investors in Albania), the International development Association (the World Bank) has approved a credit of USD 10 million to the Albanian Government under its Private Sector Recovery Project to support a Political Risks Guarantee Facility, to be administered by the Albanian Guarantee Agency(AGA), a statutory corporation owned by the Government of Albania.

This is a Program to provide guarantees to private sector entities that have financial exposure in Albania for a productive purpose. The guarantee covers a range of political risks, including the risk of civil disturbance of the kind experienced in March of 2004.

BILATERAL AGREEMENTS ON PROMOTION AND PROTECTION OF RECIPROCAL INVESTMENTS AND THOSE ON AVOIDANCE OF DOUBLE TAXATION

Albania has signed a number of Bilateral Agreements on the Promotion and protection of Reciprocal Investments as an instrument for promotion foreign investment and co-operation. The following is a list of countries with which Albania has signed the Agreement (as per end 2004)

Austria	Israel	Malaysia
Bulgaria	Italy	Turkey

China	Netherlands	United Kingdom
Croatia	Poland	USA (OPIC)
Egypt	Rumania	Slovenia
France	Sweden	Switzerland
Germany	Greece	Tunisia

On the avoidance of double taxation Albania has signed Agreements with the following states (as per September 1996 - as ratified by the Albanian Parliament):

Croatia (1995)	Czech Republic (2004)
Greece (1995)	Russian Federation (1995)
Hungary (1992)	Italy (1995)
Malaysia (1995)	Poland (1995)
Turkey (1995)	Rumania (1995)

TAXATION SYSTEM

There are two level of taxation in Albania:

- at national level
- at regional level (municipality level)

Taxes at national level are by far the most important one, while those at municipality level are mostly related with hotels, restaurants, advertising, cleaning and ambulatory trade. National tax system in Albania can be classified as follows:

DIRECT TAXES:

a) On income:

- corporate income tax (tax on profit)
- personal income tax

b) On assets:

- tax on buildings
- tax on agriculture land

Both these taxes are marginal and normally doesn't play any important role

INDIRECT TAXES:

- value added tax
- excise tax
- custom duties on imports

Legal acts The main legal acts that determine the Albanian tax system are the followings

- Law nr. 7681, dated 4.3.1993 "On the administration of taxes and fees in the Republic of Albania"
- Law nr. 7677, dated 3.3.1993 " On the tax on profit"
- Law nr. 7678, dated 3.3.1993 " On excise tax"
- Law nr. 7679, dated 3.3.1993 " On small business tax"
- Law nr. 7928, dated 27.4.1995 " On value added tax"
- Law nr.7805, dated " On Property tax"

and their amendments. There are a number of circulators issued by the Ministry of Finance on the implementation of the legal acts concerning the tax system.

CORPORATE INCOME TAX (TAX ON PROFIT)

This tax applies to all legal persons, Albanian or foreigner, that exercise economic activity in territory of Albania and for that reason are considered as resident in Albania for tax purposes. This applies equally to companies with their seat in Albania and to branches of foreign companies. A tax on profit of 30% is level on profits made by resident companies in Albania, irrespective of their legal form. Normally the tax on profit is prepaid each quarter and by the end of the year the balance is set off. For companies that exercise economic activity in tourism, this tax is 40%. Companies that exercise economic activity in oil and gas exploitation pay an average of about 50% tax on profits depending on the quantity produced. Taxable income is determined according to the Law No.7671, dated 19.1.1993 "On the Accounting" and is in line with standard western business practices.

PERSONAL INCOME TAX

This tax is a progressive one. Foreigners are considered as residents in Albania and liable for personal income tax if they have an income in Albania and spend a period of more than 183 days in the country. The minimum wage and remuneration taxable is 10000 lek/month. The maximum level of personal tax is 20%. Other kind of income are taxed at 10%. Exempt the creative work is taxed at the level of 5%.

PROPERTY TAX

The tax on buildings and Agriculture land by Law 7805 on Property Tax, Revenues Tax on agriculture land which varies depending on the quality and dimensions of the agriculture activity. The tax on the building is paid by the owners of the buildings . It varies from 3 to 6 lek/m2 year for living houses depending on whether the house is ingle building, buildings in co-ownership or in the country side. For buildings for manufacturing activities or service activities including trade activity, the tax rate varies from 50 to 100 lek/m2 year. Tax on agriculture land varies depending on the quality of agriculture land from 1500 to 6000 lek/ha year.

VALUE ADDED TAX

The value added tax entered in force in July 1, 1996 and substituted the turnover tax that was applied up to that moment. The basic purpose of VAT law was to adapt the Albanian legislation to EU VAT directives and regulations. The value added tax is levied on all legal and natural persons that performs goods or services supply and is calculated based on the total sum paid for the goods or services. The tax rate is 20%.(Law 8240 dates 16.9.2004) For exports and international services the tax rates in 0%. Following the EU model certain transaction are VAT exempt e.g. services and supplies of goods related to financial activities, transaction related to shares, stocks, bonds and other securities, transactions related to bank accounts, transfers, cheques, transaction related to life insurance policy, management of pension funds, rental of residential property etc.

Business are required to register for this tax if their annual turnover exceeds 5 milion LEK (1 January 2005) Also goods supplied under the temporary importation regime for job processing activities, are VAT-exempt. VAT must be paid within the first 14 days of the next month. First, the taxpayer must have carried forward a VAT tax credit for six consecutive month, and second, the total refund claimed must exceed 400,00 lek

EXCISE TAX

Excise tax is applied on limited number of goods such as tobacco, cigars, cigarettes, alcoholic drinks, soft and fresh drinks, electrical energy, derivatives of petroleum and coffee. This tax is applied only for goods produced in Albania or imported. For goods produced in Albania the excise tax is calculated on the bases of the value of each lot of goods sold and for imported goods it is calculated on the bases of the custom value. Excise tax is not applied on above mentioned goods when they are exported. Excise tax for tobacco and tobacco products is 50% to 70% when produced in Albania and 100% to 105% when imported. Alcoholic drinks have an excise tax of 40% to 105% when produced in Albania and an additional of 25% when imported.

For derivatives of petroleum the excise tax is in the range of 25% to 85% and for some specials derivatives up to 300 %.Normally the excise tax stimulates the domestic production of goods rather than import of goods

The Government has prepared e new law on excise. In this law there will be applied the same excise system for both the products that are produced on the country and those imported.

TAX ON SMALL BUSINESS

This tax is applied on individuals exercising private economic activities. It includes learned professions as well as small scale individual ambulatory trade activity. It is calculated on the bases of the total revenues and varies from 2% to about 10% depending on the type of activity.

DIRECT TAXES ON BUSINESS

GENERAL REVIEW

There are three main direct taxes paid by registered taxpayers in the Republic of Albania .

Tax on profit, which is paid by taxpayers who exceed the VAT registration threshold.

Simplified tax on profit , which is paid by registered taxpayers having an annual circulation that does not exceed the VAT registration threshold.

Local tax on small business , which is paid by registered taxpayers having an annual circulation that does not exceed the VAT registration threshold.

The VAT registration threshold is 8 million lek per calendar year.

2.1. Principle of residence

The definition of tax residence criteria for individuals, legal entities and physical persons is closely related with the place where they pay their taxes.

Under the law, taxable Albanian residents are taxed in Albania on all incomes realized on a world level (incomes deriving inside or outside Albania). Non-residents are taxed in Albania only on incomes deriving from within the Republic of Albania .

In particular, for persons who are residents in countries with which Albania has signed Agreements (Treaties) to eliminate double taxes and when these agreements have entered in force, the provisions of these agreements will be adopted.

- The individual is regarded as an Albanian resident for tax purposes, when he has a permanent place of residence, when he has his own family, i.e. when he has vital and economic interests vested in Albania (place of vital interests), although he may work outside the country for indefinite periods of time, or have foreign citizenship.

- For tax purposes, an Albanian resident is also considered an individual who stays in Albania for a tax year, whether for the entire period or a part of it totaling above 183 days, regardless of citizenship or place of vital interests. The calculation of duration of stay in Albania includes the days of his physical presence, i.e. not only workdays, but also days of arrival, departure and holidays.

To conclude, a taxable Albanian resident is considered every individual (regardless of nationality or citizenship), who meets one or both of the above-mentioned requirements.

A legal entity is considered a taxable Albanian resident if:

- Its headquarters (head office) are in the Republic of Albania ; and/or

- Its place of business management is in the Republic of Albania .

A person is considered an Albanian taxable resident when he runs his own business and is registered as a physical trader in the Albanian Court and the Albanian Tax organs.

2.2. Subjects that pay direct taxes on business

- ***Tax on Profit***

As we pointed out, all taxpayers registered in tax organs, whose annual circulation exceeds the VAT registration threshold are subject to the tax on profit. This category of taxpayers includes:

• Legal entities created according to the Law " On trade companies" and that are registered to the VAT ;

• Legal entities established on the basis of Civil Code which have profit activities in the territory of the Republic of Albania ;

• All other legal entities established or recognized as such by special laws;

• Partnerships as defined by law;

• Legal entities, partnerships or all other groupings of persons established or organized on the basis of a foreign law and exercising their activity in the territory of the Republic of Albania through a permanent headquarter.

• Every other person regardless of their legal registration form, including traders, who are not subject to simplified tax on profits, but who are otherwise registered as Value Added Tax subjects.

• ***Simplified tax on profits***

The simplified tax on profits applies to all taxpayers who are not registered, or bound by law to register as taxpayers for Value Added Tax.

• ***Local tax on small business***

Subject to local tax on small business is every person who runs a business in the territory under the jurisdiction of a local government entity in the Republic of Albania at any given time of a calendar year and who is not subject to Value Added Tax.

2.3 Registration

• All taxpayers are registered once, in the moment they begin their economic activity, before starting their business. Taxpayers of local tax on small business and/or of simplified tariff on earnings are excluded from this rule in the year 2005. These taxpayers must re-register within the 20-th of March. If the taxpayers are not registered or re-registered in the right time the tax authorities do their registration. This registration has the same effects as if the taxpayers would have done the registration their self.

• From January 1 -st , 2006, the local tax on small business, the registration for the first time of the taxpayers is done after they are furnished from the local authorities with the License for Activity Exercise.

In the law No.8438, Dated 28.12.1998 "On the tariff of incomes" and in the law No.8978, Dated. 12.12.2002 "On local tax on small business" it was defined that all the subjects that paid these taxes would re-register every year near the tax authorities. With the 2005 Fiscal Package, these subjects are obliged to register only once in the beginning of their activity.

2.4 Direct tax levels on business

• Tax level on profit for the fiscal year that begins in January 1-rst 2005 – December 31-rst 2005 is 23%, and 20% for the coming years.

• Simplified tax on profit is 3% of the taxpayer gross incomes. For the tax basis on which this tax is calculated, no discounting expense is recognized .

• The local tax on small business is a fixed, annual and mandatory quota. Every business, whenever it is located, is taxed separately. Categories and their respective tax levels are given in the following table. The Municipality Council or the Communal Council of the territory where the business is located may increase or decrease the indicator level value by no more than 30%. Each increase or decrease equally applies to all business categories.

Indicator levels of local tax on small businesses (in '000 Lek)

No.	Type of Business	Cat. I	Cat. II	Cat. III
A	RETAIL SALE	60	20	15
B	Wholesale	60	20	15
C	Production	35	15	10
Ç	Services	20	10	10
D	Freelances	45	30	15
DH	Ambulant vendors in the area of trade and services	15	10	10
E	Transport:			
	1.Passenger transport:			
	Vehicles up to 5 seats (including driver)		35	
	Vehicles from 6 to 9 seats (including driver)		70	
	Vehicles with 10 to 25 seats (including driver)		80	
	Vehicles with 26 up to 42 seats (including driver)		90	
	Vehicles with over 42 seats (including driver)		95	
	2.Freight transport:			
	Vehicles up to 2 tons		55	
	Vehicles from 2,1 to 5 tons		80	
	Vehicles from 5,1 to 10 tons		95	

Vehicles from 10,1 to 16 tons	100
Vehicles with over 16 tons	150
3.Water transport	
Transport by sea within the country	110
Transport by lake within the country	95
Cruise ships/boats	30

Under category I: Municipality of Tirana , and Durrësi

Under category II: Municipalities: Shkodra, Korça, Vlora, Saranda, Gjirokastra, Elbasani, Fieri, Lushnja, Pogradeci, Berati, Lezha and Kavaja

Under category III: All the other Municipalities

Indicator tax level in communes is 50% for each category.

2.5. Tax Exemption

• ***The following are exempted from tax on profit :***

• Units/institutions of central and local government;

• Bank of Albania .

• Legal entities which exercise activities of a religious, humanitarian, charity, scientific or educational character, whose wealth or profits are not used for profits by its leaders or members.

• Labor organizations (unions, confederates) chamber of commerce, industry or agriculture, and any other organization similar in function, which do not have profit purposes.

• International organizations and their representations in the Republic of Albania, agencies of technical cooperation and their representatives, who are acknowledged as such by the Albanian State on the basis of legal provisions, whose tax exemption has been envisaged by special agreements.

• Persons envisaged in international agreements ratified by the People's Assembly.

• Foundations and financial non-banking institutions founded or delegated with a decision of Council of Ministers, whose main objective have the support of government development politics through crediting.

• Picture studios, licensed and subsided from the National Center of Cinematography.

• ***The following are exempted from simplified tax on profits:***

• Ambulant vendors.

- Persons exercising individual transport.
- Individuals that gather waste of metals, glasses, paper and individuals who gather herbs and spices, etc.
- Individuals that produce fire wood, mountain stones, etc,

The new law No. 9326, Date 06.12.2004 "For some amendments and changes in the law "On tariff on incomes", predicts that all subjects that have an annual turnover less than 3 million Leks are no longer excluded from he simplified tax on profit.

2.6. Establishing the taxable profit

- ***For taxpayers of the tax on profits:***

The financial balance sheet and its annexes will provide the basis to establish the taxable profit for a certain tax period. The financial balance sheet must comply with law no. 7661, of 19.1.1993 " On Accounting " valuable till January 1-rst, 2006 , with the provisions of law no. 8438, of 28.12.1998 "On Income Tax" as well as other sub-legal acts issued by the Minister of Finance for purpose of calculating the taxable profit. After January 1-rst, 2006, will come into act the law No.9228, date, 29.04.2004, "On accounting and Financial Declarations". In principle, the taxable profit or net income, is the difference between total incomes (incomes from normal activity and extraordinary incomes), including the value of profits and advantages in nature, with effective and recognized expenditures, for the purpose of income realization and protection. Under recognized expenditures fall all those expenditures made for business purposes, that is, expenditures that intend to realize and secure incomes. In order to be recognized or deductible expenditures should meet these conditions:

- They must be made to the direct benefit of the economic activity out of which incomes are achieved or to have been related to the normal course of the taxpayer's activity.
- They must be effectively made or faced and based on legally recognized justifying documents.
- The must be reflected by an accounting action, reducing the net active.
- In any case the taxpayer must evidence expenditures with relevant legal documentation

- ***For taxpayers of Simplified Tax on Profits***

This category of taxpayers it is taxed for the gross incomes. So, every taxpayer must declare before 31-th of March of every year his gross incomes, for all his businesses that are objects of the Simplified Tax on Profit.

The taxpayer is obligated hold the books of purchase and sell, where the every day sales and buys are registered. These books are kept for every location of the activity.

2.7. Special provisions for Tax on Profits

2.7.1. Amortization

Amortization of assets is one of the major items of recognized, deductible business expenses.

Amortization of business assets is calculated by:

- Owner of assets

- Person who runs the risk, in the case of rented assets (usually long-term), with loans or leasing contracts;

Such assets as land, building grounds, works of art, artifacts, jewellery, precious metals or stones are not amortized.

The following are individually amortized and in a linear manner :

- Purchase or construction costs; building improvement, renovation and reconstruction costs, as well as costs of machineries and equipment with a utilization lifetime of above 20 years. The amortization norm of these assets is 5%. Similar amortization applies to water pipelines, oil pipelines, gas pipelines, the higher voltage transmission lines, and other similar assets;

- All the following business assets such as patents, trademarks, expenses for starting a business, "the good name" in cases when the latter is purchased etc. are amortized by a 10% permissible norm for fiscal effects.

The calculation basis for the amortization of both "a" and "b" categories of the above-mentioned activities is the initial value of the asset (historical cost) to which are added the asset's improvement, renovations and restructuring costs.

The following are amortized on a group basis:

- Computers, information systems, computer programs and all data protection software and equipment. The amortization norm on this asset category is 25%.

- All other assets which are not grouped under the above-mentioned "a", "b" and "c", such as production and service machineries and equipments, all means of transportation, are amortized with a permissible norm for fiscal effect at 10%.

The calculation basis for the amortization of categories "c" and "d" of above-mentioned assets is the remaining accounting value of the asset group (the initial value minus amortization), to which are added the improvement, renovation and reconstruction costs of group assets and from which the incomes from sales and compensations received are deduced.

2.7.2. Bad debts

"Bad debt" implies a payment request (debt obligation), which becomes an obligation that can be totally or partially unpaid because of the debtor's bad financial situation, his placement in bankruptcy or because of any other reasons not depending on the creditor.

A bad debt must meet the following conditions in order to be recognized as such during the activity year, i.e. to reduce the taxable profit:

- The total sum of this debt must be included previously in the taxpayer's incomes.

- All necessary legal efforts must have been made for its payment;

• When this debt has been deleted from accounting books;

2.7.3. Participations that are exempted from tax on profits

In order to avoid double tax, dividends and profit-shares gained by companies and Albanian resident partnerships (beneficiaries) are exempted from tax on profits, provided that these dividends be paid by an Albanian resident tax company or the profit be shared by an Albanian resident tax company (i.e. these dividends or profit-shares are distributed after tax on profits in Albania has been paid) and the beneficiaries of dividends or distributed profit should possess no les than 25% of the stock or capital of the company or partnership making the distribution.

Hence, dividends and profit-shares made by a company or partnership (i.e. beneficiaries) are exempted from the tax on profits, when all three following conditions are met:

• The beneficiary is an Albanian tax resident;

• The payer (company or partnership making the distribution of dividencs is an Albanian tax resident;

• The beneficiary owns no less than 25% of the payer's stock capital, right to vote, or initial capital (in the case of partnerships).

2.7.4. Recapturing losses

If taxable profit in a certain tax period turns out as negative, that is if expenses are bigger than incomes, the resulting losses may be covered by the profits of three consecutive years.

If a loss is not recaptured for three consecutive years in a row (and the entity results in losses again), it cannot be extended farther and thus affecting the results of other years, prior to the application of tax on profit.
The law prohibits the transfer of company loss, because allowing carriage of losses should be linked only with the taxpayer who suffers the loss. That is, if during a tax period the direct and /or indirect property of the core capital, or the rights to vote of a person changes by more than 25% in value or number, the right of loss transfer for that tax period and the preceding periods is lost.

2.7.5 Crediting foreign tax

Crediting foreign tax has to do with crediting and recognition of taxes that taxpayers residing in the Republic of Albania have paid in other countries (outside the territory of the Republic of Albania) on profits that they have made in those countries. But this reduction or recognition cannot exceed the Albanian tax level to be applied on those incomes if they had been made within the territory of the Republic of Albania .

2.8. Tax payment and its final calculation

• ***Tax on profits***

During the activity year the tax on profits is paid by the taxpayer one month in advance. To determine the monthly payment amount of tax on profit the law has foreseen a formula, which takes into account the tax on profit the taxpayer has paid in the last two preceding years.

During the coming tax period, the taxpayer pays the respective monthly tax on profit to the tax organ accounts no later than the 15 th of each month, accounting for the next month, according to the calculation formula described above.

The final calculation of the tax on profits is based on the factual data included in the tax declaration (Annex A) and other supporting documents, such as the balance sheet and its annexes, data from tax controls, as well as any other legal document that helps to determine the tax obligation.

If the tax declared on the basis of the annual income declaration is far bigger than the advance payments made during the year, the taxpayer is obliged to pay the difference at the moment he presents the declaration. If the advance payment amounts turn out to be far bigger than those declared in the annual income declaration, or those resulting from a tax control, the tax organs are obliged to recognize these sums for overdue payment of tax obligations or for the payment of future obligations, including the advance payment amount for the coming periods. Upon taxpayer's request, these sums could be returned to him within 60 days after receiving the tax declaration.

- ***Simplified tax on profits***

Taxpayers pay the rate of their annual obligation considering the estimation of the flows for the calendarian year. These rates are paid as follows:

- Not later than 20-th of April, 20-th of July and 20-th of October, respectively in the first, second and the third quarter of the year

- Not later than the 20-th of December for the fourth quarter of the respective year.

- Possible differences that are related with the changes of the turnover, are declared and paid in the moment of presentation of the tax declaration that cannot be submitted later 31-th of March of the coming year.

When a business starts during a taxable period, the calculation of rates is based in the estimated circulation according to the predicts that are made by the taxpayer and the estimations done by the tax authorities. The payment is done according to the deadlines specified above. When a business delivers e declaration for the close down of its activity, the payment of the tax is done not later than 10 days from the day of declaration delivery.

The gathered taxes are shell out in the state budget and are transferred to the municipalities or communes' budget, once a month, where the taxpayer is registered or has his activity going. Law No. 9326, Date 06.12.2004, “For some amendments and changes in the law “Tariff on Incomes”, changed, predicts the payment of this tariff in four rates than two that were predicted in the old law. The new law approved with the new 2005 Fiscal Package does not put any limitation in the sum of payment. In case that the activity closes down, the taxpayer must pay the debt 5 days earlier than the deadline specified by the law.

- ***Local tax on small business***

Local tax on small business is paid in two equal rates. The first rate has to be paid within the 30-th of April and the one not later than the 20-th October of the respective year. The place and the way of tax payment it is defined with a special instruction.

If a taxpayer begins its commercial activity during the year, the taxes are paid for effective working months according to the Instruction of the Minister of Finances.

The law predicts the reduction of the tax level, if the taxpayers pay their obligation, before the deadlines stated below:

- If the taxpayer pays the whole sum of his annual obligation within the 1-rst of February, the sum that has to be paid is reduced by 5%

- If the taxpayer pays the whole sum of his annual obligation within the 1-rst of March, the sum that has to be paid is reduced by 3%

If the information given from the taxpayer is incorrect and if the fixed sum to be paid is more than the one paid, the authorities must notify the taxpayer. The taxpayer must pay his tax obligation within 15 days from the day that he was noticed. In the same way, if a business shuts down and the value of the tax obligation is lower than the value paid than the tax authorities must reimburse the difference within 30 days from the day the business shuts down.

The new law No. 9327, Date 06.12.2004, "For some changes and amendments in the law No.8978, Date 12.12.2002 "On local tax on small business" predicts a delay of the deadlines for the payment of the rates of this tax.

The old law predicted the reduction of the annual obligation, in different levels from the ones presented above; this reduction was related with the ending of the re-registration process and the gaining of the registration certificate from the taxpayers. With coming into act of the law No. 9327, Date. 06.12.2004, approved with the 2005 Fiscal Package, we see a unification in the reduction of the sum of annual obligation, based only in the above mentioned deadlines.

2.9. Record Keeping

For the purpose of determining the tax calculation basis, the registered taxpayers should keep the required legal records and documentation. Models of the basic documents that are used for the calculation of the tariffs are given in Annex B

- ***Taxpayers of tax on profit***

This taxpayer category is taxed on net incomes (that is on net profit). To this effect, they should keep accounting records, issue the balance sheet with its annexes, which should comply with the law "On accounting" and the provisions of the law "On incomes tax".

Being subject to VAT, these taxpayers are obliged to abide by the rules of the law "On Value Added Tax" related to the tax bill and its use.

- ***Taxpayers of simplified tax on profit***

This taxpayer category is not obliged to keep accounting records and issue the balance sheet, since the tax object is not the net profit, but the realized turnover (gross incomes).

The taxpayer should keep a series of records and documentation regarding the activity. The taxpayer should keep the following records and documents:

- Purchase documents, which include the VAT bills, simple bills, and tax bills, as evidence of the purchases made;

• Sales documents, simple tax bills, tax bills, and daily summaries of registering cash box (for sales from cash boxes).

• Purchase book and sales book.

Small business taxpayers are obliged to issue the following documents for each sale of goods or services made:

• Tax coupon in cases when the taxpayer is equipped with a registering cash box. This coupon is given to the buyer for each sale made.

• Tax bill when the taxpayer is not equipped with a registering cash box;

• A simple tax bill issued only by taxpayers selling goods or services to clients who are not the final consumers of those goods or services but purchase them for the purpose of processing or re-sale, i.e. they are registered tax entities. • At the end of each day's work, the taxpayer should record in the purchase book the total of purchases made during that day, as well as other expenses made, such as rent, electricity, salary payment, etc.

• At the end of each day's work, the taxpayer should record in the sales book the total value of sales made by him, respectively grouping them as sales with simple tax bill, sales with cash box (the daily total of cash box) and sales with tax bill.

• **Tax on fortune games, casinos and hippodromes**

Taxpayers exercising an activity in the realm of fortune games, casinos and hippodromes, like all other taxpayers, are subject to tax legislation provisions. Like all other taxpayers, they pay all taxes and tariffs specified in fiscal laws (such as VAT, tax on profits, various national and local taxes, etc).

Except usual tax and tariffs, every person that benefits from the fortune games and casinos, pays a tariff equal to 20% of the earnings. This tariff is taken from the owner of the game or casino, whom is obliged to shell out within 24 hours near tax authorities.

2005 Fiscal Package, and respectively the law No.9326, Date 06.12.2004, "For some amendments and changes in the law No. 8483, Date. 24.12.1998 “On Tariff on Incomes”, predicts a reduce of tax level by 5%

2005 Fiscal Package, and respectively the law No. 9326, Date 06.12.2004, "For some amendments and changes in the law No. 8483, Date 24.12.1998, “On Tariff on Incomes” predicts a reduce of the simplified tariff on profit by 1%.

Letters “g“ and “h” are part of the exclusions from the tax on profit in the 2005 Fiscal Package according to the law No. 9326, Dated. 06.12.2004 “For some Changes and Amendments in the law No. 8583, Dated.28.12.1998 “On Tax on Incomes”.

BANKING SYSTEM

Albania is trying to develop a diversified modern financial system. The operators in the Albanian financial system can be classified as follows:

1. the central issuing bank
2. commercial banks including savings bank
3. stock market
4. investment funds
5. insurance and reinsurance companies
6. credit associations (co-operatives)

BANKS

Law NR. 7559, dated 22.4.1992 " On the Bank of Albania" and Law NR. 7560, dated 28.4.1992 transformed bank system from a centrally planned, single tier system, to a Western two-tier system with the Bank of Albania as the central bank and second level or commercial banks. Law NR 8076, dated 22.2.1996 and law NR. 8075 dated 22.2.1996 further developed the banking sector. The activities of the Bank of Albania have paralleled those of central banks in other market economies. The main principle behind the legislation is that banks should operate on a fully commercial base whether they deal with public or private sector.

BANK ESTABLISHMENT

Joint banks or totally private banks with Albanian or foreign capital can be established. The licence to establish and operate a bank is obtained upon written application at the Bank of Albania. In accordance with a form issued by the Bank of Albania a list of documents must be presented together with the request for getting a license. Actually in Albania there are three state-owned commercial banks, two joint banks with participation of foreign capitals, three foreign private banks and the branch of the National Bank of Greece. Other foreign banks or branches of foreign banks have got the license and are in the process of establishment. There are programs for the privatisation of second level state-owned banks.

ALBANIAN BANK SYSTEM

The structure of the bank system in Albania at the end of the year `91 was typical of a centralised and planed economy. It included four state institutions: (i) Bank of the State of Albania, which applied at the same time the functions of the central bank and of the commercial bank: (ii) Bank for Agriculture and Development, which credited co-operatives and the state farms: (iii) Savings Bank, the holder of the almost individuals deposits: (iv) Albanian Commercial Bank, which performed the transactions of the foreign market. Bank of the State of Albania changed in Bank of Albania and has only the functions of a central bank.

The approving of the new law on Central Bank and of law on bank activity in April 1992 which brought the creation of the two level bank system.

On 1 January 1993 its commercial operations joint with Albanian Commercial Bank and created the National Commercial Bank of Albania.

In September of 1993, Bank for Agriculture and Development restructured and its deposits and good assets transferred in a new bank, Commercial Rural Bank. In Albania till at the end of the year 1993 existed: a central bank, three state owned bank and the Bank for Agriculture and Development without any activity. Bank of Albania estimated the important role that the foreign equity, management and technology can played in the modernisation of the bank system in Albania. At this stage an important forward step was the creation of the first common bank in country at the end of the year 1992.

At the end of the March 2005 the system bank of Albania presented as follows:

1 **National Commercial Bank of Albania (NCBA):** has a network from 7 branches in all around the country. The most part of its passives, the deposits of enterprises and an important part of its loan are for the enterprises of the private and state sector. It applies short-term loans for enterprises in supporting their production and commercial activity and long term loans for the most important investment projects.
NBCA has created relationships with 21 analogue banks - 19 in Europe and 2 in USA. Also it has ownership interests in the equity of the Italian - Albanian Bank and of Islamic Arab-Albanian Bank possessing 40% of the shares of each of them.

2 **Albanian Savings Bank:** has 33 branches in all the country and the biggest bank network in the Republic of Albania. Actually the deposits of the individuals firstly compose its passives. Its portfolio of the loans consists mainly I the short and middle term loans for the private sector. It issues Eurocard, MasterCard, travel cheques, American Express, Thomas Cook and Eurocheques. Both, National Commercial Bank and Savings Bank performs exchange money transactions with enterprises and individuals.

3 **Rural Commercial Bank:** is created as the result of the restructuring and the recapitalising of the Bank for Agriculture and Development. RCB performed commercial bank commonly activity, especially in the agricultural sector. It didn't offer transaction of the exchange money, even it accepted deposits in foreign money by its clients. During the first three months of the year 2005 the RCB was devised I two parts. The good part represented by deposits and liquids was gathered with Savings Bank. The other resting part of actives and passives were been transferred into the Credit Treatment Agency to be liquidated.

4 **Ital. – Albanian Bank** is the first common bank. Its shareholders are National Commercial Bank of Albania holds 40% of the shares, Bank of Rome holds 40 % of shares and European Bank for Reconstruction holds 20 % of shares. This bank acts as an universal bank offering the performing of deposits, transfers, commercial credits and exchange money transactions.

5 **Islamic Arab- Albanian Bank** is also a common bank. NCBA holds 40% of the shares and the foreign banks and individuals hold the other shares. It doesn't offer credits and doesn't accept deposits with time limit. It operates according to the bank Islamic principles.

6 **Dardania Bank** is the first private bank in country and up to now has developed a simple bank activity.

7 **Bank of Tirana** begins its activity in Tirana on September 1996 with a paid equity of 2 million USD recently is growing to 4 million USD. Its main shareholder is the Bank of Pireu in Greece. This bank offers universal commercial bank transactions and operates as consulate.

8 **National Bank of Greece** begins its activity at the end of September 1996. Its insure an complete --- of the bank transactions.

During `97, the Albanian Bank System was growing with two other foreign private banks (International Commercial Bank and Alpha Credit Bank). These two banks begin their activity respectively in May `97 and in January 2005. Both are universal banks and sitting in the city of Tirana. At this stage the number of the banks is growing in seven and the general number of the banks that actually operate is nine.

BANK OF ALBANIA AS A MONETARY AUTHORITY

According to the Law NR. 8269, dt. 23.12.2004 "On Bank of Albania" , the Bank of Albania is responsibility for the monetary police and its implementation; the issuing of the domestic money; the administration of the foreign currency reserves; the adjustment of the commercial banks and their supervisory; the keeping of the government accounts, etc. The main aim of the monetary police in Albania is the holding of the inflation under the control and the stability of prices. The intermediate and operational objectives of the inflation control are: the control of the monetary offer and of the monetary base, superfluous reserves, net foreign assets, the real percentage of the interests and the credit limit for economy.

The main used instruments for the implementation of the monetary police are: the obligatory reserve, the limit of the credit for the commercial banks, the minimum of the interest percentage for the state owned banks, Lombard credit and of Refinancial, the agreements of buying again, the transactions of the secondary market.

CREDIT POLICY

Substantially all Albanian banks provide a full range of services and operations for their clients and operate in accordance with the private-sector banking practices. The majority of commercial banks generally lend their funds preferably to private persons although they can also finance major public works. The most common credits are of short and medium terms.

Indications on credit and deposit interest rates of some commercial banks (as per first quarter 1999)

Lending rates, Per annum in %

Short and Medium term credit	*in Lek*	*in USD*
The Ital.-Albania Bank	28%-30%	10.5%-12.5%
The Tirana Bank	28%	10%

Deposit rates, Per annum in %

	in LEK	*in USD*
Current deposits	12%-13.5%	1.5%-2.5%
6-M deposits	16.5%	2.255-4%
12-M deposits	18 %	4.1%

STOCK MARKET

Tirana stock exchange was established on May 1996 and is a relatively new institution. For the moment governmental bonds, treasury bills with 12month maturity and privatisation vouchers are traded. A National Stock Exchange Commission controls the activity of the stock exchange and co-operates in the development of its regulations

Indication on security rates, as per March 1999.

3-M Treasury bills	17.95%-19.0%
6-M Treasury bills	18.90%-20.5%
12-M Treasury bills	20.80%-21.3%

Government bonds

20 Years 1.5%

INVESTMENT FUNDS

Law no. 7979, dated 26.7.1995 ,regulates the establishment and operation of Investment Funds.

Investment Funds are joint stock companies involved in investment, reinvestment, hold or exchange of privatisation vouchers. The minimum capital requirement is the equivalent in lek of USD 20 000. Foreign entities and companies whose capital is partly owned by foreigners may subscribe no more than 50% of the basic capital of the Fund.

The Fund is managed by a licensed administrator in accordance with the management contract. The administrator must be a subject not employed in the investment fund. The investment fund must appoint a licensed depositor to carry out depositor's duties, as well as a certified public accountant. Normally the organisation of an Investment Fund follows the rules found in the company Law for joint stock companies, except for some specific rules and regulation as specified in the Investment Law

ADDRESSES

Institution	*Address (Tirana, Albania)*	*Tel (00355/42)*	*Fax (00355/42)*
Bank of Albania	Sheshi "Skenderbej" Nr. 1	22230, 22752, 22152, 22153, 23205,35565	23587, 23695
National Commercial Bank	Bulevardi "Zhan D`Ark"	35100, 23133, 35113, 35114, 35116, 35118	
Savings Bank	Rr. "Deshmoret e 4 Shkurtit", Nr. 6	245 40, 226 60	
National Bank of Greece, Tirana Branch	Qendra e Bisnesit "Veve", Bulevard "Deshmoret e Kombit", nr. 72	336 21, 336 22, 336 23, 336 24, 336 25	
Dardania Bank	Qendra e Bisnesit "Veve", Bulevard "Deshmoret e Kombit"	287 59 Telex: 2298 DB BANC AB	305 66
Islamic Arab- Albanian Bank	Rr."Deshmoret e Kombit", nr. 8, P.O. Box 128	274 08, 284 60	284 60
Italo- Albanian Bank	Rr. Barrikadave,	339 65, 339 66	
Bank of Tirana	Bulevard "Deshmoret e Kombit", nr. 55/1,	334 43,334 67,334 41, 334 92	334 17
American Bank of Albania	Rr. "Ismail Qemali" nr. 27 P.O.Box 8319, *E-mail: aba@icc.al.eu.org*	48753, 48754, 48755,48756	48762
FEFAD Bank	Rr. "Sami Frasheri", Tirana e Re, P.O. Box 2395	304 99, 33496 Telex: +355 42 21 51	334 81
Tirana Burs	Sheshi "Skenderbej", Nr.1 *E-mail: emeka@capmark. tirana.al*	355 68 ext. 179	23558
First Investment Bank (Bulgaria Bank)	Bulevard "Deshmoret e Kombit", nr. 64	564 23, 56424	56422

ECONOMIC & BUSINESS ENVIRONMENT

Albania is an unusual country even by the standards of other former communist bloc countries such as Poland, Hungary, Russia etc.. For the 15 years prior to its change from a centrally planned dictatorship to a democratic, free market economy, it was isolated from both the East and West. During this period the country relied on minimal trade with Comecon pact countries and attempted to maintain a self-sufficiency policy with the effects that car now been seen in everyday life in Albania.

In the West we take for granted the flow of new information, new skills, techniques and experience through training programs, television, newspapers and magazines. During this period in Albania there was no such flow of new information. So the skills and knowledge the people of Albania possess today are based upon things they learned over fifteen years ago.

During the fifty years of brutal rule by the Hoxha regime, the ability of the average person to take responsibility for his own decisions was removed and taken over by the state. The State decided where you lived, where you worked, what you ate, etc.. To expect the Albanian people to quickly come to terms with their new rights of individual freedom and choice, is frankly expecting too much. The majority of appointees given responsibility for senior posts within the government and civil service need time to consider that such responsibility means they must now take the decisions.

The basic education standards achieved in Albania are very good, however they are based on text book theory and not practical experience. Those Albanian's who have moved into the private sector are quickly learning the practical skills needed to operate in a free market economy. Those who have remained in the state sector are, at the moment, prevented by bureaucracy from developing the same skills, however the culture is slowly changing. This makes life particularly difficult for foreign investors because of the Governments active role in business activity in Albania. All business opportunities outside of service and retail must be negotiated with either a state body or institution.

DECISION MAKING IN ALBANIA.

For fifty years the vast majority of Albanians, and certainly all those currently working for the state, have had no basic right to make decisions. They have not experienced the role of taking responsibility for their own actions. It is therefore important for Western businessmen to understand the basis on which business is conducted in Albania today. Most decision making within the government and state institutions is based upon 90% politics & personalities and only 10% on commerce.

Therefore to gain a decision in your favour it is important to establish who the political players are and the key personalities you must influence. Under no circumstances should this approach ever be taken as the need to bribe or pay someone for their support. It is simply a question of identifying the people who will influence and make the decision on your proposal and convince them that the benefits and merits of it are genuine and in the interests of Albania.

It is going to take many years for the people of Albania to come to terms with the new working environment that they are creating. It must be the responsibility of western businessmen to encourage them to understand the merits of personal decision making and taking responsibility for the posts that they work in.

MAKING THE FIRST MOVE.

Once you or your company has decided to take a serious look at the business opportunities Albania has to offer, it is vital that you research the specific field of interest, prior to visiting the country. There are, within the United Kingdom, a number of sources of information that can assist you in this task.

Once you have completed your research and decided that you wish to visit Albania, you should establish contact with the Ministries, Institutions and private sector companies you wish to meet whilst on your visit. We would always recommend that the first visit be no shorter than 5 working days. The reason for this is that transportation, office facilities and scheduling meetings is very time consuming and delays can often occur.

Having established your program and the individuals you wish to meet with, you will then need to arrange your flight and accommodation for the visit. Failing this it is possible to arrange a room at a private apartment, sharing with a local family. This of course is the cheapest, and can often be the best way to learn about local culture and customs.

It is likely that your first visit to Albania will focus on Tirana, the Capital city. If this is the case then it is unlikely that you will need a car during your stay, as most offices and government buildings are within walking distance from the centre. You will however need to arrange for an interpreter to accompany you to meetings. Although many people speak good English, it is still advisable to take the interpreter with you.

If you hold a European Union, EFTA member country or United States of America passport, you are no longer required to obtain a visa for entry into Albania.

YOUR FIRST TRIP TO ALBANIA.

Most of the scheduled flights from the UK arrive in Albania, mid afternoon. Upon arrival at the passport control office you are required to pay a USD$5.00 entry tax, have your passport stamped and then move into the luggage collection room. Porters will hand carry the luggage into the collection room and you are then asked to pass through the customs section. Once you clear customs you must then exit the terminal. If this is your first visit then you should brace yourself for the crowds of people immediately outside the main entrance door. You will be barraged by taxi drivers offering their services and locals seeking to carry your bags to the vehicle. They are extremely persistent and can often make first time visitors feel very insecure, be firm if you do not wish them to assist you. If you have not arranged for someone to meet with you at the airport, then you will need to hire a taxi, the going rate for the journey to Tirana is USD$20.00.

If this is your first trip to Albania, then you should brace yourself for the journey from the airport to Tirana. The country is severely underdeveloped and what little infrastructure there is, has been poorly maintained. The majority of buildings appear to have fallen into disrepair, the roads are very poor quality and the streets are very dirty. However, in contrast there are huge tracks of untouched countryside offering some of the most beautiful scenery in Central Europe.

The law and order situation in Albania and particularly in Tirana and Durres is now firmly under the control of the local police force. As long as common sense prevails, it is as safe as any European city, if not safer. The culture that exists across Albania is one of the utmost respect for foreigners and as such it is very rare to hear of any incidents of crime against foreign nationals.

When you have completed your visit, it is advisable to arrive at the airport an hour prior to your flight departure. You are required to pay an exit tax of USD$10.00 once you have checked in. There is a duty free shop and drinks bar in the main departure lounge.

LOCAL CUSTOMS

- The Albanian's nod their heads for NO and shake their heads for YES.

This can get very confusing, especially as over recent years with western influence many people nod for Yes and shake their heads for No. Always try to check an individual's response with a verbal Yes or No. Albanian for Yes is Po and No is Jo.

- The Albanians are extremely nervous about dealing with foreign businessmen; it is very important that your credibility is established quickly with them. Demonstrate that you have real proven experience in the fields you are discussing and if proposing to go into a Joint Venture or Direct Investment establish financial credibility very early on in the negotiations.

- When dealing with foreigners it is considered impolite to refer to someone by their first name, they will always refer to you as Mr * and you will be expected to do likewise. Although again due to western influence this is becoming less common.

- Private ownership of cars has only been permitted during the last three years and it would appear that the Italian driving system has been copied. Albanian drivers have an irritating habit of sounding their horn at every opportunity and display no regard for the safety of pedestrians.

- The high number of unemployed means that the majority of the ever increasing number of private cafes and bars are full with locals. Espresso, Cappuccino and Turkish coffee are served in most cafes. Soft drinks such as Pepsi, Coca-Cola, 7 Up etc. are also readily available.

- Privately run restaurants have now sprung up all over the capital, the majority of high quality, however they are expensive by Albanian living standards. The most popular are Italian, French and Chinese, although it is worth seeking out the few traditional Albanian cuisine restaurants.

HOW TO MAKE CONTACTS WHILE IN TIRANA.

On your first visit to Albania it is important to establish as many new contacts as possible. There are a variety of channels in which this can be achieved. First stop should be the British Charge d'affaires Office, Ministry of Industry and Trade, then the Albanian Chamber of Commerce. In addition to this you should visit the Hotel reception desks, where it is possible to buy copies of the ATA (State Press) news bulletins and local information brochures.

FIXING APPOINTMENTS WITH MINISTERS.

As a businessman, it is becoming more and more difficult to arrange a direct meeting with Ministers in Tirana. The reason for this is very simple; for the first two years of the transition, Ministers were eager to talk to as many people form foreign companies as possible. Unfortunately a large number of unscrupulous businessmen took advantage of this hospitality and had photographs taken in order that they could return to their own country and claim they had a special relationship with the Minister.

The Prime Minister has now decreed that Ministers should only meet with businessmen at a time when a project proposal is coming to its final conclusion. This said, it is still possible to arrange a meeting if a formal letter is sent to the Minister explaining the reasons for the meeting and that it is in his interest to meet with you.

UNDERSTANDING THE BUREAUCRACY.

If at the end of your visit you anticipate that you will be making concrete business proposals either now or in the future, it is necessary to understand the administrative procedures that will effect your project's chances of success.

If your proposal is solely concerned with individuals or companies in the private sector, you should be able to proceed relatively quickly. However, foreign proposals that require some form of State approval can be long and time consuming. It is necessary to engage the services of an Albanian lawyer to advise you on the laws effecting your proposed project.

For fifty years the Albanian State has employed only one law, that of the constitution, established by Enver Hoxha. The constitution was effectively Hoxha's law for ruling Albania and was not to be questioned or interpreted. Since there was only one law, the need for lawyers and judges was limited. Since the transition period commenced the government has slowly but surely drafted and approved laws for all sectors of economic, political and social life.

Because the legal profession in Albania is so new and inexperienced there is no interpretation of law. Whatever is published as the law is taken as sacro- sanct and non-negotiable. Thus when it comes to negotiating a contract with a government body you will be told that the conditions under which they can agree are published in the Laws. For this reason it is necessary to obtain English versions of all the legislation that will have a bearing on your particular project.

The second reason for requiring local legal services is that all documentation relating to the proposal, must be presented in Albanian and the translation must be notarised by the local court.

Each Ministry and local authority has a series of administrative procedures through which your proposal must pass, before it can be agreed upon. In certain circumstances a proposal, once it has passed through these procedures, must be approved by the Council of Ministers. The Council of Ministers sits once a week and is responsible for approving projects that under the legislation are deemed to be of national importance. The problem is that, what you might consider a straight forward business proposal, may under Albanian legislation be considered not in the nations interests. An example of this is, when a foreign company wishes to lease a piece of land for a project. If it is under 5 hectares in size the local authority can approve the lease contract. If the site is larger than 5 hectares the Council of Minister must approve it and only then is the local authority allowed to sign the lease contract.

So it is very important that you establish as quickly as possible the administrative procedures that your proposal will be subjected to. Once this has been achieved and you have decided to proceed, you will need to establish a local company in order to present your final proposal.

MAINTAINING PROGRESS IN YOUR ABSENCE.

It is important that, as you embark upon the process of putting forward a business proposal to a State body, your interests are being looked after once you have left the country. The ideal approach to take is to stay in Albania until such time as the proposal is either agreed or rejected. However, this is a very costly exercise and cannot guarantee the desired result. It therefore makes sense to appoint a local person to take responsibility for your projects progress when you are out of Albania.

His task should be to maintain contact with those individuals involved from the state sector and ensure that documents are presented at the appropriate time. He should also be responsible for arranging meetings and local facilities when you return to Albania. Someone who has respect in the local community and is known in Government circles will be able to push your project through the system much quicker than you could on your own. If you fail to make use of a local person during your absence, you will find that your project has not progressed since you were last in Albania.

THE WORLD BANK IN ALBANIA

AGRICULTURE, RURAL DEVELOPMENT AND THE ENVIRONMENT

Albania is a relatively small, very mountainous country with a population of about 3.1 million people. Only 24 percent of its land is classified as agricultural land, while 36 percent is forests and 15 percent is pastureland. Yet, agriculture provides the income basis for most of the population and serves as an employment safety net. The rural population is estimated to comprise about 54 percent of the total population while more than 60 percent of the labor force works in agriculture and related fields.

The agriculture sector continues to play an important role in the economy, providing for 53 percent of the GDP. Initially, the agricultural sector experienced high growth rates, which are still around 5 percent annually. The rapid growth and recovery during the early stages of the transition resulted mostly form the ability of farmers to quickly adapt to the changes brought about through the privatization by modifying their production structures. However, production has sometimes taken place at the expense of long term sustainability. Production continues to take place with limited use of improved seeds, fertilizers, and other inputs.

Albania has some advantages for the development of its agriculture. Among these are (a) a favorable geographic location relative to the European Union, particularly Italy and Greece, (b) comparably low wage levels, (c) a relatively educated rural population, many of whom have worked in other European countries for some period of time, (d) creativeness among Albanian farmers in adapting rapidly to changing circumstances, and (e) fertile soils and favorable climate in some regions. Based on these advantages, the major opportunities for growth in the agricultural sector are in the production of higher value crops, livestock, processing, and some agricultural niche markets.

The World Bank continues to aid in the development of the agricultrual and rural sectors by addressing different areas through initiation, implementation, and evaluation of World Bank financed projects.

TRANSPORT

Albania inherited a poor road and highway system from the Communist period. Only nine percent of rural households own a car or truck or have access to one. Over the last several years the government has invested in national highways running East-West and North-South. However, there are not enough of these investments and the quality of existing roads makes travel slow and difficult.

The main objectives for the sector include: (i) establishing a modern infrastructure network for an effective transport system to facilitate growth; (ii) increasing efficiency of cost recovery in transport operations by reducing the demand on the state budget; (iii) streamlining of transport operations with an aim of increasing economic efficiency, road safety, and environment protection; and (iv) promoting cooperation with the private sector and the development in teh context of the Stability Pact.

Despite visible progress in improving parts of Albania's road network, major deficiencies remain. A Road Maintenance Project (2002) as well as a Supplemental Credit to Road Maintenance (2003) supports improved maintenance of national and rural roads through gradual contracting of routine road maintenance, also ensuring adequate policies for financing road maintenance. Through a proposed Transport Project, the World Bank is committed to the improvement of the Durres-Morine road. This investment is widely perceived as a critical investment for the growth of the impoverished northeastern Albania.

In addition to road improvements, the Bank is also supporting the port sector through the ongoing Durres Port Project. The ongoing Trade and Transportation Facilitation in South East Europe Project - a part of a regional program joining eight Balkan countries--aims to reduce non-tariff costs of trade and transport and reduce corruption and smuggling at border crossings. A planned Transport Strategy will take stock of overall transport sector issues and needs, especially in the context of Albania's alignment with EU structures.

ENERGY

Over the transition period from a centrally-planed to a market-based economy, the country of Albania, like most other transitional countries experienced deterioration in a number of sectors, including the energy sector. In an attempt to address the fundamental issues affecting the energy sector, the Government of Albania is initiating an action to reverse the deterioration in sector performance. Despite the encouraging start, however, the sector's problems are so deep-rooted that sustained efforts will be needed for a considerable period of time, supported by critically needed investments. It will take time to implement the legislative and regulatory framework needed to attract private investment to the sector. Consequently, donor assistance will be required for several years.

The World Bank has so far taken the lead role in the sector, and is well placed to continue this role. A Power Transmission and Distribution Project has approved in 1996, but suspended in 2004, mainly because the government failed to reduce illegal electricity use and improve collection of electricity bills. The Bank lifted the suspension of disbursements in June 2005, after the government and KESH met the first quarter of 2005 Action Plan targets. At the same time, the Bank decided to prepare a new operation to support the government's efforts to resolve the crisis.

A Power Sector Rehabilitation and Restructuring Project, which was approved in June 2002 supports technical assistance, procurement and installation of meter boxes, and rehabilitation of priority components of the transmission and distribution networks in the Durres, Elbasan, and Kucova regions. At the government's requests, the Bank will also support efforts to add critically-needed thermal generation capacity. A planned Thermal Power Project will finance part of the construction cost of a new 100 MW thermal power station. The Bank will help the government raise additional financing from other donors for the construction of the new thermal power plant and will continue to play a key role in sector dialogue.

PRIVATE AND FINANCIAL SECTOR DEVELOPMENT

A primary World Bank Country Assistance Strategy (CAS) objective is to promote sustainable sector growth, reflecting on the National Strategy for Socio-Economic Development's (NSSED) theory, which treats the private sector as the driving force behind growth. Relative political stability and commitment to reforms since 2005 have led to robust growth in private sector activity. However, to sustain private sector growth leading to poverty reduction, it is necessary to improve the business environment and complete the structural reform agenda (especially enterprise and financial sector privatization). A Foreign Investment Advisory Sector (FIAS) study identified poor governance and weak institutions as the overarching problem deterring foreign direct investments (FDI).

In an attempt to overcome such obstacles, the World Bank's CAS is geared towards the creation of more accountable and transparent institutions. The Bank Group is supporting the government's efforts to improve the institutional and legal framework by assessing administrative barriers to investment (FIAS) and subsequently streamlining administrative procedures (PRSC II, 2003);

improving the legal framework for bankruptcy, resolution of debt, and commercial disputes through the ongoing Financial Sector Adjustment Credit, 2002 and PRSC I and II, 2002-2003, respectively; and establishing with the Multilateral Investment Guarantee Agency (MIGA) an investment promotion agency.

Microenterprises and small enterprises dominate Albania's economy. A number of donor initiatives, including Southeast Europe Enterprise Development (SEED) are specifically working to assist micro, small, and medium enterprises. The need for a business climate extends to rural areas, where many of Albania's poor live, highlighting the need for a sound rural strategy. Improving infrastructure, especially in rural areas is also essential for enabling business environment.

Although the necessity for growth and reform is evident in the enterprise sector, tangible progress continues in the financial sector reforms. Since 2004, the government has liquidated the insolvent state-owned Rural Commercial Bank, privatized the National Commercial Bank to an investor consortium that included the IFC and EBRD, and put the Savings Bank - the last remaining state-owned and Albania's largest - under a governance contract in preparation for its privatization, which is well advanced at this point. Close IDA-IFC cooperation has been instrumental in helping Albania move forward with financial sector privatization. The IFC is helping the government market the Savings Bank while planning to invest in it. The ongoing Financial Sector Institution Building Technical Assistance Project and the proposed Financial Sector Adjustment Credit (2002), which will be presented to the Board with the CAS, will also support the government in privatizing the Savings Bank as well as INSIG. Meanwhile, the government of Albania, IFC and EBRD are in the process of negotiations for acquiring up to 40 percent in the share capital of INSIG. Respective agreements for the final transfer of the shares will mark the first stage of pre-privatization of INSIG.

WATER SUPPLY AND SANITATION

Albania can be considered a water-abundant country. Its overall renewable resources amount to 41.7 billion cubic meters or 13,300 cubic meter per capita, out of which about 65% are generated within Albania and the remaining from upstream countries (namely, Serbia and Montenegro and FYROM). Resources are unevenly distributed throughout the country. The major water resource is surface water, and is found in rivers, lakes, and lagoons. The most important rivers are the Drin, the Mati, the Ishmi, the Erzeni, the Shkumbini, the Semani, the Vjose, and the Bistrica.

The lack of adequate monitoring system, the rapid changes in economic activities, and the continuous movements in population make it difficult to assess the use of water resources. Available data suggests that irrigation and mining rely mostly on sufrace water, while households and industry on groundwater from aquifers. Domestic water demand is increasing not only because of population growth but also because of the increase in the level of water losses, estimated to be greater than 50 percent in all cities.

Albania's water sector is plagued by a variety of problems facing the power sector, such as high consumption, wastage and misuse, illegal connections, below-cost tariffs, inadequate revenue collection, and insufficient investment in physical infrastructure. Consequently, despite Albania's abundant water resources, water supply in urban areas is intermittent and less than half of the rural population has access to piped water. The lack of reliable water supply hampers private investment and endangers public health, especially that of the poor. Without sector reform and investment in physical infrastructure, the ongoing deterioration will lead to crisis situations in many urban and rural areas.

The Bank, in close cooperation with other donors, is taking the lead in helping the government tackle policy reforms, focusing on cost recovery and private sector and community participation. The government has prepared, with Bank assistance, a Water Supply Action Plan and a comprehensive Water Supply and Sanitation Strategy. The Municipal Water and Wastewater Project (January 2003) tests private sector participation in water supply and sanitation through a management contract for four cities - Durres, Fier, Lezhe, and Saranda. Alongside this project, the World Bank is also committed to a variety of other projects in support of water supply rehabilitation throughout the country.

GOVERNANCE, ADMINISTRATIVE REFORM AND ANTICORRUPTION

A merit-oriented, depolicized civil service plays an essential role in enabling the public sector to deliver services and limiting the spread of corruption. Through its analytical studies, policy dialogue and lending operations, the World Bank is helping governments in many countries in Europe and Central Asia to begin to instill the features of transparent and accountable civil service institutions.

One of the Country Assistance Strategy (CAS) objectives in Albania is to improve governance and strengthen institutions. The World Bank - in close coordination with other donors - has focused on building critical central capacities, including public administration and the civil service, public expenditure management, and legal and judicial institutions. The Bank will extend institution building efforts to selected priority sectors - education, health, power, water, and transport - through sector-specific operations. Bank operations are also designed to support Albania's decentralization process, and to build capacity at local levels.

Fighting corruption - both a symptom of and a contributor to weak institutions - remains a part of the the Bank's strategy in the country. Since 2005, as part of a broad governance and anticorruption agenda defined and supported by the Friends of Albania, the Bank has helped the government develop and implement its Anti-Corruption Plan (ACP), which includes 150 specific actions affecting economic policy, rule of law, public administration, public finance, customs administration, procurement, audit, and public awareness. The Bank has undertaken surveys of public officials in order to establish baseline measurements of the performance of the public administration and its constituent parts. Surveys continue to be implemented due to raised concerns of weak governance and poor business climate reflected in recent data from the second Business Environment and Enterprise Performance Survey (BEEPS), covering the period 1999-2002, which showed an increase in perceived administrative corruption and state capture in Albania compared to the first BEEPS, which covered the period 1996-1999. However, the overall remaining corruption suggests that long-term efforts are required. An April 2002 report produced under the guidance of the Southeast European Legal Development Initiative indicates once again that Albanians rank corruption as the country's top problem. As a result, the Bank intends to continue supporting anticorruption efforts through a number of operations (including PRSCs II and III) and nonlending acitvities. In particular, building on the NSSED process, the Bank's future operations will focus on increasing transparency and accountability as a means to strengthen institutions and reduce corruption.

In response, the Albanian Government has demonstrated commitment through an agreement to be resurveyed in the coming years in an attempt to systematically monitor medium-term improvements in the functioning of the public administration. The World Bank has also supported the Government of Albania undertake a survey of salaries in the public sector, the private sector and within the local offices of the donor community; a survey which has provided important information in designing salary reform measures in Albania.

The foundations for public administration reform are in place, following the adoption of the Civil Service Law in November 1999. The Bank is supporting better public expenditure management -

essential to poverty reduction. The government is improving budget formulation by adopting a Medium-Term Expenditure Framework (MTEF), which adds a strategic focus to the budget process. The Bank is also supporting better budget execution and financial accountability by improving the treasury, accounting, and internal audit.

The fundamentals for legal and judicial reform are in place: the Constitution of November 2005 provides for judicial independence, strengthened through the 2005 Law on Judicial Organization, amended in 1999. However, there is a need for continued institutional strengthening. There is slow progress in law enforcement, including enforcement of property rights. Corruption and incompetence in the judiciary remain serious problems and major obstacles to economic growth.

HUMAN DEVELOPMENT

Over the past decade Albania has experienced expansionary as well as recessive economic trends, accompanied by changes in education, healthcare and social protection systems; during which time the World Bank provided support for improvement in the previously mentioned fields. The country program under the Human Development umbrella attempts to address the myriad of challenges that touch on the fundamental aspects of human capital development and households well-being.

An education trend during the transition consisted of a decline in gross enrollment rates for basic and secondary education. Overall basic education enrollments declined from over 90 percent prior to the transition to 88 percent in 2004. Secondary enrollment rates in 1989 were 79 percent, and they fell to roughly 40 percent by 2004. Albania, however, has joined the Education for All (EFA) Fast Track Initiative, being one of the 18 countries invited. Bank interventions in the education sector are grounded in a comprehensive education sector review. Albania's Education Sector: Problems and Promises (2000). The ongoing Education Reform Project (2000) aims to improve the capacity of the Ministry of Education and Science (MOES) to plan and manage the delivery of education services. The MOES is a pilot ministry for civil service reform, supported by the ongoing Public Administration Reform Project. Crucial reforms for improving planning and management and increasing the access of the poor to quality education are also supported by the PRSC program.

The Bank is helping the government translate its health goals into actions that protect the basic health needs of the most vulnerable population. Although Albania entered the transition with a relatively healthy population, life expectancy has since fallen, and infant and under-five mortality rates remain relatively high, especially in rural areas. The ongoing Health Recovery and Development Project (2005) is focused on the secondary and tertiary health care systems, while being adjusted during implementation to better align the project with National Strategy for Socio-Economic Development (NSSED) priorities.

The World Bank supports the government's efforts to create a fiscally sustainable social protection system that effectively targets the poor and vulnerable. The government's comprehensive pension reform program aims to create an affordable and equitable pension system while reducing reliance on budget subsidies. The PRSCs support the implementation of Albania's pension reform package, as well as improved targeting of cash economic assistance (ndihme ekonomike). The Bank also supports the government's development of a sustainable framework for community-based social services, which are primarily being developed under the ongoing Social Service Delivery Project (2005).

POVERTY REDUCTION AND ECONOMIC MANAGEMENT

Albania has enjoyed strong economic performance in the last five years, growing at an average of above 7 percent annually for most of the period. Inflation remained at levels of 4 percent less, exports and imports grew steadily, and both the current account and the domestically financed deficit improved significantly. Several structural reforms have also been carried out in the last five years, and have involved banking, land reform and privatization. Almost all small and medium enterprises have been privatized and significant progress has been made in the privatization of strategic sectors, like telecommunications. Regulation in the financial sector as well as core public sector functions has been strengthened, and the Government has adopted a new bankruptcy law and deposit insurance scheme. Significant steps have also been taken in the area of public administration, and a comprehensive civil service law has been adopted. Legal and judicial capacities have been strengthened, accountability rules have been tightened, and anti-corruption action plan is under implementation. Despite the impressive performance of the economy, poverty in Albania has remained high and per capita income, at around US$1,230 in 2002, one of the lowest among transition economies.

Poverty in Albania has marked spatial and regional dimensions, with rural areas in the Mountain region being consistently poorer than the rest of the country, according to all definitions of poverty. Poverty headcount in rural areas is 66 percent higher than in Tirana, and 50 percent higher than in other urban areas. Per capita consumption in rural areas, at 7,224 Leks, is about four-fifths of the consumption levels in urban areas. Households in the most remote districts in the Mountain region in the north and northeast of the country do not fare well in terms of poverty, and almost half of residents in this area are poor, and more than a fifth live in extreme poverty. Also, the depth of poverty in this area is much more pronounced than in any of the other regions, with a poverty gap index of over 11 percent. Average consumption in the mountainous region is two-thirds of consumption levels in Tirana, and about 20-30 percent lower than the rest of the country. Poverty rates and depth in all other regions are around or below the national averages.

The preparation of Albania's Poverty Reduction Strategy Paper, known in Albania as the National Strategy for Social and Economic Development (NSSED) was the first national development strategy that explicitly addressed poverty - outlining medium-term actions to reach long-term goals. THe NSSED, which was completed in November 2005, rests on two pillars: governance and strong economic growth. It also emphasizes policy interventions to improve education, healthcare, and infrastructure, while calling for stronger public accountability and increased public participation in decision making to empower the poor. The NSSED creates a better environment for advancing reforms and reducing poverty, by strengthening country onwership of the reform program; reinforcing a long-term vision; focusing on results; and encouraging partnerships.

Albania's prospects for growth, development and poverty reduction, however, are good, especially in view of a more favorable and stable political climate in Southeastern Europe and enhanced prospects for a closer association with the European Union. In the medium term, economic growth is projected to remian strong, with GDP growing by about 5 percent a year. An increase in exports and private sector activities is expected to lead growth in the next three years. Albania's strong growth should contribute to attracting more investment, generating income-earning opportunities and reducing poverty.

In support of Albania's NSSED, the World Bank has launched, implemented and continues to prepare projects geared towards poverty reduction and economic development.

TRAVEL TO ALBANIA

US STATE DEPARTMENT SUGGESTIONS

TRAVEL WARNING: The Department of State warns against all travel to Albania because the overall security situation remains unstable. U.S. citizens are urged to consider their personal security situations, and if appropriate, to leave Albania.

Given the possibility that the U.S. Embassy's personnel and facilities could be the targets of a terrorist attack, on August 14, 2005, the Department of State ordered the departure of Embassy personnel in nonemergency positions and families of Embassy personnel, and later further reduced its staff. As a result of the continued reduction in staff, the Embassy has suspended normal operations and is able to offer only emergency services to American citizens.

Following incidents of violence in Tirana in September 2005, in the wake of the assassination of a political leader, the situation in Albania remains volatile and the possibility exists that there may be further incidents of violence. American citizens resident in Albania are strongly advised to avoid crowds and demonstrations at all costs and exercise extreme caution at all times. The northeastern area of Albania, including the towns of Tropoja and Bajram Curri and the area near the Kosovo border, remains outside effective government control. Travel to this area is exceedingly dangerous. Even persons traveling to this area solely to render humanitarian assistance to refugees have been attacked by bandits.

COUNTRY DESCRIPTION: Albania continues to undergo profound social, political, and economic change. Facilities for tourism are not well developed and many of the goods and services taken for granted in other European countries are not yet available. Hotel accommodations are limited outside of Tirana.

ENTRY/EXIT REQUIREMENTS: A passport is required, but a visa is not necessary for a tourist stay of up to 30 days. An extension of up to 180 days may be granted by applying at the local police station. After 180 days, the Ministry of Interior accepts extension requests. There is a departure fee of $10, payable in U.S. dollars or local currency (the lek). For additional information, please contact the Embassy of the Republic of Albania at 2100 S Street, N.W., Washington, D.C. 20008, tel: (202) 223-4942.

MEDICAL FACILITIES: Medical facilities are limited, and medicine is in short supply. There are periodic outbreaks of polio, cholera, and dysentery. Doctors and hospitals generally expect immediate cash payment for health services. U.S. medical insurance is not always valid outside the United States. The Medicare/Medicaid program does not provide payment for medical services outside the United States.

Check with your own insurance company to confirm whether your policy applies overseas, including provision for medical evacuation. Ascertain whether payment will be made to the overseas hospital or doctor or whether you will be reimbursed later for expenses you incur. Some insurance policies also include coverage for psychiatric treatment and for disposition of remains in the event of death. Useful information on medical emergencies abroad, including overseas insurance programs, is provided in the Department of State, Bureau of Consular Affairs brochure *Medical Information for Americans Traveling Abroad*, available via its home page and autofax service.

Information on vaccinations and other health precautions may be obtained from the Centers for Disease Control and Prevention's international traveler's hotline at 1-877-FYI-TRIP (1-877-394-8747), via their autofax service at 1-888-CDC-FAXX (1-888-232-3229), or its Internet home page at http://www.cdc.gov.

CRIME INFORMATION: Albania has a high rate of violent crime. Street crime is fairly common and occurs particularly at night. Crime is generally directed at targets of opportunity, not at Americans specifically. Armed carjackings are a matter of considerable concern, especially for drivers of four-wheel drive and sport-utility vehicles, which criminals covet. Persons who are carjacked should surrender their vehicles without resistance. Those resisting carjackings or attempting to run roadblocks have been shot and wounded, some seriously.

The loss or theft of a U.S. passport should be reported immediately to the local police and the nearest U.S. Embassy or Consulate. Useful information on safeguarding valuables and protecting personal safety while traveling abroad is provided in the Department of State's pamphlet *A Safe Trip Abroad*. It is available from the Superintendent of Documents, U.S. Government Printing Office, Washington, D.C. 20402, via the Internet at http://www.access.gpo.gov/su_docs, or http://travel.state.gov.

ROAD SAFETY/TRAVEL CONDITIONS: Major roads are passable, but often in poor repair. Buses travel between most major cities almost exclusively during the day, but may be unreliable and uncomfortable. Travelers have reported attacks by bands of thieves in all parts of the country at all times of day and night. There are no commercial domestic flights and few rail connections.

Safety of Public Transportation: Poor
Urban Road Condition/Maintenance: Poor
Rural Road Condition/Maintenance: Poor
Availability of Roadside Assistance: Poor

AVIATION SAFETY OVERSIGHT: As there is no direct commercial air service at present, or economic authority to operate such service between the United States and Albania, the U.S. Federal Aviation Administration (FAA) has not assessed Albania's Civil Aviation Authority for compliance with international aviation safety standards for oversight of Albania's air carrier operations. For further information, travelers may contact the Department of Transportation within the U.S. at 1-800-322-7873, or visit the FAA Internet home page at http://www.faa.gov/avr/iasa/index.htm. The U.S. Department of Defense (DOD) separately assesses some foreign air carriers for suitability as official providers of air services. For information regarding the DOD policy on specific carriers, travelers may contact DOD at 618-256-4801.

CRIMINAL PENALTIES: U.S. citizens are subject to the laws of the country in which they are traveling. Penalties for possession, use and dealing of illegal drugs in Albania are severe, and convicted offenders can expect jail sentences and fines.

DUAL NATIONALITY: The Albanian government considers any person born in Albania of Albanian parents to be an Albanian citizen. This has in the past delayed notification of the Embassy in certain consular cases.

CURRENCY REGULATIONS: Credit cards and travelers checks are not accepted in Albania, except at the major new hotels in Tirana. Travelers checks can be changed at banks in larger towns.

CHILDREN'S ISSUES: For information on international adoption of children, international parental child abduction, and international child support enforcement issues, please refer to our Internet site at http://travel.state.gov//children's_issues.html, or telephone (202) 736-7000.

REGISTRATION AND EMBASSY LOCATION: U.S. citizens visiting or remaining in Albania are strongly recommended to register at the U.S. Embassy and obtain updated information on travel and security within Albania. Americans are asked to inform the Embassy should they depart Albania. The U.S. Embassy in Tirana is located at Rruga E Elbasanit 103, Tel: (355)(42) 32875, Fax: (355)(42) 32222.

ALBANIA TELEPHONE CODES

Albania country code: 355

- 42 Tirana
- 52 Durrës
- 545 Elbasan
- 726 Gjirokastra
- 824 Korça
- 224 Shkodra
- 623 Berat
- 574 Kavaja
- 63 Vlora

IMPORTANT NUMBERS

- 19 for the Police
- 17 for a medical emergency

TOURISM IN ALBANIA

Albania has during the past fifty years tried its hardest to keep foreigners out of its country. Only now has it recognised that tourism can play an important role in the development of its economy. With its unspoilt beaches and stunning mountainous scenery Albania is set to become a destination for future tourist and travellers. In order to achieved this, however, a fundamental change is taking place through the development of new facilities to cater for the expected increase in tourists.

As such new hotels and guest houses are being constructed across the country. In the short term however, it is likely that Tirana will remain as the starting point for foreign travellers and to this end a number of new developments are taking place.

In February 1995 the Tirana International Hotel re-opened after a year of reconstruction and is operated and managed by the Turin Hotel Group. It is also planned to open a Casino in the basement of the hotel.

In April 1995 the Kuwait company, Mak Albania, completed its first construction with the opening of the Chateau Linza Motel, located at the foot of the Dajti mountain. The Motel has quite stunning views and on clear days you can in fact see the Adriatic coast near Durres. The Motel is designed for travelling businessmen and boasts a number of meeting and conference rooms together with a large restaurant and swimming pool.

In August 1995 the Austrian company Rogner constructed a brand new Four Star hotel along the main boulevard in Tirana. Named the Europapark Hotel this is truly western standard and provides additional facilities for the businessman including office accommodation.

In 2004 Mak Albania is scheduled to open the newly constructed 5 Star hotel for the Inter Continental Group at the foot of the national park in Tirana.

In 1994 a Norwegian company established La Vikinga Ferries to operate a modern ferry service between Bari, Italy and Durres, Albania using a Catamaran boat.

Development guide for the Albanian government in respect of tourism for the next 10 years.

The plan has identified three key sites that will provide the Albanian's with a focus for tourism development. These are the Lalzit bay, north of Durres, Lagore and portalanero either side of Saranda in the south. The report itself only deals with the coastline and has recommended that there be no more than 20,000 beds built in total. 10,000 on the Adriatic coast and 10,000 on the southern coast next to Corfu.

The site north of Durres has been identified as having no more than 1,500 to 2,000 beds and that they must be tourist villages. Each village must have no more than 200/300 beds and be no higher than 2 - 3 storeys.

HOTEL INFORMATION

Rozafa Hotel - 2hrs 30mins from Tirana
Situated in Shkoder. It is a six storey building not in good condition. It needs modernisation and refurbishment. It has two dining halls, a bar, a souvenir shop etc. The hotel is near the Albanian-Yugoslav border post of Hani I Hotit, about a forty five minute drive.

The Hunting Lodge - 2hrs from Tirana
Situated in Lezha, about 4 miles west of the town. It is a one storey high building made of timber. It was set up in the early forties, commissioned by Count Ciano Mussolini's son-in-law. Very few foreigners go there for the night because there are not many rooms with showers or bathrooms, though some still retain the old furniture, which is nice. This hotel is daily frequented by foreigners as the food there is generally very good. It has two dining halls decorated with trophies of wild life. One of the halls is a recent addition but the old one is more comfortable and better furnished. In the past this lodge was frequented by wild fowl's as there is a water-bird reservation nearby along with a fazanry. The hotel is near by the Adriatic sea but the water there is polluted by the waste water of the paper factory of Lissus (the ancient name of Lezha).

The New Hotel - 8 Hrs from Tirana
Situated in Kukes. This is a new hotel built in the last year and is open to foreigners. The hotel is about 1 hour drive from the Albanian-Yugoslav border post of Qafe Morina.

Gjergj Kastrioti - 40 Mins from Tirana
Situated in the town of Kruja. It is a small hotel which badly needs modernisation. It has two dining halls and a bar.

DURRES.

Durres is the ancient Dyrrachium, a Greek colony of the sixth century B.C. It is also the main harbour of Albania and is some forty minutes from Tirana Airport.

The Adriatic Hotel - 45mins from Tirana
Situated in the harbour town of Durres this is the biggest hotel in the area and in the past was generally considered the best in the country. It was built in the fifties. It is a 4 storey building that

has most of its rooms facing the sea, which is no more than 20 metres away. It has a nice spacious dining hall, a bar, a tavern, a souvenir shop, a book shop with books in foreign languages. There are two tennis courts behind the hotel.

The Durres Hotel and The Apollonia Hotel - 45 mins from Tirana
Situated in Central Durres, these hotels are adjoining and share the same dining hall.

Blue Moon - Durres
Probably one of the best small hotels in Albania today. This villa was purchased from the state by a Kuwaiti businessman who wanted a secure rest place on the beach. Situated in the former Government Bloc, the building was totally refurbished with the finest possible fixtures and fittings in 1994. It was then sold onto an Albanian businessman who turned it into a small hotel with 8 rooms. Service is excellent, private facilties with all bedrooms and secure parking.

The Butrinti Hotel - 45mins from Tirana Also situated in central Durres, this hotel is generally frequented by locals.

Tirana Hotel

Situated in Tirana the capital of Albania. Recently re-opened following a refurbishment program undertaken by Turin Hotel Group of Italy. It is the tallest building ever constructed in Albania. Most of the rooms face "Skanderbeg" Square, the main square of the capital. It has a big dining room, 2 smaller ones, 3 bars, where coffee and light refreshments are served, a tavern, a spacious lobby, a souvenir shop. There is a money exchange desk at the reception together with access to telephone and fax facilities. It is about a 30 minute drive from Tirana Airport.

Dajti Hotel
Also situated in the capital, it is the oldest hotel in Albania, mainly frequented by businessmen and diplomats from abroad. The rooms are bigger than in other hotels. There are two dining halls, a bar, a tavern, a souvenir shop. There are also two other duty free shops belonging to the French. This Hotel takes American Express.

Europapark Hotel
Recently opened Four star hotel in the centre of Tirana, offering western standard accommodation, service and food.

Arberia Hotel
Also situated in Tirana, this is mainly frequented by local people.

Apollonia Hotel - 3hrs from Tirana
Situated in Fier. This is a small hotel not in very good condition and is rarely used by foreigners.

Ardenica Monastery - 2hrs 30mins from Tirana
Situated in the district of Fier, this has recently been converted into a small hotel with a capacity of only 32 beds.

Korabi Hotel - 7hrs from Tirana
Situated in Peshkopia, this is a very small hotel.

Skampa Hotel - 1hr 30mins from Tirana, 100 rooms.
Situated in Elbasan which is in the centre of Albania. Elbasan is an historical region and possess the country's only Hot Springs.

Tomori Hotel - 2hrs 30mins from Tirana
Situated in the town of Berat, again this is a small hotel.

Guri I Kuq Hotel - 3hrs 20mins from Tirana, 120 rooms.
Situated in Pogradec on the shores of Lake Ohrid. In terms of location the is probably one of Albania's most idyllic positions for tourism. With a similar environment to that of the lakes in Switzerland. It is about 40 minutes from the Albanian-Yugoslav border post of Struga.

Illiria Hotel - 4hrs from Tirana
Situated in the town of Korca. This is a large hotel however has not been maintained very well and needs extensive modernisation. It is some 45 minutes from the Albanian border post of Kapashtica.

Cajupi Hotel - 5hrs 30mins from Tirana, 50 rooms
Situated in the town of Gjirokastra, considered to be the worst hotel in the country for management and service. The town of Gjirokastra is an area of vast historical interest and is said to be one of the most picturesque regions in the country. This hotel is near the Albanian-Greek border post of Kakavia, some 30 minutes away.

Vlora - 3hrs 30mins from Tirana
The Hotel "Adriatik" is located in central Vlore and can be booked by Telephone 355.42.10 (Tirana central) ext. 2415. It has 38 rooms with 81 beds. It also has a bar, restaurant, and parking available.

Butrinti Hotel - 7hrs from Tirana
Situated in the Adriatic coastal town of Saranda. This hotel is in good condition with most of the rooms facing the sea front. Corfu Island is less than 4 miles away.

SUPPLEMENTS

INTERNATIONAL PARTNERSHIPS RELATED TO LAND

Donor	Dates	Budget	Description
European Union PHARE		300 mill euro	FEOGA Agricultural support EDHIR democracy ECHO Humanitarian
European Union CARDS	2001-2004	187 mill euro	Justice and public order Public administration Trade and transport Environmental institutions Democracy
European Investment Bank			Basic infrastructure, energy ports, water supply
International Monetary Fund		$60 mill	Enterprise privatization Poverty reduction facility
World Bank IDA		$719 mill	Poverty reduction support credit Fisheries Energy, transport NSSED sustainable development
World Bank IFC		$130 mill	Financial sector SME lending Industrial rehabilitation
UN Development Program	2006-2010		Millennium Development Goals Regional government capacity Environmental protection institutions
USAID			Agro-business capacity

			SME credit Local government administration capacity Rule of law
German government		320 mill euro	Water and sewer infrastructure Energy, hydropower
Greek government		50 mill euro	Agriculture and rural infrastructure
Italian government		353 mill euro	Electricity, water, sewer, roads
Japan		$52 mill	Agriculture sector adjustment
Switzerland			

Environment and Infrastructure

Project	Donor	End date	Budget	Description
National Water Strategy	PHARE AL9306	1997	400,000 ecu	Preparation of national Water Strategy
Feasibility Study for Sewage Treatment in Vlora	PHARE AL9306	1997	492,000 ecu	Reduce soil and water contamination by uncontrolled waste water disposal
Feasibility Study for Sewage Treatment in Pogradec	PHARE AL9306	1997	299,400 ecu	Reduce soil and water contamination by uncontrolled waste water disposal
Cleaning of Golem Beach	PHARE AL9306	1997	50,000 ecu	Demonstration coastal project
Master Plan for Dajti National Park	PHARE AL9306	1997	50,000 ecu	Protected land management planning
Karavasta Lagoon Wetland Management	PHARE AL9306	1997	346 200 ecu	Karavasta Ramsar biodiversity protected land/water management
Institutional Support for Environmental Protection	PHARE AL9306	1995	695,800 ecu	Organization, training and technical development of State Committee on Environmental Protection; national Environmental Action Plan
Strengthen Regional Environmental	PHARE AL9306	1997	92,200 ecu	Organization, training and technical development of regional staff

Agencies	AL9306			development of regional staff
Additional equipment Regional Environmental Agencies	PHARE AL9306	1998	98,300 ecu	Equip the offices of the REAs
Benchmark survey of Patos-Marinze oilfield	PHARE AL9306	1997		Pollution control planning and feasibility
Comprehensive Impact Assessment of Uranium Exploration	PHARE	1999	125, 000 ecu	Develop Environmental Impact Assessment methodology
Equipment for Scientific Laboratories	Med-Pol UNEP		$40,000	Chemical laboratories for monitoring of Mediterranean coastal waters
Urban Waste Management	EU LIFE 96	1999	591,000 ecu	Landfills in six municipalities
Mediterranean Wetlands	EU LIFE MedWet	1998		Environmental, development and social study of Kune-Vaini lagoons
Biodiversity Protection	GEF W Bk	1999	$96,000	Prepare the Biodiversity Strategy and Action Plan
Lake Ohrid Conservation	GEF W Bk	2003	$184,000	Lake water monitoring and watershed management, institutional capacity and public participation
Durres Industrial Chemical Pollution	Italy		$7,600	Removal of toxic waste from port and creation of safe storage
Environmental Regulatory Framework	PHARE COP96	1999	200,000 ecu	Strengthening of Environmental Protection agencies -- enforcement
Environmental Institutional Strengthening	PHARE COP97	2001	300,000 ecu	National Environment Action Plan implementation, policy formation for sustainable development
Conservation of Coastal Wetlands	GEF/PNU MedWet	2003	$1.7 million	Mediterranean Region -- six countries -- legal framework and methodologies; Narta Lagoon monitoring
Update national Environmental Action Plan	METAP W Bk	2001	$200,000	Develop a comprehensive national environmental policy

Environment Ministry Enforcement	DFID	2002	400,000 lb	Reorganization, training and management of the new Ministry of Environmental Protection
Institutional Strengthening of Environment Improvement	W Bk	2005	$250,000	Hot spot of Porto Romano, Durres, as model for handling of dangerous waste
Integrated Water Management and Ecosystem Management	W Bk	Start 2005	$4.87 mill	Wetlands in the Kune-Vain marsh area
Fier Arsenic Cleanup	EU	2005	1 million euro	Disposal of arsenic from nitrate fertilizer plant
Environmental Hot Spot Clean Up in Vlora	UNEP MAP	2005	$300,000	Develop remediation plan for clean up of Vlora PVC factory
Prespa lake Trans-boundary Ecosystems	UNDP GEF	2005	$928,000	Protected lands regulation and watershed management
Biosecurity National Framework	UNEP GEF	2006	$185,000/ $123,000	Prepare national Bio-Safety Framework with risk assessment, management and public participation
Institutional Strengthening of Environmental Ministry	DIFD	2005	£300,000	Strengthen the National Environmental inspectorate for monitoring and enforcement
Effective Institute of Environment	Netherld	2006	1 mill euro	Rehabilitation of Institute of Environment for monitoring
Strengthen Environmental Monitoring	EU CARDS	Planned 2005	2.5 mill euro	Monitoring system
Landfill for Hazardous Wastes	EU CARDS	2007	600,000 euro	Design of hazardous waste storage facility
Wastewater Treatment Plant Balsh Oil refinery	EU CARDS	2007	900,000 euro	Rehabilitation of the refinery facility
Construction of Landfill for Hazardous Waste	EU CARDS		3.5 million euro	Construction of hazardous waste facility

National Center and Network Environmental Monitoring	EU CARDS		2.5 million euro	National environmental monitoring network tied into European system
Environmental Laws Harmonization	EU CARDS	2007	2.5 million euro	Prepare environmental legislation and sub-acts to relate with European system
Technical Assistance to Ministry of Environment	Italy			Proposed 2 million euro under Cooperation Protocol Italy/Albania
Butrint National Park Biodiversity	W Bk	2005	$25,000	Feasibility and project design
Capacity development Biodiversity Strategy	GEF		$324,000	Review progress of Biodiversity Strategy and prepare second report
Karavasta Lagoon Management	W Bk	2005	$25,000	Preparation of project design
Ecosystem Management Lake Shkodra	W Bk	2006	$175 000	Trans-boundary pollution control and Biodiversity
Solid Waste Management Korce	SIDA	2006	15 million S krone	Solid waste management plan and institutional organization

Forest and Pasture

Private Forestry Development	USAID	1996		Communal and private forest transfer Communal Forest Users Associations
Forestry Project	W Bk Italy	1997-2003	$8 mill $8.5	Institutional capacity of Forest Directorate; communal forest transfer
Natural Resources Development	W Bk	Start 2005	$80 mill	Continue communal forest transfer Integrated management of watersheds
Korce TransBorder Wildlife				International Land Coalition

Agriculture

Project	Donor	End date	Budget	Description

Rural Development in Remote Mountains	DFID Oxfam			Small infrastructure projects
Mountain Area Development Program	DFIC IFAD		$23 mill	Poverty reduction and non-farm employment, irrigation rehabilitation
Northeastern District Rural development	IFAD		$18.2 mill	
Strengthening Business Capacity in Agriculture	USAID	2004 2005	$2.7 mill $2.0 mill	Assistance to dairy producers
Community Works Project	EU	2002		Albanian Development Fund managed small infrastructure projects
Hellenic Plan for the Balkans	Greece			Rural drinking water
Assistance to Trade Associations	USAID IFDC	1992-98		Creation of farm producers associations
Assistance to Trade Associations	USAID IFDC	1998-2002		
Assistance to Trade Associations	USAID IFDC	2002-2003		Agriculture producers associations and credit unions

Immovable Property Registration System

Project	Donor	End date	Budget	Description
Land Markets in Albania	USAID	1994-2001		Organization of IPRS First registration rural zones
Support for Immovable Property Registration System	PHARE	1994-2001		IPRS mapping capability First registration of rural zones
Registry Organizational Improvement	USAID	2002-2004	$5 mill	First registration or urban and rural zones

Project	Donor	End date	Budget	Description
Korce Region First Registration	EU	2004-2005		First registration

Urban Land Use

Project	Donor	End date	Budget	Description
Land Use Policy	PHARE			Institutional capacity and GIS
Integrated Development Tirana-Durres	EU CARDS	Planned 2005	1 mill euro	Sustainable integrated development master plan for the corridor
Assistance to the Port of Durres	EU CARDS	Planned 2005	2 mill euro	Update the Port Master Plan

Local Government

Project	Donor	End date	Budget	Description
Local Government Assistance	USAID	2005		Local budget and finance Property inventory
Civil registry and address system	EU CARDS	Planned 2005	2.5 mill euro	Address system
Local Community Development Program	EU CARDS	Planned 2005	7.5 mill euro	Infrastructure projects

IMPORTANT BUSINESS AND LEGAL CONTACTS

CONTACT FOR MORE INFORMATION

Donald Brown
Economic and Commercial Officer
U.S.A. Embassy Tirana, Albania
Rruga Elbasanit, Nr. 103
Tirana, Albania
+355 4 224 7285
BrownDA8@state.gov

LAW FIRMS

Durres

Tivari & Harecari1

Address: Rr. Sulejman Kadiu, L. 2 2001 Durres, Albania

Contact: +355(0)52227085 (tel) +355(0)52227085 (fax) info@studioligjore.info; info@lawfirmalbania.com www.studioligjore.info; www.lawfirmalbania.com

Services: Certified Translations. Notary Services.

Attorneys: 1 . 2 . Mr. Idlir Tivari Ms. Elda Harecari

TIRANA

Boga & Associates2

Address: Rr. Ibrahim Rugova (P.O. Box 8264) Tirana, Albania

Contact: +355(0)42251050 (tel) +355(0)42251055 (fax) www.bogalaw.com

Services:

Attorneys: 1 . 2 . Mr. Genc Boga Mr. 3 . 4 . Gerhard Velaj Mr. Sokol 5 . Elmazaj Ms. Alketa Uruci Ms. Renata Leka

Celibashi & Associates3

Address: Rr. Egnatia, Don Bosko P. 9, 5th Floor, H. 3 (Near Tring TV) Tirana, Albania

Contact:

Services: Certified Translations. Notary Services.

Attorneys: 1 . Mr. Aurel Celibashi

CLO Legal Solutions 4

Address: Blvd. Bajram Curri P. Palma e Arte, 5th Floor Tirana, Albania

Contact: +355(0)44314122 (tel) +355(0)44314122 (fax) www.cenameri.com

Services: Certified Translations.

Attorneys: 1 . Mr. Bledar Cenameri

Duraj Law Firm 5

Address: Blvd. Gjergj Fishta P. Gora 1, Kt. 2 Tirana, Albania

Contact: +35544532512 (tel) +35544532512 (fax) info@durajlaw.com www.durajlaw.com

Services:

Attorneys: 1 . Mr. Alban Duraj

6 Fatmir Braka Partners & Associates

Address: Rr. Ismail Qemali P. 11/1, Apr. 1 Tirana, Albania

Contact: julian.mertiri@studiobraka.com www.studiobraka.com

Services: Certified Translations. Notary Services.

Attorneys: 1 . Mr. Fatmir Braka

7 **Hakani & Associates**

Address: Rr. Vaso Pasha P. 13/1, Katui i Zyrave, Apt. 4 Tirana, Albania

Contact: +355(0)42240200 (tel) +355(0)42253422 (fax) www.hakani-attorneys.al

Services:	Court Reporter/Stenographer.	**Attorneys:**	1 .	Mr. Arben Hakani

8 **Haxhia & Hajdari**

Address:	Blvd. Deshmoret e Kombit Twin Towers, 2, Suite 9/1 & 2 Tirana, Albania	**Contact:**	+355(0)42280170 (tel) +355(0)42280171 (fax) venerajaupllari@lawfirmh-h.com.al www.lawfirmh-h.com.al
Services:	Certified Translations. Notary Services.	**Attorneys:**	1 . 2 . 3 . 4 . Mr. Artan Hajdari Mr. Envi Hicka Mr. Maksim R. Haxhia Ms. Eris Hysi

9 **Hoxha, Memi & Hoxha**

Address:	Rr. Nikolla Tupe P.O. Box 48 Tirana, Albania	**Contact:**	+35542274558 (tel) +35542244047 (fax) info@hmh.al www.hmh.al
Services:	Certified Translations. Notary Services.	**Attorneys:**	1 . 2 . Mr. Shpati Hoxha Ms. Eris Hoxha

10 **Isufi International & Associates**

Address:	Rr. Ismail Qemali Kulla Fratari, Nr. 27 Tirana, Albania	**Contact:**	+355(0)662100000 (tel) +355(0)4226935 (fax) info@isufilaw.eu www.isufilaw.eu
Services:	Certified Translations. Notary Services.	**Attorneys:**	1 . Mr. Naim Isufi

K & H Lawfirm Address: Rr. Petro Nini Luarasi,
Nr. 51 Tirana, Albania Contact: +355(0)42237064 (tel) +355(0)4240893 (fax) info@kh-lawfirm.com www.kh-lawfirm.com 11 Attorneys: Services: Mr. Andi Mani 1 . Kalo & Associates Address: G-Kam Business Center Rr. Kavajes,
4th Floor Tirana, Albania Contact: +355(0)42233532 (tel)
www.kalo-attorneys.com
12 Attorneys: Services: Certified Translations.

Mr. Perparim Kalo 1 . Kushe Law Firm Address: Rr. Barrikadave P.
118, Kt. 3 Tirana, Albania Contact: +355(0)42247561 (tel) info@kushe.al www.kushe.al
13 Attorneys:
Services:
Certified Translations.
Notary Services. Mr. Muharrem Kushe 1 . LLF Legal & Tax Address: Rr. Gjin Bue Shpata Tirana, Albania Contact: www.llf-al.com
14 Attorneys:
Services: Certified Translations.

Mr. Erjon Lena 1 . Puto, Topi & Partners Address: Rr. Gjin Bue Shpata, Nr. 3/2 1006 Tirana, Albania Contact: +355(0)44529797 (tel) +355(0)44529797 (fax) www.putopartners.com
15 Attorneys:
Services:
Certified Translations.
Notary Services.
Court Reporter/Stenographer. Mr. Erlir Puto 1 . Tonucci & Partners Albania Address: Rr. Abdi Toptani Torre Drin, 2nd Floor Tirana, Albania Contact: +355(0)42250711/2/4 (tel)

+355(0)42250713 (fax) www.tonucci.com 16 Attorneys: Services: Certified Translations. Notary Services.

Court Reporter/Stenographer. Mr. Artur Asllani 1 .
VLORE Zoto Law Office
Address: Blvd. Ismail Qemali P. 538 Vlore, Albania Contact: +355(0)33227262 (tel) +355(0)33227262 (fax) zotosoffice@gmail.com www.studiozoto.al 17

Services: Certified Translations. **Attorneys:** 1 . Mr. Ilir Zoto

http://tirana.usembassy.gov/list_of_attorneys.html Page 3 of 3

ATTORNEYS

2015

The U.S. Embassy in Tirana, Albania, assumes no responsibility or liability for the professional ability or reputation of, or the quality of services provided by, the following persons or firms. Inclusion on this list is in no way an endorsement by the Department of State or the U.S. Embassy. Names are listed alphabetically, and the order in which they appear has no other significance. The information in the list on professional credentials, areas of expertise and language ability are provided directly by the lawyers. You may receive additional information about the individuals on the list by contacting the Albanian National Chamber of Advocates (http://www.dhka.org.al/).

1 HARECARI, ELDA (MS.)

Law Firm:	Tivari & Harecari		
Address:	Rr. Sulejman Kadiu, L. 2	Contact:	+355(0)52227085 (tel)
	2001 Durres, Albania		+355(0)52227085 (fax)
			+355(0)684055889
			info@studioligjore.info; info@lawfirmalbania.com
			www.studioligjore.info; www.lawfirmalbania.com
Cases:			

Adoptions; Aeronautical/Maritime; Auto/Accidents; Child Custody; Child Protection; Civil Law; Commercial/Business Law; Contracts; Criminal Law; Damages; Estates; Family Law; Foreign Claims; Foreign Investments; Government Relations; Insurance; Labor Relations; Marketing Agreements; Marriage/Divorce; Narcotics; Parental Child Abduction; Patents/Trademarks/Copyrights; Taxes; Transportation Law;

2 TIVARI, IDLIR (MR.)

Law Firm:	Tivari & Harecari		
Address:	Rr. Sulejman Kadiu, L. 2	Contact:	+355(0)52227085 (tel)
	2001 Durres, Albania		+355(0)52227085 (fax)

+355(0)684055889
info@studioligjore.info; info@lawfirmalbania.com
www.studioligjore.info; www.lawfirmalbania.com

Cases:

Adoptions; Aeronautical/Maritime; Auto/Accidents; Child Custody; Child Protection; Civil Law; Commercial/Business Law; Contracts; Criminal Law; Damages; Estates; Family Law; Foreign Claims; Foreign Investments; Government Relations; Insurance; Labor Relations; Marketing Agreements; Marriage/Divorce; Narcotics; Parental Child Abduction; Patents/Trademarks/Copyrights; Taxes; Transportation Law;

ELBASAN

3 GJORGA, MERITA (MS.)

Law Firm: Individual

Address: L. Aqif Pasha, P. 31/1 Elbasan, Albania

Contact: +355(0)684051156 meritagjorga@yahoo.com;

Cases:

Adoptions; Auto/Accidents; Child Custody; Child Protection; Civil Law; Commercial/Business Law; Contracts; Criminal Law; Damages; Family Law; Insurance; Labor Relations; Marriage/Divorce; Narcotics; Parental Child Abduction; Taxes;

TIRANA

4 ASLLANI, Artur (Mr.)

Law Firm: Tonucci & Partners Albania

Address: Rr. Abdi Toptani Torre Drin, 2nd Floor Tirana, Albania

Contact: +355(0)42250711/2/4 (tel) +355(0)42250713 (fax) +355(0)682093083 www.tonucci.com

Cases:

Aeronautical/Maritime; Auto/Accidents; Banking/Financial; Civil Law; Collections; Commercial/Business Law; Contracts; Corporations; Criminal Law; Damages; Estates; Family Law; Foreign Claims; Foreign Investments; Government Relations; Immigration; Insurance; Labor Relations; Marketing Agreements; Marriage/Divorce; Patents/Trademarks/Copyrights; Sports; Taxes; Transportation Law;

5 BOGA, Genc (Mr.)

Address: Law Firm: Rr. Ibrahim Rugova (P.O. Box 8264) Tirana, Albania Boga & Associates

Contact: +355(0)42251050 (tel) +355(0)42251055 (fax) +355(0)682020481 www.bogalaw.com

Cases:

Aeronautical/Maritime; Banking/Financial; Civil Law; Commercial/Business Law; Contracts; Corporations; Estates; Foreign Investments; Government Relations; Immigration; Insurance; Labor Relations; Marketing Agreements; Patents/Trademarks/Copyrights; Sports; Taxes; Transportation Law;

6 BRAKA, Fatmir (Mr.)

Law Firm: Fatmir Braka Partners &

Address: Rr. Ismail Qemali P. 11/1, Apr. 1 Tirana, Albania

Contact: +355(0)684066838 julian.mertiri@studiobraka.com www.studiobraka.com

Cases:

Aeronautical/Maritime; Auto/Accidents; Banking/Financial; Civil Law; Collections; Commercial/Business Law; Contracts; Corporations; Criminal Law; Damages; Estates; Family Law; Foreign Claims; Foreign Investments; Government Relations; Immigration; Labor Relations; Marketing Agreements; Marriage/Divorce; Narcotics; Sports;

7 CELIBASHI, AUREL (MR.)

Law Firm: Celibashi & Associates Address: Rr. Egnatia, Don Bosko Contact: +355(0)693082255; +355(0)672011401
P. 9, 5th Floor, H. 3 (Near Tring TV) Tirana, Albania
Cases:

Auto/Accidents; Civil Law; Contracts; Criminal Law; Damages; Family Law; Foreign Claims; Marriage/Divorce; Narcotics;

8 CENAMERI, Bledar (Mr.)

Address: Law Firm: Blvd. Bajram Curri P. Palma e Arte, 5th Floor Tirana, Albania CLO Legal Solutions

Contact: +355(0)44314122 (tel) +355(0)44314122 (fax) +355(0)694085520 www.cenameri.com

Cases:

Adoptions; Aeronautical/Maritime; Auto/Accidents; Banking/Financial; Child Custody; Child Protection; Civil Law; Collections; Commercial/Business Law; Contracts; Corporations; Criminal Law; Damages; Estates; Family Law; Foreign Claims; Foreign InvestmentsInsurance; Labor Relations; Marketing Agreements; Marriage/Divorce; Patents/Trademarks/Copyrights; Taxes; Transportation Law; Adoptions; Auto/Accidents; Civil Law; Commercial/Business Law; Contracts; Corporations; Criminal Law; Damages; Estates; Family Law; Insurance; Labor Relations; Marriage/Divorce; Narcotics; Patents/Trademarks/Copyrights;

Law Firm: Duraj Law Firm

Address: Blvd. Gjergj Fishta P. Gora 1, Kt. 2 Tirana, Albania

Contact: +35544532512 (tel) +35544532512 (fax) +355692737706 info@durajlaw.com www.durajlaw.com

Cases:

10 ELMAZAJ, SOKOL (MR.)

Law Firm: Boga & Associates

Address: Rr. Ibrahim Rugova
(P.O. Box 8264)
Tirana, Albania

Contact: +355(0)42251050 (tel)
+355(0)42251055 (fax)
+355(0)682007603
www.bogalaw.com

Cases:

Aeronautical/Maritime; Civil Law; Commercial/Business Law; Contracts; Corporations; Estates; Foreign Claims; Patents/Trademarks/Copyrights;

11 HAJDARI, ARTAN (MR.)

Address: Law Firm: Blvd. Deshmoret e Kombit Twin Towers, 2, Suite 9/1 & 2 Tirana, Albania Haxhia & Hajdari

Contact: +355(0)42280170 (tel) +355(0)42280171 (fax) venerajaupllari@lawfirmh-h.com.al www.lawfirmh-h.com.al

Cases:

Adoptions; Aeronautical/Maritime; Auto/Accidents; Banking/Financial; Child Custody; Child Protection; Civil Law; Collections; Commercial/Business Law; Contracts; Corporations; Criminal Law; Damages; Estates; Family Law; Foreign Claims; Foreign InvestmentsInsurance; Labor Relations; Marketing Agreements; Marriage/Divorce; Narcotics; Parental Child Abduction; Patents/Trademarks/Copyrights; Sports; Taxes; Transportation Law; Traffic Law.

12 HAKANI, ARBEN (MR.)

Law Firm: Hakani & Associates

Address: Rr. Vaso Pasha
P. 13/1, Katui i Zyrave, Apt. 4
Tirana, Albania

Contact: +355(0)42240200 (tel)
+355(0)42253422 (fax)
+355(0)682024555
www.hakani-attorneys.al

Cases:

Adoptions; Child Custody; Civil Law; Commercial/Business Law; Contracts; Damages; Estates; Family Law; Labor Relations; Marketing Agreements; Marriage/Divorce;

13 HAXHIA, MAKSIM R. (MR.)

Address: Law Firm: Blvd. Deshmoret e Kombit Twin Towers, 2, Suite 9/1 & 2 Tirana, Albania Haxhia & Hajdari

Contact: +355(0)42280170 (tel) +355(0)42280171 (fax) venerajaupllari@lawfirmh-h.com.al www.lawfirmh-h.com.al

Cases:

Adoptions; Aeronautical/Maritime; Auto/Accidents; Banking/Financial; Child Custody; Child Protection; Civil Law; Collections; Commercial/Business Law; Contracts; Corporations; Criminal Law; Damages; Estates; Family Law; Foreign Claims; Foreign InvestmentsInsurance; Labor

Relations; Marketing Agreements; Marriage/Divorce; Narcotics; Parental Child Abduction; Patents/Trademarks/Copyrights; Sports; Taxes; Transportation Law; Traffic Law.

Address: Law Firm:	Blvd. Deshmoret e Kombit Twin Towers, 2, Suite 9/1 & 2 Tirana, Albania Haxhia & Hajdari	Contact:	+355(0)42280170 (tel) +355(0)42280171 (fax) venerajaupllari@lawfirmh-h.com.al www.lawfirmh-h.com.al

Cases:

Adoptions; Aeronautical/Maritime; Auto/Accidents; Banking/Financial; Child Custody; Child Protection; Civil Law; Collections; Commercial/Business Law; Contracts; Corporations; Criminal Law; Damages; Estates; Family Law; Foreign Claims; Foreign InvestmentsInsurance; Labor Relations; Marketing Agreements; Marriage/Divorce; Narcotics; Parental Child Abduction; Patents/Trademarks/Copyrights; Sports; Taxes; Transportation Law; Traffic Law.

15 HOXHA, Eris (Ms.)

Address: Law Firm:	Rr. Nikolla Tupe P.O. Box 48 Tirana, Albania Hoxha, Memi & Hoxha	Contact:	+35542274558 (tel) +35542244047 (fax) info@hmh.al www.hmh.al

Cases:

Banking/Financial; Commercial/Business Law; Contracts; Corporations; Foreign Investments; Government Relations; Immigration; Insurance; Labor Relations; Marketing Agreements; Taxes;

16 HOXHA, Shpati (Mr.)

Address: Law Firm:	Rr. Nikolla Tupe P.O. Box 48 Tirana, Albania Hoxha, Memi & Hoxha	Contact:	+35542274558 (tel) +35542244047 (fax) +355692054943 info@hmh.al www.hmh.al

Cases:

Banking/Financial; Civil Law; Collections; Commercial/Business Law; Contracts; Corporations; Estates; Foreign Claims; Foreign Investments; Government Relations; Immigration; Insurance; Labor Relations; Marketing Agreements; Patents/Trademarks/Copyrights; Sports; Taxes;

17 HYSI, Eris (Ms.)

Address: Law Firm:	Blvd. Deshmoret e Kombit Twin Towers, 2, Suite 9/1 & 2 Tirana, Albania Haxhia & Hajdari	Contact:	+355(0)42280170 (tel) +355(0)42280171 (fax) venerajaupllari@lawfirmh-h.com.al www.lawfirmh-h.com.al

Cases:

Adoptions; Aeronautical/Maritime; Auto/Accidents; Banking/Financial; Child Custody; Child Protection; Civil Law; Collections; Commercial/Business Law; Contracts; Corporations; Criminal Law; Damages; Estates; Family Law; Foreign Claims; Foreign InvestmentsInsurance; Labor Relations; Marketing Agreements; Marriage/Divorce; Narcotics; Parental Child Abduction; Patents/Trademarks/Copyrights; Sports; Taxes; Transportation Law; Traffic Law.

Law Firm: Isufi International & Associates

Address: Rr. Ismail Qemali Kulla Fratari, Nr. 27 Tirana, Albania

Contact: +355(0)662100000 (tel) +355(0)4226935 (fax) +355(0)682045790 info@isufilaw.eu www.isufilaw.eu

Cases:

Adoptions; Aeronautical/Maritime; Auto/Accidents; Banking/Financial; Civil Law; Collections; Commercial/Business Law; Contracts; Corporations; Criminal Law; Damages; Estates; Family Law; Foreign Claims; Foreign Investments; Government Relations; ImmigratiInsurance; Labor Relations; Marketing Agreements; Marriage/Divorce; Narcotics; Patents/Trademarks/Copyrights; Sports; Taxes; Transportation Law; Traffic Law.

19 KALO, Perparim (Mr.)

Law Firm: Kalo & Associates

Address: G-Kam Business Center Rr. Kavajes, 4th Floor Tirana, Albania

Contact: +355(0)42233532 (tel) +355(0)692090090 www.kalo-attorneys.com

Cases:

Adoptions; Banking/Financial; Civil Law; Collections; Commercial/Business Law; Contracts; Corporations; Damages; Family Law; Foreign Claims; Foreign Investments; Government Relations; Immigration; Insurance; Labor Relations; Marketing Agreements; Marriage/Divorce; Narcotics; Patents/Trademarks/Copyrights; Sports; Taxes; Transportation Law;

20 KUSHE, Muharrem (Mr.)

Law Firm: Kushe Law Firm

Address: Rr. Barrikadave P. 118, Kt. 3 Tirana, Albania

Contact: +355(0)42247561 (tel) info@kushe.al www.kushe.al

Cases:

Adoptions; Auto/Accidents; Banking/Financial; Child Custody; Child Protection; Civil Law; Commercial/Business Law; Contracts; Corporations; Criminal Law; Damages; Estates; Family Law; Foreign Investments; Government Relations; Immigration; Insurance; Labor Relations; Marketing Agreements; Marriage/Divorce; Narcotics; Parental Child Abduction; Patents/Trademarks/Copyrights; Taxes; Transportation Law;

21 LEKA, Renata (Ms.)

Address: Rr. Ibrahim Rugova (P.O. Box 8264) Tirana, Albania

Law Firm: Boga & Associates

Contact: +355(0)42251050 (tel) +355(0)42251055 (fax) +355(0)682007604 www.bogalaw.com

Cases:

Banking/Financial; Civil Law; Commercial/Business Law; Contracts; Corporations; Estates; Foreign Investments; Immigration; Insurance; Labor Relations; Marketing Agreements; Patents/Trademarks/Copyrights; Sports; Taxes; Transportation Law;

22 LENA, Erjon (Mr.)

Address: Rr. Gjin Bue Shpata Tirana, Albania

Law Firm: LLF Legal & Tax

Contact: +355(0)695337456 www.llf-al.com

Cases:

Adoptions; Auto/Accidents; Banking/Financial; Civil Law; Collections; Commercial/Business Law; Contracts; Corporations; Criminal Law; Family Law; Foreign Claims; Foreign Investments; Labor Relations; Marriage/Divorce; Patents/Trademarks/Copyrights; Sports; Taxes; Transportation Law; Traffic Law.

Law Firm: K & H Lawfirm

Address: Rr. Petro Nini Luarasi, Nr. 51 Tirana, Albania

Contact: +355(0)42237064 (tel) +355(0)4240893 (fax) +355(0)692361034; +355(0)694008039 info@kh-lawfirm.com www.kh-lawfirm.com

Cases:

Banking/Financial; Child Custody; Child Protection; Civil Law; Collections; Commercial/Business Law; Contracts; Corporations; Damages; Family Law; Foreign Claims; Foreign Investments; Government Relations; Insurance; Labor Relations; Marriage/Divorce; Patents/Trademarks/Copyrights; Taxes;

24 PENGILI, Enkeleda (Ms.)

Cases:
Address: Blvd. Bajram Curri, Nr. 10 Tirana, Albania
Law Firm: Individual

Contact: +355(0)699959663 e.pengili@gmail.com;

Adoptions; Auto/Accidents; Banking/Financial; Child Custody; Child Protection; Civil Law; Collections; Commercial/Business Law; Contracts; Corporations; Damages; Estates; Family Law; Foreign Investments; Immigration; Insurance; Labor Relations; Marketing Agreements; Marriage/Divorce; Parental Child Abduction; Patents/Trademarks/Copyrights;

25 PUTO, Erlir (Mr.)

Address: Rr. Gjin Bue Shpata, Nr. 3/2 1006 Tirana, Albania
Law Firm: Puto, Topi & Partners

Contact: +355(0)44529797 (tel) +355(0)44529797 (fax) +355(0)682090608 www.putopartners.com

Cases:

Adoptions; Auto/Accidents; Banking/Financial; Civil Law; Commercial/Business Law; Contracts; Corporations; Damages; Estates; Family Law; Foreign Claims; Foreign Investments; Government Relations; Immigration; Insurance; Labor Relations; Marketing Agreements; Marriage/Divorce; Patents/Trademarks/Copyrights; Taxes;

26 URUCI, Alketa (Ms.)

Address: Rr. Ibrahim Rugova (P.O. Box 8264) Tirana, Albania
Law Firm: Boga & Associates

Contact: +355(0)42251050 (tel) +355(0)42251055 (fax) +355(0)682026554 www.bogalaw.com

Cases:

Banking/Financial; Civil Law; Commercial/Business Law; Contracts; Corporations; Foreign Investments; Government Relations; Immigration; Labor Relations; Taxes; Transportation Law;

27 VEIZI, Julian (Mr.)

Law Firm: Individual

Address: Rr. Irfan Tomini P. 32, Shk. 4, Apt. 45 Tirana, Albania
Contact: +355(0)692144516 julianvezi@gmail.com;

Cases:

Adoptions; Aeronautical/Maritime; Auto/Accidents; Banking/Financial; Child Custody; Child Protection; Civil Law; Collections; Commercial/Business Law; Contracts; Corporations; Criminal Law; Damages; Estates; Family Law; Foreign Claims; Foreign InvestmentsInsurance; Labor Relations; Marketing Agreements; Marriage/Divorce; Narcotics; Parental Child Abduction; Patents/Trademarks/Copyrights; Taxes; Banking/Financial; Civil Law; Collections; Commercial/Business Law; Contracts; Corporations; Damages; Estates; Labor Relations; Patents/Trademarks/Copyrights; Sports; Taxes; Transportation Law;

Law Firm: Boga & Associates
Address: Rr. Ibrahim Rugova (P.O. Box 8264) Tirana, Albania
Contact: +355(0)42251050 (tel) +355(0)42251055 (fax) +355(0)682007605 www.bogalaw.com

Cases:

VLORE

29 ZOTO, Ilir (Mr.)
Law Firm: Zoto Law Office
Address: Blvd. Ismail Qemali P. 538 Vlore, Albania
Contact: +355(0)33227262 (tel) +355(0)33227262 (fax) +355(0)693820555 zotosoffice@gmail.com www.studiozoto.al

Cases:

Adoptions; Aeronautical/Maritime; Auto/Accidents; Banking/Financial; Child Custody; Child Protection; Civil Law; Commercial/Business Law; Contracts; Criminal Law; Damages; Family Law; Foreign Claims; Foreign Investments; Immigration; Insurance; Labor Relations; Marriage/Divorce; Narcotics; Parental Child Abduction; Taxes;

USEFUL CONTACTS

H.E. Ambassador
Albanian Embassy
4th Floor
38 Gloucester Gardens
London SW1
England
Tel: +44 171 730 5709
Fax: +44 171 730 5747
Michelle Gillen
Albania Desk Officer
Department of Trade and Industry
Kingsgate House
Victoria Street
London SW1
England

Tel: +44 171 215 4849
Fax: +44 171 215 8598
British Charge d'Affaires Office
Rruga Vaso Pasha
Tirana
Albania
Tel/Fax: +355 42 34973
Adrian Cohen
Managing Director
ITS Travel Services
540 Royal Exchange
Old Bank Street
Manchester
England
Tel: +44 161 839 1111
Fax: +44 161 839 0000

GOVERNMENT CONTACTS

Office	Location	Tel No	Fax No
OFFICE OF THE PRESIDENT	Bulevardi Deshmoret e Kombit, Tirana	+355-42-28491	+355-42-33761
OFFICE OF THE PRIME MINISTER	Bulevardi Deshmoret e Kombit, Tirana	+355-42-34816	+355-42-34818
MINISTRY OF AGRICULTURE & FOOD	Ministria e Bujqesise, Tirana	+355-42-32796	+355-42-27924
MINISTRY OF CONSTRUCTION & TOURISM	Ministria e Ndertimit dhe Turizmit, Tirana	+355-42-32477	+355-42-27879
MINISTRY OF CULTURE, YOUTH AND WOMEN	Ministria e Kultures, Rinise dhe Sporteve, Tirana	+355-42-32488	+355-42-32488
MINISTRY OF DEFENSE	Ministria e Mbrojtjes, Tirana	+355-42-32675	+355-42-28481
MINISTRY OF EDUCATION	Ministria e Arsimit, Tirana	+355-42-34845	+355-42-32002
MINISTRY OF FINANCE	Ministria e Finances, Tirana	+355-42-28405	+355-42-28494
MINISTRY OF FOREIGN AFFAIRS	Ministria e Puneve te Jashtme, Tirana	+355-42-28311	+355-42-32971
MINISTRY OF INDUSTRY, TRANSPORT & TRADE	Ministria e Industrise, Transportit dhe Tregtise, Tirana	+355-42-32503	+355-42-27773
MINISTRY OF HEALTH AND ENVIRONMENTAL PROTECTION	Ministria e Shendetesise dhe Mbrojtjes se Ambjentit, Tirana	+355-42-32937	+355-42-32554
MINISTRY OF MINERAL AND ENERGY RESOURCES	Ministria e Burimeve Minerare dhe Energjitike, Tirana	+355-42-32833	+355-42-34052
MINISTRY OF JUSTICE	Ministria e Drejtesise, Tirana	+355-42-32704	+355-42-28359

MINISTRY OF LABOUR	Rruga e Kavaje, Tirana	+355-42-33429	+355-42-28340
MINISTRY OF INTERNAL AFFAIRS	Ministria e Brendshme, Tirana	+355-42-32794	+355-42-34983
MINISTRY OF HIGHER EDUCATION & SCIENCE	Mine Peza Street, No.4, Tirana	+355-42-32461	+355-42-27975
STATE CONTROL COMMISSION	Komisioni i Kontrollit, Tirana	+355-42-32491	+355-42-32491
GENERAL DIRECTORATE OF TELECOMMUNICATION	Myslym Shyri Str., No.42, Tirana	+355-42-32169	+355-42-33323
DEPARTMENT OF ECONOMIC DEVELOPMENT	Ministry of Finance	+335-42-28467	+335-42-28362

ALBANIAN EMBASSIES

AUSTRIA
Vienna
Tel. +43 1 364628
Fax. +43 1 3691229

BULGARIA
Sofia
Tel. +359 2 441110
Fax. +359 2 443349

CHINA
Beijing
Tel. +86 1 5321120
Fax. +86 1 5321116

CZECH REPUBLIC
Prague
Tel. +42 2 379329

EGYPT
Cairo
Tel. +20 2 3415651

FRANCE
Paris
Tel. +33 1 45535096
Fax. +33 1 45535132

GERMANY
Bonn
Tel. +49 228 351044

GREECE
Athens
Tel. +30 1 7234412
Fax. +30 1 7234457

HUNGARY
Budapest
Tel. +36 1 1227251

ITALY
Rome
Tel. +39 6 8380725
Tel. +39 6 8390201
Fax. +39 6 8313024

POLAND
Warsaw
Tel. +48 22 498516
Fax. +48 22 498516

ROMANIA
Bucarest
Tel. +40 90 793180

SWEDEN
Stockholm
Tel. +46 8 7310920
Fax. +46 8 7310930

SWITZERLAND
Geneva
Tel. +41 22 7311143

TURKEY
Ankara
Tel. +90 4 1466527
Fax. +90 4 1466516

Istanbul
Tel. +90 1 1615726
Fax. +90 1 1616109

UNITED STATES
Washington, DC
Tel. 1 202 223 4942

Permanent Mission to the U.N.
New York
Tel. 1 212 249 2059
Fax. 1 212 517 5204

HOTELS IN ALBANIA

TIRANA

Dajti
Bulevardi Dëshmoret e Kombt
84 rooms
Tel. 42 33326/27662
Fax 42 32012

Tirana International
Sheshi Skenderbe
163 rooms
Tel. 42 34295
Fax 42 34447

Europapark
Bulevardi Dëshmoret e Kombt
Tel. 42 35035
Fax 42 35050

Arbëria
Bulevardi Dëshmoret e Kombt
95 rooms
Tel. 42 42813
Fax. 42 42813

Diplomati
10 rooms
Tel. 42 35542
Fax 42 42457

Chataeu Linza Motel
Linza, mountain resort

6 km from Tirana
Tel. 42 35142
Fax 42 35143

BERAT
Tomorri
45 rooms
Tel. 624 62602

DURRËS
Adriatik
57 rooms
Tel. 52 23612
Fax. 52 23051

Durrësi
92 rooms
Tel. 52 23051
Fax 52 23612

Apollonia
96 rooms
Tel. 52 23051
Fax 52 23612

Hotel Restorant Pameba
14 rooms
Tel/Fax 52 24149

Blue Moon
Plazhi i Durrësit (Durrës Beach), Vila 14

ELBASAN
Skampa
99 rooms
Tel. 545 2651
Fax 545 2093

GJIROKASTRA
Çajupi
36 rooms
Tel. 726 3621
Fax 726 3626

KORÇA
Iliria
108 rooms
Tel. 824 2473
Fax 824 2855

KRUJA
Skenderbeu
38 rooms
Tel. 4210 (through Tirana operator)

KUKËS
Kukës
44 rooms
Tel. 4210 (through Tirana operator) ext. 699, 251, 269

LEZHA
Hunting Lodge
13 rooms
Tel. 4210 (through Tirana operator) ext.483

Llogara Tourist Village
22 rooms (chalets)
Tel. 63 2415

LUSHNJA
Ardenica Inn
10 rooms, located in an old monastery, Restaurant service
Tel. 4210 (through Tirana operator) ext. 2140

POGRADEC
Enkelana
60 rooms
Tel. 4210 (through Tirana operator) ext. 269, 259

SARANDA
Butrinti
75 rooms
Tel. 4210 (through Tirana operator) ext. 538, 417

SHKODRA
Rozafa
82 rooms
Tel. 224 2354
Fax 224 3590

VLORA
Adriatik
38 rooms
Tel. 63 2415

Grand Hotel Dhermi
Dhermi (Vlora)
50 rooms, underwater sports, boats, canoes and windsurf equipment for hire, restaurant,
disco
Tel. 39 366 3275. 4 (dial through Italy)

USEFUL BUSINESS CONTACTS IN EUROPE

Albania		
U.S. Commercial Officer Frederick Baron Econ/Commercial Officer U.S. Embassy Tirana Mailing Box A PSC 59 APO AE 09624 Street: Rruga Labinoti 103 Tirana Telephone: 355-42-33520 Fax: 355-42-32222	CEEBIC Employee Omer Dashi U. S. Embassy Tirana Riugahabinot 103, Tirana Telephone: 355-42-33-520 Fax: 355-42-32-222	Commercial Officer in the U.S. Mr. Arben Tashko First Secretary Embassy of Albania 1511 K Street, NW Suite 1010 Washington, DC 20005 Tel: (202) 223-4942 Fax: (202) 628-7342
Bosnia and Herzegovina		
U.S. Commercial Officer Patrick Hughes Mailing: (Bosnia) Vienna	CEEBIC Employee Edin Fetahovic U.S. Embassy Sarajevo	Commercial Officer in the U.S. Malik Skaljic Counselor/Deputy Chief of Mission

Department of State Washington, D.C. 20521-9900 Street: 43 Ul. Dure Dakovica Sarajevo, Bosnia and Herzegovina Tel: (387-71) 659-743 Fax: (387-71) 659-722	43 Ul. Dure Dakovica Sarajevo, Bosnia and Herzegovina Tel: (387-71) 659-743 Fax: (387-71) 659-722	Embassy of Bosnia and Herzegovina 1707 L Street, N.W., Suite 760 Washington, D.C. 20036 Tel: (202) 833-3612 Fax: (202) 833-2061
Bulgaria		
U.S. Commercial Officer Susan Weidner Senior Commercial Officer U.S. Embassy Sofia 1 A Stamboliski Blvd Sofia Telephone: 359-2-963-4062/2014 Fax: 359-2-980-6850 E-Mail:osofia@doc.gov	CEEBIC Employee Georgi Peev 1 A Stamboliski Blvd, Sofia Telephone: 359-2-88-48-01 Fax: 359-2-980-6850 E-Mail: osofia@doc.gov	Commercial Officer in the U.S. Mr. Panteley Penev Commercial Counselor Embassy of Bulgaria 1621 22nd Street, NW Washington, DC 20008 Tel: (202) 387-7969 Fax: (202) 234-7973
Czech Republic		
U.S. Commercial Officer Michael Murphy Senior Commercial Officer Kathy Kriger Commercial Officer Paula Potts Assistant Commercial Attache U.S. Embassy Prague Hybernska 7a 117 16 Prague 1 Telephone: (420-2) 2421-9844, 2421-9846 Fax: (420-2) 2421-9965	CEEBIC Contact U.S. Embassy Prague Hybernska 7a, 117 16 Prague 1 Telephone: (420-2) 2421-9844 Fax: (420-2) 2421-9965	Commercial Officer in the U.S. Mr. Miroslav Toman Head of Commercial and Economic Section Embassy of the Czech Republic 3900 Spring of Freedom Ave, NW Washington, DC 20008 Tel: (202) 274-9111 Fax: (202) 244-2147 Mrs. Zuzana Novakova First Secretary 1109-1111 Madison Ave. New York, NY 10028 Tel: (212) 717-5643 Fax: (212) 717-5064
Croatia		
U.S. Commercial Officer Patrick Hughes Commercial Officer U.S. Embassy Zagreb Mailing: APO AE 09213-5080 Street: Andrije Hebranga 2 Zagreb Telephone: 385-1-45-55-500 Fax: 385-1-45-53-126	CEEBIC Employee Damir Novinic, Commercial Assistant U.S. Embassy Zagreb Andrije Hebranga 2, Zagreb Telephone: 385-1-45-55-500 Fax: 385-1-45-53-126	Commercial Officer in the U.S. Mr. Aleksandar Heina Economic Counselor 2343 Massachusetts Ave. NW Washington, DC 20008 Tel: (202) 588-5899 Fax: (202) 588-8936
Estonia		
U.S. Commercial Officer David Katz Econ/Commercial Officer U.S. Embassy Tallinn Mailing: Box T APO AE 09723 Street: Kentmanni 20 Tallinn Telephone: 372-6-312021 Fax: 372-6-312025	CEEBIC Employee Reene Sepp U.S. Embassy Tallinn Kentmanni 20, Tallinn Telephone: 372-6-31-20-21 Fax: 372-6-31-20-25	Commercial Officer in the U.S. Mr. Jaan Salvlaid First Secretary, Economic Embassy of Estonia 2131 Massachussetts Ave., NW Washington, DC 20008 Tel: (202) 588-0101 Fax: (202) 588-0108
FYR Macedonia		
	CEEBIC Employee Arben Gega	Commercial Officer in the U.S. Embassy of the Former Yugoslav Republic of

	U.S. Embassy Skopje Ilindenska bb Skopje, F.Y.R. Macedonia Telephone: 389-91-116-180 Fax: 389-91-117-103	Macedonia 3050 K St., NW Ste 210 Washington, DC 20007 Tel: (202) 337-3063 Fax:(202) 337-3093
Hungary		
U.S. Commercial Officer John Fogarasi Senior Commercial Officer U.S. Embassy Budapest Mailing: Department of State Washington, D.C. 20521-5270 Street: Bajza utca 31 H 1062 Budapest Telephone: 36-1-3228600/1217 Fax: 36-1-3422529 or 36-1-3328934	CEEBIC Employee Gabor Kaczmarczyk U.S. Embassy Budapest Bajza utca 31, 1062 Budapest Telephone: 36-1-302-6100 Fax: 36-1-302-0089	Commercial Officer in the U.S. Mr. Pal Kepisz Head of Commercial Representation Economic Affaris Embassy of Hungary 2401 Calvert Street, NW Suite 1021 Washington, DC 20008 Tel: (202) 387-3191 Fax: (202) 387-3140 Mr. Tibor Zselinszky Commerical Counselor Embassy of Hungary 150 East 58th Street 33rd Floor New York, NY 10022 Tel: (212) 752-3060 Tel: (212) 486-2958 Mr. Gyorgy Szabo Commercial Attache Embassy of Hungary Hungarian Commercial Office 1130 Prudential Plaza 130 East Randolph Drive Chicago, IL 60601 Tel: (312) 856-0274 Fax: (312) 856-1080
Latvia		
U.S. Commercial Officer Mary Ruth Coleman Economic Officer U.S. Embassy Riga Mailing: Box R APO AE 09723 Street: Raina Blvd. 7 Riga Local Tel: 371-7-211-572 Telephone: 371-882-0046 (cellular) Fax: 371-782-0047 (cellular)	CEEBIC Employee Anna Zisser U.S. Embassy Riga Raina Blvd. 7, Riga Telephone: 371-7-211-572 Fax: 371-782-0047	Commercial Officer in the U.S. Mr. Normunds Popens Commercial Attache Embassy of Latvia 4325 17th Street Washington, DC 20051
Lithuania		
U.S. Commercial Officer John Stepanchuk Economic Officer U.S. Embassy Vilnius Mailing: Box V APO AE 09723 Street: Akmenu 6 Vilnius Telephone: 370-2-223-031	CEEBIC Employee Jonas Vasilevicius America Center Pranciskonu 3/6, 2005 Vilnius Telephone: 370-2-223-031 x149 Fax: 370-670-6084	Commercial Officer in the U.S. Ms. Dalia Grybauskaite Minister for Economic Affairs Embassy of Lithuania 2622 16th Street Washington, DC 20009 Tel: (202) 234-5860 Fax: (202) 328-0466

Fax: 370-670-6084		
Poland		
U.S. Commercial Officer Maria Andrews Senior Commercial Officer David Ponsar Commercial Officer Alain Bobet Commercial Attache U.S. Embassy Warsaw al. Jerozolimskie 56/C 00-803 Warsaw Telephone: 48-22-625-4374 Fax: 48-22-621-6327	CEEBIC Employee Anna Janczewska (Warsaw) U.S. Embassy Warsaw al. Jerozolimskie 56/C 00-803 Warsaw Telephone: 48-22-625-4374 Fax: 48-22-621-6327 Barbara Blocka (Krakow) U.S. Consulate Krakow ul. Stolarska 9, 31-043 Krakow Tel/Fax:48-12-421-4909 Telex: 325350 KRUSA PL	Commercial Officer in the U.S. Mr. Andrzej Ilczuk Economic Counselor Embassy of the Republic of Poland 1503 21st Street, NW Washington, DC 20036 Tel: (202) 467-6690 Fax: (202) 833-8343 Mr. Andrzej Laganowski Commercial Counselor Embassy of the Republic of Poland 100 Park Avenue, 19th Floor New York, NY 10017 Tel: (212) 370-5300 Fax: (212) 818-9623
Romania		
U.S. Commercial Officer Bill Crawford Senior Commercial Officer U.S. Embassy Bucharest Mailing: APO AE 09213-5260 Street: Strada Tudor Arghezi 7-9 Bucharest Telephone: 40-1-2104042 Fax: 40-1-2100395 Telex: 11416		Commercial Officer in the U.S. Mr. Adrian Constantinescu Minister Counselor Mr. Marian Voicu Commercial Counselor Embassy of Romania 1607 23rd Street, NW Washington, DC 20008 Tel: (202) 332-4848 or 4852 Fax: (202) 332-4858
Slovak Republic		
U.S. Commercial Officer Gene Young Econ/Commercial Officer U.S. Embassy Bratislava Hviezdoslavovo Namesite 4 811 02 Bratislava Tel: 421-7-533-5990 Fax: 421-7-533-0096	CEEBIC Employee Pavol Matusek American Business Center Grosslingova 35, 811 09 Bratislava Telephone: 421-7-361-079 Fax: 421-7-361-085	Commercial Officer in the U.S. Ms. Ingrid Brockova Second Secretary, Economic Officer Embassy of the Slovak Republic 2201 Wisconsin Ave, NW Washington, DC 20007 Tel: (202) 965-5160 Fax: (202) 965-5166 Mr. Jaroslav Smiesny Trade Representative Economic and Commercial Section Embassy of the Slovak Republic 10 East 40th Street Suite 3601 New York, NY 10016 Tel: (212) 679-7044 Fax: (212) 679-7045
Slovenia		
U.S. Commercial Officer Paul Reid Political/Econ Officer U.S. Embassy Ljubljana Prazakova 4 Ljubljana Telephone: 386-61-301427 Fax: 386-61-301401	CEEBIC Employee Marko Mlakar U.S. Embassy Ljubljana Prazakova 4, Ljubljana Telephone: 386-61-301-427 Fax: 386-61-301-401	Commercial Officer in the U.S. Mr. Marjan Smonig, Counselor Republic of Slovenia 1525 New Hampshire Ave., NW Washington, DC 20036 Tel: (202) 667-5363 Fax: (202) 667-4563
Additional Contacts		
World Bank	EBRD	

Janice Mazur Office of the U.S. Executive Director The World Bank Tel: (202)458-0118, 458-0120 Fax: (202)477-2967	Dean Peterson Senior Commercial Officer Office of the U.S. Director One Exchange Square London, EC2A 2 EH, UK Tel: (44-171) 338-6569 Fax: (44-171) 338-6487	

BASIC TITLES ON ALBANIA

IMPORTANT!
All publications are updated annually!
Please contact IBP, Inc. at ibpusa3@gmail.com for the latest ISBNs and additional information

TITLE
Albania A "Spy" Guide - Strategic Information and Developments
Albania A Spy" Guide"
Albania Air Force Handbook
Albania Air Force Handbook
Albania Army Weapon Systems Handbook
Albania Army Weapon Systems Handbook
Albania Army Weapon Systems Handbook
Albania Banking & Financial Market Handbook
Albania Banking & Financial Market Handbook
Albania Business and Investment Opportunities Yearbook
Albania Business and Investment Opportunities Yearbook
Albania Business and Investment Opportunities Yearbook Volume 1 Strategic Information and Opportunities
Albania Business and Investment Opportunities Yearbook Volume 2 Leading Export-Import, Business, Investment Opportunities and Projects
Albania Business Intelligence Report - Practical Information, Opportunities, Contacts
Albania Business Intelligence Report - Practical Information, Opportunities, Contacts
Albania Business Law Handbook - Strategic Information and Basic Laws
Albania Business Law Handbook - Strategic Information and Basic Laws
Albania Business Law Handbook - Strategic Information and Basic Laws
Albania Business Law Handbook - Strategic Information and Basic Laws
Albania Business Law Handbook Volume 2 Investment and Trade Laws Volume 2 Investment and Trade Laws
Albania Business Success Guide - Basic Practical Information and Contacts
Albania Company Laws and Regulations Handbook
Albania Company Laws and Regulations Handbook - Strategic Information and Basic Laws
Albania Constitution and Citizenship Laws Handbook - Strategic Information and Basic Laws
Albania Country Study Guide - Strategic Information and Developments
Albania Country Study Guide - Strategic Information and Developments
Albania Country Study Guide - Strategic Information and Developments Volume 1 Strategic Information and Developments
Albania Criminal Laws, Regulations and Procedures Handbook - Strategic Information,

TITLE
Regulations, Procedures
Albania Customs, Trade Regulations and Procedures Handbook
Albania Customs, Trade Regulations and Procedures Handbook
Albania Diplomatic Handbook - Strategic Information and Developments
Albania Diplomatic Handbook - Strategic Information and Developments
Albania Ecology & Nature Protection Handbook
Albania Ecology & Nature Protection Handbook
Albania Ecology & Nature Protection Laws and Regulation Handbook
Albania Electoral, Political Parties Laws and Regulations Handbook - Strategic Information, Regulations, Procedures
Albania Energy Policy, Laws and Regulation Handbook
Albania Energy Policy, Laws and Regulations Handbook
Albania Energy Policy, Laws and Regulations Handbook
Albania Export-Import Trade and Business Directory
Albania Export-Import Trade and Business Directory
Albania Fishing and Aquaculture Industry Handbook - Strategic Information, Regulations, Opportunities
Albania Fishing Industry Business and Investment Opportunities Handbook
Albania Fishing Industry Business and Investment Opportunities Handbook
Albania Foreign Policy and Government Guide
Albania Foreign Policy and Government Guide
Albania Government and Business Contacts Handbook
Albania Government and Business Contacts Handbook
Albania Immigration Laws and Regulations Handbook - Strategic Information and Basic Laws
Albania Industrial and Business Directory
Albania Industrial and Business Directory
Albania Insolvency (Bankruptcy) Laws and Regulations Handbook - Strategic Information and Basic Laws
Albania Internet and E-Commerce Investment and Business Guide - Strategic and Practical Information: Regulations and Opportunities
Albania Internet and E-Commerce Investment and Business Guide - Strategic and Practical Information: Regulations and Opportunities
Albania Investment and Business Guide - Strategic and Practical Information
Albania Investment and Business Guide - Strategic and Practical Information
Albania Investment and Business Guide - Strategic and Practical Information
Albania Investment and Business Guide - Strategic and Practical Information
Albania Investment and Business Guide Volume 2 Business, Investment Opportunities and Incentives
Albania Investment and Business Profile - Basic Information and Contacts for Succesful investment and Business Activity
Albania Investment and Trade Laws and Regulations Handbook
Albania Investment, Trade Strategy and Agreements Handbook - Strategic Information and Basic Agreements
Albania Labor Laws and Regulations Handbook - Strategic Information and Basic Laws

TITLE
Albania Land Ownership and Agriculture Laws Handbook
Albania Mineral & Mining Sector Investment and Business Guide - Strategic and Practical Information
Albania Mineral & Mining Sector Investment and Business Guide - Strategic and Practical Information
Albania Mining Laws and Regulations Handbook
Albania National Defense and Armed Forces Handbook
Albania National Defense and Armed Forces Handbook
Albania National Development Strategy Handbook: Important Programs and Developments
Albania Oil & Gas Sector Business & Investment Opportunities Yearbook
Albania Oil & Gas Sector Business & Investment Opportunities Yearbook
Albania President Handbook - Strategic Information and Developments
Albania Privatization Programs and Regulations Handbook
Albania Privatization Programs and Regulations Handbook
Albania Recent Economic and Political Developments Yearbook
Albania Recent Economic and Political Developments Yearbook
Albania Recent Economic and Political Developments Yearbook
Albania Starting Business (Incorporating) in....Guide
Albania Tax Guide
Albania Tax Guide
Albania Tax Guide Volume 1 Strategic Information and Basic Regulations
Albania Taxation Laws and Regulations Handbook
Albania Telecom Laws and Regulations Handbook
Albania Telecommunication Industry Business Opportunities Handbook
Albania Telecommunication Industry Business Opportunities Handbook
Albania Transportation Policy and Regulations Handbook
Albania: How to Invest, Start and Run Profitable Business in Albania Guide - Practical Information, Opportunities, Contacts

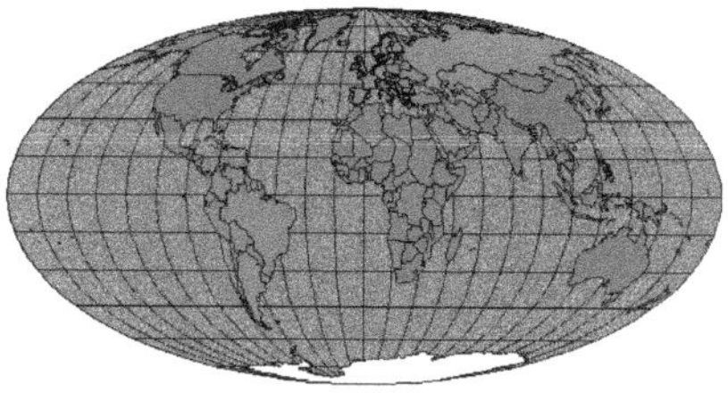

WORLD MINING LAWS AND REGULATIONS HANDBOOK LIBRARY

Price: $149.95 Each

Title
1. Afghanistan Mining Laws and Regulations Handbook
2. Albania Mining Laws and Regulations Handbook
3. Algeria Mining Laws and Regulations Handbook
4. Angola Mining Laws and Regulations Handbook
5. Argentina Mining Laws and Regulations Handbook
6. Armenia Mining Laws and Regulations Handbook
7. Australia Mining Laws and Regulations Handbook
8. Austria Mining Laws and Regulations Handbook
9. Azerbaijan Mining Laws and Regulations Handbook
10. Bahrain Mining Laws and Regulations Handbook
11. Bangladesh Mining Laws and Regulations Handbook
12. Belarus Mining Laws and Regulations Handbook
13. Belgium Mining Laws and Regulations Handbook
14. Benin Mining Laws and Regulations Handbook
15. Bolivia Mining Laws and Regulations Handbook
16. Bosnia and Herzegovina Mining Laws and Regulations Handbook
17. Botswana Mining Laws and Regulations Handbook
18. Brazil Mining Laws and Regulations Handbook
19. Brunei Mining Laws and Regulations Handbook
20. Bulgaria Mining Laws and Regulations Handbook
21. Burkina Faso Mining Laws and Regulations Handbook
22. Burundi Mining Laws and Regulations Handbook
23. Cambodia Mining Laws and Regulations Handbook
24. Cameroon Mining Laws and Regulations Handbook

Title
25. Canada Mining Laws and Regulations Handbook
26. Cape Verde Mining Laws and Regulations Handbook
27. Cayman Islands Mining Laws and Regulations Handbook
28. Central African Republic Mining Laws and Regulations Handbook
29. Chad Mining Laws and Regulations Handbook
30. Chile Mining Laws and Regulations Handbook
31. China Mining Laws and Regulations Handbook
32. Colombia Mining Laws and Regulations Handbook
33. Comoros Mining Laws and Regulations Handbook
34. Congo Mining Laws and Regulations Handbook
35. Congo, Dem. Republic Mining Laws and Regulations Handbook
36. Cook Islands Mining Laws and Regulations Handbook
37. Costa Rica Mining Laws and Regulations Handbook
38. Cote d'Ivoire Mining Laws and Regulations Handbook
39. Croatia Mining Laws and Regulations Handbook
40. Cuba Mining Laws and Regulations Handbook
41. Czech Republic Mining Laws and Regulations Handbook
42. Denmark Mining Laws and Regulations Handbook
43. Djibouti Mining Laws and Regulations Handbook
44. Dominican Republic Mining Laws and Regulations Handbook
45. Dubai Mining Laws and Regulations Handbook
46. Ecuador Mining Laws and Regulations Handbook
47. Egypt Mining Laws and Regulations Handbook

For additional analytical, business and investment opportunities information, please contact Global Investment & Business Center, USA at (202) 546-2103. Fax: (202) 546-3275. E-mail: rusric@erols.com

Title
48. El Salvador Mining Laws and Regulations Handbook
49. Equatorial Guinea Mining Laws and Regulations Handbook
50. Eritrea Mining Laws and Regulations Handbook
51. Estonia Mining Laws and Regulations Handbook
52. Ethiopia Mining Laws and Regulations Handbook
53. Fiji Mining Laws and Regulations Handbook
54. Finland Mining Laws and Regulations Handbook
55. France Mining Laws and Regulations Handbook
56. Gabon Mining Laws and Regulations Handbook
57. Gambia Mining Laws and Regulations Handbook
58. Georgia Mining Laws and Regulations Handbook
59. Germany Mining Laws and Regulations Handbook
60. Ghana Mining Laws and Regulations Handbook
61. Greece Mining Laws and Regulations Handbook
62. Guatemala Mining Laws and Regulations Handbook
63. Guinea Mining Laws and Regulations Handbook
64. Guinea-Bissau Mining Laws and Regulations Handbook
65. Guyana Mining Laws and Regulations Handbook
66. Haiti Mining Laws and Regulations Handbook
67. Honduras Mining Laws and Regulations Handbook
68. Hungary Mining Laws and Regulations Handbook
69. Iceland Mining Laws and Regulations Handbook
70. India Mining Laws and Regulations Handbook
71. Indonesia Mining Laws and Regulations Handbook
72. Iran Mining Laws and Regulations Handbook
73. Iraq Mining Laws and Regulations Handbook
74. Ireland Mining Laws and Regulations Handbook
75. Israel Mining Laws and Regulations Handbook
76. Italy Mining Laws and Regulations Handbook
77. Jamaica Mining Laws and Regulations Handbook
78. Japan Mining Laws and Regulations Handbook
79. Jordan Mining Laws and Regulations Handbook
80. Kazakhstan Mining Laws and Regulations Handbook
81. Kenya Mining Laws and Regulations Handbook
82. Korea, North Mining Laws and Regulations Handbook
83. Korea, South Mining Laws and Regulations

Title
Handbook
84. Kuwait Mining Laws and Regulations Handbook
85. Kyrgyzstan Mining Laws and Regulations Handbook
86. Laos Mining Laws and Regulations Handbook
87. Latvia Mining Laws and Regulations Handbook
88. Lesotho Mining Laws and Regulations Handbook
89. Liberia Mining Laws and Regulations Handbook
90. Libya Mining Laws and Regulations Handbook
91. Lithuania Mining Laws and Regulations Handbook
92. Macedonia Republic Mining Laws and Regulations Handbook
93. Madagascar Mining Laws and Regulations Handbook
94. Malawi Mining Laws and Regulations Handbook
95. Malaysia Mining Laws and Regulations Handbook
96. Mali Mining Laws and Regulations Handbook
97. Mauritania Mining Laws and Regulations Handbook
98. Mauritius Mining Laws and Regulations Handbook
99. Mayotte Mining Laws and Regulations Handbook
100. Mexico Mining Laws and Regulations Handbook
101. Micronesia Mining Laws and Regulations Handbook
102. Moldova Mining Laws and Regulations Handbook
103. Mongolia Mining Laws and Regulations Handbook
104. Morocco Mining Laws and Regulations Handbook
105. Mozambique Mining Laws and Regulations Handbook
106. Myanmar Mining Laws and Regulations Handbook
107. Namibia Mining Laws and Regulations Handbook
108. Nepal Mining Laws and Regulations Handbook
109. Netherlands Mining Laws and Regulations Handbook
110. New Zealand Mining Laws and Regulations Handbook
111. Nicaragua Mining Laws and Regulations Handbook
112. Niger Mining Laws and Regulations Handbook
113. Nigeria Mining Laws and Regulations Handbook
114. Norway Mining Laws and Regulations Handbook
115. Oman Mining Laws and Regulations Handbook

Title
116. Pakistan Mining Laws and Regulations Handbook
117. Papua New Guinea Mining Laws and Regulations Handbook
118. Paraguay Mining Laws and Regulations Handbook
119. Peru Mining Laws and Regulations Handbook
120. Philippines Mining Laws and Regulations Handbook
121. Poland Mining Laws and Regulations Handbook
122. Portugal Mining Laws and Regulations Handbook
123. Qatar Mining Laws and Regulations Handbook
124. Romania Mining Laws and Regulations Handbook
125. Russia Mining Laws and Regulations Handbook
126. Rwanda Mining Laws and Regulations Handbook
127. Sao Tome and Principe Mining Laws and Regulations Handbook
128. Saudi Arabia Mining Laws and Regulations Handbook
129. Scotland Mining Laws and Regulations Handbook
130. Senegal Mining Laws and Regulations Handbook
131. Serbia Mining Laws and Regulations Handbook
132. Sierra Leone Mining Laws and Regulations Handbook
133. Slovakia Mining Laws and Regulations Handbook
134. Slovenia Mining Laws and Regulations Handbook
135. Somalia Mining Laws and Regulations Handbook
136. South Africa Mining Laws and Regulations Handbook
137. Spain Mining Laws and Regulations Handbook
138. Sri Lanka Mining Laws and Regulations Handbook
139. Sudan Mining Laws and Regulations Handbook
140. Suriname Mining Laws and Regulations Handbook
141. Swaziland Mining Laws and Regulations Handbook
142. Sweden Mining Laws and Regulations Handbook
143. Syria Mining Laws and Regulations Handbook
144. Taiwan Mining Laws and Regulations Handbook
145. Tajikistan Mining Laws and Regulations Handbook
146. Tanzania Mining Laws and Regulations Handbook
147. Thailand Mining Laws and Regulations Handbook
148. Togo Mining Laws and Regulations Handbook
149. Trinidad and Tobago Mining Laws and Regulations Handbook
150. Tunisia Mining Laws and Regulations Handbook
151. Turkey Mining Laws and Regulations Handbook
152. Turkmenistan Mining Laws and Regulations Handbook
153. Uganda Mining Laws and Regulations Handbook
154. Ukraine Mining Laws and Regulations Handbook
155. United Arab Emirates Mining Laws and Regulations Handbook
156. United Kingdom Mining Laws and Regulations Handbook
157. United States Mining Laws and Regulations Handbook
158. Uruguay Mining Laws and Regulations Handbook
159. Uzbekistan Mining Laws and Regulations Handbook
160. Venezuela Mining Laws and Regulations Handbook
161. Vietnam Mining Laws and Regulations Handbook
162. Yemen Mining Laws and Regulations Handbook
163. Zambia Mining Laws and Regulations Handbook
164. Zimbabwe Mining Laws and Regulations Handbook

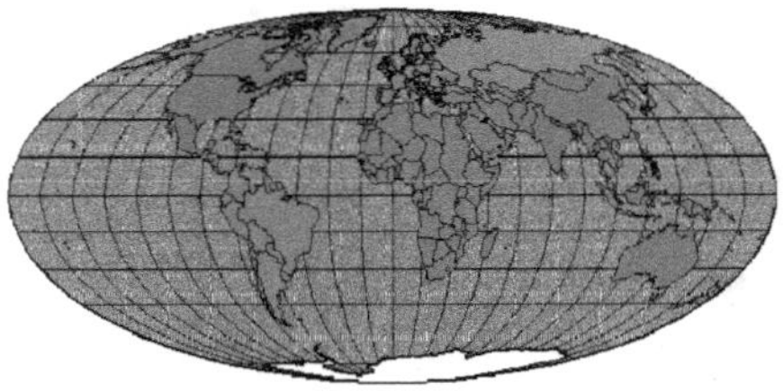

WORLD BUSINESS AND INVESTMENT OPPORTUNITIES YEARBOOK LIBRARY

World Business Information Catalog, USA: http://www.ibpus.com
Email: ibpusa3@gmail.com

Price: $99.95 Each

TITLE
Abkhazia (Republic of Abkhazia) Business and Investment Opportunities Yearbook Volume 1 Strategic, Practical Information and Opportunities
Afghanistan Business and Investment Opportunities Yearbook Volume 1 Strategic, Practical Information and Opportunities
Aland Business and Investment Opportunities Yearbook Volume 1 Strategic, Practical Information and Opportunities
Albania Business and Investment Opportunities Yearbook Volume 1 Strategic, Practical Information and Opportunities
Algeria Business and Investment Opportunities Yearbook Volume 1 Strategic, Practical Information and Opportunities
Andorra Business and Investment Opportunities Yearbook Volume 1 Strategic, Practical Information and Opportunities
Angola Business and Investment Opportunities Yearbook Volume 1 Strategic, Practical Information and Opportunities
Anguilla Business and Investment Opportunities Yearbook Volume 1 Strategic, Practical Information and Opportunities
Antigua and Barbuda Business and Investment Opportunities Yearbook Volume 1 Strategic, Practical Information and Opportunities
Antilles (Netherlands) Business and Investment Opportunities Yearbook Volume 1 Strategic, Practical Information and Opportunities
Argentina Business and Investment Opportunities Yearbook Volume 1 Strategic, Practical Information and Opportunities
Armenia Business and Investment Opportunities Yearbook Volume 1 Strategic, Practical Information and Opportunities
Aruba Business and Investment Opportunities Yearbook Volume 1 Strategic, Practical Information and Opportunities
Australia Business and Investment Opportunities Yearbook Volume 1 Strategic, Practical Information and Opportunities
Austria Business and Investment Opportunities Yearbook Volume 1 Strategic, Practical Information and Opportunities
Azerbaijan Business and Investment Opportunities Yearbook Volume 1 Strategic, Practical Information and Opportunities
Bahamas Business and Investment Opportunities Yearbook Volume 1 Strategic, Practical Information and Opportunities
Bahrain Business and Investment Opportunities Yearbook Volume 1 Strategic, Practical Information and Opportunities
Bangladesh Business and Investment Opportunities Yearbook Volume 1 Strategic, Practical Information and Opportunities
Barbados Business and Investment Opportunities Yearbook Volume 1 Strategic, Practical Information and Opportunities
Belarus Business and Investment Opportunities Yearbook Volume 1 Strategic, Practical Information and Opportunities

For additional analytical, business and investment opportunities information,
Please contact Global Investment & Business Center, USA
at (202) 546-2103. Fax: (202) 546-3275. E-mail: ibpusa3@gmail.com

TITLE
Belgium Business and Investment Opportunities Yearbook Volume 1 Strategic, Practical Information and Opportunities
Belize Business and Investment Opportunities Yearbook Volume 1 Strategic, Practical Information and Opportunities
Benin Business and Investment Opportunities Yearbook Volume 1 Strategic, Practical Information and Opportunities
Bermuda Business and Investment Opportunities Yearbook Volume 1 Strategic, Practical Information and Opportunities
Bhutan Business and Investment Opportunities Yearbook Volume 1 Strategic, Practical Information and Opportunities
Bolivia Business and Investment Opportunities Yearbook Volume 1 Strategic, Practical Information and Opportunities
Bosnia and Herzegovina Business and Investment Opportunities Yearbook Volume 1 Strategic, Practical Information and Opportunities
Botswana Business and Investment Opportunities Yearbook Volume 1 Strategic, Practical Information and Opportunities
Brazil Business and Investment Opportunities Yearbook Volume 1 Strategic, Practical Information and Opportunities
Brunei Business and Investment Opportunities Yearbook Volume 1 Strategic, Practical Information and Opportunities
Bulgaria Business and Investment Opportunities Yearbook Volume 1 Strategic, Practical Information and Opportunities
Burkina Faso Business and Investment Opportunities Yearbook Volume 1 Strategic, Practical Information and Opportunities
Burundi Business and Investment Opportunities Yearbook Volume 1 Strategic, Practical Information and Opportunities
Cambodia Business and Investment Opportunities Yearbook Volume 1 Strategic, Practical Information and Opportunities
Cameroon Business and Investment Opportunities Yearbook Volume 1 Strategic, Practical Information and Opportunities
Canada Business and Investment Opportunities Yearbook Volume 1 Strategic, Practical Information and Opportunities
Cape Verde Business and Investment Opportunities Yearbook Volume 1 Strategic, Practical Information and Opportunities
Cayman Islands Business and Investment Opportunities Yearbook Volume 1 Strategic, Practical Information and Opportunities
Central African Republic Business and Investment Opportunities Yearbook Volume 1 Strategic, Practical Information and Opportunities
Chad Business and Investment Opportunities Yearbook Volume 1 Strategic, Practical Information and Opportunities
Chile Business and Investment Opportunities Yearbook Volume 1 Strategic, Practical Information and Opportunities
China Business and Investment Opportunities Yearbook Volume 1 Strategic, Practical Information and Opportunities
Colombia Business and Investment Opportunities Yearbook Volume 1 Strategic, Practical Information and Opportunities
Comoros Business and Investment Opportunities Yearbook Volume 1 Strategic, Practical Information and Opportunities
Congo Business and Investment Opportunities Yearbook Volume 1 Strategic, Practical Information and Opportunities
Congo, Democratic Republic Business and Investment Opportunities Yearbook Volume 1 Strategic, Practical Information and Opportunities
Cook Islands Business and Investment Opportunities Yearbook Volume 1 Strategic, Practical Information and Opportunities
Costa Rica Business and Investment Opportunities Yearbook Volume 1 Strategic, Practical Information and Opportunities

TITLE
Cote d'Ivoire Business and Investment Opportunities Yearbook Volume 1 Strategic, Practical Information and Opportunities
Croatia Business and Investment Opportunities Yearbook Volume 1 Strategic, Practical Information and Opportunities
Cuba Business and Investment Opportunities Yearbook Volume 1 Strategic, Practical Information and Opportunities
Cyprus Business and Investment Opportunities Yearbook Volume 1 Strategic, Practical Information and Opportunities
Czech Republic Business and Investment Opportunities Yearbook Volume 1 Strategic, Practical Information and Opportunities
Denmark Business and Investment Opportunities Yearbook Volume 1 Strategic, Practical Information and Opportunities
Djibouti Business and Investment Opportunities Yearbook Volume 1 Strategic, Practical Information and Opportunities
Dominica Business and Investment Opportunities Yearbook Volume 1 Strategic, Practical Information and Opportunities
Dominican Republic Business and Investment Opportunities Yearbook Volume 1 Strategic, Practical Information and Opportunities
Ecuador Business and Investment Opportunities Yearbook Volume 1 Strategic, Practical Information and Opportunities
Egypt Business and Investment Opportunities Yearbook Volume 1 Strategic, Practical Information and Opportunities
El Salvador Business and Investment Opportunities Yearbook Volume 1 Strategic, Practical Information and Opportunities
Equatorial Guinea Business and Investment Opportunities Yearbook Volume 1 Strategic, Practical Information and Opportunities
Eritrea Business and Investment Opportunities Yearbook Volume 1 Strategic, Practical Information and Opportunities
Estonia Business and Investment Opportunities Yearbook Volume 1 Strategic, Practical Information and Opportunities
Ethiopia Business and Investment Opportunities Yearbook Volume 1 Strategic, Practical Information and Opportunities
Falkland Islands Business and Investment Opportunities Yearbook Volume 1 Strategic, Practical Information and Opportunities
Faroes Islands Business and Investment Opportunities Yearbook Volume 1 Strategic, Practical Information and Opportunities
Fiji Business and Investment Opportunities Yearbook Volume 1 Strategic, Practical Information and Opportunities
Finland Business and Investment Opportunities Yearbook Volume 1 Strategic, Practical Information and Opportunities
France Business and Investment Opportunities Yearbook Volume 1 Strategic, Practical Information and Opportunities
Gabon Business and Investment Opportunities Yearbook Volume 1 Strategic, Practical Information and Opportunities
Gambia Business and Investment Opportunities Yearbook Volume 1 Strategic, Practical Information and Opportunities
Georgia Business and Investment Opportunities Yearbook Volume 1 Strategic, Practical Information and Opportunities
Germany Business and Investment Opportunities Yearbook Volume 1 Strategic, Practical Information and Opportunities
Ghana Business and Investment Opportunities Yearbook Volume 1 Strategic, Practical Information and Opportunities
Gibraltar Business and Investment Opportunities Yearbook Volume 1 Strategic, Practical Information and Opportunities
Greece Business and Investment Opportunities Yearbook Volume 1 Strategic, Practical Information and Opportunities

TITLE
Greenland Business and Investment Opportunities Yearbook Volume 1 Strategic, Practical Information and Opportunities
Grenada Business and Investment Opportunities Yearbook Volume 1 Strategic, Practical Information and Opportunities
Guam Business and Investment Opportunities Yearbook Volume 1 Strategic, Practical Information and Opportunities
Guatemala Business and Investment Opportunities Yearbook Volume 1 Strategic, Practical Information and Opportunities
Guernsey Business and Investment Opportunities Yearbook Volume 1 Strategic, Practical Information and Opportunities
Guinea Business and Investment Opportunities Yearbook Volume 1 Strategic, Practical Information and Opportunities
Guinea-Bissau Business and Investment Opportunities Yearbook Volume 1 Strategic, Practical Information and Opportunities
Guyana Business and Investment Opportunities Yearbook Volume 1 Strategic, Practical Information and Opportunities
Haiti Business and Investment Opportunities Yearbook Volume 1 Strategic, Practical Information and Opportunities
Honduras Business and Investment Opportunities Yearbook Volume 1 Strategic, Practical Information and Opportunities
Hungary Business and Investment Opportunities Yearbook Volume 1 Strategic, Practical Information and Opportunities
Iceland Business and Investment Opportunities Yearbook Volume 1 Strategic, Practical Information and Opportunities
India Business and Investment Opportunities Yearbook Volume 1 Strategic, Practical Information and Opportunities
Indonesia Business and Investment Opportunities Yearbook Volume 1 Strategic, Practical Information and Opportunities
Iran Business and Investment Opportunities Yearbook Volume 1 Strategic, Practical Information and Opportunities
Iraq Business and Investment Opportunities Yearbook Volume 1 Strategic, Practical Information and Opportunities
Ireland Business and Investment Opportunities Yearbook Volume 1 Strategic, Practical Information and Opportunities
Israel Business and Investment Opportunities Yearbook Volume 1 Strategic, Practical Information and Opportunities
Italy Business and Investment Opportunities Yearbook Volume 1 Strategic, Practical Information and Opportunities
Jamaica Business and Investment Opportunities Yearbook Volume 1 Strategic, Practical Information and Opportunities
Japan Business and Investment Opportunities Yearbook Volume 1 Strategic, Practical Information and Opportunities
Jersey Business and Investment Opportunities Yearbook Volume 1 Strategic, Practical Information and Opportunities
Jordan Business and Investment Opportunities Yearbook Volume 1 Strategic, Practical Information and Opportunities
Kazakhstan Business and Investment Opportunities Yearbook Volume 1 Strategic, Practical Information and Opportunities
Kenya Business and Investment Opportunities Yearbook Volume 1 Strategic, Practical Information and Opportunities
Kiribati Business and Investment Opportunities Yearbook Volume 1 Strategic, Practical Information and Opportunities
Korea, North Business and Investment Opportunities Yearbook Volume 1 Strategic, Practical Information and Opportunities
Korea, South Business and Investment Opportunities Yearbook Volume 1 Strategic, Practical Information and Opportunities

TITLE
Kosovo Business and Investment Opportunities Yearbook Volume 1 Strategic, Practical Information and Opportunities
Kurdistan Business and Investment Opportunities Yearbook Volume 1 Strategic, Practical Information and Opportunities
Kuwait Business and Investment Opportunities Yearbook Volume 1 Strategic, Practical Information and Opportunities
Kyrgyzstan Business and Investment Opportunities Yearbook Volume 1 Strategic, Practical Information and Opportunities
Laos Business and Investment Opportunities Yearbook Volume 1 Strategic, Practical Information and Opportunities
Latvia Business and Investment Opportunities Yearbook Volume 1 Strategic, Practical Information and Opportunities
Lebanon Business and Investment Opportunities Yearbook Volume 1 Strategic, Practical Information and Opportunities
Lesotho Business and Investment Opportunities Yearbook Volume 1 Strategic, Practical Information and Opportunities
Liberia Business and Investment Opportunities Yearbook Volume 1 Strategic, Practical Information and Opportunities
Libya Business and Investment Opportunities Yearbook Volume 1 Strategic, Practical Information and Opportunities
Liechtenstein Business and Investment Opportunities Yearbook Volume 1 Strategic, Practical Information and Opportunities
Lithuania Business and Investment Opportunities Yearbook Volume 1 Strategic, Practical Information and Opportunities
Luxembourg Business and Investment Opportunities Yearbook Volume 1 Strategic, Practical Information and Opportunities
Macao Business and Investment Opportunities Yearbook Volume 1 Strategic, Practical Information and Opportunities
Macedonia Business and Investment Opportunities Yearbook Volume 1 Strategic, Practical Information and Opportunities
Madagascar Business and Investment Opportunities Yearbook Volume 1 Strategic, Practical Information and Opportunities
Madeira Business and Investment Opportunities Yearbook Volume 1 Strategic, Practical Information and Opportunities
Malawi Business and Investment Opportunities Yearbook Volume 1 Strategic, Practical Information and Opportunities
Malaysia Business and Investment Opportunities Yearbook Volume 1 Strategic, Practical Information and Opportunities
Maldives Business and Investment Opportunities Yearbook Volume 1 Strategic, Practical Information and Opportunities
Mali Business and Investment Opportunities Yearbook Volume 1 Strategic, Practical Information and Opportunities
Malta Business and Investment Opportunities Yearbook Volume 1 Strategic, Practical Information and Opportunities
Man Business and Investment Opportunities Yearbook Volume 1 Strategic, Practical Information and Opportunities
Marshall Islands Business and Investment Opportunities Yearbook Volume 1 Strategic, Practical Information and Opportunities
Mauritania Business and Investment Opportunities Yearbook Volume 1 Strategic, Practical Information and Opportunities
Mauritius Business and Investment Opportunities Yearbook Volume 1 Strategic, Practical Information and Opportunities
Mayotte Business and Investment Opportunities Yearbook Volume 1 Strategic, Practical Information and Opportunities
Mexico Business and Investment Opportunities Yearbook Volume 1 Strategic, Practical Information and Opportunities

TITLE
Micronesia Business and Investment Opportunities Yearbook Volume 1 Strategic, Practical Information and Opportunities
Moldova Business and Investment Opportunities Yearbook Volume 1 Strategic, Practical Information and Opportunities
Monaco Business and Investment Opportunities Yearbook Volume 1 Strategic, Practical Information and Opportunities
Mongolia Business and Investment Opportunities Yearbook Volume 1 Strategic, Practical Information and Opportunities
Montserrat Business and Investment Opportunities Yearbook Volume 1 Strategic, Practical Information and Opportunities
Montenegro Business and Investment Opportunities Yearbook Volume 1 Strategic, Practical Information and Opportunities
Morocco Business and Investment Opportunities Yearbook Volume 1 Strategic, Practical Information and Opportunities
Mozambique Business and Investment Opportunities Yearbook Volume 1 Strategic, Practical Information and Opportunities
Myanmar Business and Investment Opportunities Yearbook Volume 1 Strategic, Practical Information and Opportunities
Nagorno-Karabakh Republic Business and Investment Opportunities Yearbook Volume 1 Strategic, Practical Information and Opportunities
Namibia Business and Investment Opportunities Yearbook Volume 1 Strategic, Practical Information and Opportunities
Nauru Business and Investment Opportunities Yearbook Volume 1 Strategic, Practical Information and Opportunities
Nepal Business and Investment Opportunities Yearbook Volume 1 Strategic, Practical Information and Opportunities
Netherlands Business and Investment Opportunities Yearbook Volume 1 Strategic, Practical Information and Opportunities
New Caledonia Business and Investment Opportunities Yearbook Volume 1 Strategic, Practical Information and Opportunities
New Zealand Business and Investment Opportunities Yearbook Volume 1 Strategic, Practical Information and Opportunities
Nicaragua Business and Investment Opportunities Yearbook Volume 1 Strategic, Practical Information and Opportunities
Niger Business and Investment Opportunities Yearbook Volume 1 Strategic, Practical Information and Opportunities
Nigeria Business and Investment Opportunities Yearbook Volume 1 Strategic, Practical Information and Opportunities
Niue Business and Investment Opportunities Yearbook Volume 1 Strategic, Practical Information and Opportunities
Northern Cyprus (Turkish Republic of Northern Cyprus) Business and Investment Opportunities Yearbook Volume 1 Strategic, Practical Information and Opportunities
Northern Mariana Islands Business and Investment Opportunities Yearbook Volume 1 Strategic, Practical Information and Opportunities
Norway Business and Investment Opportunities Yearbook Volume 1 Strategic, Practical Information and Opportunities
Oman Business and Investment Opportunities Yearbook Volume 1 Strategic, Practical Information and Opportunities
Pakistan Business and Investment Opportunities Yearbook Volume 1 Strategic, Practical Information and Opportunities
Palau Business and Investment Opportunities Yearbook Volume 1 Strategic, Practical Information and Opportunities
Palestine (West Bank & Gaza) Business and Investment Opportunities Yearbook Volume 1 Strategic, Practical Information and Opportunities
Panama Business and Investment Opportunities Yearbook Volume 1 Strategic, Practical Information and Opportunities

TITLE
Papua New Guinea Business and Investment Opportunities Yearbook Volume 1 Strategic, Practical Information and Opportunities
Paraguay Business and Investment Opportunities Yearbook Volume 1 Strategic, Practical Information and Opportunities
Peru Business and Investment Opportunities Yearbook Volume 1 Strategic, Practical Information and Opportunities
Philippines Business and Investment Opportunities Yearbook Volume 1 Strategic, Practical Information and Opportunities
Pitcairn Islands Business and Investment Opportunities Yearbook Volume 1 Strategic, Practical Information and Opportunities
Poland Business and Investment Opportunities Yearbook Volume 1 Strategic, Practical Information and Opportunities
Polynesia French Business and Investment Opportunities Yearbook Volume 1 Strategic, Practical Information and Opportunities
Portugal Business and Investment Opportunities Yearbook Volume 1 Strategic, Practical Information and Opportunities
Qatar Business and Investment Opportunities Yearbook Volume 1 Strategic, Practical Information and Opportunities
Romania Business and Investment Opportunities Yearbook Volume 1 Strategic, Practical Information and Opportunities
Russia Business and Investment Opportunities Yearbook Volume 1 Strategic, Practical Information and Opportunities
Rwanda Business and Investment Opportunities Yearbook Volume 1 Strategic, Practical Information and Opportunities
Sahrawi Arab Democratic Republic Volume 1 Strategic Information and Developments
Saint Kitts and Nevis Business and Investment Opportunities Yearbook Volume 1 Strategic, Practical Information and Opportunities
Saint Lucia Business and Investment Opportunities Yearbook Volume 1 Strategic, Practical Information and Opportunities
Saint Vincent and The Grenadines Business and Investment Opportunities Yearbook Volume 1 Strategic, Practical Information and Opportunities
Samoa (American) A Business and Investment Opportunities Yearbook Volume 1 Strategic, Practical Information and Opportunities
Samoa (Western) Business and Investment Opportunities Yearbook Volume 1 Strategic, Practical Information and Opportunities
San Marino Business and Investment Opportunities Yearbook Volume 1 Strategic, Practical Information and Opportunities
Sao Tome and Principe Business and Investment Opportunities Yearbook Volume 1 Strategic, Practical Information and Opportunities
Saudi Arabia Business and Investment Opportunities Yearbook Volume 1 Strategic, Practical Information and Opportunities
Scotland Business and Investment Opportunities Yearbook Volume 1 Strategic, Practical Information and Opportunities
Senegal Business and Investment Opportunities Yearbook Volume 1 Strategic, Practical Information and Opportunities
Serbia Business and Investment Opportunities Yearbook Volume 1 Strategic, Practical Information and Opportunities
Seychelles Business and Investment Opportunities Yearbook Volume 1 Strategic, Practical Information and Opportunities
Sierra Leone Business and Investment Opportunities Yearbook Volume 1 Strategic, Practical Information and Opportunities
Singapore Business and Investment Opportunities Yearbook Volume 1 Strategic, Practical Information and Opportunities
Slovakia Business and Investment Opportunities Yearbook Volume 1 Strategic, Practical Information and Opportunities

TITLE
Slovenia Business and Investment Opportunities Yearbook Volume 1 Strategic, Practical Information and Opportunities
Solomon Islands Business and Investment Opportunities Yearbook Volume 1 Strategic, Practical Information and Opportunities
Somalia Business and Investment Opportunities Yearbook Volume 1 Strategic, Practical Information and Opportunities
South Africa Business and Investment Opportunities Yearbook Volume 1 Strategic, Practical Information and Opportunities
Spain Business and Investment Opportunities Yearbook Volume 1 Strategic, Practical Information and Opportunities
Sri Lanka Business and Investment Opportunities Yearbook Volume 1 Strategic, Practical Information and Opportunities
St. Helena Business and Investment Opportunities Yearbook Volume 1 Strategic, Practical Information and Opportunities
St. Pierre & Miquelon Business and Investment Opportunities Yearbook Volume 1 Strategic, Practical Information and Opportunities
Sudan (Republic of the Sudan) Business and Investment Opportunities Yearbook Volume 1 Strategic, Practical Information and Opportunities
Sudan South Business and Investment Opportunities Yearbook Volume 1 Strategic, Practical Information and Opportunities
Suriname Business and Investment Opportunities Yearbook Volume 1 Strategic, Practical Information and Opportunities
Swaziland Business and Investment Opportunities Yearbook Volume 1 Strategic, Practical Information and Opportunities
Sweden Business and Investment Opportunities Yearbook Volume 1 Strategic, Practical Information and Opportunities
Switzerland Business and Investment Opportunities Yearbook Volume 1 Strategic, Practical Information and Opportunities
Syria Business and Investment Opportunities Yearbook Volume 1 Strategic, Practical Information and Opportunities
Taiwan Business and Investment Opportunities Yearbook Volume 1 Strategic, Practical Information and Opportunities
Tajikistan Business and Investment Opportunities Yearbook Volume 1 Strategic, Practical Information and Opportunities
Tanzania Business and Investment Opportunities Yearbook Volume 1 Strategic, Practical Information and Opportunities
Thailand Business and Investment Opportunities Yearbook Volume 1 Strategic, Practical Information and Opportunities
Timor Leste (Democratic Republic of Timor-Leste) Business and Investment Opportunities Yearbook Volume 1 Strategic, Practical Information and Opportunities
Togo Business and Investment Opportunities Yearbook Volume 1 Strategic, Practical Information and Opportunities
Tonga Business and Investment Opportunities Yearbook Volume 1 Strategic, Practical Information and Opportunities
Trinidad and Tobago Business and Investment Opportunities Yearbook Volume 1 Strategic, Practical Information and Opportunities
Tunisia Business and Investment Opportunities Yearbook Volume 1 Strategic, Practical Information and Opportunities
Turkey Business and Investment Opportunities Yearbook Volume 1 Strategic, Practical Information and Opportunities
Turkmenistan Business and Investment Opportunities Yearbook Volume 1 Strategic, Practical Information and Opportunities
Turks & Caicos Business and Investment Opportunities Yearbook Volume 1 Strategic, Practical Information and Opportunities
Tuvalu Business and Investment Opportunities Yearbook Volume 1 Strategic, Practical Information and Opportunities

TITLE
Uganda Business and Investment Opportunities Yearbook Volume 1 Strategic, Practical Information and Opportunities
Ukraine Business and Investment Opportunities Yearbook Volume 1 Strategic, Practical Information and Opportunities
United Arab Emirates Business and Investment Opportunities Yearbook Volume 1 Strategic, Practical Information and Opportunities
United Kingdom Business and Investment Opportunities Yearbook Volume 1 Strategic, Practical Information and Opportunities
United States Business and Investment Opportunities Yearbook Volume 1 Strategic, Practical Information and Opportunities
Uruguay Business and Investment Opportunities Yearbook Volume 1 Strategic, Practical Information and Opportunities
Uzbekistan Business and Investment Opportunities Yearbook Volume 1 Strategic, Practical Information and Opportunities
Vanuatu Business and Investment Opportunities Yearbook Volume 1 Strategic, Practical Information and Opportunities
Vatican City (Holy See) Business and Investment Opportunities Yearbook Volume 1 Strategic, Practical Information and Opportunities
Venezuela Business and Investment Opportunities Yearbook Volume 1 Strategic, Practical Information and Opportunities
Vietnam Business and Investment Opportunities Yearbook Volume 1 Strategic, Practical Information and Opportunities
Virgin Islands, British Business and Investment Opportunities Yearbook Volume 1 Strategic, Practical Information and Opportunities
Wake Atoll Business and Investment Opportunities Yearbook Volume 1 Strategic, Practical Information and Opportunities
Wallis & Futuna Business and Investment Opportunities Yearbook Volume 1 Strategic, Practical Information and Opportunities
Western Sahara Business and Investment Opportunities Yearbook Volume 1 Strategic, Practical Information and Opportunities
Yemen Business and Investment Opportunities Yearbook Volume 1 Strategic, Practical Information and Opportunities
Zambia Business and Investment Opportunities Yearbook Volume 1 Strategic, Practical Information and Opportunities
Zimbabwe Business and Investment Opportunities Yearbook Volume 1 Strategic, Practical Information and Opportunities

www.ingramcontent.com/pod-product-compliance
Lightning Source LLC
LaVergne TN
LVHW080034210926
848481LV00011B/3186
* 9 7 8 1 4 3 3 0 7 6 8 8 6 *